TEACHER EDITION

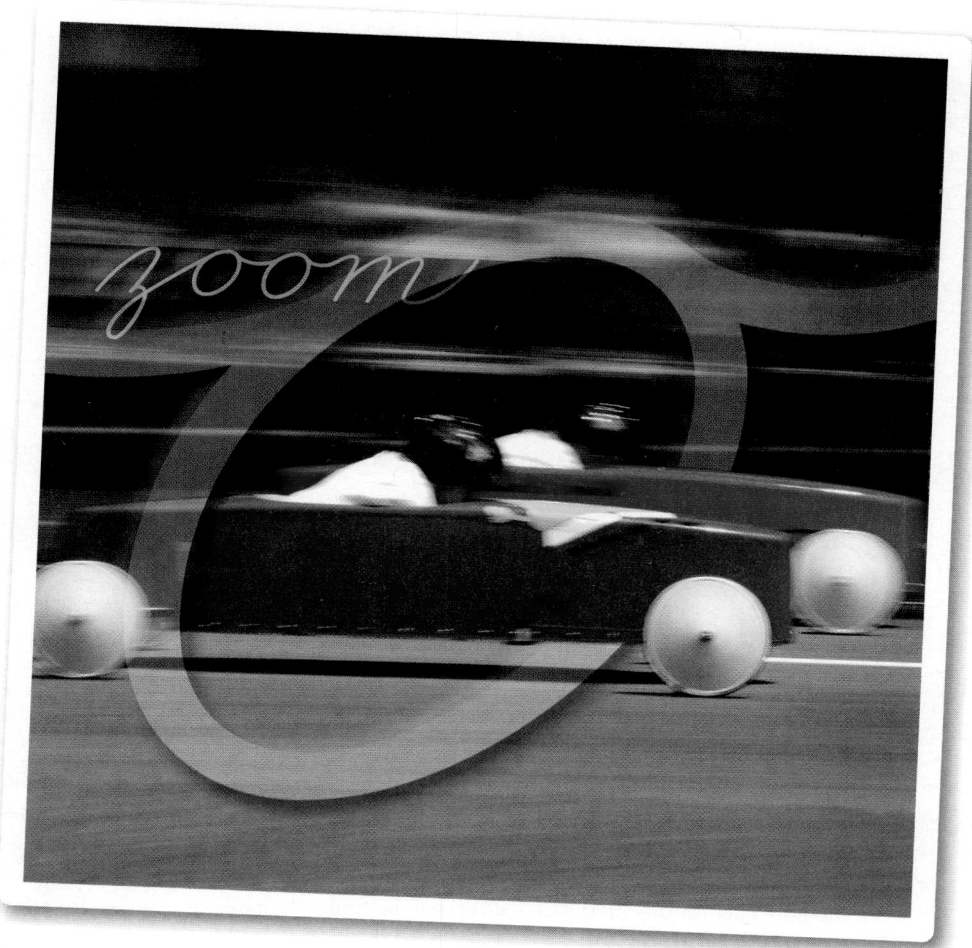

ZB Zaner-Bloser

Occupational Therapy Consultants

Asha Asher, MA OTR/L, FAOTA, M.Ed. (Special Education), Cincinnati, OH

Mary Benbow, M.S., OTR, La Jolla, CA

Jane Case-Smith, Ed.D., OTR/L, FAOTA, Former Chair of the Occupational Therapy Division, Ohio State University

North Shore Pediatric Therapy

ELL Consultants

Ellen Riojas Clark, Ph.D., Professor of Bicultural-Bilingual Studies, University of Texas at San Antonio

Bertha Pérez, Ed.D., Professor Emeritus of Literacy, University of Texas at San Antonio

Occupational Therapy Advisory Board

Carol Armann, OTR/L, Marietta, OH

Kathleen A. Benton-Sanchez, M.P.A., OTR/L, Nashville, TN

Sherry Eisenbach, OT/L, Portland, OR

Elizabeth Gerich, OTR/L, Plymouth, MN

Sheila Martins, OTR/L, North Las Vegas, NV

Leslie N. Parker, OTR/L, Huntington, WV

Tricia Shibuya, OTR/L, Las Vegas, NV

Denaysa Sisemore, M.S., OTR/L, Windsor, CO

Cheryl Weaver, CAS, M.S.Ed., OTR/L, Macedon, NY

Reviewers

Amy Bass, National Heritage Academies, Byron Center, MI

Donetta S. Brown, Birmingham City Schools, AL

Kelly Caravelli, Poway Unified School District, San Diego, CA

Michelle Corsi, East Windsor Regional Schools, NJ

Naomi Drewitz, East Windsor Regional Schools, NJ

Shan Glandon, Tulsa, OK

Karen Jackson, School District of Philadelphia, PA

Liz Knowles, Ed.D., 21st Century Curriculum Designs, LLC, Del Ray Beach, FL

Rita Olsen, Chicago Public Schools, IL

Geraldine A. Pappas, Detroit Public Schools, MI

Michael E. Pizzingrillo, Roman Catholic Diocese of Brooklyn, NY

Deborah C. Thomas, Ed.D., Montgomery Public Schools, AL

Ellen Lerch Thomsen, Roanoke County Public Schools, VA

Iefay Williams, School District of Philadelphia, PA

Credits

Photo: ©Getty Images: Cover, title page; ©iStockphoto.com/Christopher Futcher: Z3; ©Getty Images/KidStock: Z19; ©George Anderson Photography: Z21

ISBN 978-1-4531-1806-1

ZB Code 16

Zaner-Bloser, Inc.
800.421.3018
www.zaner-bloser.com

Printed in the United States of America

3 4 5 330 19 18 17

Table of Contents

Introduction to Zaner-Bloser Handwriting

	Teacher	Student
Handwriting: A Research-Based Foundational Literacy Skill	Z6	
Program Components	Z8	
Multisensory Support Materials	Z9	
Digital Tools	Z10	
Instructional Plan	Z12	
Basic Strokes	Z18	
Letter Groupings	Z19	
Differentiated Instruction	Z20	
Developing Effective Partnerships Between Classroom Teachers and Occupational Therapists	Z22	
When Should I Call the OT?	Z23	
Handwriting Instruction and English Language Learners	Z24	
National Handwriting Contest	Z26	
Grade 3 Handwriting at a Glance	T5	5

Unit 1: Reviewing Manuscript Writing

	Teacher	Student
Writing Positions	T6	6
Manuscript Keys to Legibility	T7	7
Write Ll, Ii, Tt	T8	8
Write Oo, Aa, Dd	T9	9
Write Cc, Ee, Ff	T10	10
Write Gg, Jj, Qq	T11	11
Write Uu, Ss, Bb, Pp	T12	12
Write Rr, Nn, Mm, Hh	T13	13
Write Vv, Yy, Ww	T14	14
Write Xx, Kk, Zz	T15	15
Manuscript Review and Application	T16	16

Unit 2: Cursive Writing: Getting Started

	Teacher	Student
Pretest: Write a Poem	T18	18
Welcome to Cursive Writing	T20	20
Cursive Letters and Numerals	T22	22
Reading Cursive Writing	T24	24
Writing Positions: Left-Handed Writers	T26	26
Writing Positions: Right-Handed Writers	T27	27

Unit 2: Cursive Writing: Getting Started (continued)

	Teacher	Student
Basic Strokes: Undercurve	T28	28
Basic Strokes: Downcurve	T29	29
Basic Strokes: Overcurve	T30	30
Basic Strokes: Slant	T31	31
Keys to Legibility: Shape	T32	32
Keys to Legibility: Size	T33	33
Keys to Legibility: Spacing	T34	34
Keys to Legibility: Slant	T35	35

Unit 3: Cursive Letters

	Teacher	Student
Writing Lowercase Cursive Letters	T36	36
Write Undercurve Letters *i, t, u, w, e, l, b, h, f, k, r, s, j, p*	T38	38
Joinings	T53	53
Review	T54	54
Application	T55	55
Cursive Writing in the Real World	T56	56
Manuscript Maintenance	T57	57
Keys to Legibility	T58	58
Write Downcurve Letters *a, d, g, o, c, q*	T60	60
Joinings	T67	67
Review	T68	68
Application	T69	69
Cursive Writing in the Real World	T70	70
Write Overcurve Letters *n, m, y, x, v, z*	T71	71
Review	T78	78
Application	T79	79
Keys to Legibility	T80	80
Review Lowercase Letters	T82	82
Joinings	T84	84
Cursive Numerals	T86	86
Manuscript Maintenance	T88	88
Writing Uppercase Cursive Letters	T90	90
Write Downcurve Letters *A, O, D, C, E*	T92	92
Review	T98	98
Application	T99	99
Write Curve Forward Letters *N, M, H, K, U, Y, Z, V, W, X*	T100	100
Joinings	T111	111
Review	T112	112
Application	T113	113
Cursive Writing in the Real World	T114	114

	Teacher	Student
Manuscript Maintenance	T115	115
Keys to Legibility	T116	116
Write Overcurve and Doublecurve Letters *I, J, Q, T, F*	T118	118
Review	T124	124
Application	T125	125
Write Undercurve-Loop Letters *G, S, L*	T126	126
Write Undercurve-Slant Letters *P, R, B*	T130	130
Joinings	T133	133
Review	T134	134
Application	T135	135
Cursive Writing in the Real World	T136	136
Review Uppercase Cursive Letters	T137	137
Keys to Legibility	T138	138
Manuscript Maintenance	T140	140
Unit 4: Using What You Have Learned		
Friendly Letter	T142	142
Compare and Contrast	T144	144
Fiction or Nonfiction?	T146	146
Last Weekend	T148	148
How To	T150	150
Handwriting and the Writing Process	T151	151
Writing Quickly	T152	152
Writing Easily	T154	154
Posttest: Write a Poem	T156	156
Write the Sentence	T158	158
Record of Student's Handwriting Skills	T159	159
Appendix		
Handwriting Instruction Checklist	T160	
Cursive Evaluation Rubric	T161	
Corrective Strategies	T162	
Glossary of Handwriting Terms	T166	
Glossary of Occupational Therapy Terms	T168	
Scope and Sequence	T170	
Index	T174	160

Handwriting: A Research-Based Foundational Literacy Skill

How does handwriting instruction benefit students?

Handwriting is more than a fine motor skill. Research shows that handwriting instruction and handwriting skill impact students' overall literacy development and that early fine motor writing skills predict later academic achievement.

Reading and math acquisition
Preschool students who have greater ease with fine motor writing tasks have better academic skills in second grade in both reading and math (Dinehart & Manfra, 2013).

Letter formation
Handwriting practice is a key component of the motor learning necessary to form letters and numerals correctly (Asher, 2006).

Handwriting speed and output
When students develop the fine motor skills that accompany learning to write by hand, their writing speed and output increase (Graham & Harris, 2005; Graham & Weintraub, 1996).

Fluency, automaticity, and the quality of higher-order written language skills
As students' handwriting becomes more fluent and automatic, they can devote more attentional resources to complex writing tasks, and their written language improves (Christensen & Jones, 2000).

Other research suggests that handwriting is significantly related to writing fluency and quality for both primary and intermediate elementary students (Graham, Berninger, Abbott, Abbott, & Whitaker, 1997).

Deliver high-quality, developmentally appropriate handwriting instruction in 15 minutes per day or less.

Zaner-Bloser Handwriting is a complete program that

- uses **academic language and modeling** with fewer, more specific stroke descriptions than other programs.
- teaches **vertical manuscript** that resembles **environmental print** to promote literacy development.
- meets the needs of all students by teaching in an **appropriate developmental sequence** and allowing for **differentiation**, based on learning style, language acquisition, and motor development.
- provides **easy-to-use digital teaching tools** to engage students and support teachers.

Handwriting Research: Impact on the Brain and Literacy Development

Handwriting Research contains more than 20 recent research articles about the importance of writing by hand and handwriting instruction.

References

Asher, A. (2006). Handwriting instruction in elementary schools. *American Journal of Occupational Therapy, 60*, 461–471.

Christensen, C., & Jones, D. (2000). Handwriting: An underestimated skill in the development of written language. *Handwriting Today, 2*, 56–69.

Dinehart, L., & Manfra, L. (2013). Associations between low-income children's fine motor skills in preschool and academic performance in 2nd grade. *Early Education and Development, 24*(2), 138–161.

Graham, S., Berninger, V. W., Abbott, R. D., Abbott, S. P., & Whitaker, D. (1997). Role of mechanics in composing of elementary school students: A new methodological approach. *Journal of Educational Psychology, 89*(1), 170–182.

Graham, S., & Harris, K. R. (2005). Improving the writing performance of young struggling writers. *The Journal of Special Education, 39*, 19–33.

Graham, S., & Weintraub, N. (1996). A review of handwriting research: Progress and prospects from 1980–1994. *Educational Psychology Review, 8*, 7–87.

Grade 3
Manuscript Review and Transition to Cursive

Grade 4
Cursive Reinforcement

Grade 5
Manuscript Maintenance and Cursive Mastery

Grade 6
Manuscript and Cursive Maintenance

Begin cursive handwriting instruction in Grade 2 or Grade 3.

Program Components

Teacher Edition offers easy, step-by-step instruction, content area writing in various text types, integration of technology, and embedded professional development including Support for English Language Learners, Tips From an Occupational Therapist, and multisensory activities.

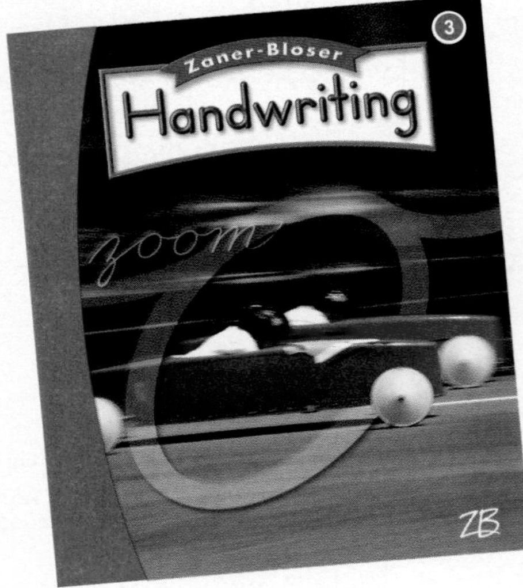

Student Edition includes easy step-by-step instruction and self-evaluation, provides meaningful practice and application, and engages students with colorful, fun activities.

Practice Masters provides more practice for every letter and skill and offers school-to-home activities and support materials.

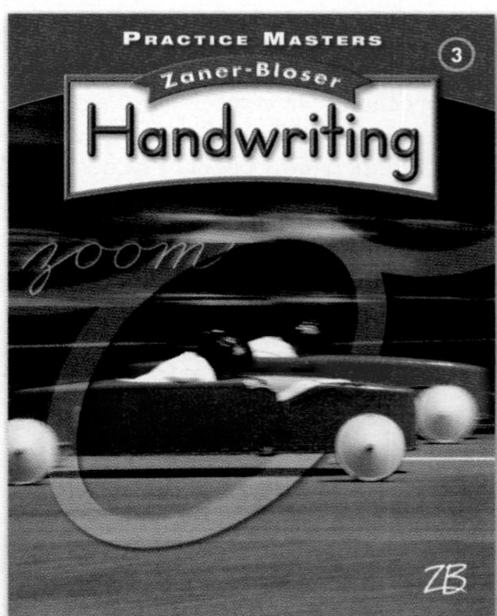

Also available in Spanish

La escritura offers parallel handwriting instruction in Spanish.

Now with . . .
Handwriting Tutor

Scan the QR codes throughout the Teacher Edition and Student Edition with a mobile device to watch animated letter models and how-to videos. For system requirements, go to **www.zaner-bloser.com /system-requirements**.

Multisensory Support Materials

A full selection of classroom, multisensory practice materials to provide extra support for teaching handwriting and make learning fun:

A. Alphabet Wall Strips, Grades K–6
B. Alphabet Desk Strips, Grades K–4
C. Adhesive Desk Strips, Grades 1–4
D. Manuscript/Cursive Card Sets, Grades 1–4
E. Home Handwriting Pack, Grades K–4
F. Poster Super Pack
Also available in Spanish.
G. Story Journals
H. Writing Journals
I. Paper, Grades K–6
J. Animal Alphabet Cards, Grades K–2
K. Touch and Trace Cards (Manuscript and Cursive), Grades PreK–3
L. Wikki Stix®
M. Handwriting Research: Impact on the Brain and Literacy Development
N. Handwriting Correspondence Course

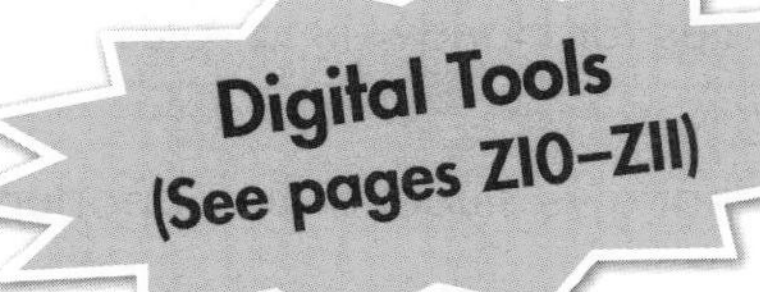

Digital Tools

Zaner-Bloser Online eResources Center

Go to **resources.zaner-bloser.com/hw** to access a variety of **free,** downloadable classroom resources.

- Assessments
- Corrective Strategies
- Detailed Stroke Descriptions
- Handwriting Tutor Cards
- Songs and videos (Readiness–Grade 1)
- Professional Development and more!

Digital Resources for Handwriting*

Available for purchase for Grades K–6

Digital Resources for Handwriting engages students and supports teachers in handwriting instruction.

- **Letter and numeral formation animations** feature audio and visual stroke descriptions in English and Spanish to reinforce instruction.
- **Short instructional videos** provide tips and lessons on the Keys to Legibility, self-evaluation strategies, writing quickly, and more.
- **Fun, interactive activities** bring letters to life.

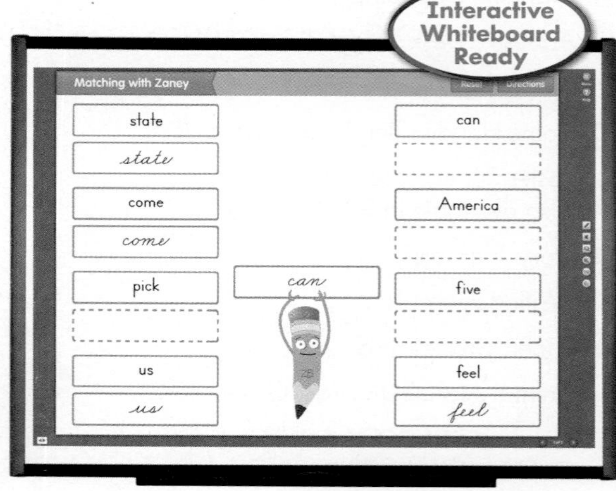

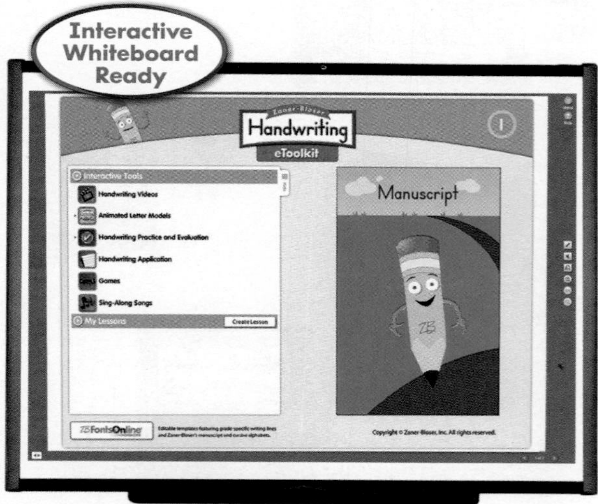

Handwriting eToolkit™*

Available for purchase for Grades K–3

The **Handwriting eToolkit** is a robust digital solution that can be used as a standalone handwriting instruction option or in conjunction with the Teacher and Student print editions or Practice Masters. It includes all of the features in the Digital Resources for Handwriting, plus the ability to

- **print handwriting practice pages** that give students the opportunity to apply the skills they learn.
- **build and save custom lessons** that incorporate interactive tools, including videos, letter models, practice activities, games, and sing-along songs.
- **create, save, and print worksheets and activities** using Zaner-Bloser's manuscript and cursive alphabets with ZB FontsOnline Plus.

*The Digital Resources and eToolkit are designed for whole-class or small-group instruction and can be used with any interactive whiteboard or projector.

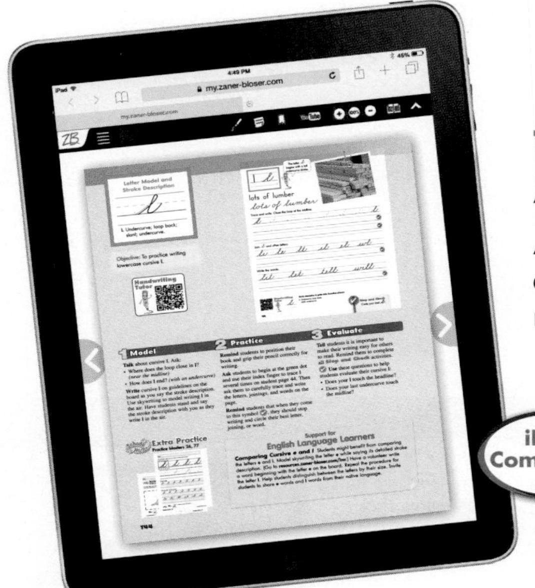

Teacher Edition eBook

Available for purchase for Grades K–6

Accessible online, the interactive **Teacher Edition eBook** makes it easy for teachers to plan and review handwriting lessons from home or at school.

ZB FontsOnline Plus™

ZB FontsOnline Plus allows teachers to create documents using Zaner-Bloser's manuscript and cursive alphabets. ZB FontsOnline Plus provides grade-specific templates for a variety of documents and includes Spanish characters.

Available for separate purchase and as part of the eToolkit.

Zaner-Bloser Handwriting Apps

Zaner-Bloser Handwriting apps enable students to practice writing uppercase and lowercase letterforms and numerals in a fun and engaging way. Automatic feedback and a built-in reward motivate students and help them improve their handwriting. Download the apps from the Apple App Store® for English Manuscript, English Cursive, Spanish Manuscript, and Spanish Cursive. The apps are available for iPhone® and iPad®.

Student Edition

Zaner-Bloser Handwriting guides students through a step-by-step process for learning handwriting, a vital literacy skill. The engaging, colorful Student Edition provides developmentally appropriate practice to increase legibility through regular self-evaluation and develop fluency and automaticity.

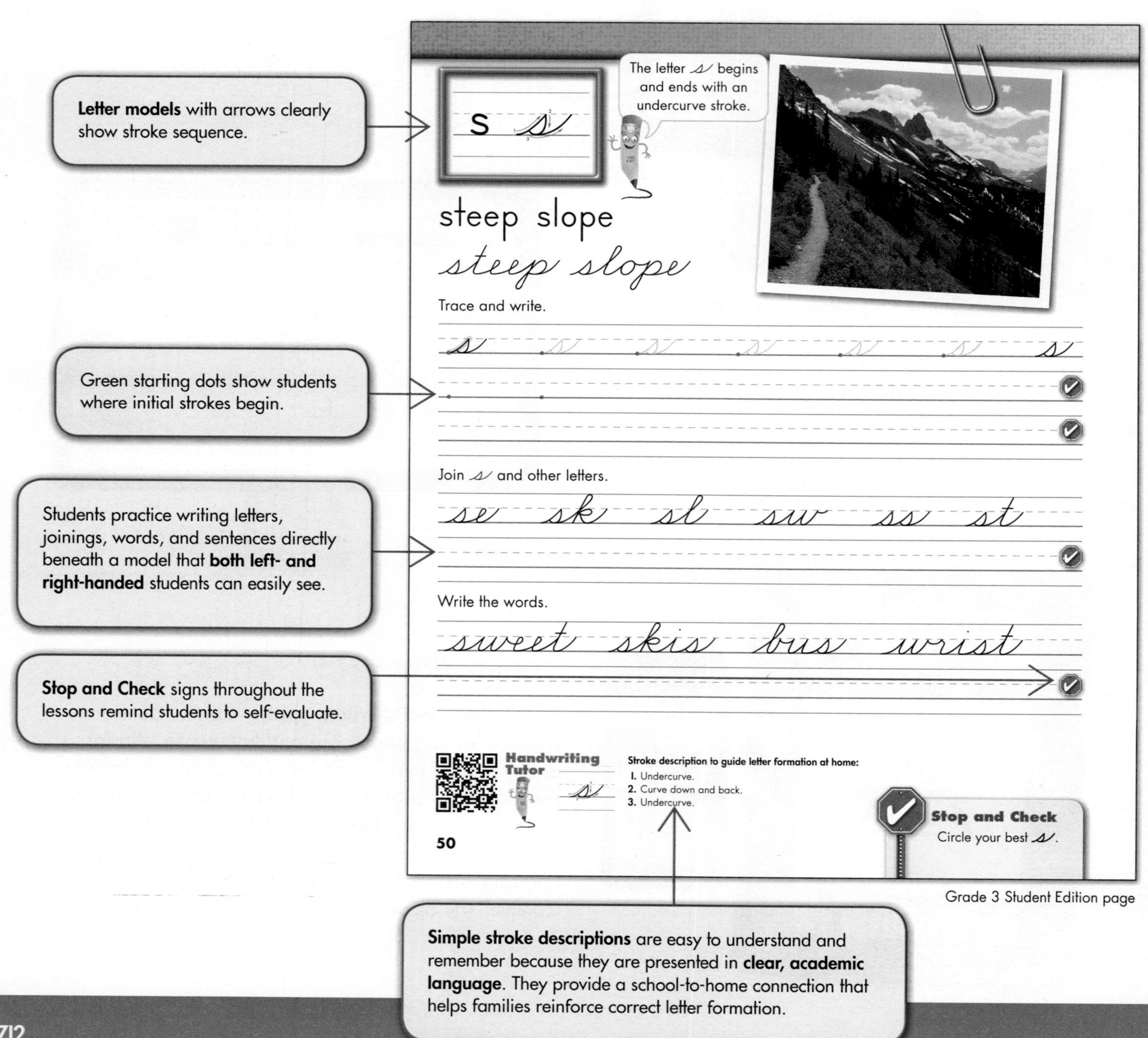

The letter s begins and ends with an undercurve stroke.
s s
steep slope
steep slope
Trace and write.
Join s and other letters.
se sk sl sw ss st
Write the words.
sweet skis bus wrist
Handwriting Tutor
Stroke description to guide letter formation at home:
1. Undercurve.
2. Curve down and back.
3. Undercurve.
50
Stop and Check
Circle your best s.

Grade 3 Student Edition page

Letter models with arrows clearly show stroke sequence.

Green starting dots show students where initial strokes begin.

Students practice writing letters, joinings, words, and sentences directly beneath a model that **both left- and right-handed** students can easily see.

Stop and Check signs throughout the lessons remind students to self-evaluate.

Simple stroke descriptions are easy to understand and remember because they are presented in **clear, academic language**. They provide a school-to-home connection that helps families reinforce correct letter formation.

automaticity

Review activities for all upper- and lowercase letters and numerals reinforce learning and develop automaticity.

Application activities provide opportunities for students to apply the handwriting skills they have learned.

Writing Quickly promotes speed and automaticity so that students can do well in high-pressure testing situations where they must write quickly and maintain legibility.

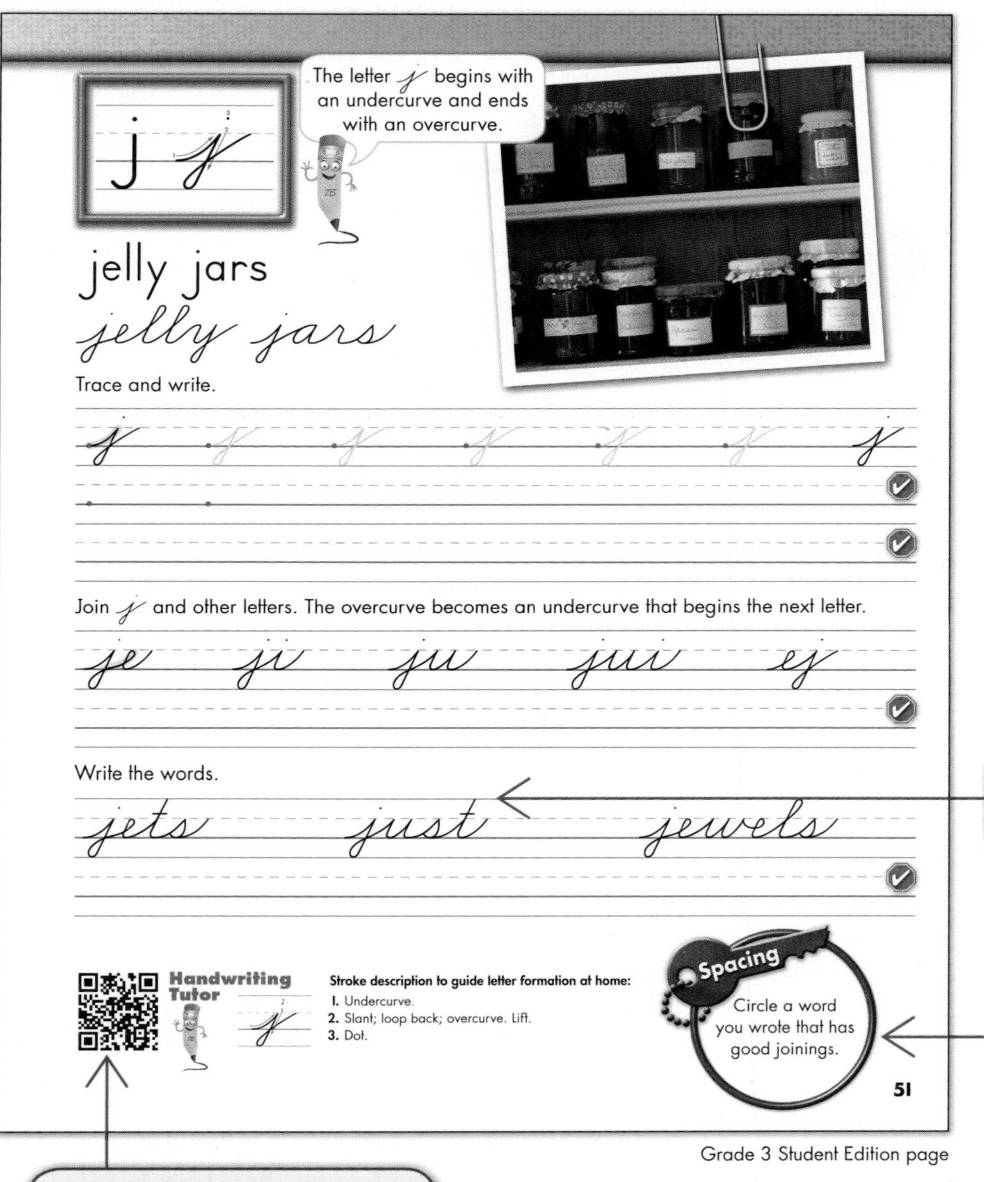

The letter j begins with an undercurve and ends with an overcurve.
jelly jars
jelly jars
Trace and write.
Join j and other letters. The overcurve becomes an undercurve that begins the next letter.
je ji ju jui ej
Write the words.
jets just jewels
Handwriting Tutor
Stroke description to guide letter formation at home:
1. Undercurve.
2. Slant; loop back; overcurve. Lift.
3. Dot.
Spacing
Circle a word you wrote that has good joinings.
51

Grade 3 Student Edition page

High-frequency words are included to enhance reading development.

Students are reminded to self-evaluate by focusing on the **Keys to Legibility** throughout the year so that Shape, Size, Spacing, and Slant continually improve.

Handwriting Tutor provides students with access to animated letter models and how-to videos.

The Keys to Legibility

Four Keys to Legibility—**Shape, Size, Spacing,** and **Slant**—are the basis of Zaner-Bloser's unique instructional system. The Keys form an assessment rubric for teachers and students.

Students are introduced to the four Keys at the beginning of the year. As letters are introduced, students self-evaluate the shape, size, spacing, and slant of their handwriting for continual improvement.

Keys are used in the Teacher Edition as prompts for the teacher to remind the students about shape, size, spacing, and slant.

Consistent terminology, such as the names of the guidelines and the Keys to Legibility, appears throughout the Student Edition and across all grades.

Handwriting Tutor
Size
Look at the size of each letter.
Use the guidelines to help you make each letter the correct size.
Tall letters touch the headline.
b d h
Short letters touch the midline.
a m g u
Some letters have descenders that go below the baseline and touch the next headline.
f q y
Circle the tall letters.
a c d e f g h k
Circle the short letters.
l n d q s t u w
Circle the letters that have descenders.
p q s t u x y z
33

Grade 3 Student Edition page

Writing in the Text Types

Authentic writing activities help students prepare for the rigors of written assessments. In Unit 4, students have multiple opportunities to apply their handwriting skills in a meaningful context through **Narrative, Informative/ Explanatory,** and **Opinion** writing tasks.

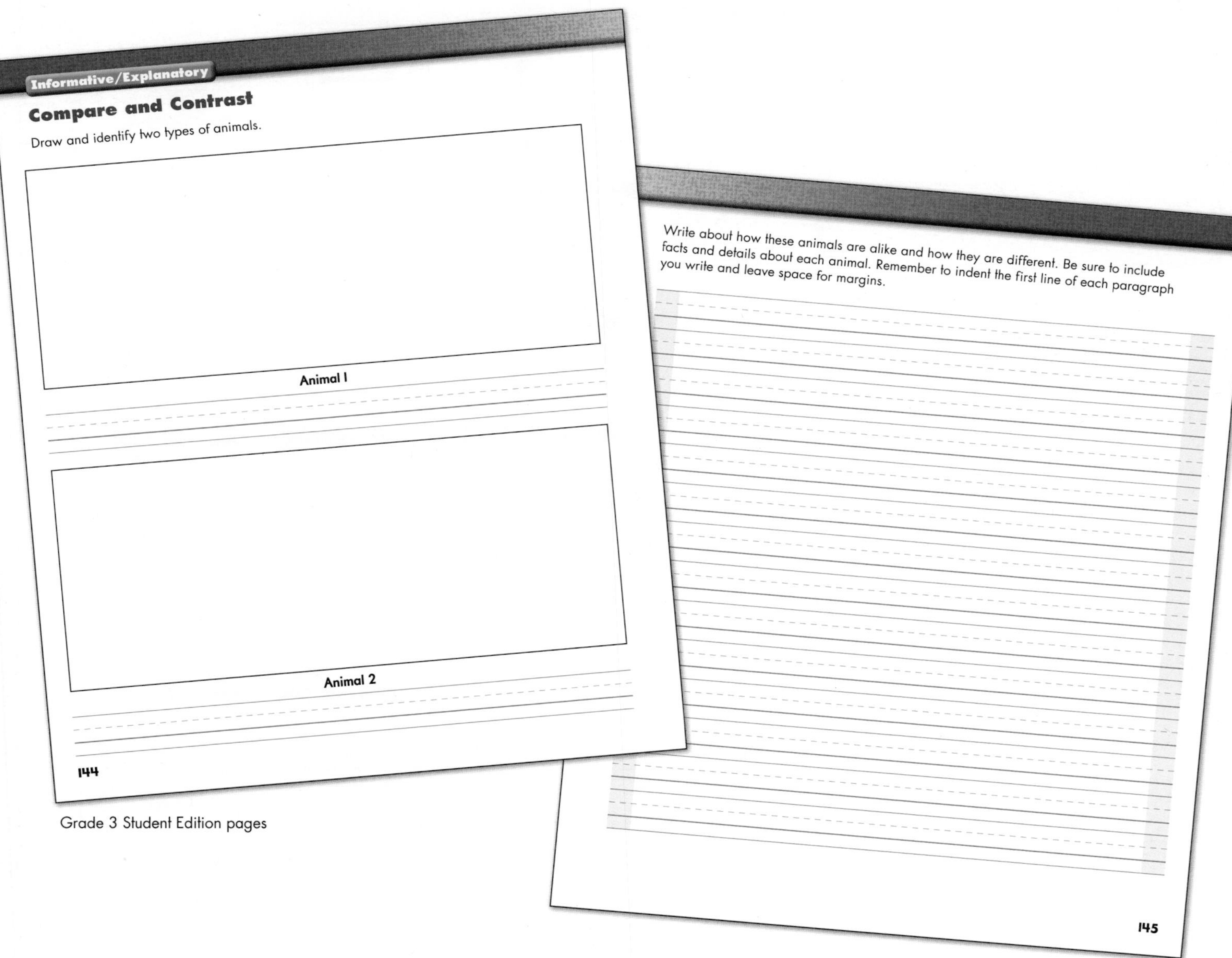

Grade 3 Student Edition pages

Teacher Edition

Confidently teach handwriting in **15 minutes per day or less** with the easy-to-use Teacher Edition. The three-step lesson presents a clear, simple instructional plan—Model, Practice, Evaluate. **Zaner-Bloser Handwriting** works with any language arts curriculum to fully support reading and writing instruction.

Short, **clear stroke descriptions** use academic language and give teachers the exact words to use when modeling.

Clearly stated objectives guide instruction.

Handwriting Tutor provides access to animated letter models and how-to videos.

Skywriting with large muscle movements reinforces the motor patterns used to form strokes and letters.

Letter Model and Stroke Description

1. Undercurve.
2. Slant; undercurve. Lift.
3. Slide right.

Objective: To practice writing lowercase cursive **t**.

Handwriting Tutor

The letter t begins with a tall undercurve stroke.
test tubes
test tubes
Trace and write.
Join t and other letters. Notice the undercurve-to-undercurve joinings.
it it it it it it
tt tt tt ti ti ti
Handwriting Tutor
Stroke description to guide letter formation at home:
1. Undercurve.
2. Slant, undercurve. Lift.
3. Slide right.
40
Stop and Check
Circle your best t.

1 Model

Talk about cursive **t**. Ask:

- In the letter **t**, what stroke follows the slant? *(undercurve)*
- How does **t** end? *(with a slide right)*

Write cursive **t** on guidelines on the board as you say the stroke description. Use skywriting to model writing **t** in the air. Have students stand and say the stroke description with you as they write **t** in the air.

2 Practice

Remind students to position their book and grip their pencil correctly for writing.

Ask students to begin at the green dot and use their index finger to trace **t** several times on student page 40. Then ask them to carefully trace and write with pencil the letters and joinings on the page.

Remind students that when they come to this symbol ✓, they should stop writing and circle their best letter or joining.

3 Evaluate

Tell students it is important to make their writing easy for others to read. Remind them to complete all **Stop and Check** activities.

✓ **Use** these questions to help students evaluate their cursive **t**:

- Does your first undercurve end at the headline?
- Is your slant stroke pulled toward the baseline?
- Is your slide right stroke just above the midline?

School Home Extra Practice
Practice Masters 22, 75

Support for
English Language Learners

Sound Recognition Students will benefit from hearing the sound of the letter **t** pronounced so they will recognize the same sound when it is used in words. Provide students with pictures of objects or point to things in the classroom that begin with the letter **t**, such as **table, toy, time,** and **toe**. Say the words, and emphasize the /t/ sound. Invite students to repeat after you, and encourage them to skywrite the letter **t** as they say the words.

T40

Grade 3 Teacher Edition page

The Teacher Edition provides many opportunities to differentiate instruction:

- Support for English Language Learners
- Tips From an Occupational Therapist
- Handwriting Coach
- Practice Masters

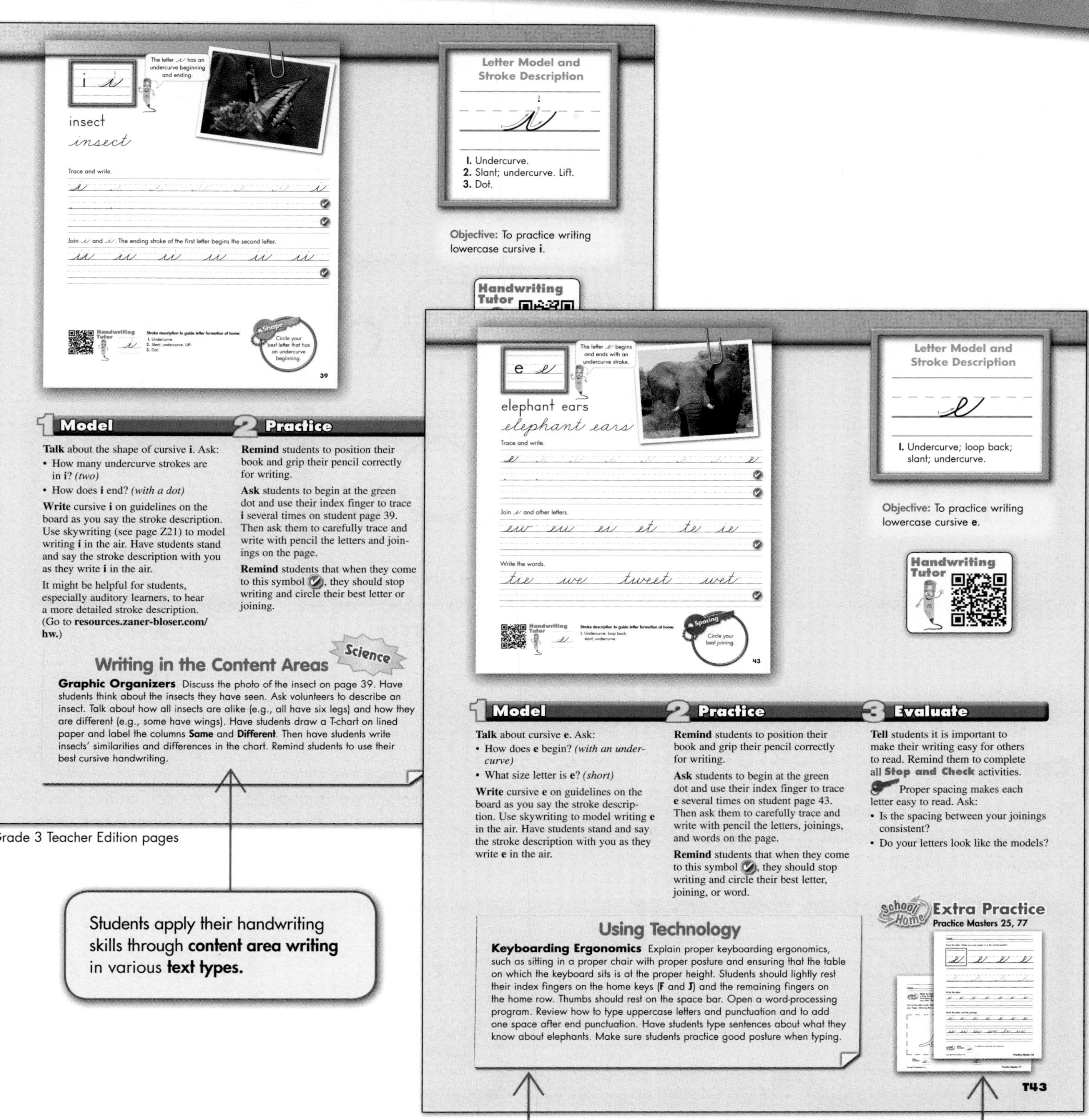

Grade 3 Teacher Edition pages

Students apply their handwriting skills through **content area writing** in various **text types.**

Meaningful activities in each unit develop and reinforce **digital literacy skills,** including keyboarding, word-processing, and online publishing.

Practice Masters allow the teacher to match additional practice to students' needs.

Basic Strokes

Manuscript

Four basic lines, or strokes, are used to form all manuscript letters and numerals—vertical, horizontal, circle, and slant.

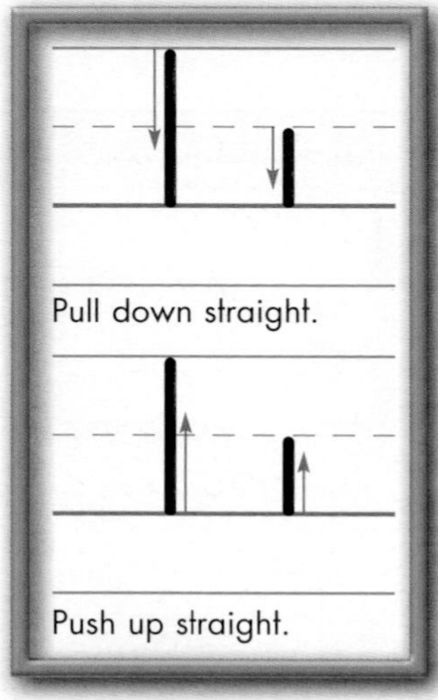

Vertical

Slide right.

Slide left.

Horizontal

Circle

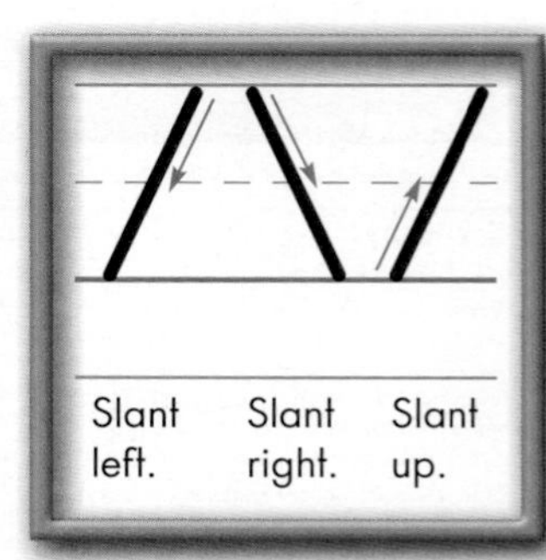

Slant

Cursive Chant

Undercurves swing.
Downcurves dive.
Overcurves bounce.
Slants just slide.
Undercurve, downcurve,
Overcurve, slant.
As you write in cursive,
Remember this chant.

Cursive

Four basic strokes are used to form all cursive letters and numerals. These four strokes are undercurve, downcurve, overcurve, and slant.

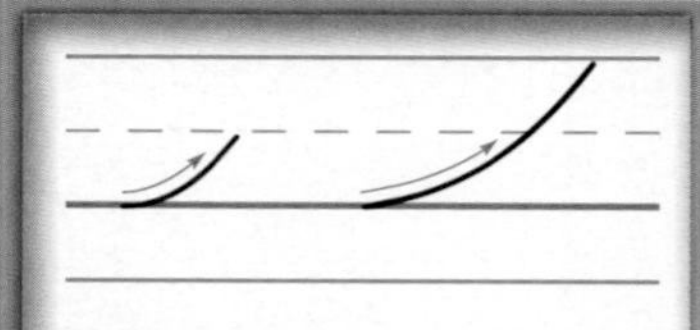

1. Touch the baseline; curve under and up to the midline (or headline).

Undercurve

1. Touch the midline (or headline); curve left and down to the baseline.

Downcurve

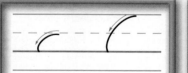

1. Touch the baseline; curve up and right to the midline (or headline).

Overcurve

1. Touch the midline (or headline); slant left to the baseline.

Slant

Zaner-Bloser Handwriting provides options to begin cursive writing instruction in Grade 2 or Grade 3.

Letter Groupings

For both manuscript and cursive handwriting, Zaner-Bloser presents the letters of the alphabet in groups. Each group shares common strokes, formation patterns, and visual attributes. When a child sees an individual letter, such as manuscript **a,** and attempts to write it, he or she may look at the letter and try to copy its shape. In many cases, this practice results in self-invented and inefficient methods for writing letters, such as starting the letter at the baseline instead of the midline or using a forward circle line instead of a backward circle line. By presenting **a** with other letters that contain backward circle lines, such as **o** and **d,** children are able to see patterns and learn to write letters correctly and efficiently.

Manuscript Groupings

Manuscript groupings are based on the strokes used to form the lowercase letter form of each lowercase/uppercase letter pair.

- Vertical and horizontal strokes: **l, i, t (L, I, T)**
- Forward circle and backward circle strokes: **o, a, d, c, e, f, g, j, q, u, s, b, p, r, n, m, h (O, A, D, C, E, F, G, J, Q, U, S, B, P, R, N, M, H)**
- Slant strokes: **v, y, w, x, k, z (V, Y, W, X, K, Z)**

Cursive Groupings

Cursive groupings are based on the initial stroke used to form each letter.

Lowercase

- Undercurve letters: *i, t, u, w, e, l, b, h, f, k, r, s, j, p*
- Downcurve letters: *a, d, g, o, c, q*
- Overcurve letters: *n, m, y, x, v, z*

Uppercase

- Downcurve letters: *A, O, D, C, E*
- Curve forward letters: *N, M, H, K, U, Y, Z, V, W, X*
- Overcurve letters: *I, J, Q*
- Undercurve-Loop letters: *G, S, L*
- Doublecurve letters: *T, F*
- Undercurve-Slant letters: *P, R, B*

Suggested Activities for Differentiated Instruction

Kinesthetic Learners

- Walk out the letter strokes on the floor.
- Form letters in the air using full arm movement.
- Make letter models with clay, string, or Wikki Stix®.
- Use different writing instruments, such as crayons, markers, and varied sizes of pencils.
- Trace large strokes, letters, and joinings on the board and on paper—first with fingers, then with chalk or other media.

The activities suggested for kinesthetic learners are also appropriate for students who experience attention deficit.

Auditory Learners

- Verbalize each stroke in the letter as that letter is presented.
- Encourage the student to verbalize the letter strokes and to explain how strokes are alike and how they are different in the letterforms.
- Ask students to write each letter as you verbalize the strokes.
- Be consistent in the language you use to describe letters, strokes, shapes, and joinings.

Visual Learners

- Encourage students first to look at the letter as a whole and to ask themselves if the letter is tall or short, fat or skinny. Does all of the letter rest on the baseline, is it a tall letter, or is it a letter with a descender? How many and what kinds of strokes are in the letter?
- Have students look at each individual stroke carefully before they attempt to write the letter.

Go Online Go to **resources.zaner-bloser.com/hw** to access 12 lively sing-along songs, printable song lyrics, and optional practice pages to help students with all learning styles—kinesthetic, auditory, and visual—develop handwriting skills. (Available for Readiness–Grade 1)

Students With Reversal Tendencies

Directionality

A problem with directionality (moving from left to right across the page) interferes with a student's ability to form letters correctly and to write text that makes sense. To develop correct directionality, try these techniques:

- Provide opportunities for the student to write at the board within a confined area, with frequent arrows as a reminder of left-to-right progression.
- Prepare sheets of paper on which the left edges and the beginning stroke of a letter are colored green.

Letter Reversals

Determine which letters a student reverses most often. Make a list of these reversals and concentrate on them either on an individual basis or by grouping together the students who are reversing the same letters.

- Emphasize each step of the stroke description before the students write a letter.
- Provide a letter for tracing that has been colored according to stroke order. Repeat the stroke description with the students as they write the letter.
- Encourage the students to write the letter as they verbalize the stroke description.

Left-Handed Students

Three important techniques assist the left-handed student in writing.

Paper Position
For manuscript writing, the lower right corner of the paper should point toward the left of the body's midsection. Downstrokes are pulled toward the left elbow.

For cursive writing, the lower right corner of the paper should point toward the body's midsection. Downstrokes are pulled toward the left elbow.

Cursive paper position shown

Pencil Position
The top of the pencil should point toward the left elbow. The pen or pencil should be held at least one inch above the point. This allows students to see what they are writing.

Arm Position
Holding the left arm close to the body and keeping the hand below the line of writing prevents "hooking" the wrist and smearing the writing.

Featured Activity: Skywriting

Skywriting is a technique that allows students to use their large muscles to practice the motor patterns used to form strokes and letters. To skywrite, hold up the index and middle fingers of the writing hand and raise the whole arm.

Students should follow the teacher in forming the featured strokes and letters at a large size in the air. As they skywrite, students should repeat the name of each stroke after the teacher. The teacher should either reverse the motion or turn his or her back so that it is not necessary for students to mirror the teacher's actions.

Kinesthetic learners especially benefit from skywriting to practice a letter's formation before writing it on paper. Auditory and visual learners benefit from teacher modeling of skywriting.

Skywriting is also a great warm-up activity for whole-class handwriting instruction.

Developing Effective Partnerships Between Classroom Teachers and Occupational Therapists

Illegible handwriting is one of the most common reasons students are referred to occupational therapy.[1] A few students may lag behind their peers in speed and legibility, but how do you know when it's serious? And then what do you do? Working as a team, you and an occupational therapist can help each student thrive.

How can teachers and occupational therapists collaborate to support students?

Sometimes students struggle because they have never received instruction in letter formation or have received conflicting, ad hoc instructions.[2] Providing developmentally appropriate classroom instruction can resolve handwriting difficulties for many students, especially if a school has consistent instruction across the grade spans.[3]

Occupational therapists can work with teachers to provide interventions that won't conflict with the handwriting program in use. Sometimes an occupational therapist will work one-on-one or perhaps in small groups with struggling students. Collaborating with an occupational therapist in a classroom setting can lead to successful outcomes for all students.[4, 5]

Because teachers have daily interactions with their students, they can easily identify which students are still struggling to form legible letters and words even with direct handwriting instruction. An occupational therapist can help identify and treat underlying problems, facilitate development of handwriting skills, and help devise accommodations to enable the student to successfully participate in classroom activities and the educational process.[6]

An occupational therapist may want to observe struggling students "in action." They might inquire about the writing paper students use or examine how students grip their pencil or orient their posture to write. An occupational therapist should also spend time in the classroom to understand its daily routines and physical design.

Occupational therapists are trained to examine the underlying cause of a student's handwriting difficulties in order to target effective interventions.[7] For instance, does the student struggle with isolating the movements of each finger or with planning how to execute the next step in forming the shape of each letter? Occupational therapists intervene differently depending on the conclusion of their analysis of students in the act of writing. They are also trained to determine whether handwriting difficulties signal a more serious underlying disorder, which can help students get the range of services necessary for their school success.[8, 9]

Handwriting is a complex task for children, and teachers and school-based occupational therapists are equal partners in student success. Use the checklist on page Z23 to help you determine when to consult an occupational therapist.

References

1 Cahill, S. M. (2009). Where does handwriting fit in? Strategies to support academic achievement. *Intervention in School and Clinic, 44*(4), 223–228.

2 Asher, A. V. (2006). Handwriting instruction in elementary schools. *The American Journal of Occupational Therapy, 60*, 461–471.

3 Graham, S., & Harris, K. R. (2005). Improving the writing performance of young struggling writers. *The Journal of Special Education, 39*(1), 24–26.

4 Asher. (2006).

5 Case-Smith, J., Holland, T., Lane, A., & White, S. (2012). Effect of a coteaching handwriting program for first graders: One-group pretest-posttest design. *The American Journal of Occupational Therapy, 66*(4), 369–405.

6 Asher, A. (2016). When Should I Call the Occupational Therapist? *Zaner-Bloser Handwriting* (K ed., p. Z23). Columbus, OH: Zaner-Bloser.

7 Pape, L., & Ryba, K. (2004). *Practical Considerations for School-Based Occupational Therapists*. Bethesda, MD: American Occupational Therapy Association, Inc.

8 Fuentes, C. T., Mostofsky, S. H., & Bastian, A. J. (2009). Children with autism show specific handwriting impairments. *Neurology, 73*(19), 1532–1537.

9 Dinehart, L.H.B. (2014). Handwriting in early childhood education: Current research and future implications. *Journal of Early Childhood Literacy, 15* (1), 97–118. doi:10.1177/1468798414522825

When Should I Call the Occupational Therapist?

Developed by Asha Asher, MA OTR/L, FAOTA, M.Ed. (Special Education), Cincinnati, Ohio

Use the following checklist to help you determine when the occupational therapist should be consulted for assistance in remediating specific problems that interfere with a student's handwriting development.

If you've tried this...	And this happens... Then consult the OT
Provided chair/desk of the appropriate height (i.e., the student can sit with feet flat on the floor, back snug against the chair back, and the desk slightly higher than the student's elbow)	The student assumes improper posture (e.g., head on the desk, sits on feet, sits at the edge of the chair)
Provided direct instruction of letter formations followed by regular guided practice	Written output is below grade-level expectations in either quality, quantity, or both (e.g., writing is difficult to read, student produces one sentence when peers have produced five sentences)
Allowed the student to experiment with writing tools of differing widths to choose one that the student finds most comfortable to use	Student continues to have an awkward pencil grasp AND written output is below grade-level expectations
Allowed student to experiment with writing paper that has lines of differing widths so the student can choose one that works best for him/her	Quality of student writing does not match grade-level expectations
Provided student with opportunities to refine fine motor control by incorporating various activities in the daily program (i.e., cutting, coloring, using small manipulatives such as peg boards, blocks, construction sets)	Student's fine-motor control is below that of peers (e.g., does not show stable hand preference, quality of student writing does not match grade-level expectations)
Provided opportunities to refine pencil control (vertical, horizontal, circle, oblique cross)	Quality of student writing does not match grade-level expectations (student uses too much or too little pressure, letters are formed from the baseline up, or piecemeal)
Provided adequate handwriting instruction	Quality of student writing does not match grade-level expectations (e.g., reversals beyond grade 2, uneven sizing or spacing of letters, omits or repeats letters)
Provided structured classroom expectations	Student's behavior often deteriorates only when written work is required

Handwriting Instruction and English Language Learners

By Ellen Riojas Clark, Ph.D., and Bertha Pérez, Ed.D.

Handwriting is an important communication skill that reinforces reading, spelling, and writing. Because of its foundational nature, this skill is important for all children, including English Language Learners (ELLs).

It is essential to know your students' first language (L1) literacy levels. Students who are literate in their first language can draw upon those literacy concepts and skills as they learn to write English (L2). Even when the writing systems are different, research shows that concepts about the meaning and constancy of letters/symbols and skills, such as alphabet knowledge and phonological awareness, will transfer to another language (Cummins, 1992; Cisero & Royer, 1995).

Handwriting instruction will give ELLs a tool for writing. **Zaner-Bloser Handwriting** and **Zaner-Bloser La escritura** use continuous-stroke vertical manuscript to teach the distinctive shapes and features of letters. This instructional approach will lead to mastery of basic writing skills (manuscript and cursive), improved letter recognition, and fluency in writing. Learning to write the vertical manuscript—the letters children see in books and environmental print—strengthens the L2 reading-writing connection.

The more a teacher understands the mechanics of English spelling and writing, the more successful their ELL students will be (Kroese, Mather, & Sammons, 2006). Teachers can assist students with L1 literacy skills to use those skills to write in English (August & Shanahan, 2008). For example, ELLs who know Spanish or other Roman alphabets can use those letter names and sounds to identify the same letters in English.

English orthography might not be easy for ELLs who use a non-alphabetic system, but teachers can assist students to make the connections (Moats & Tolman, 2008). Some ELLs' L1 may be written in a different script (such as Chinese or Arabic) or may be organized from right to left (Cloud, Genesee, & Hamayan, 2009). For these ELLs, use visuals to demonstrate handwriting strokes.

The more students attempt to write in English, the more handwriting practice they will acquire. Visual aids such as graphic organizers can help students generate ideas for writing (Sigueza, 2005). In addition, concrete content and language can also help students understand ideas they may wish to express in their writing. It is important to integrate concrete content and language (Morahan & Clayton, 2003). The use of ELLs' background knowledge as a cultural resource (Gonzalez, Moll, & Amanti, 2005) will anchor their writing to their conceptual learning.

ELLs need time and special techniques to acquire the proper handwriting strokes. Teachers can demonstrate the academic language used to teach handwriting (shape, size, spacing, and slant) through Total Physical Response (TPR) and other second language approaches. As you work with ELL students, implement the following:

- Allow the students to watch you forming the letters. Use visuals to demonstrate proper stroke sequence. Say the stroke sequence aloud as you form the letter.

- Use TPR to describe letter formation. For example, point to your head when referencing the headline on the handwriting grid. Say, "Your **head** is the **top** of your body. The **headline** is the **top** line." Similarly, you can demonstrate strokes with TPR. As you say "Slide right," slide your feet across the floor.
- Ask students to describe and demonstrate the steps in creating the letter, whether in L1 or L2.
- Conclude the lesson by having the students apply the new handwriting skill in a meaningful context.

Finally, as the students practice their handwriting, guide your ELLs

- to access their prior knowledge (Jefferies & Merkley, 2001) about what to write about.
- to write as a class, in pairs, or independently (Morahan & Clayton, 2003).
- to use their native language when necessary.
- to write about what they know.

References

August, D. & Shanahan, T. (Eds.). (2008). *Developing reading and writing in second-language learners.* New York: Routledge.

Cisero, C. & Royer, J. (1995). The development and cross-language transfer of phonological awareness. *Contemporary Educational Psychology, 20*(3), 275–303.

Cloud, N., Genesee, & Hamayan, E. (2009). *Literacy instruction for English language learners: A teacher's guide to research-based practices.* Portsmouth, NH: Heinemann.

Cummins, J. (1992). Bilingualism and second language learning. *Annual Review of Applied Linguistics, 13,* 51–70.

Gonzalez, N., Moll, L., & Amanti, C. (Eds.). (2005). *Funds of knowledge: Theorizing practices in households, communities, and classrooms.* Mahwah, NJ: Lawrence Erlbaum Associates.

Jefferies, D., & Merkley, D. (2001). Guidelines for implementing a graphic organizer. *The Reading Teacher, 54*(4), 350–357.

Kroese, J., Mather, N., & Sammons, J. (2006). The relationship between nonword spelling abilities of K–3 teachers and student spelling outcomes. *Learning Disabilities: A Multidisciplinary Journal, 14*(2), 85–89.

Moats, L., & Tolman, C. (2008). *English gets a bad rap!* Retrieved from colorincolorado.org/article/28650.

Morahan, M., & Clayton, C. (2003). *Bilingual students in the elementary classroom: A reference for the practicum student at Boston College Lynch School of Education.* Title III Project ALL, Boston College Lynch School of Education.

Sigueza, T. (2005). *Graphic organizers.* Retrieved from colorincolorado.org/article/13354.

La escritura: Parallel Spanish Handwriting Instruction

La escritura for Grades K–3 provides parallel instruction to the English program so that Spanish-speaking students with limited English can progress in handwriting, a critical literacy skill, alongside their English-speaking peers.

A parallel **La escritura** Student Edition and a **La escritura** Teacher Guide are available. The Teacher Guide includes reduced student pages and Spanish translations of all objectives, stroke descriptions, and self-evaluation questions.

Spanish posters and Practice Masters are also available.

Ellen Riojas Clark holds a Ph.D. in curriculum and instruction from The University of Texas at Austin. Dr. Clark is Professor Emeritus of Bicultural Bilingual Studies at The University of Texas at San Antonio. Her research interests include the relationship between the constructs of self-concept, ethnic identity, self-efficacy, and good teaching; bilingual education teacher training; and the identification of gifted language-minority children.

Bertha Pérez, Ed.D., began her career as a classroom teacher in San Antonio, Texas. Later, she earned her doctorate from the University of Massachusetts at Amherst and served as professor of reading and biliteracy at San José State University, The University of Texas at El Paso, and The University of Texas at San Antonio. As a result of her literacy and biliteracy research, Dr. Pérez has become an authority on biliteracy and assisting English language learners to develop biliteracy.

Zaner-Bloser National Handwriting Contest

Legible handwriting is something to be proud of!

Develop, celebrate, and reward legible handwriting—enter the Zaner-Bloser National Handwriting Contest! The annual contest measures the handwriting abilities of students in Grades K–8 in schools using **Zaner-Bloser Handwriting** materials.

State and national recognition for finalists and schools

A public school and private school National Grade-Level Semifinalist for each state is selected from State Grade-Level Winners. Nine National Grade-Level Semifinalists are selected as the top handwriting students in the country—the Grand National Grade-Level Champions.

About the contest:

- The contest is completely free of charge.
- Over 300,000 students participate each year.
- Entries can be completed in class or at home.
- Entries are judged on shape, size, spacing, and slant.
- Prizes are awarded to students and their teachers and schools.
- Every student earns a Participation Certificate.
- Students with special needs have the opportunity to compete for the **Nicholas Maxim Award**.

For complete contest information and entry materials, call 800.924.9233 or visit www.zaner-bloser.com

Previous Handwriting Contest winners

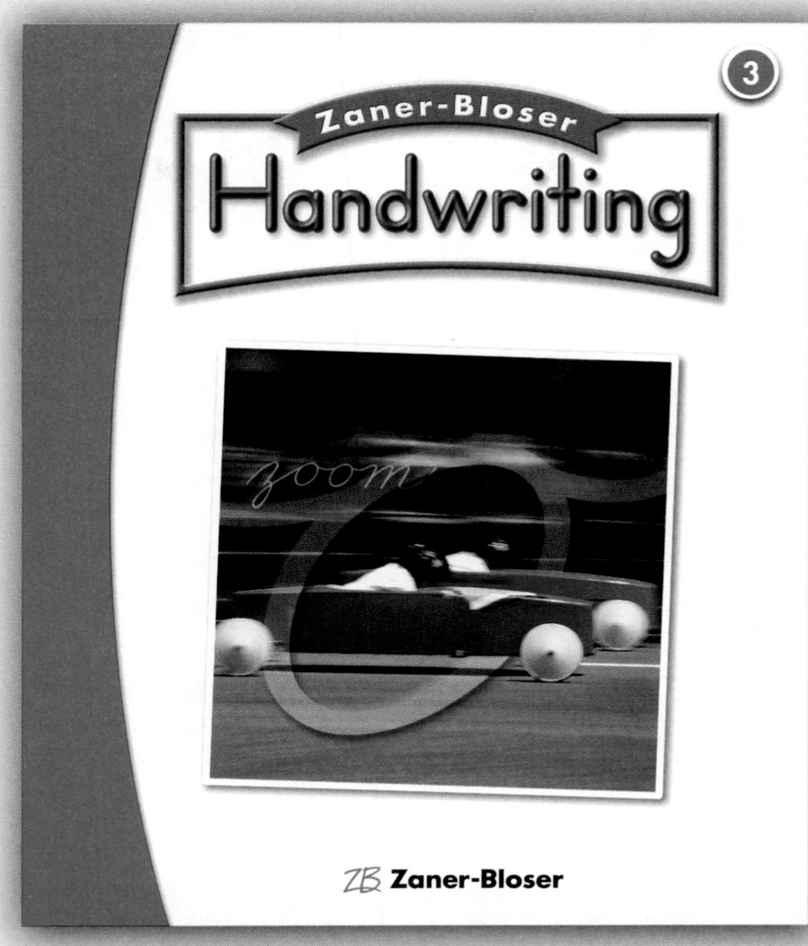

Occupational Therapy Consultants

Asha Asher, MA OTR/L, FAOTA, M.Ed. (Special Education), Cincinnati, OH
Mary Benbow, M.S., OTR, La Jolla, CA
Jane Case-Smith, Ed.D., OTR/L, FAOTA, Former Chair of the Occupational Therapy Division, Ohio State University
North Shore Pediatric Therapy

ELL Consultants

Ellen Riojas Clark, Ph.D., Professor of Bicultural-Bilingual Studies, University of Texas at San Antonio
Bertha Pérez, Ed.D., Professor Emeritus of Literacy, University of Texas at San Antonio

Occupational Therapy Advisory Board

Carol Armann, OTR/L, Marietta, OH
Kathleen A. Benton-Sanchez, M.P.A., OTR/L, Nashville, TN
Sherry Eisenbach, OT/L, Portland, OR
Elizabeth Gerich, OTR/L, Plymouth, MN
Sheila Martins, OTR/L, North Las Vegas, NV
Leslie N. Parker, OTR/L, Huntington, WV
Tricia Shibuya, OTR/L, Las Vegas, NV
Denaysa Sisemore, M.S., OTR/L, Windsor, CO
Cheryl Weaver, CAS, M.S.Ed., OTR/L, Macedon, NY

Reviewers

Amy Bass, National Heritage Academies, Byron Center, MI
Donetta S. Brown, Birmingham City Schools, AL
Kelly Caravelli, Poway Unified School District, San Diego, CA
Michelle Corsi, East Windsor Regional Schools, NJ
Naomi Drewitz, East Windsor Regional Schools, NJ
Shan Glandon, Tulsa, OK
Karen Jackson, School District of Philadelphia, PA
Liz Knowles, Ed.D., 21st Century Curriculum Designs, LLC, Del Ray Beach, FL
Rita Olsen, Chicago Public Schools, IL
Geraldine A. Pappas, Detroit Public Schools, MI
Michael E. Pizzingrillo, Roman Catholic Diocese of Brooklyn, NY
Deborah C. Thomas, Ed.D., Montgomery Public Schools, AL
Ellen Lerch Thomsen, Roanoke County Public Schools, VA
Iefay Williams, School District of Philadelphia, PA

Credits

Art: John Hovell: 33–35, 151

Photos: ©Getty Images: Cover; ©Creatas/Getty: TOC (top); ©iStockphoto.com/Claudiad: TOC (bottom); George C. Anderson Photography, Inc.: 5, 6, 26–30; ©Westend61 GmbH/Alamy: 8 (left); ©iStockphoto.com/mcpix: 8 (right); ©iStockphoto.com/maciul7: 9 (left): ©iStockphoto.com/jcyoung2: 9 (right); ©Katrina Brown/Alamy: 10; Zaner-Bloser: 11 (left), 66, 141; ©Photosindia/Getty Images: 11 (right); ©Design Pics Inc./Alamy: 12; ©RayArt Graphics/Alamy: 13; ©iStockphoto.com/compassandcamera: 14; ©JUPITERIMAGES/Brand X/Alamy: 15 (left); ©iStockphoto.com/bmcentl: 15 (right); ©scenicireland.com/Christopher Hill Photographic/Alamy: 16 (left); ©Cultura/Alamy: 16 (top right); ©Ariel Skelley/CORBIS: 18 (bottom right); ©Ian Shaw/Alamy: 17 (left); ©Bruce Laurance/Photolibrary: 17 (right); ©Digital Vision/Getty Images: 18–19; ©Akihiro Sugimoto/Photolibrary: 20–21; ©Kevin Schafer/Corbis: 22–23; ©Visions of America, LLC/Alamy: 23 (bottom); ©iStockphoto.com/Floortje: 25 (left); ©Comstock/Jupiterimages: 25 (right); ©Creatas/Getty: 39; ©iStockphoto.com/tulcarion: 40; ©Medioimages/Photodisc/Getty Images: 41; ©iStockphoto.com/sydem: 42; ©iStockphoto.com/Claudiad: 43; ©iStockphoto.com/billnoll: 44; ©Brand X Pictures/Jupiterimages: 45; ©iStockphoto.com/jeannehatch: 46; ©iStockphoto.com/ ladyminnie: 47; ©Carey Alan & Sandy/Photolibrary: 48; ©iStockphoto.com/Freder: 49; ©iStockphoto.com/Adventure_Photo: 50; ©iStockphoto.com/cinoby: 51; ©iStockphoto.com/matka_Wariatka: 52; ©iStockphoto.com/Andrea_Hill: 53; ©Matt Oldfield/Getty Images: 54; ©iStockphoto.com/Malven: 55; ©Ryan McGinnis/Alamy: 57; ©Neo Vision/Getty Images: 68; ©Alan SCHEIN/Alamy: 61; ©iStockphoto.com/stevenallan: 62; ©LWA-Sharie Kennedy/Corbis: 63; ©Brand X Pictures/Getty Images: 64; ©iStockphoto.com/alexxxl981: 65; ©Stephen Marks/Getty Images: 67; ©Big Cheese Photo/Jupiterimages: 68; ©Brand X Pictures/Jupiterimages: 69; ©iStockphoto.com/DarrenFisher: 70; ©Wes Thompson/CORBIS: 72; ©Digital Vision/Getty Images: 73; ©iStockphoto.com/iPandastudio: 74; ©age fotostock/SuperStock: 75; ©iStockphoto.com/JulienGrondin: 76; ©iStockphoto.com/SkyF: 77; ©ilian studio/Alamy: 78; ©Li Ding/Alamy: 79; ©PhotosIndia.com/Getty Images: 80; ©iStockphoto.com/mjbs: 84; ©ImagesBazaar/Alamy: 87; ©imagebroker/Alamy: 88; ©iStockphoto.com/gmnicholas: 89; ©Brandon Seidel/Alamy: 93; ©iStockphoto.com/digitalskillet: 94; ©iStockphoto.com/ManoAfrica: 95; ©Brand X/Corbis: 96; ©Jim Batty/Alamy: 97; ©Tom Schierlitz/Getty Images 98 (left); ©Martin Poole/Getty Images: 98 (right); ©iStockphoto.com/fajean: 99; ©Charles C. Place/Getty Images: 101; ©IMAGEMORE Co., Ltd./Alamy: 102; ©iStockphoto.com/francisblack: 103; ©Comstock/Getty Images: 104; ©Ariel Skelley/Getty Images: 105; ©iStockphoto.com/VCNW: 106; ©David Young-Wolff/PhotoEdit Inc.: 107; ©Comstock/Getty Images: 108; ©iStockphoto.com/DorianPhotoInc: 109; ©Jim Wehtje/Getty Images: 110; ©Comstock/Getty Images: 112; ©Corbis Premium RF/Alamy: 113; ©Siede Preis/Getty Images: 115; ©MELBA PHOTO AGENCY/Alamy: 116; ©Stewart Cohen/Getty Images: 119; ©iStockphoto.com/monkeybusinessimages: 120; ©iStockphoto.com/solarseven: 121; ©Robert Struwe/Alamy: 122; ©Penrod Studios/Alamy: 123; ©Corbis: 124; ©Hisham Ibrahim/Alamy: 124 (inset); ©iStockphoto.com/EwaWysocka: 125; ©iStockphoto.com/tibor5: 127; ©Don Despain/www.rekindlephoto.com/Alamy: 128; ©iStockphoto.com/kassandra: 129; ©iStockphoto.com/amanalang: 130; ©Digital Vision/Getty Images: 131; ©Sharon Lowe/Alamy: 132; ©Comstock/Jupiterimages: 133 (left); ©Tim Pannell/Corbis/Getty Images: 133 (right); ©Jon Parker Lee/Alamy: 134; ©Pictorial Press Ltd/Alamy: 135; ©iStockphoto.com/tainted: 136; ©Image Source/Getty Images: 138; ©Blend Images/SuperStock: 140; ©Comstock/Jupiterimages: 142, 156; ©CORBIS: 152; ©Jim Esposito/Photolibrary: 154; ©Digital Vision/Getty Images: 156–157

ISBN 978-1-4531-1798-9

ZB Code 16

Zaner-Bloser, Inc.
1-800-421-3018
www.zaner-bloser.com
Printed in the United States of America

1 2 3 4 5 997 19 18 17 16 15

Zaner-Bloser

CONTENTS

Introduction 5

Unit 1 **Reviewing Manuscript Writing**

Writing Positions 6
Manuscript Keys to Legibility 7
Write Ll, Ii, Tt 8
Write Oo, Aa, Dd 9
Write Cc, Ee, Ff 10
Write Gg, Jj, Qq 11
Write Uu, Ss, Bb, Pp 12
Write Rr, Nn, Mm, Hh 13
Write Vv, Yy, Ww 14
Write Xx, Kk, Zz 15
Manuscript Review and Application . . . 16

Unit 2 **Cursive Writing: Getting Started**

Pretest: Write a Poem 18
Welcome to Cursive Writing 20
Cursive Letters and Numerals 22
Reading Cursive Writing 24
Writing Positions: Left-Handed Writers . . 26
Writing Positions: Right-Handed Writers . 27
Basic Strokes: Undercurve 28
Basic Strokes: Downcurve 29
Basic Strokes: Overcurve 30
Basic Strokes: Slant 31
Keys to Legibility: Shape 32
Keys to Legibility: Size 33
Keys to Legibility: Spacing 34
Keys to Legibility: Slant 35

Unit 3 **Cursive Letters**

Writing Lowercase Cursive Letters 36
Write Undercurve Letters i, t, u, w, e, l, b, h, f, k, r, s, j, p 38
Joinings 53
Review 54
Application 55
Cursive Writing in the Real World 56
Manuscript Maintenance 57
Keys to Legibility 58

Write Downcurve Letters a, d, g, o, c, q 60
Joinings 67
Review 68
Application 69
Cursive Writing in the Real World 70

Write Overcurve Letters n, m, y, x, v, z 71
Review 78
Application 79
Keys to Legibility 80

Review Lowercase Letters 82
Joinings 84
Cursive Numerals 86
Manuscript Maintenance 88

Writing Uppercase Cursive Letters 90
Write Downcurve Letters A, O, D, C, E 92
Review 98
Application 99
Write Curve Forward Letters N, M, H, K, U, Y, Z, V, W, X 100
Joinings 111
Review 112
Application 113
Cursive Writing in the Real World 114
Manuscript Maintenance 115
Keys to Legibility 116

Write Overcurve and Doublecurve Letters I, J, Q, T, F 118
Review 124
Application 125

Write Undercurve-Loop Letters G, S, L . 126
Write Undercurve-Slant Letters P, R, B . . 130
Joinings 133
Review 134
Application 135
Cursive Writing in the Real World 136

Review Uppercase Cursive Letters 137
Keys to Legibility 138
Manuscript Maintenance 140

Unit 4 **Using What You Have Learned**

Friendly Letter 142
Compare and Contrast 144
Fiction or Nonfiction? 146
Last Weekend 148
How To 150
Handwriting and the Writing Process . . . 151
Writing Quickly 152
Writing Easily 154
Posttest: Write a Poem 156
Write the Sentence 158
Record of Student's Handwriting Skills . . . 159
Index 160

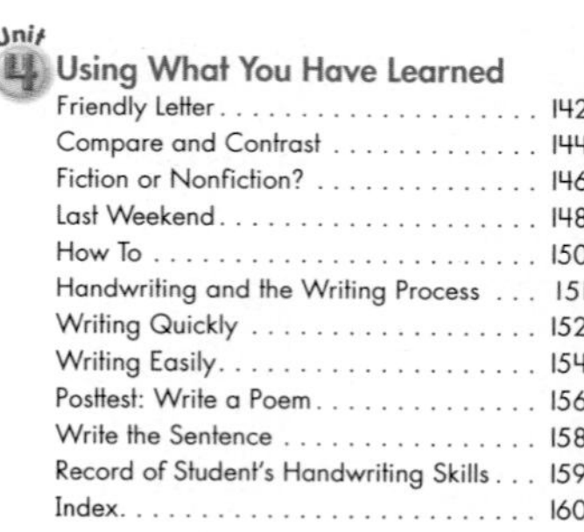

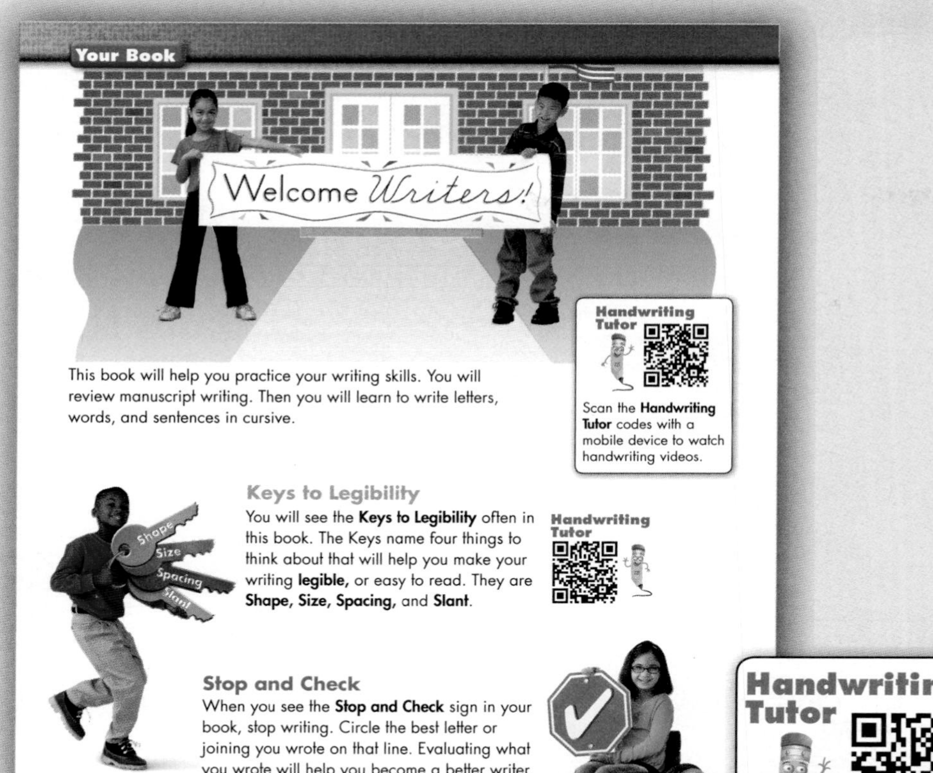

Your Book

This book will help you practice your writing skills. You will review manuscript writing. Then you will learn to write letters, words, and sentences in cursive.

Handwriting Tutor

Scan the **Handwriting Tutor** codes with a mobile device to watch handwriting videos.

Keys to Legibility

You will see the **Keys to Legibility** often in this book. The Keys name four things to think about that will help you make your writing **legible,** or easy to read. They are **Shape, Size, Spacing,** and **Slant**.

Handwriting Tutor

Stop and Check

When you see the **Stop and Check** sign in your book, stop writing. Circle the best letter or joining you wrote on that line. Evaluating what you wrote will help you become a better writer.

Handwriting Tutor

5

Students can scan the **Handwriting Tutor** codes throughout their book to watch animated letter models and how-to videos.

Handwriting Tutor

Grade 3 Handwriting at a Glance

The goal of *Zaner-Bloser Handwriting* is to teach students to write legibly. As you work through the pages of this book with students, you will be helping them learn to write letters, words, and sentences that are legible to both writers and readers. By learning and applying the four Keys to Legibility—**Shape, Size, Spacing,** and **Slant**—students will evaluate their writing and discover techniques to help them improve and refine their writing skills.

The opening pages are important for laying a foundation for writing. **Reviewing Manuscript Writing** helps students warm up for cursive writing. A **Pretest** provides an initial sample of each student's handwriting quality before the year's formal handwriting instruction. **Welcome to Cursive Writing** provides readiness information for beginning cursive writing. **Cursive Letters and Numerals** presents correct models of the forms students will write.

Writing Positions guides students in the correct positions for sitting, holding the pencil, and positioning the paper. On the pages for **Basic Strokes,** students will become familiar with the lines that form all the letters and numerals in cursive handwriting. The **Keys to Legibility** pages emphasize the qualities of good writing that will help students evaluate and improve their handwriting throughout the year.

In **Cursive Letters,** lowercase and uppercase letters are introduced separately. The letter sequence is determined by the beginning stroke of the letters. In **Cursive Numerals,** students observe models and write the cursive numerals **1** through **10** with correct strokes. Finally, students apply their knowledge in **Using What You Have Learned,** which includes activities that will help them increase their speed and fluency as they gain automaticity in handwriting.

Note that the models are provided for all writing and students have space to write directly beneath the models. **Key** or **Stop and Check** features on every letter page foster self-evaluation on a continuing basis.

Suggest that students keep a notebook or folder of the writing they do for themselves and for others.

Review student page 5 with your class as an introduction to the *Zaner-Bloser Handwriting* program. It defines and explains the visual components appearing throughout their book that will help them learn to write and evaluate with consistency.

Explain to students that in this book they will learn how to write letters, words, and sentences fluently and quickly. They will also discover ways to make their writing easy to read.

Manuscript Review

Suggest that students refer to student page 6 throughout the year as a reminder of correct paper and pencil position for manuscript writing. Demonstrate correct positions for both left-handed and right-handed writers. Then ask students to place a sheet of paper in the proper position on their desk, pick up a pencil, and write their name.

Objective: To review correct paper and pencil position for manuscript writing for left- and right-handed writers.

Handwriting Tutor

People use manuscript writing every day. Good manuscript writing is easy to read.

Be sure to place your paper in the correct position for manuscript when you write. That will help keep your writing straight up and down.

Writing Positions Manuscript

If you write with your **LEFT** hand . . .

Place the paper like this.

Slant the paper as shown in the picture.

Rest both arms on the desk. Use your right hand to move the paper as you write.

Pull the pencil toward your left elbow when you write.

Hold the pencil like this.

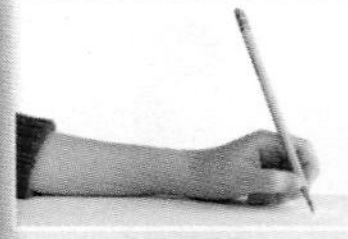

Hold the pencil with your thumb and first two fingers. Do not squeeze the pencil when you write.

If you write with your **RIGHT** hand . . .

Place the paper like this.

Place the paper straight in front of you.

Rest both arms on the desk. Use your left hand to move the paper as you write.

Pull the pencil toward the middle of your body when you write.

Hold the pencil like this.

Hold the pencil with your thumb and first two fingers. Do not squeeze the pencil when you write.

6

Writing Positions

Paper Position

Tell students that correct page placement is a critical factor in legibility. To ensure that the paper is placed correctly for both right- and left-handed students, use tape to form a frame on the desk so students will be able to place the paper in the correct position.

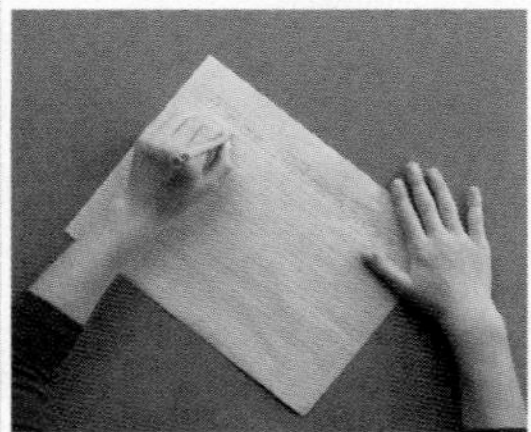

Left-Handed Writers

Right-Handed Writers

Pencil Position

Model good pencil position for students. The pencil is held between the thumb and the first two fingers, about an inch above its point. The first finger rests on the top of the pencil. The end of the bent thumb is placed against the pencil to hold it high in the hand and near the knuckle.

Left-Handed Writers

Right-Handed Writers

Alternative Pencil Position

Students who have difficulty with the traditional pencil position may prefer the alternative method of holding the pencil between their first and second fingers.

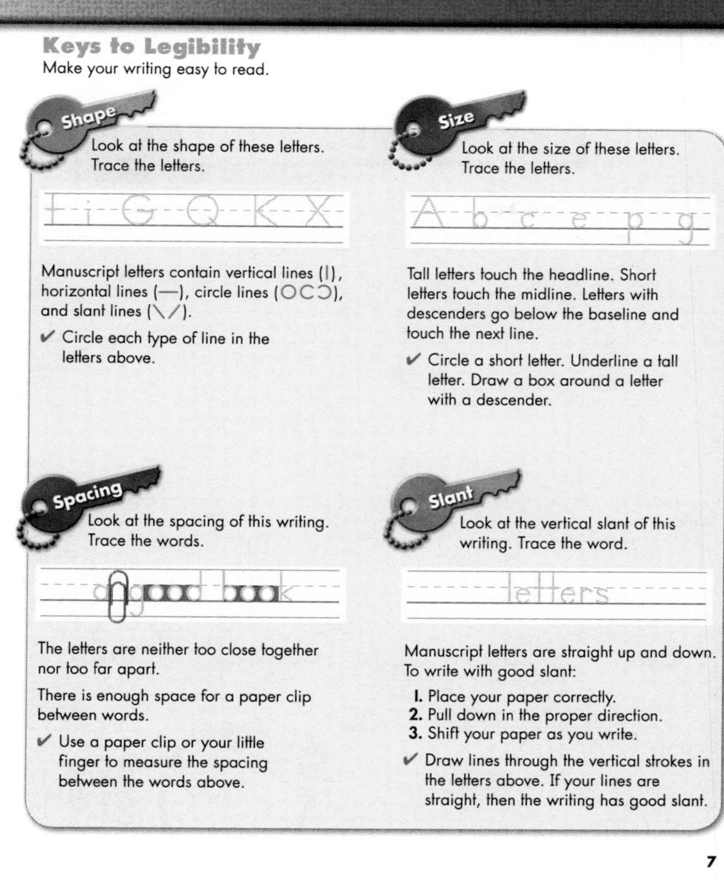
Keys to Legibility
Make your writing easy to read.

Shape
Look at the shape of these letters. Trace the letters.

I i G Q K X

Manuscript letters contain vertical lines (|), horizontal lines (—), circle lines (O C Ↄ), and slant lines (\ /).

✔ Circle each type of line in the letters above.

Size
Look at the size of these letters. Trace the letters.

A b c e p g

Tall letters touch the headline. Short letters touch the midline. Letters with descenders go below the baseline and touch the next line.

✔ Circle a short letter. Underline a tall letter. Draw a box around a letter with a descender.

Spacing
Look at the spacing of this writing. Trace the words.

a good book

The letters are neither too close together nor too far apart.

There is enough space for a paper clip between words.

✔ Use a paper clip or your little finger to measure the spacing between the words above.

Slant
Look at the vertical slant of this writing. Trace the word.

letters

Manuscript letters are straight up and down. To write with good slant:

1. Place your paper correctly.
2. Pull down in the proper direction.
3. Shift your paper as you write.

✔ Draw lines through the vertical strokes in the letters above. If your lines are straight, then the writing has good slant.

7

Keys to Legibility

Objective: To review the Keys to Legibility for manuscript writing.

Keys to Legibility

Point out the four Key sections on student page 7. Explain to students that each colored key directs them to consider certain qualities of good manuscript writing.

Emphasize to students that applying the Keys consistently as they write will promote the legibility of their writing.

Discuss the information provided for each Key. Use the board as needed to model and reinforce what students are reviewing. Then guide them to complete the exercises on the page.

Shape The basic strokes—vertical, horizontal, circle, slant—written correctly in specific combinations yield letters with correct shape.

Size Forming letters that are correctly placed on guidelines yields letters with correct size.

Spacing Letters and words that are too close together or too far apart are hard to read.

Slant In manuscript writing, letters are written with vertical slant. The correct position of the paper and the proper direction in which the strokes are pulled foster vertical slant.

Support for English Language Learners

Listening Skills Developing listening skills is an important part of language acquisition. Use commands and Total Physical Response (TPR) to help students develop listening skills. For example, use TPR to help students understand and demonstrate the Spacing Key to Legibility. Ask two students to stand and show the space between two words. The students' physical response will demonstrate their comprehension of your command and will add to their understanding of the language.

Handwriting Coach

Manuscript Writing

At the Board Use manuscript writing on the board for various purposes, especially vocabulary and dictionary study, as well as other work involving word-attack skills.

At the Desk Give a weekly assignment that requires students to use their best manuscript writing, such as filling out forms, doing map study, developing charts, preparing labels and captions, working crossword puzzles, and making posters.

See the *Keys to Legibility Poster* for more information.

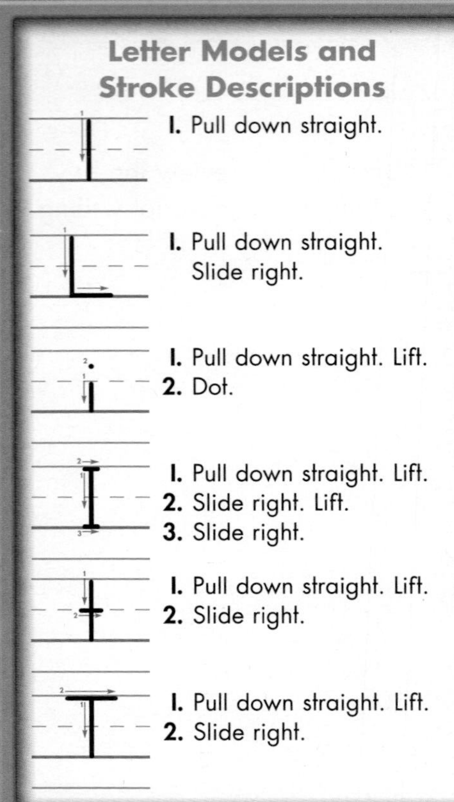
Letter Models and Stroke Descriptions
1. Pull down straight.
1. Pull down straight.
Slide right.
1. Pull down straight. Lift.
2. Dot.
1. Pull down straight. Lift.
2. Slide right. Lift.
3. Slide right.
1. Pull down straight. Lift.
2. Slide right.
1. Pull down straight. Lift.
2. Slide right.

Handwriting Tutor

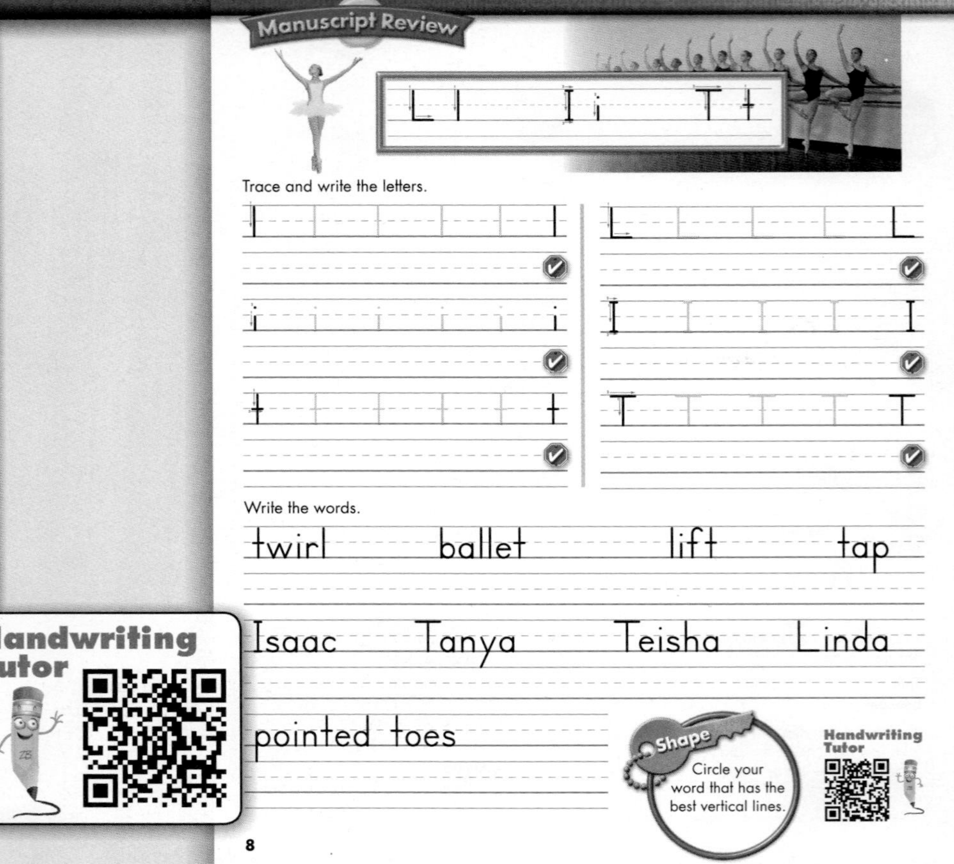
Manuscript Review

Ll Ii Tt

Trace and write the letters.

Write the words.

twirl ballet lift tap

Isaac Tanya Teisha Linda

pointed toes

Shape: Circle your word that has the best vertical lines.

Handwriting Tutor

8

Objective: To practice and master **Ll, Ii,** and **Tt**.

1 Model

Point out that the letters on student page 8 all begin by pulling straight down. Write the letters on guidelines as you say the stroke descriptions.

Repeat the stroke descriptions as students use their finger to write the letters on their desktop.

2 Practice

Remind students to position their book and grip their pencil correctly for writing.

Ask students to begin at the green starting dot and carefully trace the letters with pencil. Then have them write the letters and words on the page.

Remind students that when they come to this symbol ✓, they should stop writing and circle their best letter.

3 Evaluate

Tell students it is important to make their writing easy for others to read. Remind them to complete all **Stop and Check** activities.

Proper shape makes each letter easy to read. Ask:

- Is your **l** straight up and down?
- Does your **L** begin at the headline?
- Did you remember to dot your **i**?
- Is your **I** about the same width as the model?
- Is the vertical line in your **t** straight?
- Is the slide right stroke in **T** written on the headline?

School Home Extra Practice

Practice Master 1

Manuscript Review

Write the letters.

Write the words.

label lullaby icicle

inside twist tablet

Leslie Lancelot Iris

Iberia Tahiti Trevor

Practice Master 1

Support for English Language Learners

Total Physical Response Show students what it means to **pull down straight**. Invite students to stand with you, arms stretched up toward the ceiling. Make an arm motion as though you are pulling down straight. Have students mimic your action. Tell them they are making vertical lines. Then show students what it means to **slide right**. Move your arm in a sliding motion to the right as you say, "slide right." Have students mimic your actions. Tell them they are making horizontal lines.

Oo Aa Dd

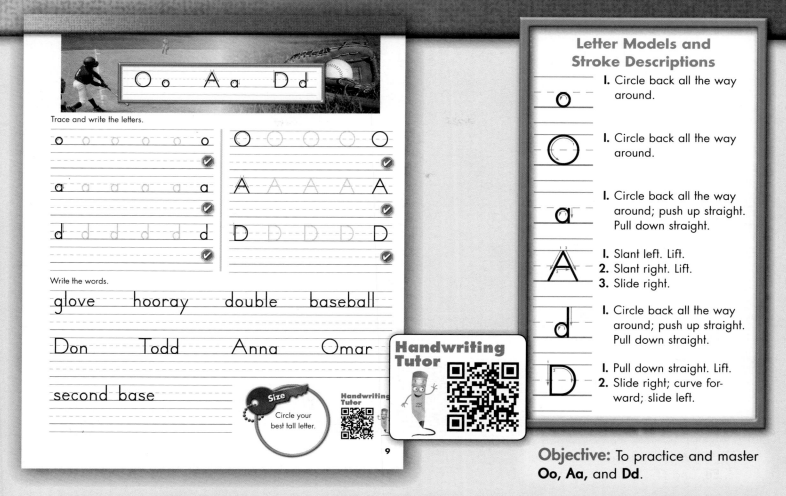

Trace and write the letters.

o o o o o o | O O O O O
a a a a a a | A A A A A
d d d d d d | D D D D D

Write the words.

glove hooray double baseball

Don Todd Anna Omar

second base

Size

Circle your best tall letter.

Handwriting Tutor

9

Letter Models and Stroke Descriptions

o
I. Circle back all the way around.

O
I. Circle back all the way around.

a
I. Circle back all the way around; push up straight. Pull down straight.

A
I. Slant left. Lift.
2. Slant right. Lift.
3. Slide right.

d
I. Circle back all the way around; push up straight. Pull down straight.

D
I. Pull down straight. Lift.
2. Slide right; curve forward; slide left.

Handwriting Tutor

Objective: To practice and master **Oo, Aa,** and **Dd**.

1 Model

Write the letters on guidelines as you say the stroke descriptions. Repeat the stroke descriptions as students use skywriting (see page Z21) to write the letters in the air.

Ask students to use their finger to trace the letters several times on student page 9.

2 Practice

Remind students to position their book and grip their pencil correctly for writing.

Ask students to begin at the green starting dot and carefully trace the letters with pencil. Then have them write the letters and words on the page.

Remind students that when they come to this symbol ✓, they should stop writing and circle their best letter.

3 Evaluate

Tell students it is important to make their writing easy for others to read. Remind them to complete all **Stop and Check** activities.

Proper size makes each letter easy to read. Ask:

- Do your **o, a,** and **d** begin just below the midline?
- Are your **O, A,** and **D** about the same width as the model?
- Does your **d** touch the headline and the baseline?

Writing in the Content Areas

Directions Display a road map of your state. Tell students to use the map to locate cities and towns that begin with the letters **O, A,** and **D** and have them write the names of those places on handwriting paper. Remind students that all proper nouns, including place names, must begin with an uppercase letter. Then have students write directions from their hometown to one of the cities or towns they located on the map. Students may write a numbered list if they wish. Remind students to use proper capitalization and punctuation in their sentences and to use their best handwriting.

Practice Master 2

Manuscript Review

o o o o | O O O O
a a a a | A A A A
d d d d | D D D D

wool odd aloha
agenda demand dazed
Oslo Oscar Andrea
Asia Dirk Denise

Practice Master 2

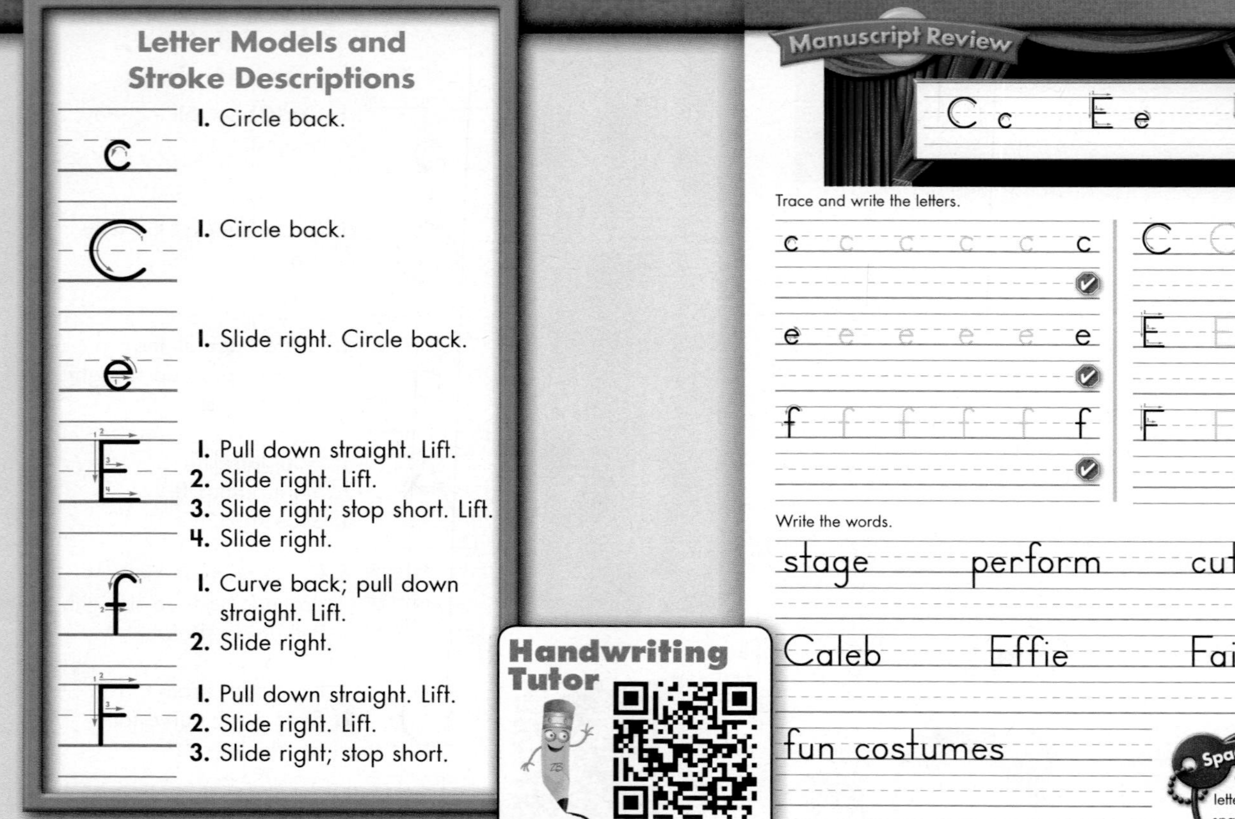

Letter Models and Stroke Descriptions
c
1. Circle back.
C
1. Circle back.
e
1. Slide right. Circle back.
E
1. Pull down straight. Lift.
2. Slide right. Lift.
3. Slide right; stop short. Lift.
4. Slide right.
f
1. Curve back; pull down straight. Lift.
2. Slide right.
F
1. Pull down straight. Lift.
2. Slide right. Lift.
3. Slide right; stop short.
Handwriting Tutor
Manuscript Review
Cc Ee Ff
Trace and write the letters.
Write the words.
stage perform cute clap
Caleb Effie Faith Ella
fun costumes
Spacing
Circle two letters with good spacing between them.
Handwriting Tutor
10

Objective: To practice and master **Cc, Ee,** and **Ff**.

1 Model

Write the letters on guidelines as you say the stroke descriptions. Repeat the stroke descriptions as students use their finger to trace the letters on their desktop.

2 Practice

Remind students to position their book and grip their pencil correctly for writing.

Ask students to begin at the green starting dot on student page 10 and carefully trace the letters with pencil. Then have them write the letters and words on the page.

Remind students that when they come to this symbol ✓, they should stop writing and circle their best letter.

3 Evaluate

Tell students it is important to make their writing easy for others to read. Remind them to complete all **Stop and Check** activities.

Proper spacing makes each letter easy to read. Ask:

- Is the space between each letter in a word consistent?
- Is there space for your fingertip between **fun** and **costumes**?

School Home Extra Practice

Practice Master 3

Manuscript Review

Write the letters.

c c c c C C C C

e e e e E E E E

f f f f F F F F

Write the words.

cactus crutch engine

evening cliff fifty

Canada Carson Enid

Elvis France Faith

Practice Master 3

Support for English Language Learners

Providing Clear Clues As you present material orally or write on the board, remember that students follow both verbal and nonverbal cues. When writing on the board, position yourself so students can see you when you are speaking. Doing so allows students to watch your facial expressions, look for other nonverbal cues, hear your intonation, and observe how you produce your sounds.

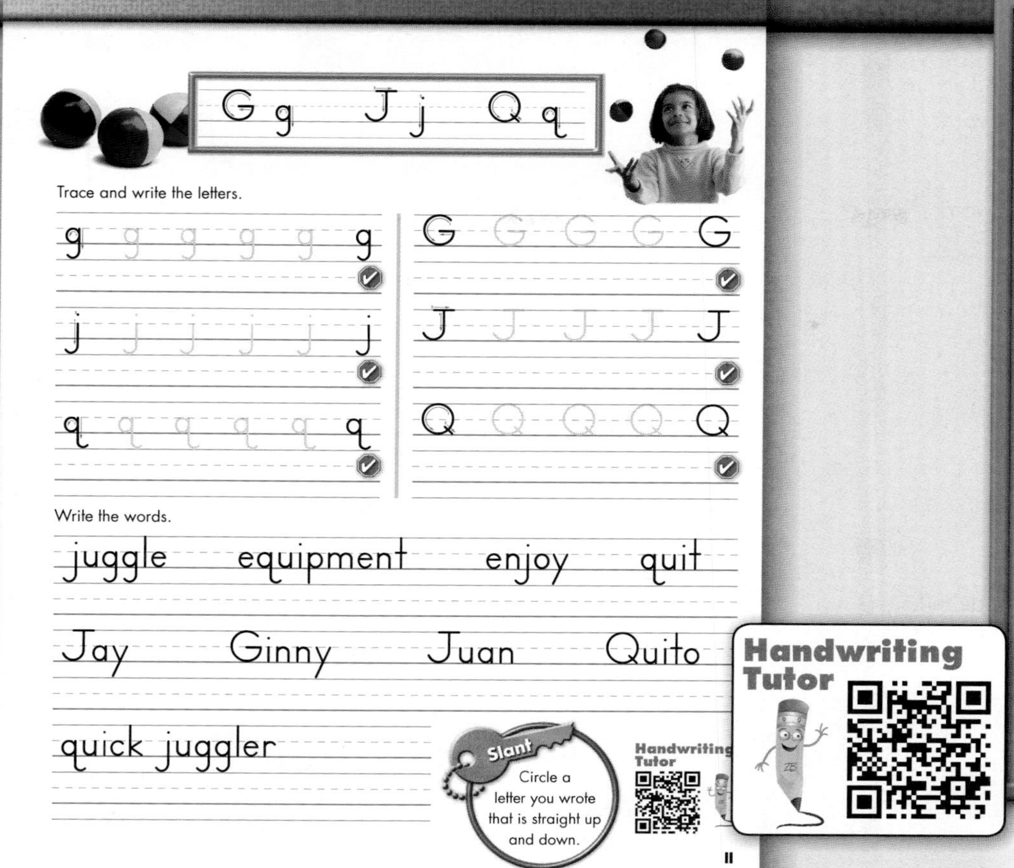
Gg Jj Qq

Trace and write the letters.

g g g g g g
G G G G G
j j j j j j
J J J J J
q q q q q q
Q Q Q Q Q

Write the words.

juggle equipment enjoy quit

Jay Ginny Juan Quito

quick juggler

Slant
Circle a letter you wrote that is straight up and down.

Handwriting Tutor

11

Handwriting Tutor

Letter Models and Stroke Descriptions

g
1. Circle back all the way around; push up straight. Pull down straight; curve back.

G
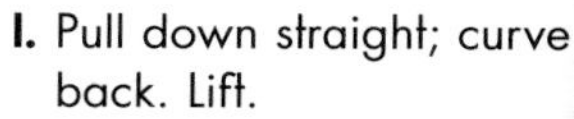
1. Circle back. Slide left.

j
1. Pull down straight; curve back. Lift.
2. Dot.

J
1. Pull down straight; curve back. Lift.
2. Slide right.

q
1. Circle back all the way around; push up straight. Pull down straight; curve forward.

Q
1. Circle back all the way around. Lift.
2. Slant right.

Objective: To practice and master **Gg, Jj,** and **Qq.**

1 Model

Write the letters on guidelines as you say the stroke descriptions. Repeat the stroke descriptions as students use skywriting to write the letters in the air.

Ask students to use their finger to trace the letters several times on student page 11.

2 Practice

Remind students to position their book and grip their pencil correctly for writing.

Ask students to begin at the green starting dot and carefully trace the letters with pencil. Then have them write the letters and words on the page.

Remind students that when they come to this symbol ✔, they should stop writing and circle their best letter.

3 Evaluate

Tell students it is important to make their writing easy for others to read. Remind them to complete all **Stop and Check** activities.

Proper slant makes each letter easy to read. Ask:

- Is the vertical line in your **g, j,** and **q** straight up and down?
- Did you pull down straight when making your **J**?

Writing in the Content Areas

Language Arts

Short Story Have students use the words from the bottom of page 11 to write a short story about Jay, Ginny, Juan, and Quito. Students should be sure to pay attention to capitalization, punctuation, and sentence formation. Remind students to use their best handwriting. Have volunteers read their stories aloud to the class or in small groups.

Extra Practice

Practice Master 4

Manuscript Review

g g g g G G G G
j j j j J J J J
q q q q Q Q Q Q

garage engineer eject
jade square quiz
Greece Gus June
Jesse Quincy Qatar

Practice Master 4

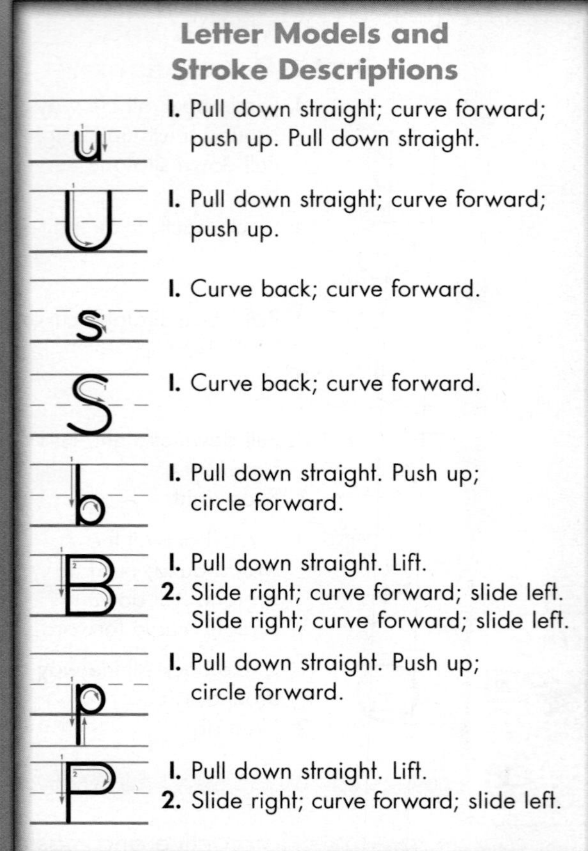

Letter Models and Stroke Descriptions

u 1. Pull down straight; curve forward; push up. Pull down straight.

U 1. Pull down straight; curve forward; push up.

s 1. Curve back; curve forward.

S 1. Curve back; curve forward.

b 1. Pull down straight. Push up; circle forward.

B 1. Pull down straight. Lift.
2. Slide right; curve forward; slide left. Slide right; curve forward; slide left.

p 1. Pull down straight. Push up; circle forward.

P 1. Pull down straight. Lift.
2. Slide right; curve forward; slide left.

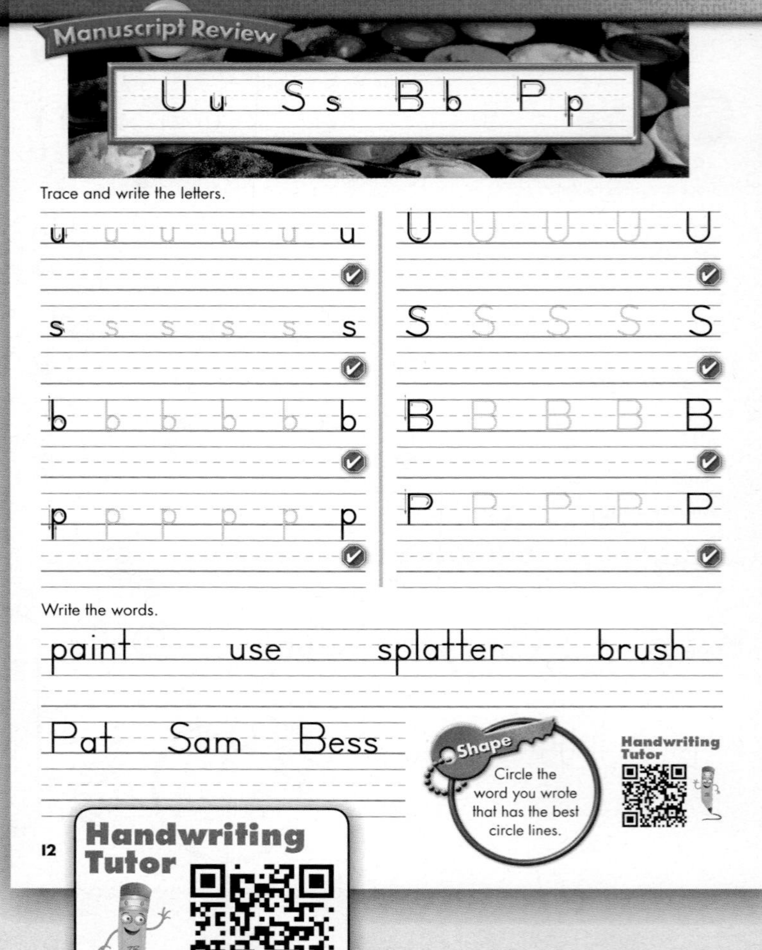

Manuscript Review

Uu Ss Bb Pp

Trace and write the letters.

u u u u u u U U U U U

s s s s s s S S S S S

b b b b b b B B B B B

p p p p p p P P P P P

Write the words.

paint use splatter brush

Pat Sam Bess

Shape: Circle the word you wrote that has the best circle lines.

Handwriting Tutor

12

Handwriting Tutor

Objective: To practice and master **Uu, Ss, Bb,** and **Pp**.

1 Model

Write the letters on guidelines as you say the stroke descriptions.

Repeat the stroke descriptions as students use their finger to trace the letters on their desktop.

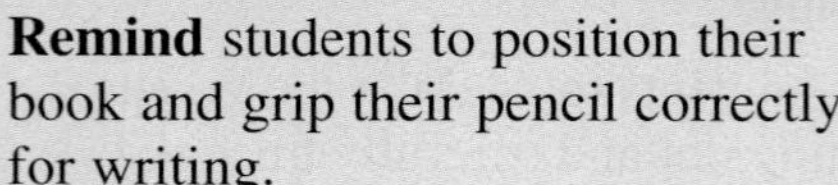

2 Practice

Remind students to position their book and grip their pencil correctly for writing.

Ask students to begin at the green starting dot on student page 12 and carefully trace the letters with pencil. Then have them write the letters and words on the page.

Remind students that when they come to this symbol ✓, they should stop writing and circle their best letter.

3 Evaluate

Tell students it is important to make their writing easy for others to read. Remind them to complete all **Stop and Check** activities.

Proper shape makes each letter easy to read. Ask:

- Does the curve of your **U** begin and end about halfway between the midline and the baseline?
- Is the top of your **S** about the same size as the bottom?
- Is the slide left stroke in your **P** on the midline?

Extra Practice

School Home

Practice Master 5

Manuscript Review

Write the letters.

u u u u U U U U

s s s s S S S S

b b b b B B B B

p p p p P P P P

Write the words.

umbrella sunset bubble

pulp Ulster Solon

Savannah Bernice Peru

Practice Master 5

Support for English Language Learners

Stroke Description Vocabulary The words **forward** and **backward** are particularly challenging for ELL students. Be sure to show students the letter model with stroke descriptions and arrows as you describe how to make strokes that curve forward and curve back. Make sure they understand the meaning of all the words used in the stroke descriptions.

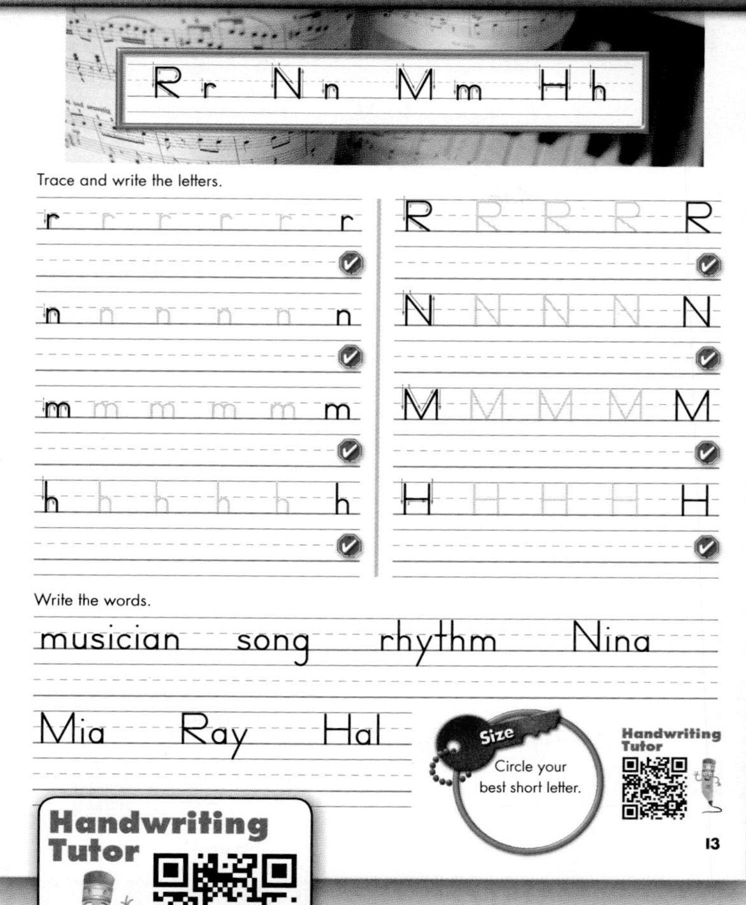
Rr Nn Mm Hh

Trace and write the letters.

r r r r r r R R R R R

n n n n n n N N N N N

m m m m m m M M M M M

h h h h h h H H H H H

Write the words.

musician song rhythm Nina

Mia Ray Hal

13

Handwriting Tutor

Letter Models and Stroke Descriptions

r
1. Pull down straight. Push up; curve forward.

R
1. Pull down straight. Lift.
2. Slide right; curve forward; slide left. Slant right.

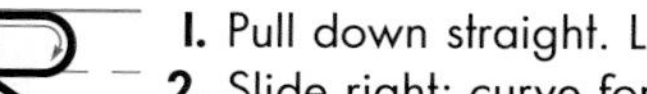

n
1. Pull down straight. Push up; curve forward; pull down straight.

N
1. Pull down straight. Lift.
2. Slant right. Push up straight.

m
1. Pull down straight. Push up; curve forward; pull down straight. Push up; curve forward; pull down straight.

M
1. Pull down straight. Lift.
2. Slant right. Slant up. Pull down straight.

h
1. Pull down straight. Push up; curve forward; pull down straight.

H
1. Pull down straight. Lift.
2. Pull down straight. Lift.
3. Slide right.

Objective: To practice and master **Rr, Nn, Mm,** and **Hh**.

1 Model

Write the letters on guidelines as you say the stroke descriptions. Repeat the stroke descriptions as students use skywriting to write the letters in the air.

Ask students to use their finger to trace the letters several times on student page 13.

2 Practice

Remind students to position their book and grip their pencil correctly for writing.

Ask students to begin at the green starting dot and carefully trace the letters with pencil. Then have them write the letters and words on the page.

Remind students that when they come to this symbol ✓, they should stop writing and circle their best letter.

3 Evaluate

Tell students it is important to make their writing easy for others to read. Remind them to complete all **Stop and Check** activities.

Proper size makes each letter easy to read. Ask:

- Are your letters about the same width as the models?
- Do your letters hit the guidelines in the same places as the model letters?

Extra Practice

Practice Master 6

Manuscript Review

r r r r R R R R
n n n n N N N N
m m m m M M M M
h h h h H H H H

murmur nation memory
hatch Ross Netherlands
Mexico Mike Holly

Practice Master 6

Tips From an Occupational Therapist

Rubber Band Rings Students at this age should be able to initiate individual finger movements and oppose each fingertip separately with the tip of the thumb. **Practice these skills by having students put small rubber bands on the fingers of their writing hand as if they were putting rings on their fingers.** Then have students take off the "rings" with the thumb of their writing hand and without the help of their other hand.

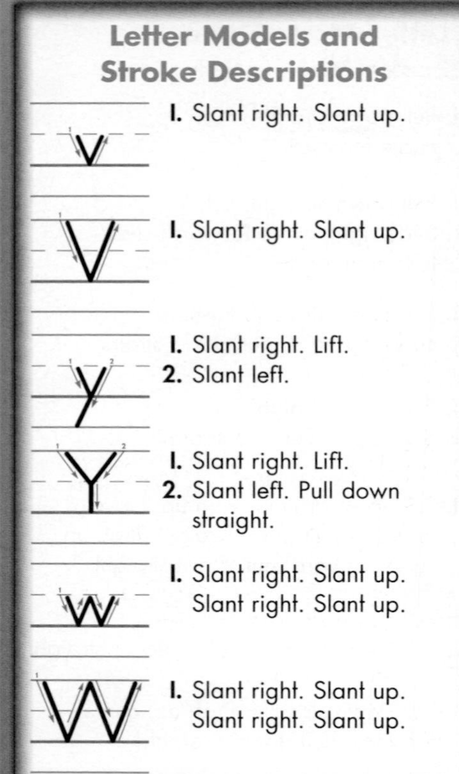

Letter Models and Stroke Descriptions
1. Slant right. Slant up.
1. Slant right. Slant up.
1. Slant right. Lift.
2. Slant left.
1. Slant right. Lift.
2. Slant left. Pull down straight.
1. Slant right. Slant up. Slant right. Slant up.
1. Slant right. Slant up. Slant right. Slant up.

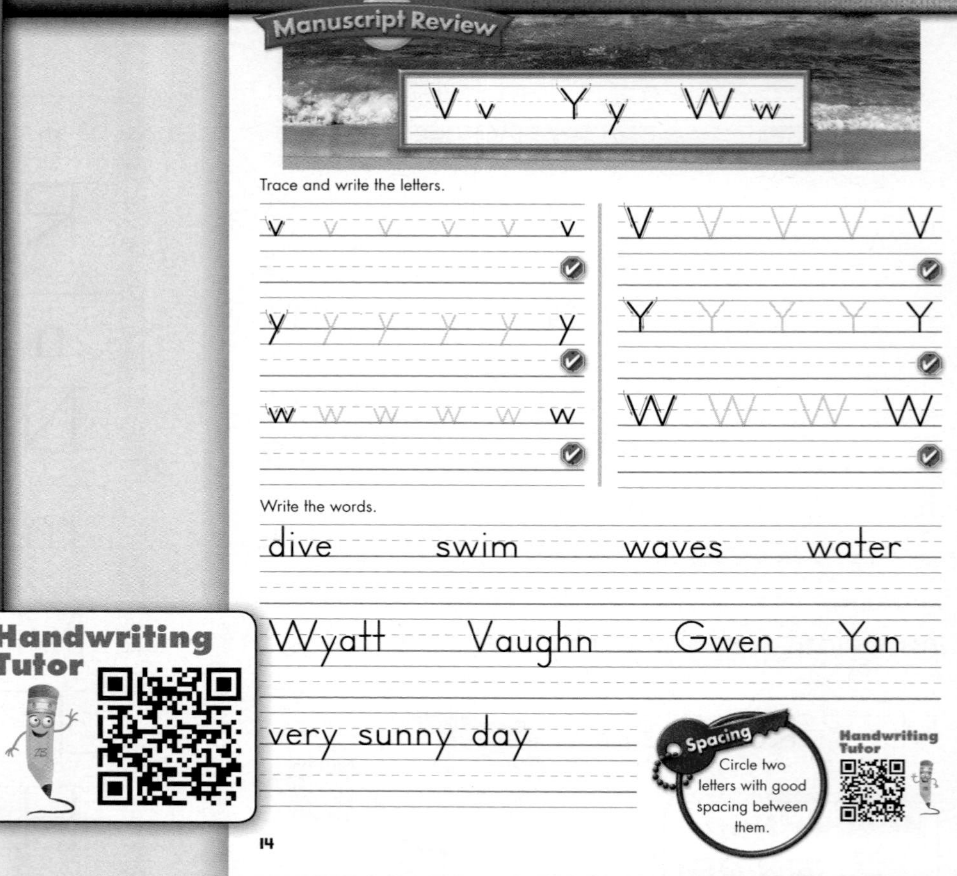

Manuscript Review
Vv Yy Ww
Trace and write the letters.
Write the words.
dive swim waves water
Wyatt Vaughn Gwen Yan
very sunny day
Handwriting Tutor
Spacing
Circle two letters with good spacing between them.
Handwriting Tutor
14

Objective: To practice and master **Vv, Yy,** and **Ww**.

1 Model

Write the letters on guidelines as you say the stroke descriptions.

Repeat the stroke descriptions as students use their finger to trace the letters on their desktop.

2 Practice

Remind students to position their book and grip their pencil correctly for writing.

Ask students to begin at the green starting dot on student page 14 and carefully trace the letters with pencil. Then have them write the letters and words on the page.

Remind students that when they come to this symbol ✓, they should stop writing and circle their best letter.

3 Evaluate

Tell students it is important to make their writing easy for others to read. Remind them to complete all **Stop and Check** activities.

Proper spacing makes each letter easy to read. Ask:

- Is your spacing between letters in a word equal?
- Do your letters look like the models?

School Home Extra Practice

Practice Master 7

Support for English Language Learners

Additional Practice Provide students with several word search puzzles. Have them solve each puzzle to practice letter and word recognition. For additional practice, have students create their own word search puzzles, and remind them to use proper strokes when making their letters.

Xx Kk Zz

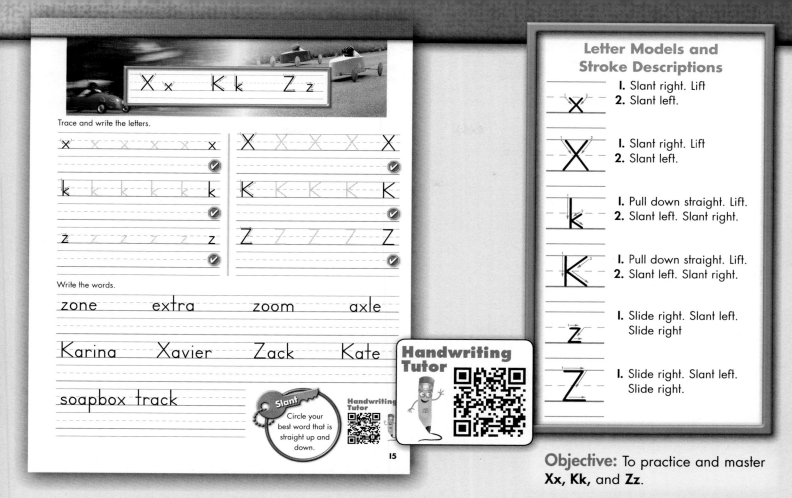

Trace and write the letters.

x x x x x x

X X X X X

k k k k k k

K K K K K

z z z z z z

Z Z Z Z Z

Write the words.

zone extra zoom axle

Karina Xavier Zack Kate

soapbox track

Slant

Circle your best word that is straight up and down.

Handwriting Tutor

15

Handwriting Tutor

Letter Models and Stroke Descriptions

x
1. Slant right. Lift
2. Slant left.

X
1. Slant right. Lift
2. Slant left.

k
1. Pull down straight. Lift.
2. Slant left. Slant right.

K
1. Pull down straight. Lift.
2. Slant left. Slant right.

z
1. Slide right. Slant left. Slide right

Z
1. Slide right. Slant left. Slide right.

Objective: To practice and master **Xx, Kk,** and **Zz**.

1 Model

Write the letters on guidelines as you say the stroke descriptions. Repeat the stroke descriptions as students use skywriting to write the letters in the air.

Ask students to use their finger to trace the letters several times on student page 15.

2 Practice

Remind students to position their book and grip their pencil correctly for writing.

Ask students to begin at the green starting dot and carefully trace the letters with pencil. Then have them write the letters and words on the page.

Remind students that when they come to this symbol ✓, they should stop writing and circle their best letter.

3 Evaluate

Tell students it is important to make their writing easy for others to read. Remind them to complete all **Stop and Check** activities.

Proper slant makes each letter easy to read. Ask:

- Are your letters and words straight up and down?

Writing in the Content Areas

Science

Explanatory Essay Discuss the photo of the soapbox on page 15. Ask a volunteer to explain what an axle is *(a bar on which a wheel or a pair of wheels turns)*. Brainstorm a list of machines that have at least one axle. Write students' ideas on the board. Then have students select one of the machines and write an **informative/explanatory** piece about it, making sure to explain how the axle helps the machine do its job. Remind students to use their best handwriting.

Extra Practice

Practice Master 8

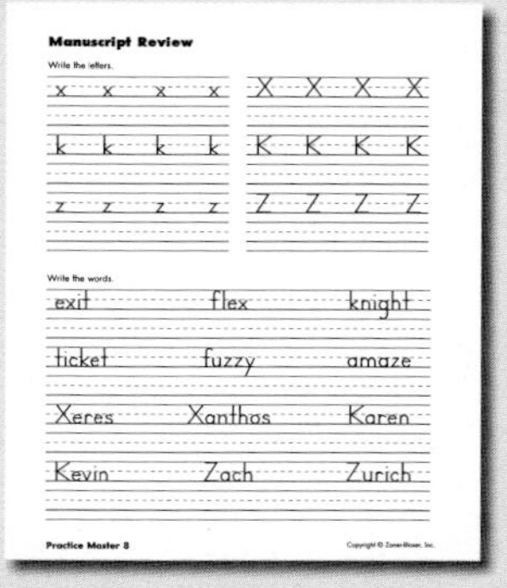

Manuscript Review

x x x x X X X X

k k k k K K K K

z z z z Z Z Z Z

exit flex knight

ticket fuzzy amaze

Xeres Xanthos Karen

Kevin Zach Zurich

Practice Master 8

Manuscript Review

Practice

Objective: To review verbs from **a** to **z**.

Manuscript Review

Practice

Verbs Here are verbs from **a** to **z**. These words name things people do.

act	eat	knit	quit	
bake	fish	leap	run	
catch	giggle	march	sing	write
dance	hug	nap	throw	fix
	illustrate	observe	understand	yell
	jump	practice	visit	zoom

Circle four things you do. Then write four sentences.
Each sentence should include one of the verbs you circled.

16

1 Review

Direct students to look at the verbs, or action words, in the box on student page 16. Point out that all the letters of the lowercase alphabet are included. Ask them to describe what they remember about the shape, size, spacing, and slant of letters and words written in manuscript.

Review the stroke descriptions and model any letters students might be having difficulty writing.

Ask a volunteer to describe one of the letters. Challenge the other students to identify the letter being described and then write it on guidelines on the board.

2 Practice

Remind students to position their book and grip their pencil correctly for writing.

Have students write their sentences using the verbs they circled on student page 16. Remind them to form the letters carefully so they will be legible.

3 Evaluate

Tell students it is important to make their writing easy for others to read.

Use these questions to help students evaluate their writing:

- Did you write with correct strokes so your letters have good shape?
- Did you use the guidelines to help make your short and tall letters the correct size?
- Do you have good space between your letters and words?
- Are your letters written straight up and down?

Support for
English Language Learners

Building Vocabulary Use the words listed on student page 16 to build vocabulary. After students write their sentences using four of the verbs, have them do more practice with the words they chose. Introduce these phrases: *I like* and *I don't like*. Then model examples of how to add the vocabulary words to those phrases to express preferences, such as saying or writing: **I like to sing. I don't like to run.**

Application

Writing a List Sometimes you write lists of things you have to do.

Things to Do

1. read my book
2. write a book report
3. illustrate it
4. color the cover

Write a list of things you plan to do soon.

I.

Stop and Check Circle your best letter.

17

Application

Objective: To write words and sentences legibly.

1 Model

Direct students to look at the Things to Do list on student page 17. Point out that each task is numbered and in the order it needs to be completed.

Ask the class to make a list of tasks for students to do in the classroom each day.

2 Practice

Remind students to position their book and grip their pencil correctly for writing.

Have students make a list on student page 17 of the things they plan to do soon. Remind them to form their letters carefully so they will be legible.

3 Evaluate

Tell students it is important to make their writing easy for others to read. Remind them to complete the **Stop and Check** activity at the end of this page.

Use these questions to help students evaluate their writing:

- Did you write each letter using correct shape?
- Are your letters the correct size?
- Did you leave the right amount of space between your letters and words?
- Did you use correct slant?

Writing in the Content Areas

Language Arts

To-Do Lists Review the types of sentences (declarative, interrogative, imperative, and exclamatory) and the end punctuation for each. Ask students why end punctuation is important. Next, have students write their to-do list from page 17 as a paragraph. Challenge them to use all four sentence types in their paragraph. For example, *I can't wait to read my book! After I finish I will write a book report. Should I illustrate it? Tell me what colors to use on the cover. I love to read!* Remind students to use their best handwriting.

Pretest

Before Writing

Point out the poem by Rachel Field on student page 18. Tell students that Field was an American writer who lived in the first half of the twentieth century and wrote many children's books, poems, and plays.

Objective: To write a poem in manuscript or cursive and compare it to posttests later in the year.

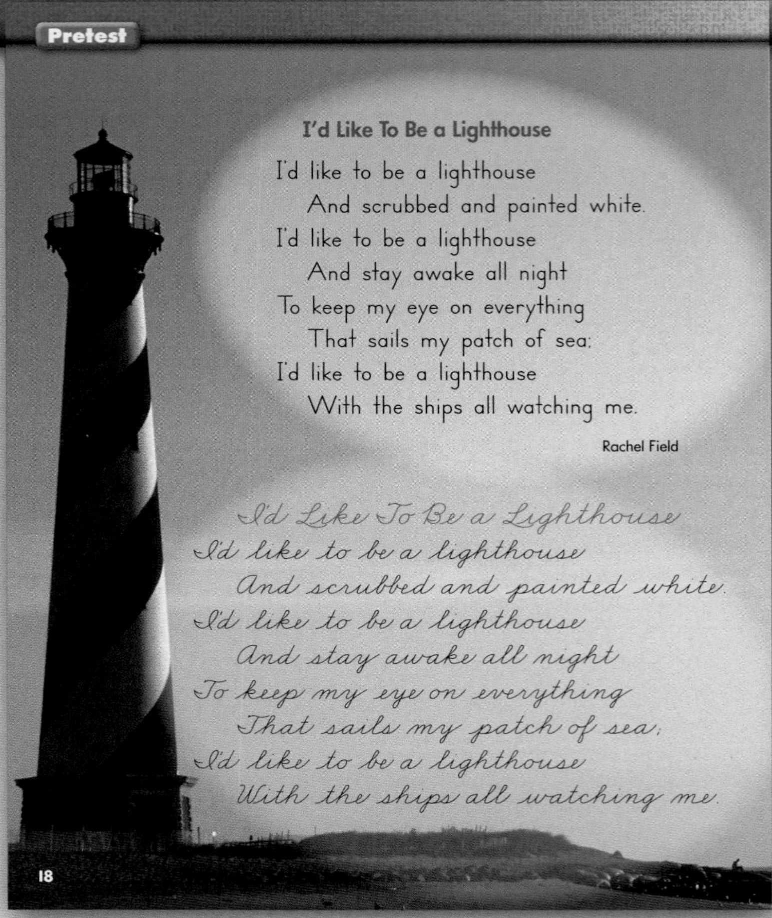
Pretest
I'd Like To Be a Lighthouse
I'd like to be a lighthouse
And scrubbed and painted white.
I'd like to be a lighthouse
And stay awake all night
To keep my eye on everything
That sails my patch of sea;
I'd like to be a lighthouse
With the ships all watching me.
Rachel Field
I'd Like To Be a Lighthouse
I'd like to be a lighthouse
And scrubbed and painted white.
I'd like to be a lighthouse
And stay awake all night
To keep my eye on everything
That sails my patch of sea;
I'd like to be a lighthouse
With the ships all watching me.
18

1 Present the Activity

Tell students they will be learning to write the letters of the alphabet and the numerals in cursive writing.

Explain to students that they will first take a handwriting pretest by writing this poem in their best handwriting. They will put this writing sample in their writing portfolio. Later in the year, they will write the same poem again and compare it to their first sample. By comparing their two writing samples, they will be able to measure their progress.

2 Pretest

Remind students this pretest will help them evaluate their writing now and later in the school year. Read the poem aloud with students. Then point out the writing area on student page 19, where they are to write the poem in their best handwriting. Encourage any students who learned cursive handwriting in second grade to write the pretest in cursive and to pay close attention to margins.

Write the title and the poem in your best manuscript or cursive handwriting. Remember to leave space for margins.
19

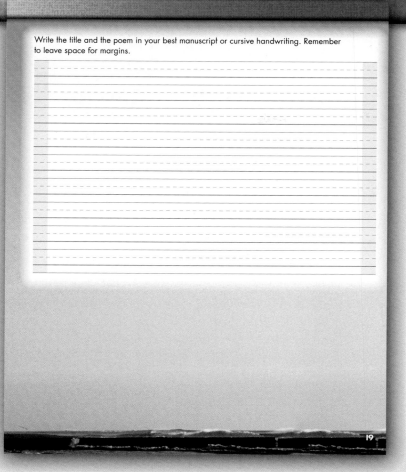

Evaluate

Observe students as they write the poem. Note that many may still be using manuscript writing some or all of the time. Use this page as an assessment of each student's current handwriting skills. Meet with students individually to help them assess their handwriting. Discuss any goals they may have for improving their handwriting.

Tips From an Occupational Therapist

Cursive New Beginnings **For students with poor manuscript handwriting skills, cursive handwriting can be a new beginning.** At first, cursive handwriting might be overwhelming to these students, but its novelty has the potential to be very motivating. These students might benefit from extra cursive handwriting practice.

Handwriting Coach

Evaluation

Self-evaluation is an important step in the handwriting process. By identifying their own strengths and weaknesses, students become independent learners. The steps in the self-evaluation process are as follows:

Question Students should ask themselves questions such as these: "Is my slant correct?" "Do my letters rest on the baseline?" Teacher modeling is vital in teaching effective questioning techniques.

Compare Students should compare their handwriting to correct models.

Evaluate Students should determine strengths and weaknesses in their handwriting based on the Keys to Legibility.

Diagnose Students should diagnose the cause of any difficulties. Possible causes include incorrect paper or pencil position, inconsistent pressure on the writing implement, and incorrect strokes.

Improve Self-evaluation should include a means of improvement through additional instruction and continued practice.

Welcome to Cursive

Encourage volunteers to read aloud the poem on student page 20. Invite discussion on the similarities and the differences they have noticed between manuscript and cursive writing.

Initiate class discussion about where students have seen cursive handwriting. Ask them when they have observed adults using cursive writing.

Objective: To notice the differences between manuscript and cursive; to begin writing cursive letters.

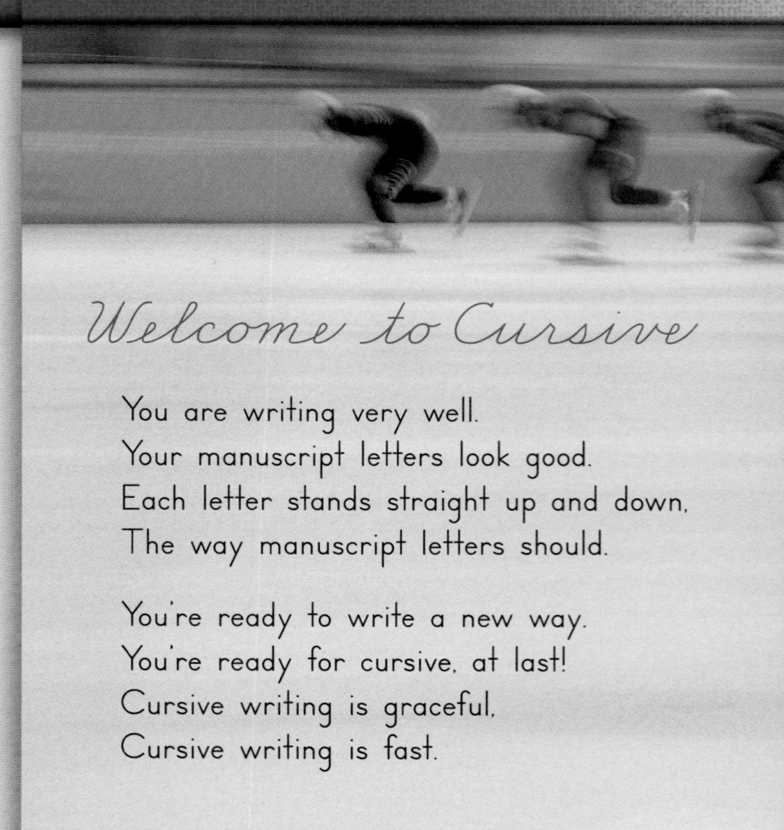

Welcome to Cursive

You are writing very well.
Your manuscript letters look good.
Each letter stands straight up and down,
The way manuscript letters should.

You're ready to write a new way.
You're ready for cursive, at last!
Cursive writing is graceful,
Cursive writing is fast.

20

Introducing Cursive

The following are some criteria to help determine whether students are ready for cursive writing.

Reading Level Does the student show reading proficiency near grade level?

Manuscript Mastery Is the student able to write legibly in manuscript?

Cursive Letter Recognition Is the student able to recognize and identify all cursive letters?

Cursive Word Reading Is the student able to read cursive words, and understand that letters preceded by **b, o, v,** and **w** are written slightly differently?

Grouping of Letters Is the student able to group letters according to size, shape, beginning stroke, and ending stroke?

Understanding of Terminology Does the student understand the terms for cursive handwriting?

Understanding of Slant Does the student understand that slant is determined by paper position, the direction in which the downstrokes are pulled, and the shifting of the paper as the writing space is filled?

Support for English Language Learners

Letter Recognition As students prepare to begin cursive, review the names of all upper and lowercase letters with them. Write each upper and lowercase manuscript letter on an index card or sentence strips that have been cut apart. Shuffle them, and put them face down on the table or floor. Have students take turns picking up a card, holding it up for everyone to see, and saying the name of the letter.

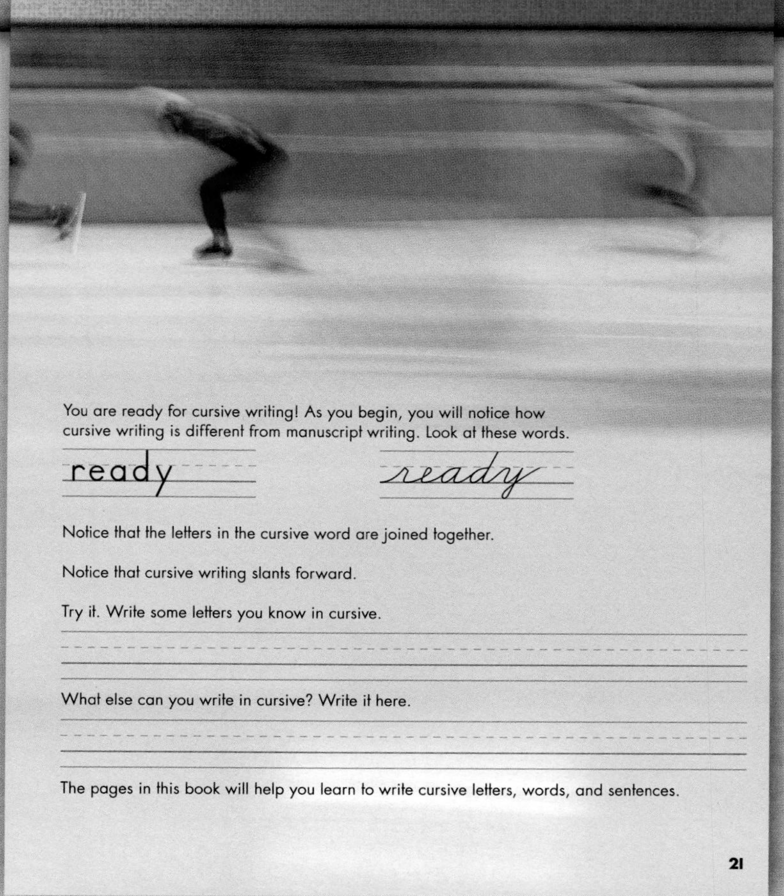

You are ready for cursive writing! As you begin, you will notice how cursive writing is different from manuscript writing. Look at these words.

ready 

Notice that the letters in the cursive word are joined together.

Notice that cursive writing slants forward.

Try it. Write some letters you know in cursive.

What else can you write in cursive? Write it here.

The pages in this book will help you learn to write cursive letters, words, and sentences.

21

1 Model

Direct students' attention to the words at the top of student page 21, and compare manuscript and cursive. Discuss the ways in which they are different. Point out that the letters in cursive are joined together and slant forward. Model writing a word or a name in manuscript and in cursive on the board. Ask students to describe how the two are different.

2 Practice

Have students write the cursive letters they know on guidelines. When they are done, ask them to write any words in cursive they know. Ask students to share the letters and words they know. Tell students they will learn to write letters, words, and sentences in cursive.

3 Evaluate

Write on the board all the lowercase letters of the alphabet in cursive, but do not write them in alphabetical order. Determine whether all students can recognize and identify all the cursive letters. Repeat the procedure using uppercase letters. This exercise will help you identify students who might need extra help when they begin learning cursive.

Writing in the Content Areas

Reflection Ask partners to discuss how they feel about learning cursive writing. Are they excited? Why? Are they fearful? Why? How do they think cursive writing will benefit them? Then have students write a journal entry describing their feelings and expectations about learning cursive. Remind students to use their best handwriting.

Cursive Letters and Numerals

Objective: To notice the similarities and differences between manuscript and cursive letters and numerals.

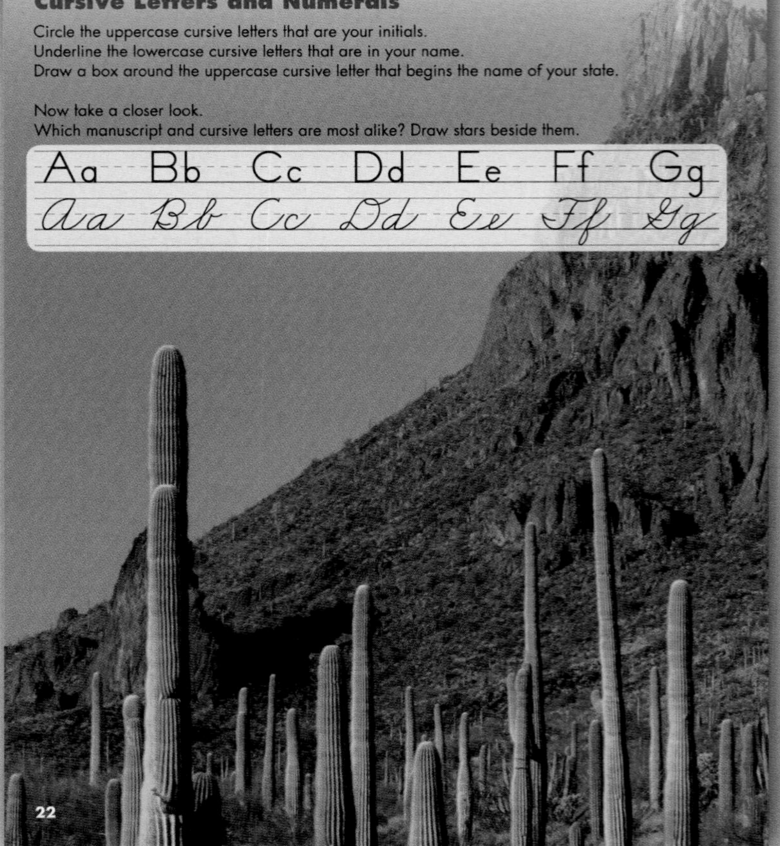

Cursive Letters and Numerals

Circle the uppercase cursive letters that are your initials.
Underline the lowercase cursive letters that are in your name.
Draw a box around the uppercase cursive letter that begins the name of your state.

Now take a closer look.
Which manuscript and cursive letters are most alike? Draw stars beside them.

Aa Bb Cc Dd Ee Ff Gg

Aa Bb Cc Dd Ee Ff Gg

22

1 Model

Project student pages 22–23 on a whiteboard or screen. Model the first instruction on page 22 by saying and circling the uppercase letters that are your initials. Then model the second instruction by underlining the lowercase letters that are in your name.

2 Practice

Have students follow each of the instructions on student page 22. Ask students having difficulty to raise their hand. Help these students locate the correct letters.

Extra Practice

Practice Master II

Zaner-Bloser Alphabet

A B C D E F G H I
J K L M N O P Q
R S T U V W X Y Z
a b c d e f g h i j
k l m n o p q r s
t u v w x y z

Practice Master II

Support for English Language Learners

Letter Recognition Keep in mind that some students who have learned a language with a non-alphabetic writing system (such as Chinese) or a non-Roman writing system (such as Russian) may benefit from a review of the complete Roman alphabet. Students will also benefit from listening to pronunciation models so they will recognize the name and pronunciation of each letter when it is used in class. As you introduce a letter in cursive, model the manuscript form as well. Help students make the connection that a cursive letter shaped like its manuscript counterpart will require similar hand movements for its formation.

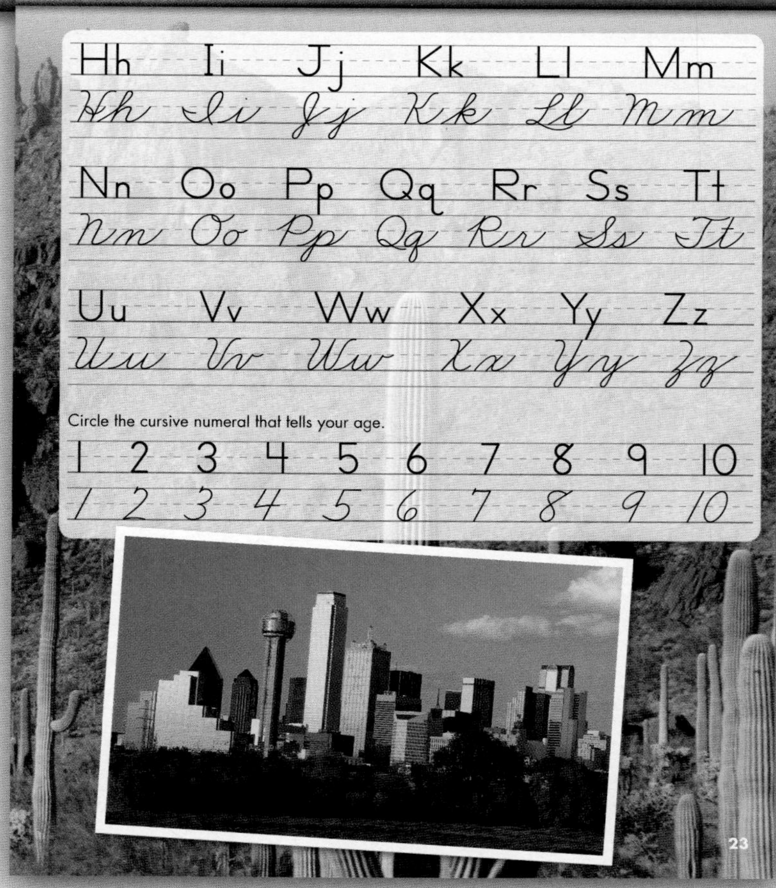
Hh Ii Jj Kk Ll Mm
Hh Ii Jj Kk Ll Mm

Nn Oo Pp Qq Rr Ss Tt
Nn Oo Pp Qq Rr Ss Tt

Uu Vv Ww Xx Yy Zz
Uu Vv Ww Xx Yy Zz

Circle the cursive numeral that tells your age.

1 2 3 4 5 6 7 8 9 10
1 2 3 4 5 6 7 8 9 10

23

Evaluate

Ask students to tell which letters they drew stars beside. Have them explain why they think those manuscript and cursive letters are most alike.

Using Technology

Digital Tools There are many handwriting programs and applications available for students to practice forming letters and writing words in cursive. You may wish to use the *Zaner-Bloser Handwriting* App. Introduce students to one of these applications on a classroom tablet or on a smartphone. Have them use a stylus or their index finger to practice tracing the letters. Encourage students to use these tools at home as well.

Reading Cursive Writing

Objective: To match uppercase and lowercase manuscript and cursive letters.

Reading Cursive Writing

Look at the orange manuscript lowercase letter.
Circle the cursive lowercase letter that matches it.

a	a	b	c	d	e	f
g	d	e	f	g	h	i
n	j	k	l	m	n	o
r	p	q	r	s	t	u
z	u	v	w	x	y	z

Look at the orange manuscript uppercase letter.
Circle the cursive uppercase letter that matches it.

B	A	B	C	D	E	F
E	D	E	F	G	H	I
M	I	J	K	L	M	N
Q	O	P	Q	R	S	T
Y	U	V	W	X	Y	Z

24

1 Model

Write a lowercase manuscript **f** on the board. Ask students to look at student page 24 and tell you the location of the **f**'s matching cursive letter. Repeat using an uppercase letter.

2 Practice

Have students follow the instructions on the page by circling each matching cursive letter.

3 Evaluate

Ask volunteers to tell the location of each matching cursive letter in the row. Let students evaluate their own page and identify any letters they might be having difficulty reading.

Poll students to find out which cursive letters are most difficult for them to read. Discuss possible reasons for this difficulty.

Support for English Language Learners

Letter Recognition Reading cursive letters can be a challenge for many students. Some may have learned to write in a cursive form that differs from that taught in this program. Others may be unfamiliar with the Roman alphabet and cursive forms. You may need to spend time helping students distinguish between the letters **o, p, b,** and **d;** as well as **p, g,** and **q**. Also, anticipate helping students distinguish between **l, t,** and **k; n** and **m; u, v,** and **w;** and **y** and **g**. Use manuscript/cursive flashcards and Zaner-Bloser manuscript/cursive *Illustrated Alphabet Strips* to help students with letter differentiation.

Read the name of a sport written in manuscript.
Circle the matching word written in cursive.

baseball	baseball	football	soccer
volleyball	diving	volleyball	skating
tennis	hockey	skiing	tennis
football	football	hockey	basketball
skating	swimming	skating	tennis

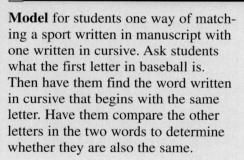

Read the name of a sport written in cursive.
Write the name in manuscript.

tennis

basketball

soccer

ice skating

25

Objective: To match manuscript and cursive words; to write cursive words in manuscript.

1 Model

Model for students one way of matching a sport written in manuscript with one written in cursive. Ask students what the first letter in baseball is. Then have them find the word written in cursive that begins with the same letter. Have them compare the other letters in the two words to determine whether they are also the same.

2 Practice

Ask students to match all the words in manuscript with those written in cursive. Remind them to compare each word letter-by-letter to find the correct match. Then have students read the words in cursive and write them on the lines in manuscript. Remind students to use their best handwriting.

3 Evaluate

Tell students it is important to make their writing easy for others to read. Remind them to go back and check their manuscript writing.

Tips From an Occupational Therapist

Large Letters When teaching cursive handwriting, **encourage correct formation by having students write very large letters on the board or on big pieces of bulletin-board paper taped to the wall.** Writing on a vertical surface improves stability through the arm and helps develop wrist and finger muscles that promote correct pencil grip. Writing in large letters allows the teacher and student to identify and correct problems with letter formation before they become habitual.

Writing Positions

Objective: To practice correct sitting, paper, and pencil positions for writing cursive.

Cursive

Left-Handed Writers

Sit like this.
Sit comfortably.
Lean forward a little.
Keep your feet flat on the floor.

Handwriting Tutor

Place the paper like this.

Handwriting Tutor

Slant the paper as shown in the picture.

Rest both arms on the desk. Use your right hand to shift the paper as you write.

Pull the pencil toward your left elbow when you write.

Hold the pencil like this.

Handwriting Tutor

Hold the pencil with your thumb and first two fingers.

Keep your first finger on top.

Bend your thumb and keep it on the side.

Do not squeeze the pencil when you write.

Handwriting Tutor

Writing Positions

Sitting Position

Using correct body position when writing will help students write better letters. They will also not tire as quickly. Encourage them to sit comfortably erect with their feet flat on the floor and their hips touching the back of the chair. Both arms should rest on the desk. Be sure students are relaxed and are holding their pencil correctly.

Paper Position

Correct paper placement is a critical factor in legibility. To ensure the paper is placed correctly for both right- and left-handed students, use tape to form a frame on the desk so students will be able to place the paper in the correct position.

Left-Handed Writers

Right-Handed Writers

Pencil Position

Model good pencil position for students. The pencil is held between the thumb and the first two fingers, about an inch above the point. The first finger rests on top of the pencil. The tip of the bent thumb is placed against the pencil to hold it high in the hand near the knuckle.

Left-Handed Writers

Right-Handed Writers

School Home **Extra Practice**
Practice Master 9

Writing Positions: Cursive

If you write with your left hand . . .

Slant your paper as shown in the picture.
Rest both arms on the desk. Use your right hand to move the paper as you write.
Pull the pencil toward your left elbow when you write.

Hold the pencil with your thumb and first two fingers.
Keep your first finger on top.
Bend your thumb, and keep it on the side.
Do not squeeze the pencil when you write.

 Practice Master 9

Right-Handed Writers

Sit like this.
Sit comfortably.
Lean forward a little.
Keep your feet flat on the floor.

Handwriting Tutor

Place the paper like this.

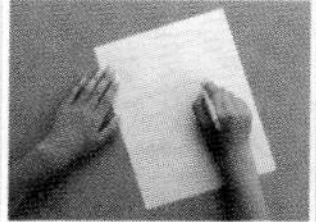

Slant the paper as shown in the picture.

Rest both arms on the desk. Use your left hand to shift the paper as you write.

Pull the pencil toward the middle of your body when you write.

Hold the pencil like this.

Hold the pencil with your thumb and first two fingers.

Keep your first finger on top.

Bend your thumb and keep it on the side.

Do not squeeze the pencil when you write.

27

Writing Positions

Alternative Pencil Position

Students who have difficulty with the traditional pencil position may prefer the alternative method of holding the pencil between the first and second fingers.

Support for English Language Learners

Conventions of Print Some students may have learned to write a language from right to left or from top to bottom. Remind students that English is written from left to right. Explain that proper sitting, paper, and pencil positions make it easier to write in English. Have students practice these positions while drawing simple lines from left to right across a sheet of paper.

Extra Practice

Practice Master 10

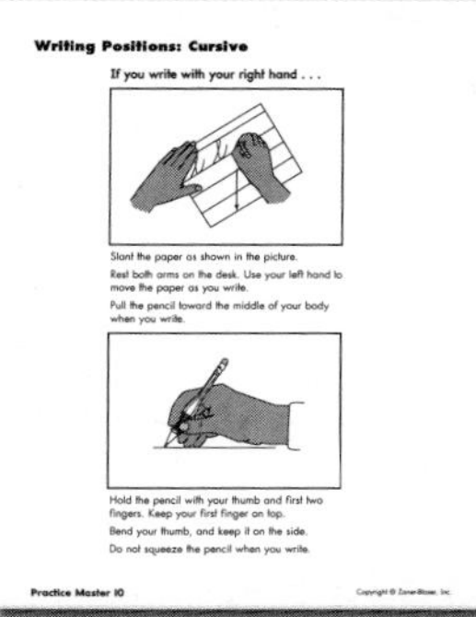

Writing Positions: Cursive

If you write with your right hand . . .

Slant the paper as shown in the picture.

Rest both arms on the desk. Use your left hand to move the paper as you write.

Pull the pencil toward the middle of your body when you write.

Hold the pencil with your thumb and first two fingers. Keep your first finger on top.

Bend your thumb, and keep it on the side.

Do not squeeze the pencil when you write.

Practice Master 10

Copyright © Zaner-Bloser, Inc.

Undercurve

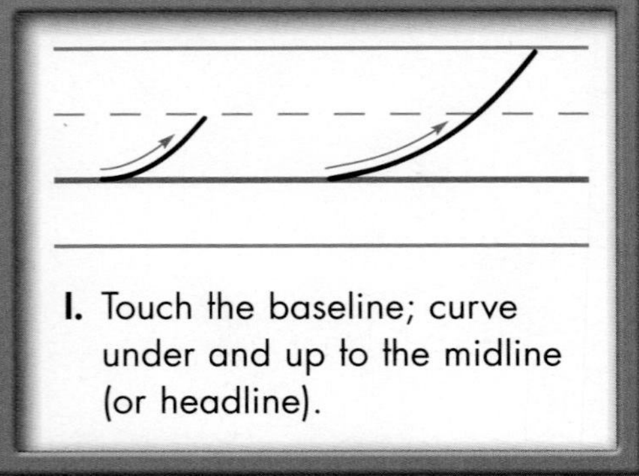

I. Touch the baseline; curve under and up to the midline (or headline).

Objective: To practice the undercurve stroke.

Basic Strokes

Undercurve

An **undercurve** is one of the basic strokes used to write cursive letters.

An undercurve stroke swings up.

Trace an undercurve stroke at the beginning of each lowercase letter.

b e f h i j k
l p r s t u w

Trace an undercurve stroke at the beginning of each uppercase letter.

B G L P R S

Trace and write undercurve strokes.

28

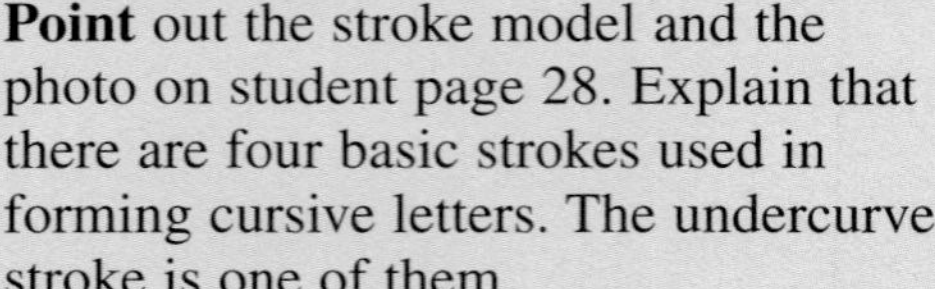

1 Model

Point out the stroke model and the photo on student page 28. Explain that there are four basic strokes used in forming cursive letters. The undercurve stroke is one of them.

Have students read the directions and trace the strokes with their index finger on the student page. If any students have difficulty identifying the stroke in a certain letter, model the letter on the board and highlight the undercurve stroke in a different color.

2 Practice

Remind students to position their book and grip their pencil correctly for writing.

Ask students to begin at the green starting dot and trace each stroke with pencil. Then have students write the two sizes of undercurve strokes on the student page.

Remind students that when they come to this symbol ✓, they should stop writing and circle their best undercurve stroke.

3 Evaluate

Tell students it is important to make their writing easy for others to read.

✓ **Use** these questions to help students evaluate their writing:

- Did you begin each stroke at the correct starting point on the baseline?
- Did you end each short undercurve stroke at the midline?
- Does each of your tall undercurve strokes end at the headline?

Extra Practice

Practice Master 12

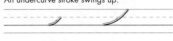

Support for English Language Learners

Stroke Description Vocabulary Some students may need extra help with the term **undercurve**. Explain that the curve in the stroke is like the curve you make while swinging on a playground swing. Point out the picture on student page 28. Model for students the motion of swinging on a playground swing by extending both your arms behind you and then swinging them forward in an arc like a swing. Have students join you in modeling the swing motion and saying **undercurve**.

Downcurve

A **downcurve** is one of the basic strokes used to write cursive letters.

A downcurve stroke dives down.

Trace a downcurve stroke at the beginning of each lowercase letter.

Trace a downcurve stroke at the beginning of each uppercase letter.

Trace and write downcurve strokes.

29

Downcurve

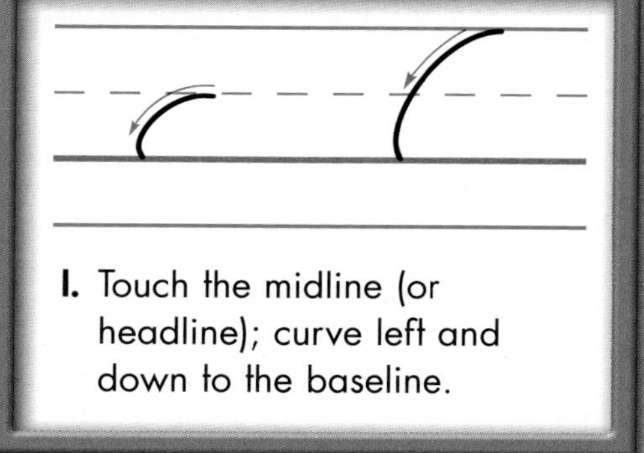

1. Touch the midline (or headline); curve left and down to the baseline.

Objective: To practice the downcurve stroke.

1 Model

Point out the stroke model and the photo on student page 29. Explain that the downcurve stroke is another basic stroke used to write cursive letters.

Have students read the directions and trace the strokes with their finger on the student page. If any students have difficulty identifying the stroke in a certain letter, model the letter on the board and highlight the downcurve stroke in a different color.

2 Practice

Remind students to position their book and grip their pencil correctly for writing.

Ask students to begin at the green starting dot and trace each stroke with pencil. Then have students write the two sizes of downcurve strokes on the student page.

Remind students that when they come to this symbol ✓, they should stop writing and circle their best downcurve stroke.

3 Evaluate

Tell students it is important to make their writing easy for others to read. Remind them to complete all **Stop and Check** activities.

✓ **Use** these questions to help students evaluate their writing:

- Did you begin each short downcurve stroke near the midline?
- Do each of your tall downcurve strokes begin near the headline?
- Do your downcurve strokes end at the baseline?

Support for English Language Learners

Stroke Description Vocabulary Some students may need extra help with the term **downcurve**. Explain that the curve in the stroke is like the curve you make while diving into a swimming pool. Point out the picture on student page 29. Model for students the motion of diving into a pool by straightening your arms over your head, putting one hand on top of the other, and bending forward at the waist. Have students join you in modeling the dive motion and saying **downcurve**.

Extra Practice

Practice Master 13

Basic Strokes

Overcurve

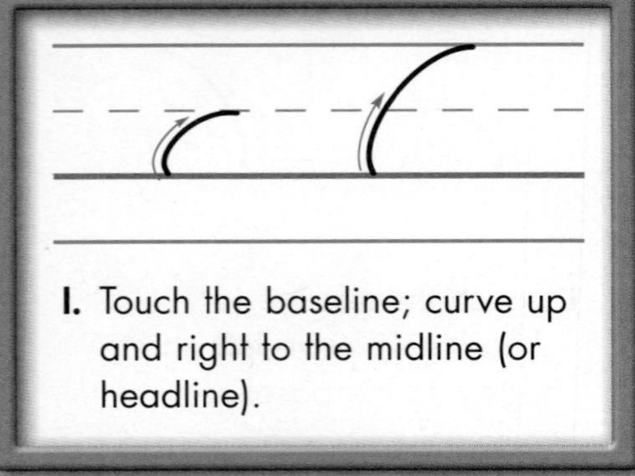

1. Touch the baseline; curve up and right to the midline (or headline).

Objective: To practice the overcurve stroke.

Basic Strokes

Overcurve

An **overcurve** is one of the basic strokes used to write cursive letters.

An overcurve stroke bounces up.

Trace an overcurve stroke at the beginning of each lowercase letter.

Trace an overcurve stroke at the beginning of each uppercase letter.

Trace and write overcurve strokes.

30

1 Model

Point out the stroke model and the photo on student page 30. Explain that the overcurve is another basic stroke used to write cursive letters.

Have students read the directions and trace the strokes with their finger on the student page. If any students have difficulty identifying the stroke in a certain letter, model the letter on the board and highlight the undercurve stroke in a different color.

2 Practice

Remind students to position their book and grip their pencil correctly for writing.

Ask students to begin at the green starting dot and trace each stroke with pencil. Then have students write the two sizes of overcurve strokes on the student page.

Remind students that when they come to this symbol ✓, they should stop writing and circle their best undercurve stroke.

 Evaluate

Tell students it is important to make their writing easy for others to read.

✓ **Use** these questions to help students evaluate their writing:

- Did you begin each stroke at the correct starting point on the baseline?
- Did you end each short overcurve stroke near the midline?
- Do each of your tall overcurve strokes end near the headline?

Support for English Language Learners

Stroke Description Vocabulary Some students may need extra help with the term **overcurve**. Explain that the curve in the stroke is like the curve you make while shooting a basket—throwing the ball into the net—in basketball. Point out the picture on student page 30. Model for students the motion of shooting a basket. Have students join you in modeling the ball-toss motion and saying **overcurve**.

Slant

A **slant** is one of the basic strokes used to write cursive letters.

A slant stroke slides.

Trace a slant stroke in each lowercase letter.

a b d f g h i

j k l m t u y

Trace a slant stroke in each uppercase letter.

A B K P R U X Y

Trace and write slant strokes.

31

Slant

I. Touch the midline (or headline); slant left to the baseline.

Objective: To practice the slant stroke.

1 Model

Point out the stroke model and the photo on student page 31. Explain that the slant stroke is another basic stroke used to write cursive letters.

Have students read the directions and trace the strokes with their finger on the student page. If any students have difficulty identifying the stroke in a certain letter, model the letter on the board and highlight the slant stroke in a different color.

2 Practice

Remind students to position their book and grip their pencil correctly for writing.

Ask students to begin at the green starting dot and trace each stroke with pencil. Then have students write the two sizes of slant strokes on the student page.

Remind students that when they come to this symbol ✓, they should stop writing and circle their best slant stroke.

3 Evaluate

Tell students it is important to make their writing easy for others to read.

✓ **Use** these questions to help students evaluate their writing:

- Did you begin each short slant stroke at the midline?
- Do each of your tall slant strokes begin at the headline?
- Do your slant strokes end at the baseline?

Support for English Language Learners

Stroke Description Vocabulary Some students may need extra help with the term **slant**. Explain that the stroke is like the angle at which you ride a sled down a hill. Point out the picture on student page 31. Bend one of your arms at the elbow and model the angle of the hill. Use the index finger of your other hand to show the downhill motion of sliding down that hill. Have students join you in modeling the angle and saying **slant**.

School Home

Extra Practice

Practice Master 15

Objective: To practice the Shape and Size Keys to Legibility.

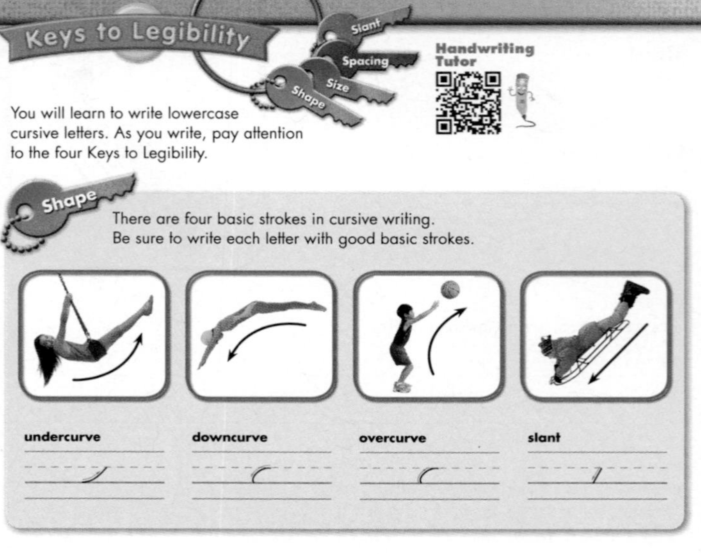

Keys to Legibility

Slant
Spacing
Size
Shape

Handwriting Tutor

You will learn to write lowercase cursive letters. As you write, pay attention to the four Keys to Legibility.

Shape

There are four basic strokes in cursive writing. Be sure to write each letter with good basic strokes.

undercurve downcurve overcurve slant

Circle each letter that has an undercurve beginning.

Circle each letter that has a downcurve beginning.

Circle each letter that has an overcurve beginning.

Circle each letter that has a slant stroke.

32

Handwriting Tutor

Handwriting Coach

Keys to Legibility

Explain to students that good handwriting is legible handwriting. The most important thing to remember is that readers must be able to read a message in order to understand its meaning.

Brainstorm with students qualities of legible handwriting. Write responses on the board. These might include neatness, carefully written letters, and letters that are not too crowded.

Point out that there are four Keys to Legibility. They are easy to remember because they all start with **s**: **Shape, Size, Spacing,** and **Slant**.

Explain that **Shape** describes the strokes that form each letter and give it a unique appearance. **Size** describes the height of letters. **Spacing** describes the space between letters, words, and sentences. **Slant** refers to the angle of writing on the paper. Using these Keys will help students improve the legibility of their writing.

1 Present the Key

Shape

Point out to students that the basic strokes they learned in the previous pages are the basis for a letter's shape.

Read and discuss with students the information and illustrations in the box on student page 32. Ask students to trace the strokes with their finger. Help students as needed to complete the activities on the page.

2 Practice Shape

Project a letter onto a chalkboard or a whiteboard. Ask students to use a piece of colored chalk or a marker to trace over the stroke you name.

Support for

English Language Learners

Handwriting Reference Journal To help students understand the meaning of the Keys to Legibility, ask them to prepare a Keys to Legibility booklet to use as a reference throughout the school year. Students can include a page for each Key: Shape, Size, Spacing, and Slant. On the top portion of the page, have students use graphics, photos, and their own drawings to illustrate the Key. Provide students with magazines and other materials. On the bottom part of the page, ask students to write letters or words as examples of the Key to Legibility.

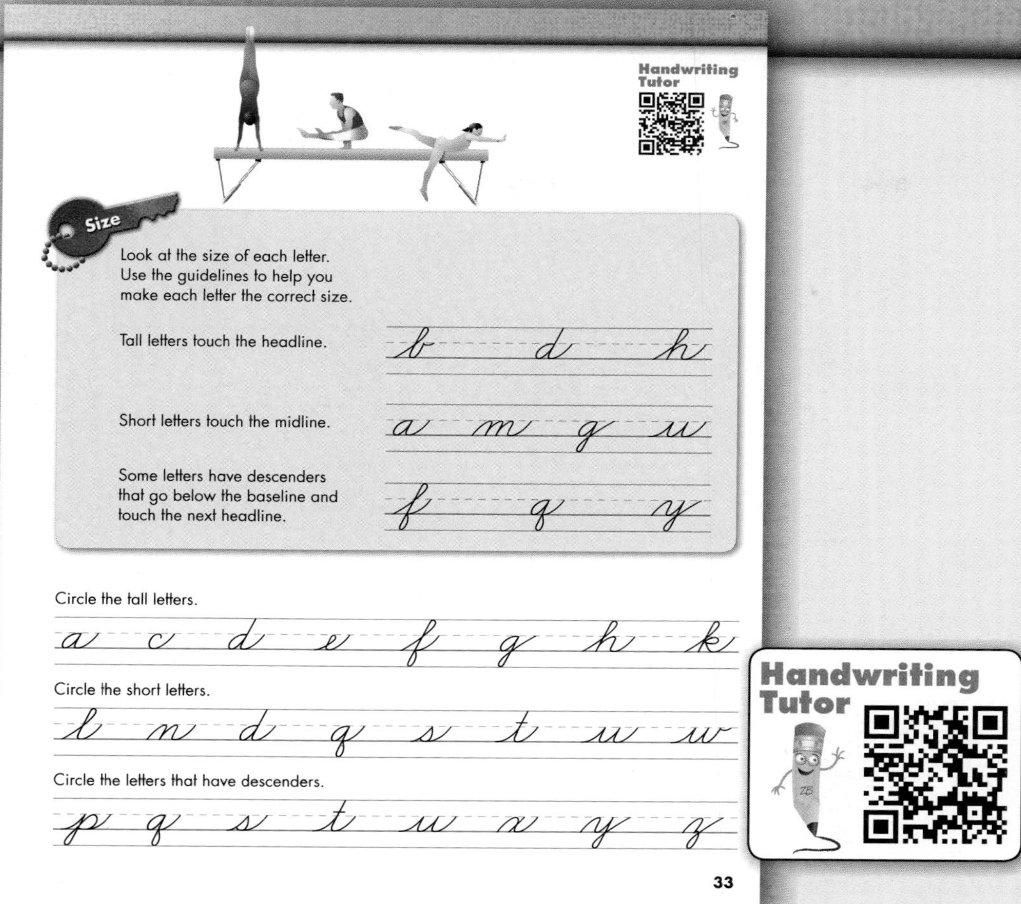

Handwriting Tutor

Size

Look at the size of each letter.
Use the guidelines to help you make each letter the correct size.

Tall letters touch the headline. *b d h*

Short letters touch the midline. *a m g u*

Some letters have descenders that go below the baseline and touch the next headline. *f q y*

Circle the tall letters.

a c d e f g h k

Circle the short letters.

l n d q s t u w

Circle the letters that have descenders.

p q s t u x y z

Handwriting Tutor

33

1 Present the Key

Size

Read and discuss the information and illustration on student page 33. Emphasize that writing letters on guidelines will help students produce letters of consistent size. Help students as needed to complete the activities on the page. For some students, it may be helpful to see letter models at a larger size. Write a few letters on guidelines on the board, and encourage students to highlight the headline, midline, and baseline in different colored chalk or marker.

2 Practice Size

Make a set of letter cards by writing uppercase and lowercase letters in cursive on paper with guidelines. Cut out each letter and tape it to an index card. Write **tall** and **short** on the board or on chart paper to form two columns. Ask students to select cards and tape them under the appropriate column. Model an example for students.

Tall: all uppercase letters and **b, d, f, h, k, l, t**

Short: a, c, e, g, i, j, m, n, o, p, q, r, s, u, v, w, x, y, z

Ask students to tell how they know whether letters are tall or short. Remind them that tall letters touch the headline and short letters touch the midline. Invite volunteers to come to the board and make a check mark beside letters with descenders that go below the baseline and touch the next headline: **f, g, j, J, p, q, y, Y, z, Z.**

Support for English Language Learners

Understanding Sizes To help students understand the different sizes of letters, have three volunteers come to the front of the room. Ask one student to stand on a chair (with your assistance). Have another sit in a chair cross-legged. Have a third student sit in a chair with one of his or her legs dangling down. Explain that the three positions represent a tall letter, a short letter, and a short letter with a descender.

Extra Practice

Practice Masters 16–17

Objective: To practice the Spacing and Slant Keys to Legibility.

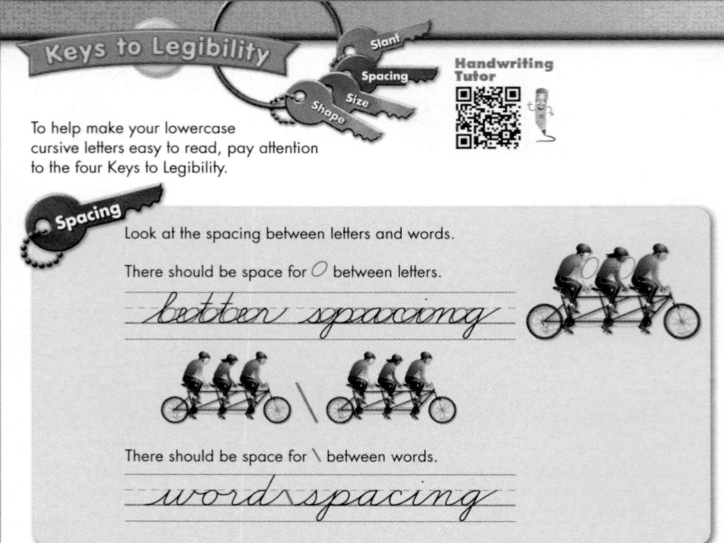

Keys to Legibility
Slant
Spacing
Size
Shape
Handwriting Tutor
To help make your lowercase cursive letters easy to read, pay attention to the four Keys to Legibility.
Spacing
Look at the spacing between letters and words.
There should be space for O between letters.
better spacing
There should be space for \ between words.
word spacing

Circle the word that has good letter spacing.

spacing spacing spacing

Circle the line that has good word spacing.

word spacing

word spacing

wordspacing

34

Handwriting Tutor

Handwriting Coach

Keys to Legibility

Review that **Shape** describes the strokes that form each letter and give it a unique appearance. **Size** describes the height of letters. **Spacing** describes the space between the letters, words, and sentences. **Slant** refers to the angle of writing on the paper. Using these Keys will help students improve the legibility of their writing.

On guidelines on the board, write words, singly or in pairs, with obvious errors in spacing. Challenge volunteers to come to the board, identify an error, and tell how it should be corrected.

1 Present the Key

Spacing

Remind students that good handwriting is legible handwriting. The most important thing to remember is that readers must be able to read a message in order to understand its meaning.

Review that spacing describes the space between letters, words, and sentences.

2 Practice Spacing

Remind students to position their book and grip their pencil correctly for writing.

Point out to students that the space between letters, words, and sentences is a vital part of legibility.

Read and discuss with students the information and illustrations in the box on student page 34. Help students as needed to complete the activities on the page.

Support for English Language Learners

Real-World Examples Have two students stand next to each other. Point to the space between them and say, "This is a small space." Gesture the meaning by placing your hands close together. Tell students that the space between letters in a word is small. Show examples in your sentence. Have two other students stand farther apart from each other. Say, "This is a big space." Gesture the meaning by placing your hands far apart. Tell students that the space between words in a sentence is big. Show examples in your sentence.

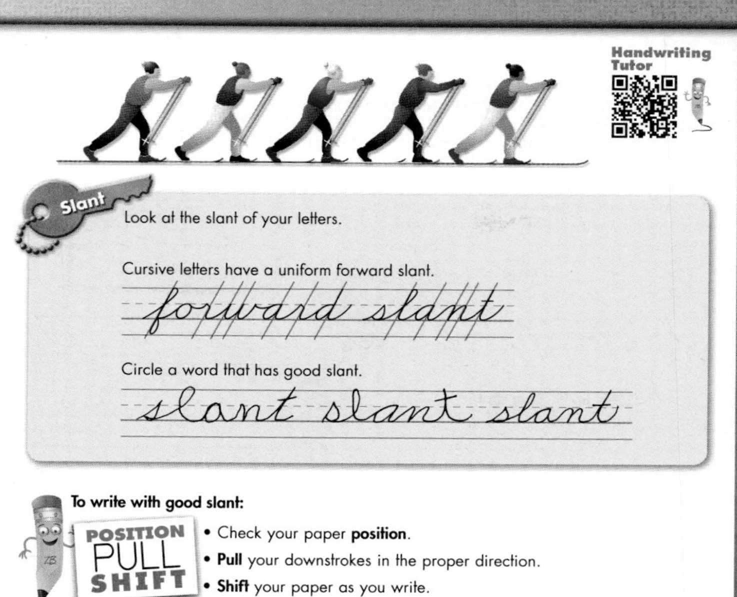

Handwriting Tutor

Slant

Look at the slant of your letters.

Cursive letters have a uniform forward slant.

forward slant

Circle a word that has good slant.

slant slant slant

To write with good slant:

POSITION PULL SHIFT

- Check your paper **position**.
- **Pull** your downstrokes in the proper direction.
- **Shift** your paper as you write.

If you are left-handed . . .

pull toward your left elbow.

If you are right-handed . . .

pull toward your midsection.

35

Handwriting Tutor

1 Present the Key

Slant

Make guide sheets to help students write with good slant. Using a thick, dark-colored marker, write slant strokes across blank guidelines (see Practice Master 109) to fill a page. Leave a finger space between the strokes. Duplicate the page, and give one copy to each student.

Encourage students to place the guide sheets under their paper as they write. The dark strokes should show through and provide a guide for writing with good slant. Invite volunteers to show writing samples with uniform slant.

2 Practice Slant

Remind students to position their book and grip their pencil correctly for writing.

Read and discuss the information and illustration on student page 35. Emphasize that writing letters and words with consistent forward slant fosters legibility. Help students as needed to complete the activities on the page. Then go over the **Position/Pull/Shift** information.

Write the same word on the board in cursive and in manuscript to help students recognize slant. Use parallel lines of colored chalk or marker to highlight the difference between manuscript verticality and cursive slant.

Support for English Language Learners

Stroke Description Vocabulary Some students may need extra help with the term **slant**. Have them take a blank sheet of paper and draw a diagonal line from the upper right corner to the lower left corner. Explain that they have just drawn a **slanted** line. Have them continue drawing diagonal lines parallel to the first one until they have filled the page to the top left and bottom right corners.

School Home **Extra Practice**

Practice Masters 18–20

Writing Lowercase Cursive Letters

Undercurve Letters

i t u
w e l
b h f
k r s
j p

Objective: To practice short and tall undercurve strokes.

Writing Lowercase Cursive Letters

Let's begin with lowercase letters.
As you learn to write in cursive, you'll learn to read it, too.
You will learn to write each letter.
Then you'll join letters and write words.

Undercurve Letters

You will learn to write these lowercase letters.
Each letter begins with an undercurve stroke.

i t u w e

l b h f k r s j p

Trace and write undercurve strokes.

Stop and Check
Circle your best short undercurve stroke.
Circle your best tall undercurve stroke.

36

1 Model

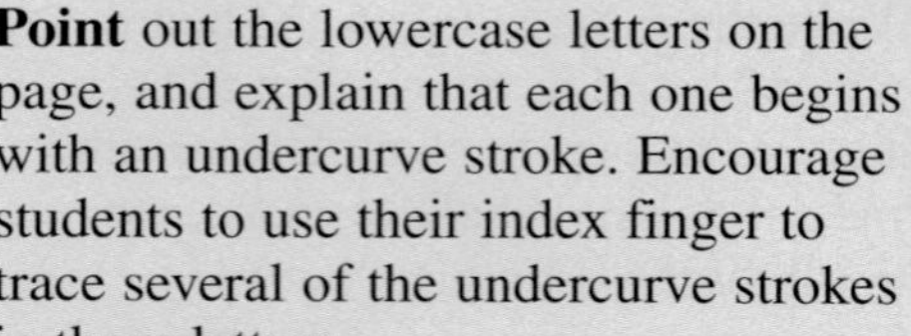

Point out the lowercase letters on the page, and explain that each one begins with an undercurve stroke. Encourage students to use their index finger to trace several of the undercurve strokes in these letters.

2 Practice

Remind students to position their book and grip their pencil correctly for writing.

Ask students to trace the undercurve strokes with pencil and then write them on the guidelines.

Remind students that when they come to this symbol ✓, they should stop writing and circle their best undercurve stroke.

3 Evaluate

Tell students it is important to make their writing easy for others to read. Remind them to complete all **Stop and Check** activities.

✓ **Use** these questions to help students evaluate their writing:

- Do your short undercurve strokes touch the midline?
- Do your tall undercurve strokes touch the headline?

Support for English Language Learners

Understanding Sizes Students might recognize the descriptors **tall** and **short,** but they might not know that these words can describe letters. To review these descriptors, place pictures illustrating *tall* and *short* on the board. Point to the tall pictures and say "tall." Point to the short pictures and say "short." Look around the room for more examples of *tall* and *short*.

After reviewing the meanings of **tall** and **short,** help students use the words to classify letters. Show students letter cards for **t, l, b, h, f,** and **k**. When you present each card, say, "This is the letter_____. It is a tall letter." Show students letter cards for **i, u, w, e, r, s, j,** and **p**. When you present each card, say, "This is the letter ____. It is a short letter."

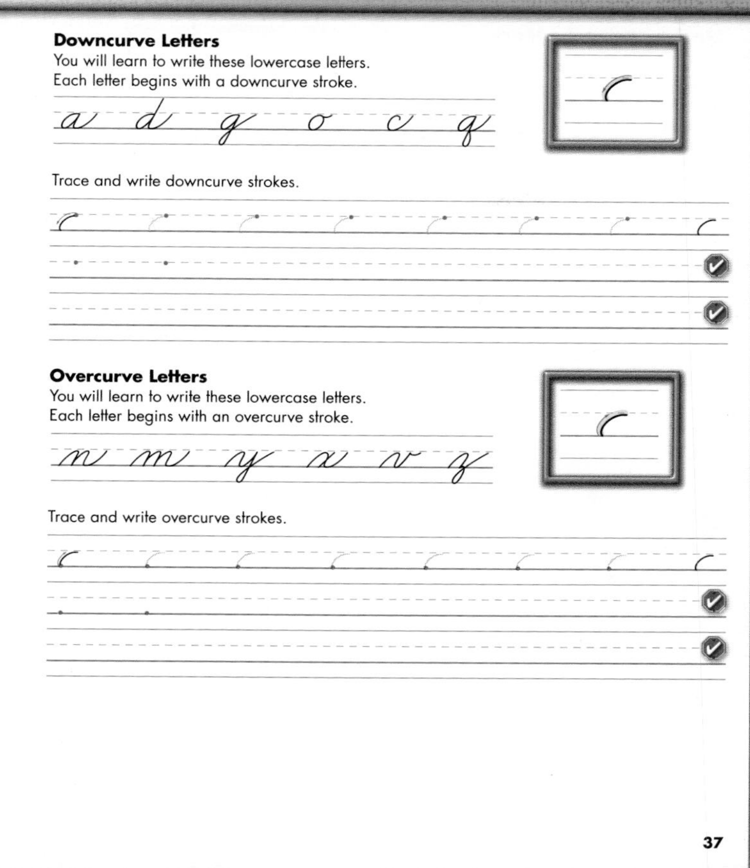

Downcurve Letters
You will learn to write these lowercase letters.
Each letter begins with a downcurve stroke.

a d g o c q

Trace and write downcurve strokes.

Overcurve Letters
You will learn to write these lowercase letters.
Each letter begins with an overcurve stroke.

n m y x v z

Trace and write overcurve strokes.

37

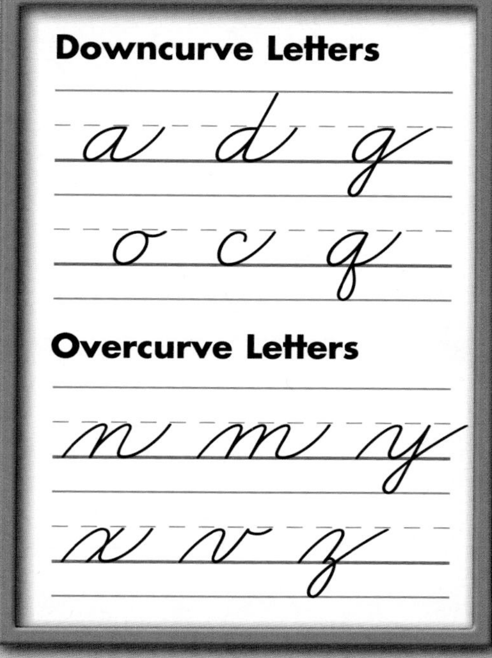

Objective: To practice short and tall downcurve and overcurve strokes.

1 Model

Point out the lowercase letters on the page, and explain that each one begins with a downcurve stroke. Encourage students to use their index finger to trace several of the downcurve strokes in these letters.

2 Practice

Remind students to position their book and grip their pencil correctly for writing.

Ask students to trace and write the downcurve strokes on the guidelines.

Remind students that when they come to this symbol ✓, they should stop writing and circle their best downcurve stroke.

Repeat steps 1 Model and 2 Practice for overcurve stroke.

3 Evaluate

Tell students it is important to make their writing easy for others to read. Remind them to complete all **Stop and Check** activities.

✓ **Use** these questions to help students evaluate their writing:

- Do your downcurves begin at the midline and end at the baseline?
- Do your overcurves begin at the baseline and end at the midline?

Tips From an Occupational Therapist

Rotating Cups This activity can help develop the arches of the hand and refine students' ability to hold and use writing implements. Provide a round cup, such as the large cap from a bottle of liquid laundry detergent. Have students hold the cup with the thumb and fingertips of their writing hand. Hold the cup from the bottom, with the open part facing up. Then, have students rotate the cup with their fingers without letting the cup touch their palm.

Undercurve Letters

Objective: To practice writing short and tall undercurve strokes.

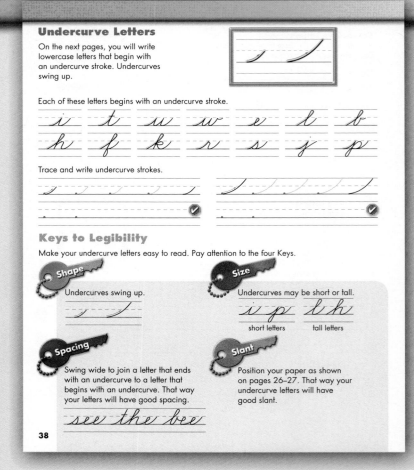

Undercurve Letters

On the next pages, you will write lowercase letters that begin with an undercurve stroke. Undercurves swing up.

Each of these letters begins with an undercurve stroke.

i t u w e l b
h f k r s j p

Trace and write undercurve strokes.

Keys to Legibility

Make your undercurve letters easy to read. Pay attention to the four Keys.

Shape
Undercurves swing up.

Size
Undercurves may be short or tall.

i p — short letters
l h — tall letters

Spacing
Swing wide to join a letter that ends with an undercurve to a letter that begins with an undercurve. That way your letters will have good spacing.

see the bee

Slant
Position your paper as shown on pages 26–27. That way your undercurve letters will have good slant.

38

1 Model

Point out lowercase letters on student page 38, and explain that each one begins with an undercurve stroke. Encourage students to use their index finger to trace several of the undercurve strokes in these letters.

2 Practice

Remind students to position their book and grip their pencil correctly for writing.

Ask students to trace the undercurve strokes with pencil and then write them on the guidelines.

Remind students that when they come to this symbol ✓, they should stop writing and circle their best undercurve.

3 Evaluate

Tell students it is important to make their writing easy for others to read. Remind them to complete all **Stop and Check** activities.

✓ **Use** these questions to help students evaluate their undercurve strokes:

- Do your short undercurve strokes touch the midline?
- Do your tall undercurve strokes touch the headline?

Support for English Language Learners

Understanding Shape and Size Help students understand what the Keys to Legibility mean. Write a sentence on the board, and read it aloud. Then use it to illustrate the following Keys.

Shape Explain that letters have shapes. Draw a circle on the board, and have students compare it to letters in your sentence. Which letters have a circular shape? Point out other letter shapes in your sentence.

Size Ask students to identify the tall letters in your sentence. Then ask them to identify the short letters.

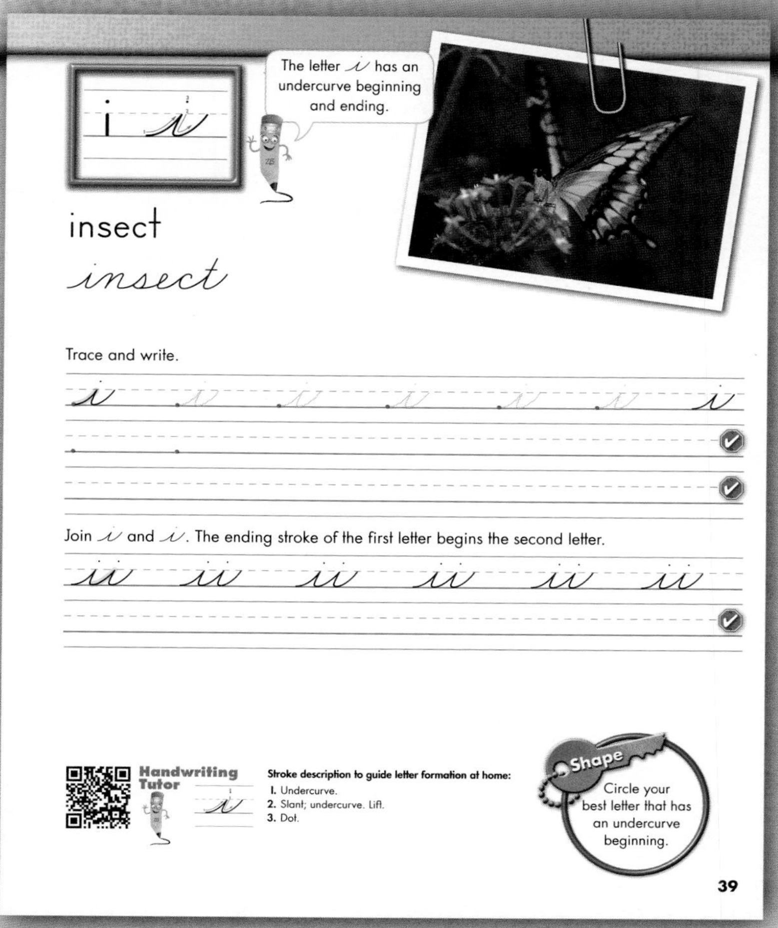

i *i*

The letter *i* has an undercurve beginning and ending.

insect

insect

Trace and write.

Join *i* and *i*. The ending stroke of the first letter begins the second letter.

Handwriting Tutor

Stroke description to guide letter formation at home:
1. Undercurve.
2. Slant; undercurve. Lift.
3. Dot.

Shape

Circle your best letter that has an undercurve beginning.

39

Letter Model and Stroke Description

1. Undercurve.
2. Slant; undercurve. Lift.
3. Dot.

Objective: To practice writing lowercase cursive **i**.

1 Model

Talk about the shape of cursive **i**. Ask:

- How many undercurve strokes are in **i**? *(two)*
- How does **i** end? *(with a dot)*

Write cursive **i** on guidelines on the board as you say the stroke description. Use skywriting (see page Z21) to model writing **i** in the air. Have students stand and say the stroke description with you as they write **i** in the air.

It might be helpful for students, especially auditory learners, to hear a more detailed stroke description. (Go to **resources.zaner-bloser.com/hw.**)

2 Practice

Remind students to position their book and grip their pencil correctly for writing.

Ask students to begin at the green dot and use their index finger to trace **i** several times on student page 39. Then ask them to carefully trace and write with pencil the letters and joinings on the page.

Remind students that when they come to this symbol ✓, they should stop writing and circle their best letter or joining.

3 Evaluate

Tell students it is important to make their writing easy for others to read. Remind them to complete all **Stop and Check** activities.

Proper shape makes each letter easy to read. Ask:

- Does your **i** begin and end with an undercurve?
- Does your ending stroke touch the midline?

Extra Practice

Practice Masters 21, 75

Writing in the Content Areas

Science

Graphic Organizers Discuss the photo of the insect on page 39. Have students think about the insects they have seen. Ask volunteers to describe an insect. Talk about how all insects are alike (e.g., all have six legs) and how they are different (e.g., some have wings). Have students draw a T-chart on lined paper and label the columns **Same** and **Different**. Then have students write insects' similarities and differences in the chart. Remind students to use their best cursive handwriting.

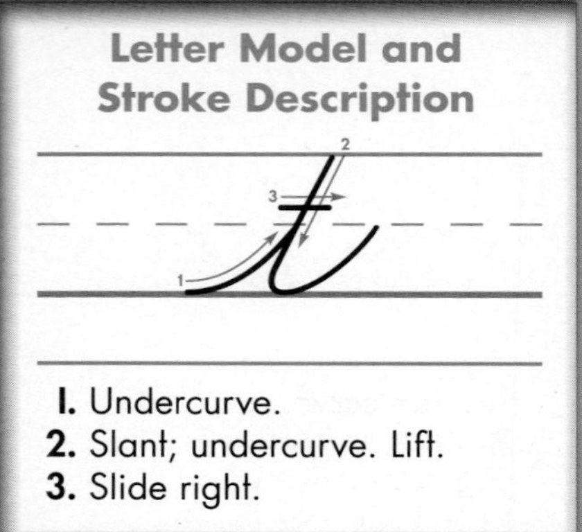

I. Undercurve.
2. Slant; undercurve. Lift.
3. Slide right.

Objective: To practice writing lowercase cursive **t**.

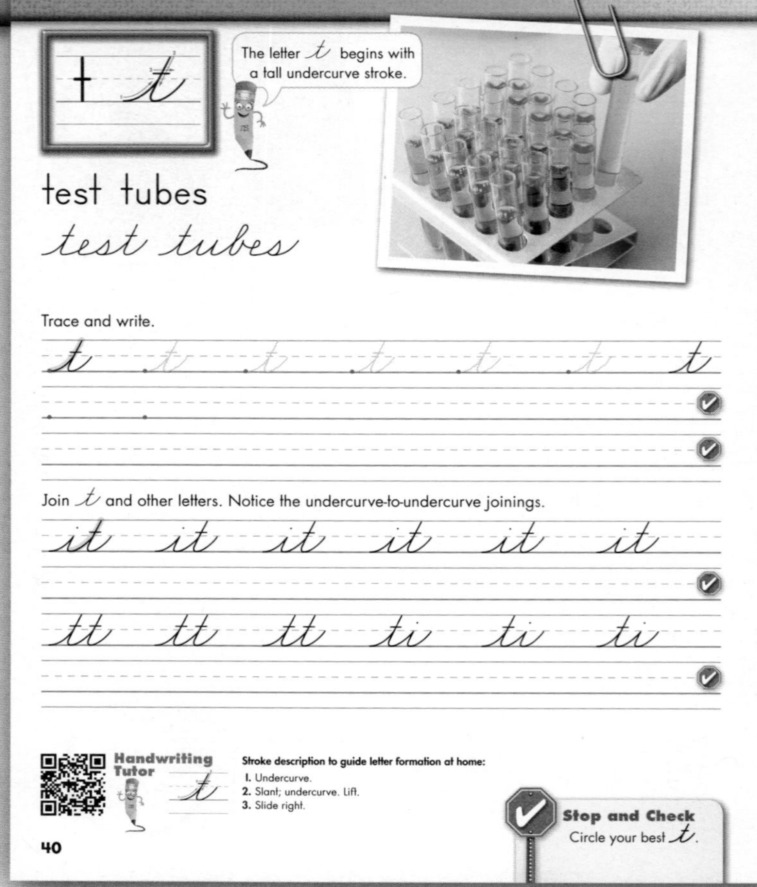

test tubes

test tubes

Trace and write.

Join *t* and other letters. Notice the undercurve-to-undercurve joinings.

it it it it it it

tt tt tt ti ti ti

Handwriting Tutor

Stroke description to guide letter formation at home:
1. Undercurve.
2. Slant; undercurve. Lift.
3. Slide right.

Stop and Check Circle your best *t*.

40

1 Model

Talk about cursive **t**. Ask:

- In the letter **t,** what stroke follows the slant? *(undercurve)*
- How does **t** end? *(with a slide right)*

Write cursive **t** on guidelines on the board as you say the stroke description. Use skywriting to model writing **t** in the air. Have students stand and say the stroke description with you as they write **t** in the air.

2 Practice

Remind students to position their book and grip their pencil correctly for writing.

Ask students to begin at the green dot and use their index finger to trace **t** several times on student page 40. Then ask them to carefully trace and write with pencil the letters and joinings on the page.

Remind students that when they come to this symbol ✓, they should stop writing and circle their best letter or joining.

3 Evaluate

Tell students it is important to make their writing easy for others to read. Remind them to complete all **Stop and Check** activities.

✓ **Use** these questions to help students evaluate their cursive **t**:

- Does your first undercurve end at the headline?
- Is your slant stroke pulled toward the baseline?
- Is your slide right stroke just above the midline?

Extra Practice

Practice Masters 22, 75

Support for English Language Learners

Sound Recognition Students will benefit from hearing the sound of the letter **t** pronounced so they will recognize the same sound when it is used in words. Provide students with pictures of objects or point to things in the classroom that begin with the letter **t,** such as **table, toy, time,** and **toe**. Say the words, and emphasize the /t/ sound. Invite students to repeat after you, and encourage them to skywrite the letter **t** as they say the words.

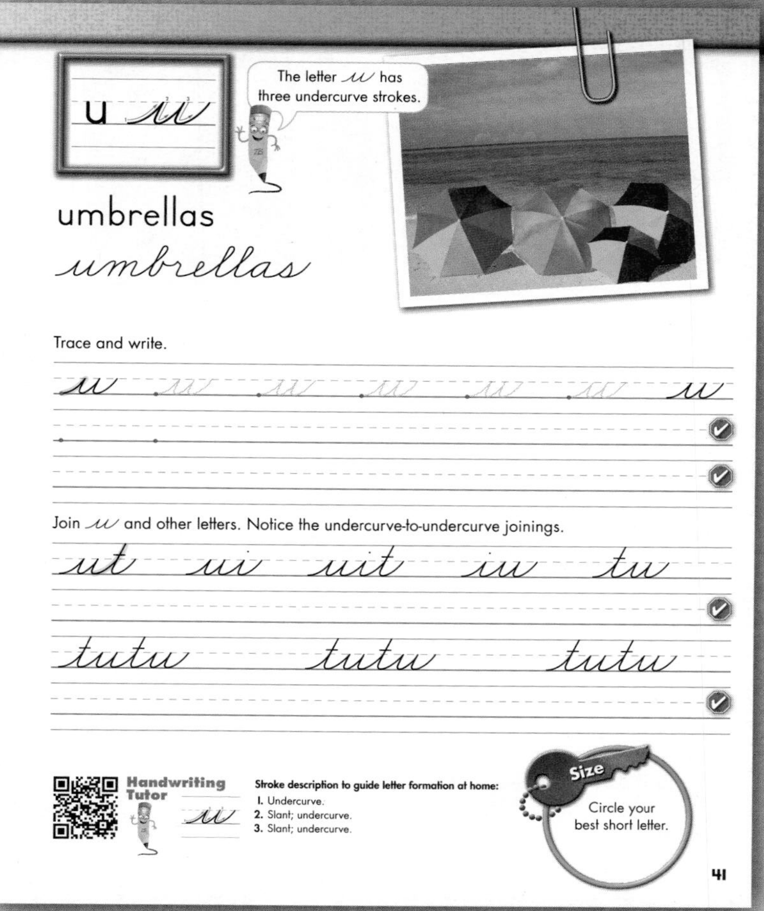

u *u*

The letter *u* has three undercurve strokes.

umbrellas

umbrellas

Trace and write.

Join *u* and other letters. Notice the undercurve-to-undercurve joinings.

ut ui uit iu tu

tutu tutu tutu

Handwriting Tutor

Stroke description to guide letter formation at home:
1. Undercurve.
2. Slant; undercurve.
3. Slant; undercurve.

Size

Circle your best short letter.

41

Letter Model and Stroke Description

1. Undercurve.
2. Slant, undercurve.
3. Slant, undercurve.

Objective: To practice writing lowercase cursive **u**.

1 Model

Talk about cursive **u**. Ask:

- In the letter **u**, what stroke follows the first slant? *(undercurve)*
- How does **u** end? *(with an undercurve)*

Write cursive **u** on guidelines on the board as you say the stroke description. Use skywriting to model writing **u** in the air. Have students stand and say the stroke description with you as they write **u** in the air.

2 Practice

Remind students to position their book and grip their pencil correctly for writing.

Ask students to begin at the green dot and use their index finger to trace **u** several times on student page 41. Then ask them to carefully trace and write with pencil the letters and joinings on the page.

Remind students that when they come to this symbol ✓, they should stop writing and circle their best letter or joining.

3 Evaluate

Tell students it is important to make their writing easy for others to read. Remind them to complete all **Stop and Check** activities.

Proper size makes each letter easy to read. Ask:

- Do your short letters touch the midline?
- Do your tall letters touch the headline?
- Do your letters look like the models?

Tips From an Occupational Therapist

Sidewalk Chalk Try to figure out fun ways to incorporate handwriting into the daily school routine. For example, if it is a nice day, take students outside and do a project using sidewalk chalk. Have students write large letters, particularly letters they are just learning, on the playground. **The use of chalk provides more muscle feedback than dry erase markers.** Practicing letter formation on small chalkboards is also beneficial.

Extra Practice

Practice Masters 23, 76

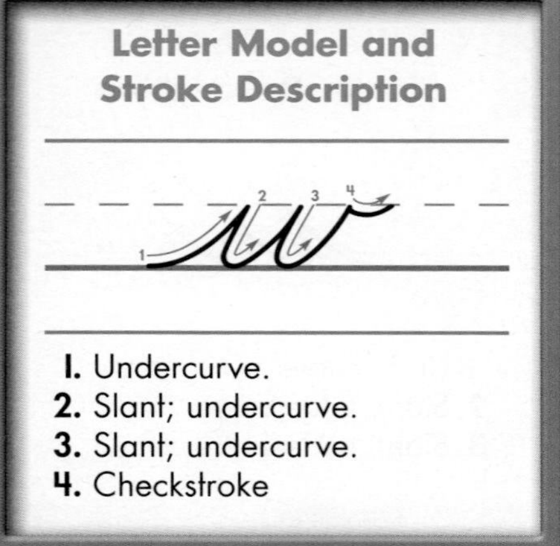

Objective: To practice writing lowercase cursive **w**.

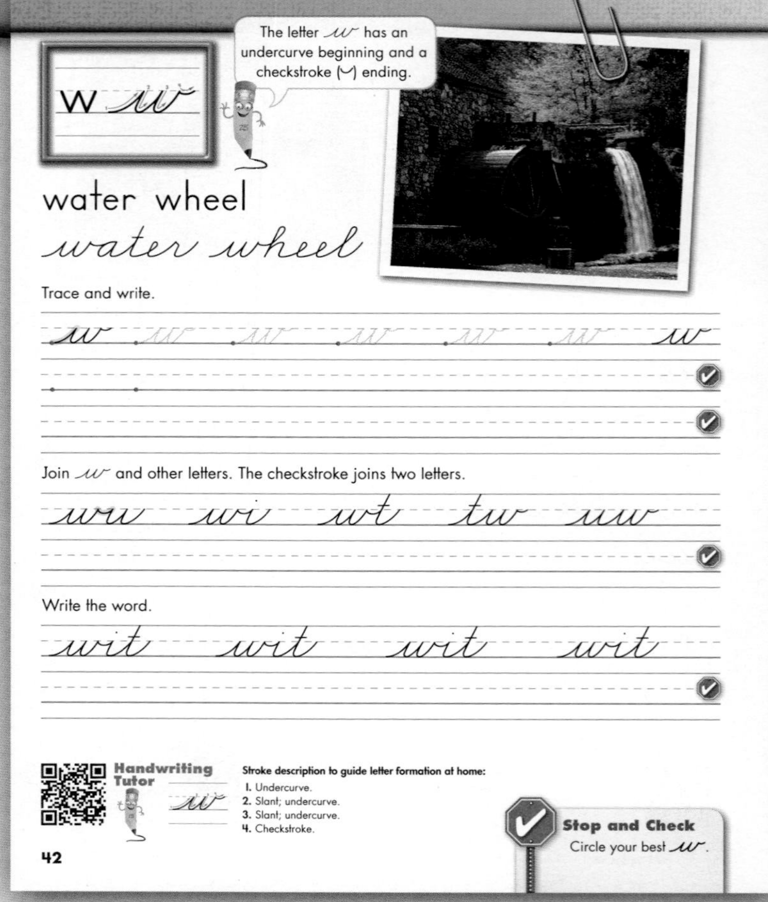

The letter w has an undercurve beginning and a checkstroke ending.
water wheel
Trace and write.
Join w and other letters. The checkstroke joins two letters.
Write the word.
Handwriting Tutor
Stroke description to guide letter formation at home:
1. Undercurve.
2. Slant; undercurve.
3. Slant; undercurve.
4. Checkstroke.
Stop and Check
Circle your best w.
42

1 Model

Talk about cursive **w**. Ask:

- How is **w** like **u**? *(Both begin with an undercurve, have slant strokes, and three undercurves.)*
- How does **w** end? *(with a checkstroke)*

Write cursive **w** on guidelines on the board as you say the stroke description. Use skywriting to model writing **w** in the air. Have students stand and say the stroke description with you as they write **w** in the air.

2 Practice

Remind students to position their book and grip their pencil correctly for writing.

Ask students to begin at the green dot and use their index finger to trace **w** several times on student page 42. Then ask them to carefully trace and write with pencil the letters, joinings, and words on the page.

Remind students that when they come to this symbol , they should stop writing and circle their best letter, joining, or word.

3 Evaluate

Tell students it is important to make their writing easy for others to read. Remind them to complete all **Stop and Check** activities.

Use these questions to help students evaluate their cursive **w**:

- Are your slant strokes pulled down to the baseline?
- Does your checkstroke begin and end at the midline?

Extra Practice

Practice Masters 24, 76

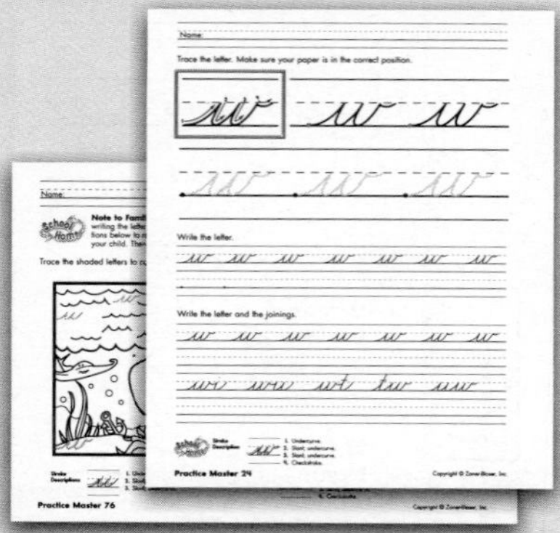

Support for English Language Learners

Digraph *ph* Point out the elephant on student page 43. Explain to students that the digraph **ph** in *elephant* is pronounced with an /f/ sound. Ask students to think of other words that contain a **ph** that sounds like **f** (**photo, graph, phone, alphabet, geography,** and so on).

e *e*

The letter *e* begins and ends with an undercurve stroke.

elephant ears

elephant ears

Trace and write.

Join *e* and other letters.

ew eu ei et te ie

Write the words.

tie we tweet wet

Handwriting Tutor

Stroke description to guide letter formation at home:

I. Undercurve; loop back; slant; undercurve.

Spacing

Circle your best joining.

43

Letter Model and Stroke Description

I. Undercurve; loop back; slant; undercurve.

Objective: To practice writing lowercase cursive **e**.

1 Model

Talk about cursive **e**. Ask:

- How does **e** begin? *(with an undercurve)*
- What size letter is **e**? *(short)*

Write cursive **e** on guidelines on the board as you say the stroke description. Use skywriting to model writing **e** in the air. Have students stand and say the stroke description with you as they write **e** in the air.

2 Practice

Remind students to position their book and grip their pencil correctly for writing.

Ask students to begin at the green dot and use their index finger to trace **e** several times on student page 43. Then ask them to carefully trace and write with pencil the letters, joinings, and words on the page.

Remind students that when they come to this symbol ✓, they should stop writing and circle their best letter, joining, or word.

3 Evaluate

Tell students it is important to make their writing easy for others to read. Remind them to complete all **Stop and Check** activities.

Proper spacing makes each letter easy to read. Ask:

- Is the spacing between your joinings consistent?
- Do your letters look like the models?

Using Technology

Keyboarding Ergonomics Explain proper keyboarding ergonomics, such as sitting in a proper chair with proper posture and ensuring that the table on which the keyboard sits is at the proper height. Students should lightly rest their index fingers on the home keys (**F** and **J**) and the remaining fingers on the home row. Thumbs should rest on the space bar. Open a word-processing program. Review how to type uppercase letters and punctuation and to add one space after end punctuation. Have students type sentences about what they know about elephants. Make sure students practice good posture when typing.

Extra Practice

Practice Masters 25, 77

Objective: To practice writing lowercase cursive **l**.

The letter l begins with a tall undercurve stroke.
lots of lumber
Trace and write. Close the loop at the midline.
Join l and other letters.
li le lt il el wl
Write the words.
lit let tell will
Handwriting Tutor
Stroke description to guide letter formation at home:
l. Undercurve; loop back; slant; undercurve.
44
Stop and Check
Circle your best l.

1 Model

Talk about cursive **l**. Ask:

- Where does the loop close in **l**? *(near the midline)*
- How does **l** end? *(with an undercurve)*

Write cursive **l** on guidelines on the board as you say the stroke description. Use skywriting to model writing **l** in the air. Have students stand and say the stroke description with you as they write **l** in the air.

2 Practice

Remind students to position their book and grip their pencil correctly for writing.

Ask students to begin at the green dot and use their index finger to trace **l** several times on student page 44. Then ask them to carefully trace and write the letters, joinings, and words on the page.

Remind students that when they come to this symbol ✓, they should stop writing and circle their best letter, joining, or word.

3 Evaluate

Tell students it is important to make their writing easy for others to read. Remind them to complete all **Stop and Check** activities.

✓ **Use** these questions to help students evaluate their cursive **l**:

- Does your **l** touch the headline?
- Does your last undercurve touch the midline?

Extra Practice

Practice Masters 26, 77

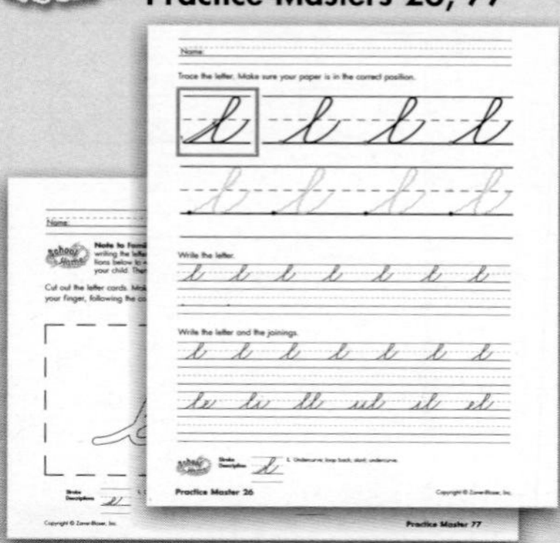

Support for English Language Learners

Comparing Cursive *e* and *l* Students might benefit from comparing the letters **e** and **l**. Model skywriting the letter **e** while saying its detailed stroke description. (Go to **resources.zaner-bloser.com/hw**.) Have a volunteer write a word beginning with the letter **e** on the board. Repeat the procedure for the letter **l**. Help students distinguish between the letters by their size. Invite students to share **e** words and **l** words from their native language.

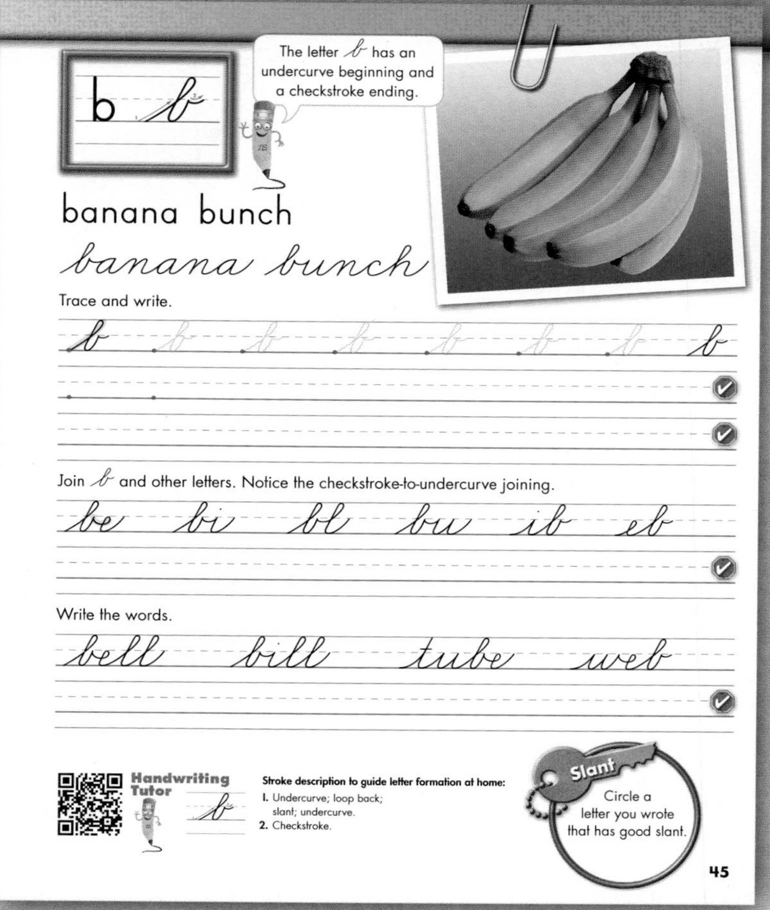
b *b*

The letter *b* has an undercurve beginning and a checkstroke ending.

banana bunch

banana bunch

Trace and write.

b b b b b b b b

Join *b* and other letters. Notice the checkstroke-to-undercurve joining.

be bi bl bu ib eb

Write the words.

bell bill tube web

Handwriting Tutor

Stroke description to guide letter formation at home:
1. Undercurve; loop back; slant; undercurve.
2. Checkstroke.

Slant

Circle a letter you wrote that has good slant.

45

Letter Model and Stroke Description

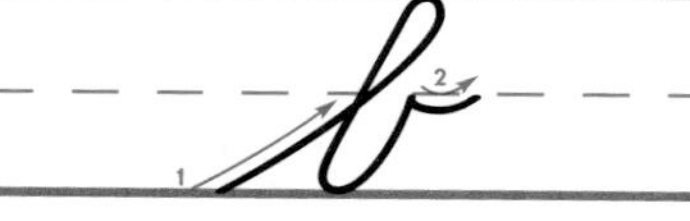

1. Undercurve; loop back; slant; undercurve.
2. Checkstroke.

Objective: To practice writing lowercase cursive **b**.

1 Model

Talk about cursive **b**. Ask:

- Where does the loop close in **b**? *(near the midline)*
- How does **b** differ from **l**? *(The letter* ***b*** *ends with a checkstroke.)*

Write cursive **b** on guidelines on the board as you say the stroke description. Use skywriting to model writing **b** in the air. Have students stand and say the stroke description with you as they write **b** in the air.

2 Practice

Remind students to position their book and grip their pencil correctly for writing.

Ask students to begin at the green dot and use their index finger to trace **b** several times on student page 45. Then have them carefully trace and write with pencil the letters, joinings, and words on the page.

Remind students that when they come to this symbol ✓, they should stop writing and circle their best letter, joining, or word.

3 Evaluate

Tell students it is important to make their writing easy for others to read. Remind them to complete all **Stop and Check** activities.

Proper slant makes each letter easy to read. Ask:

- Does your writing have good slant?
- Do your letters look like the models?

Using Technology

Anagrams Help students find sites online where they can create anagrams based on the letters they have learned so far. (Enter *anagrams* into a search engine.) Have students type the undercurve letters **i, t, u, w, e, l,** and **b** into an anagram generator. Then have them write the five longest words on lined paper. Remind students to use their best cursive handwriting. Have partners compare and comment on their cursive words.

Extra Practice

Practice Masters 27, 78

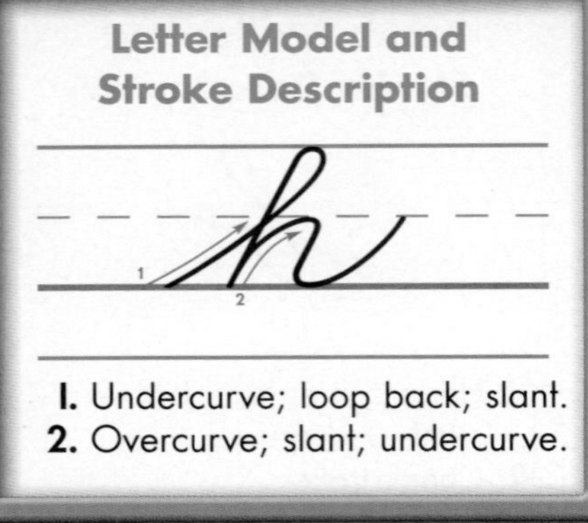

Objective: To practice writing lowercase cursive **h**.

The letter h begins and ends with an undercurve stroke.
herd of horses
Trace and write.
Join h and other letters.
he hi hu wh th ht
Write the words.
hub while the with
Handwriting Tutor
Stroke description to guide letter formation at home:
1. Undercurve; loop back; slant.
2. Overcurve; slant; undercurve.
Stop and Check
Circle your best h.
46

1 Model

Talk about cursive **h**. Ask:

- What stroke follows the first slant in **h**? *(overcurve)*
- How does **h** end? *(with an undercurve)*

Write cursive **h** on guidelines on the board as you say the stroke description. Use skywriting to model writing **h** in the air. Have students stand and say the stroke description with you as they write **h** in the air.

2 Practice

Remind students to position their book and grip their pencil correctly for writing.

Ask students to begin at the green dot and use their index finger to trace **h** several times on student page 46. Then have them carefully trace and write with pencil the letters, joinings, and words on the page.

Remind students that when they come to this symbol , they should stop writing and circle their best letter, joining, or word.

3 Evaluate

Tell students it is important to make their writing easy for others to read. Remind them to complete all **Stop and Check** activities.

Use these questions to help students evaluate their cursive **h**:

- Does your loop close near the midline?
- Does your overcurve touch the midline?

Extra Practice

Practice Masters 28, 78

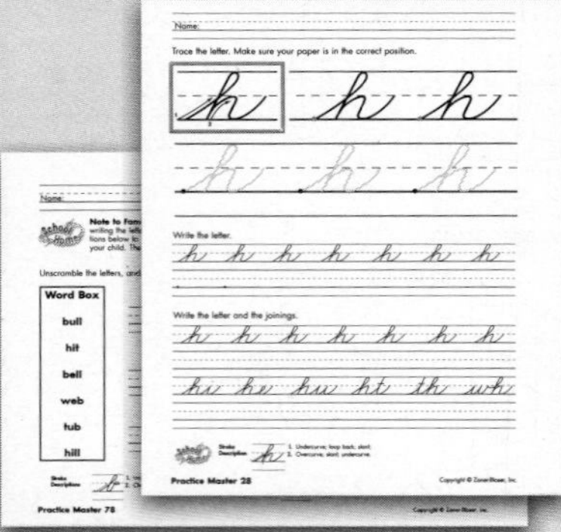

Support for English Language Learners

The Sounds of *h* Students may know that the letter **h** has the /h/ sound as in **hat, his,** and **how**. They may not realize that sometimes the sound of the letter **h** is silent in English, the same as it is in Spanish. Write the words **hat, his, how, honest, honor,** and **hour** on the board. Point to each word, say it, and have students repeat it after you. Point out to students when the **h** is pronounced and when it is silent.

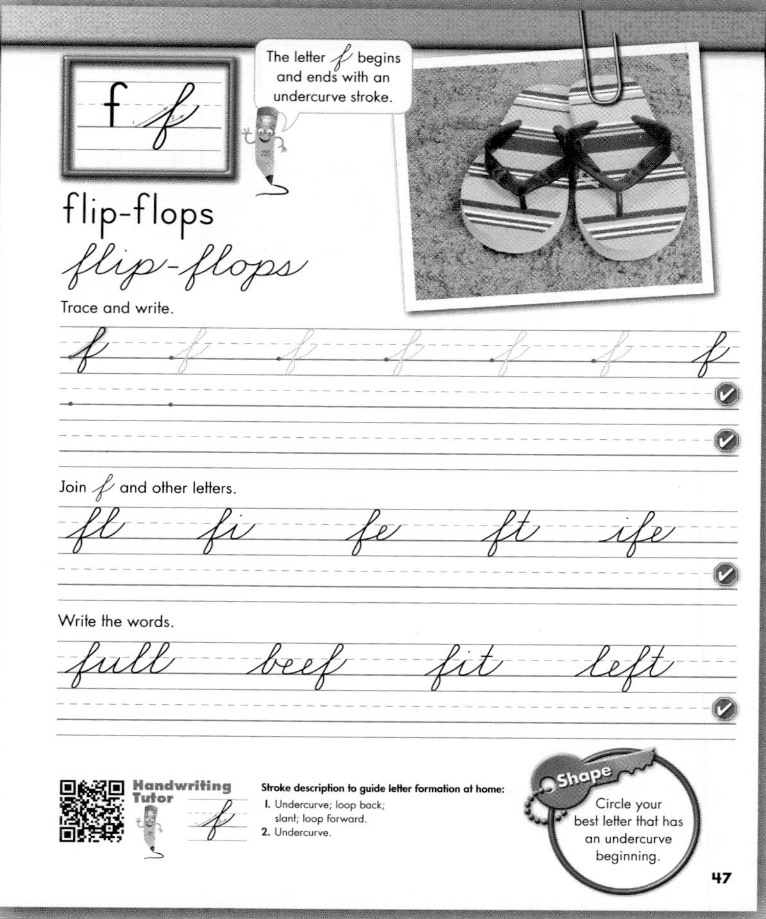

The letter *f* begins and ends with an undercurve stroke.

f *f*

flip-flops

flip-flops

Trace and write.

f f f f f f f

Join *f* and other letters.

fl fi fe ft ife

Write the words.

full beef fit left

Handwriting Tutor

Stroke description to guide letter formation at home:
1. Undercurve; loop back; slant; loop forward.
2. Undercurve.

Shape

Circle your best letter that has an undercurve beginning.

47

Letter Model and Stroke Description

1. Undercurve; loop back; slant; loop forward.
2. Undercurve.

Objective: To practice writing lowercase cursive **f**.

1 Model

Talk about cursive **f**. Ask:

- How does **f** begin and end? *(with an undercurve)*
- Where does the upper loop close in **f**? *(near the midline)*

Write cursive **f** on guidelines on the board as you say the stroke description. Use skywriting to model writing **f** in the air. Have students stand and say the stroke description with you as they write **f** in the air.

2 Practice

Remind students to position their book and grip their pencil correctly for writing.

Ask students to begin at the green dot and use their index finger to trace **f** several times on student page 47. Then have them carefully trace and write with pencil the letters, joinings, and words on the page.

Remind students that when they come to this symbol ✓, they should stop writing and circle their best letter, joining, or word.

3 Evaluate

Tell students it is important to make their writing easy for others to read. Remind them to complete all **Stop and Check** activities.

Proper shape makes each letter easy to read. Ask:

- Does your upper loop close near the midline?
- Does your lower loop close at the baseline?

Tips From an Occupational Therapist

American Sign Language This activity provides opportunities to strengthen individual finger movements and to improve visual motor skills. Find pictures of the letters of the alphabet in American Sign Language. Post the pictures around your classroom so students can see them. Help students learn the letter signs, allowing time to practice. You might want to pair students so they can test each other on the signs. As students become comfortable with signing, have them practice their spelling words in sign language.

Extra Practice

Practice Masters 29, 79

Letter Model and Stroke Description

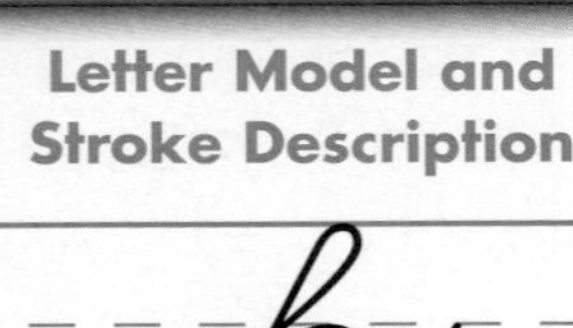

1. Undercurve; loop back; slant.
2. Overcurve; curve forward; curve under.
3. Slant right; undercurve.

Objective: To practice writing lowercase cursive **k**.

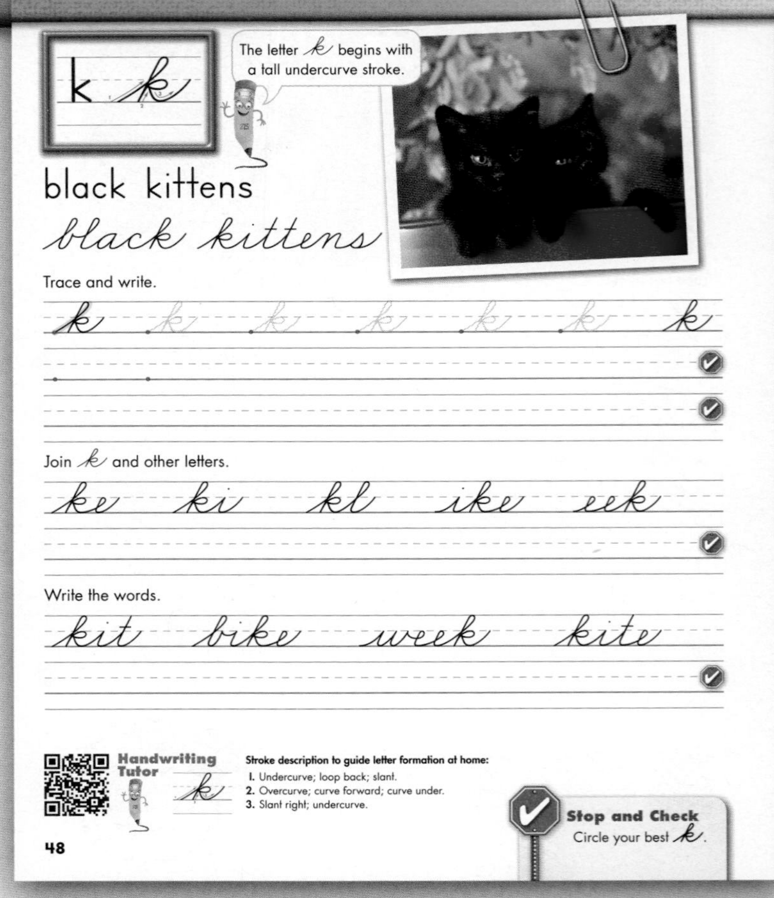

The letter k begins with a tall undercurve stroke.
black kittens
black kittens
Trace and write.
Join k and other letters.
ke ki kl ike eek
Write the words.
kit bike week kite
Handwriting Tutor
Stroke description to guide letter formation at home:
1. Undercurve; loop back; slant.
2. Overcurve; curve forward; curve under.
3. Slant right; undercurve.
48
Stop and Check
Circle your best k.

1 Model

Talk about cursive **k**. Ask:

- How does **k** begin and end? *(with an undercurve)*
- How many slants are in **k**? *(two)*

Write cursive **k** on guidelines on the board as you say the stroke description. Use skywriting to model writing **k** in the air. Have students stand and say the stroke description with you as they write cursive **k** in the air.

2 Practice

Remind students to position their book and grip their pencil correctly for writing.

Ask students to begin at the green dot and use their index finger to trace **k** several times on student page 48. Then have them carefully trace and write with pencil the letters, joinings, and words on the page.

Remind students that when they come to this symbol ✓, they should stop writing and circle their best letter, joining, or word.

3 Evaluate

Tell students it is important to make their writing easy for others to read. Remind them to complete all **Stop and Check** activities.

✓ **Use** these questions to help students evaluate their cursive **k**:

- Does your **k** begin and end with an undercurve?
- Does your upper loop close near the midline?

Extra Practice

Practice Masters 30, 79

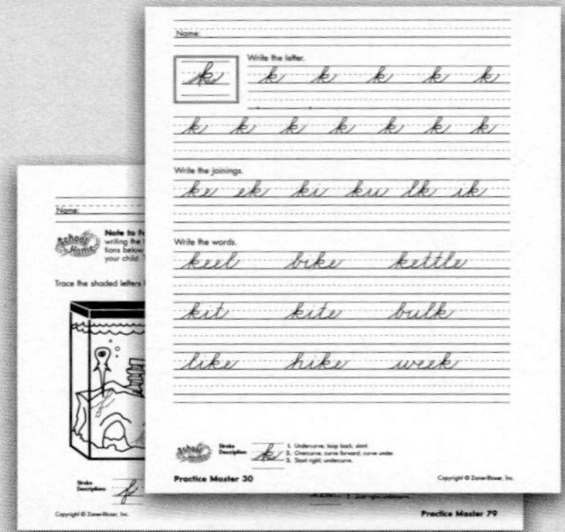

Support for English Language Learners

The Sounds of *k* Write these words that begin with **k** in two columns on the board. In the first column, write **kite, key, kind, keep, kilo, kimono,** and **kitten**. In the second column, write **knee, knob,** and **knife**. Say each word in the first column, and have students repeat it after you. Then tell students that the letter **k** is silent when it comes before the letter **n**. Pronounce **knee, knob,** and **knife**. Then have students say the words along with you. Invite students to share **k** words from their native language.

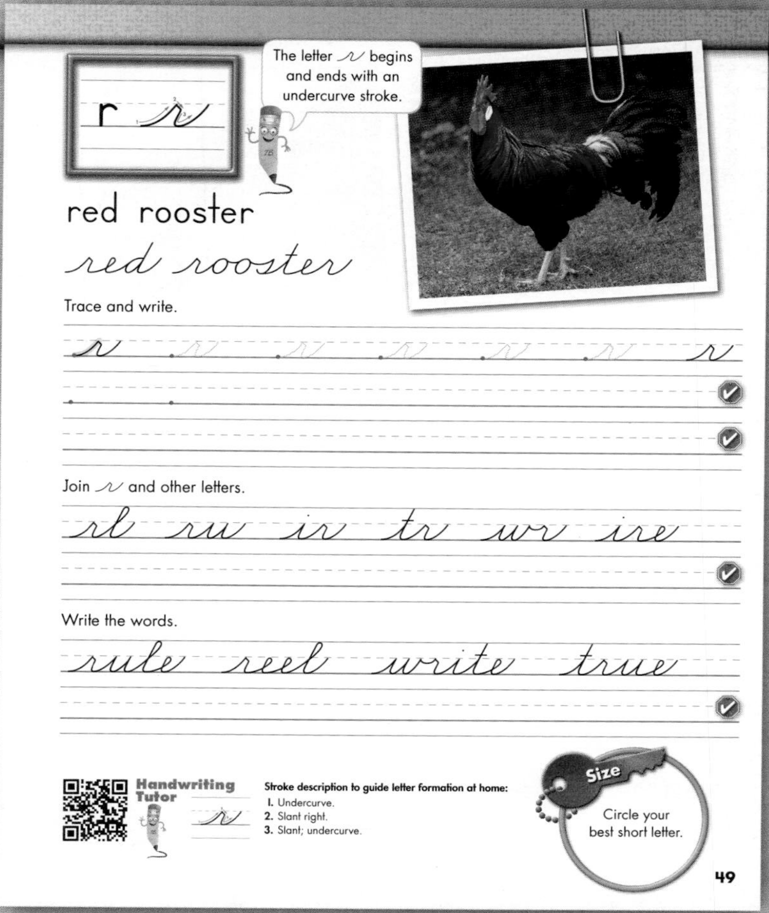
The letter begins and ends with an undercurve stroke.
red rooster
Trace and write.
Join and other letters.
Write the words.
Handwriting Tutor
Stroke description to guide letter formation at home:
1. Undercurve.
2. Slant right.
3. Slant; undercurve.
Size
Circle your best short letter.
49

Letter Model and Stroke Description

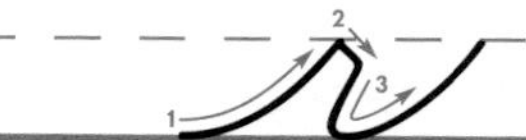

1. Undercurve.
2. Slant right.
3. Slant; undercurve.

Objective: To practice writing lowercase cursive **r**.

Handwriting Tutor

1 Model

Talk about cursive **r**. Ask:

- What stroke follows the first undercurve in **r**? *(slant right)*
- How does **r** end? *(with an undercurve)*

Write cursive **r** on guidelines on the board as you say the stroke description. Use skywriting to model writing **r** in the air. Have students stand and say the stroke description with you as they write **r** in the air.

2 Practice

Remind students to position their book and grip their pencil correctly for writing.

Ask students to begin at the green dot and use their index finger to trace **r** several times on student page 49. Then have them carefully trace and write with pencil the letters, joinings, and words on the page.

Remind students that when they come to this symbol ✓, they should stop writing and circle their best letter, joining, or word.

3 Evaluate

Tell students it is important to make their writing easy for others to read. Remind them to complete all **Stop and Check** activities.

Proper size makes each letter easy to read. Ask:

- Is your **r** about the same width as the model?
- Does your **r** touch the midline?

Writing in the Content Areas

Language Arts

Story Retelling Have students look at the photo of the rooster on page 49, and brainstorm a list of other farm animals with students. Have partners think of a story about farm animals that they know, and have them discuss details about the story, including the characters, the setting, and the plot. Then have them write a brief retelling of the story in their own words. Remind students to use their best cursive handwriting.

School Home

Extra Practice

Practice Masters 31, 80

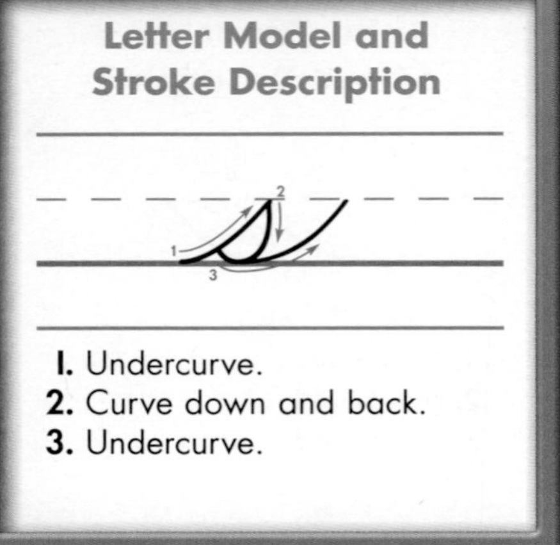

Objective: To practice writing lowercase cursive **s**.

The letter s begins and ends with an undercurve stroke.
steep slope
steep slope
Trace and write.
Join s and other letters.
se sk sl sw ss st
Write the words.
sweet skis bus wrist
Handwriting Tutor
Stroke description to guide letter formation at home:
1. Undercurve.
2. Curve down and back.
3. Undercurve.
Stop and Check
Circle your best s.
50

1 Model

Talk about cursive **s**. Ask:

- How many undercurves are in **s**? *(two)*
- Where do both undercurves end? *(at the midline)*

Write cursive **s** on guidelines on the board as you say the stroke description. Use skywriting to model writing **s** in the air. Have students stand and say the stroke description with you as they write **s** in the air.

2 Practice

Remind students to position their book and grip their pencil correctly for writing.

Ask students to begin at the green dot and use their index finger to trace **s** several times on student page 50. Then have them carefully trace and write with pencil the letters, joinings, and words on the page.

Remind students that when they come to this symbol , they should stop writing and circle their best letter, joining, or word.

3 Evaluate

Tell students it is important to make their writing easy for others to read. Remind them to complete all **Stop and Check** activities.

 **Use** these questions to help students evaluate their cursive **s**:

- Is the bottom of your **s** closed?
- Does your **s** end at the midline?

Extra Practice

Practice Masters 32, 80

Support for English Language Learners

The Sounds of *s* To help students with some of the different sounds of the letter **s**, write the words **sand, sock, yes, music, cheese,** and **rose** on the board. Next to each word, write the different sounds of **s**: /s/ as in **sand, sock,** and **yes;** and /z/ as in **music, cheese,** and **rose**. Say the words, emphasizing the **s** sounds, and then have students say them with you. Invite students to share words with equivalent sounds in their native language.

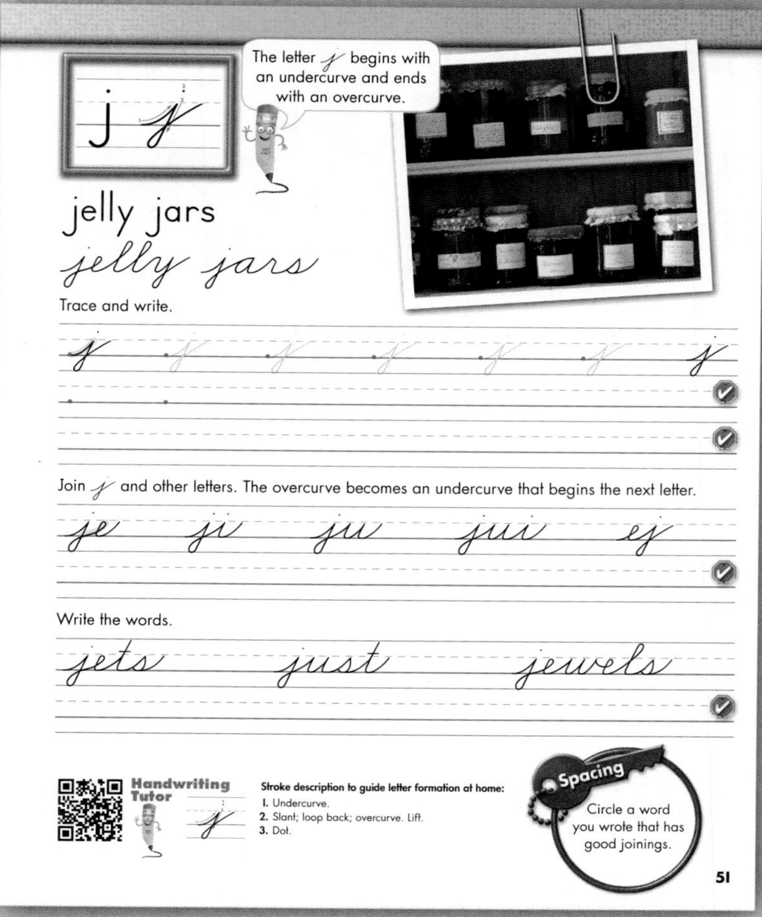

The letter j begins with an undercurve and ends with an overcurve.
jelly jars
Trace and write.
Join j and other letters. The overcurve becomes an undercurve that begins the next letter.
je ji ju jui ej
Write the words.
jets just jewels
Handwriting Tutor
Stroke description to guide letter formation at home:
1. Undercurve.
2. Slant; loop back; overcurve. Lift.
3. Dot.
Spacing
Circle a word you wrote that has good joinings.
51

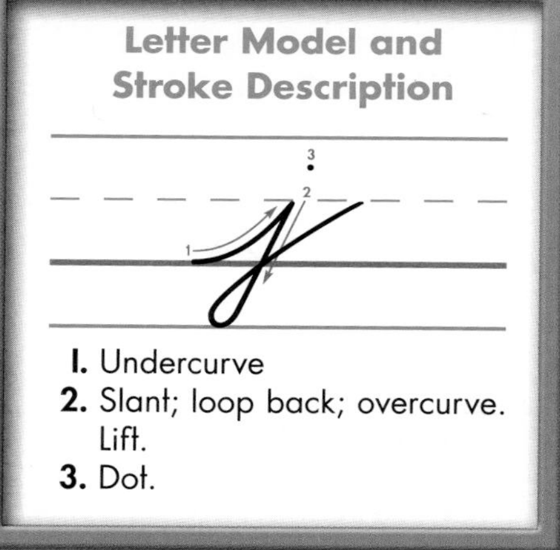

Letter Model and Stroke Description

1. Undercurve
2. Slant; loop back; overcurve. Lift.
3. Dot.

Objective: To practice writing lowercase cursive **j**.

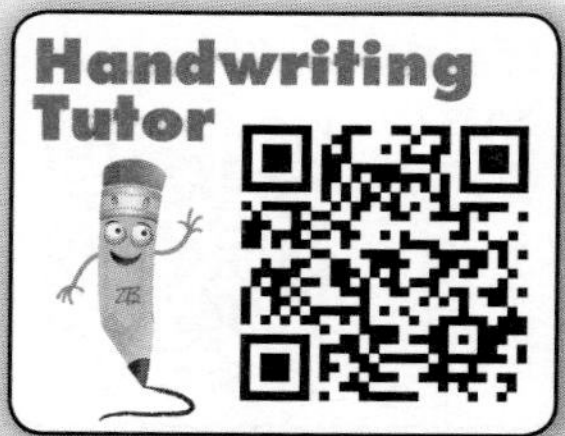

1 Model

Talk about cursive **j**. Ask:

- Where does **j** begin? *(at the baseline)*
- Where does the overcurve in **j** end? *(near the midline)*

Write cursive **j** on guidelines on the board as you say the stroke description. Use skywriting to model writing **j** in the air. Have students stand and say the stroke description with you as they write **j** in the air.

2 Practice

Remind students to position their book and grip their pencil correctly for writing.

Ask students to begin at the green dot and use their index finger to trace **j** several times on student page 51. Then have them carefully trace and write with pencil the letters, joinings, and words on the page.

Remind students that when they come to this symbol ✓, they should stop writing and circle their best letter, joining, or word.

3 Evaluate

Tell students it is important to make their writing easy for others to read. Remind them to complete all **Stop and Check** activities.

Proper spacing makes letters easy to read. Ask:

- Are your letters properly spaced?
- Do your letters look like the model?

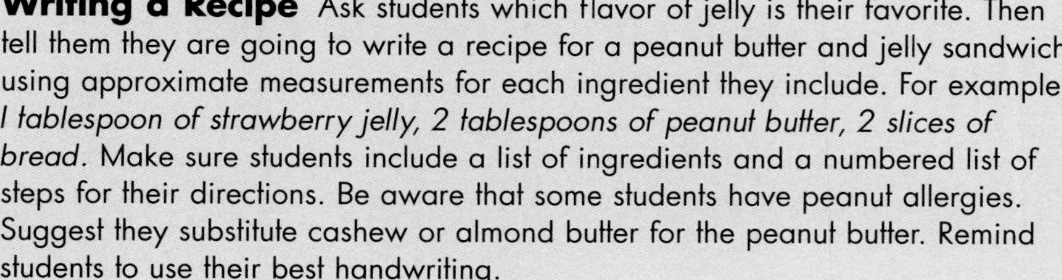

Writing in the Content Areas

Math

Writing a Recipe Ask students which flavor of jelly is their favorite. Then tell them they are going to write a recipe for a peanut butter and jelly sandwich using approximate measurements for each ingredient they include. For example, *I tablespoon of strawberry jelly, 2 tablespoons of peanut butter, 2 slices of bread.* Make sure students include a list of ingredients and a numbered list of steps for their directions. Be aware that some students have peanut allergies. Suggest they substitute cashew or almond butter for the peanut butter. Remind students to use their best handwriting.

Extra Practice

Practice Masters 33, 81

Letter Model and Stroke Description

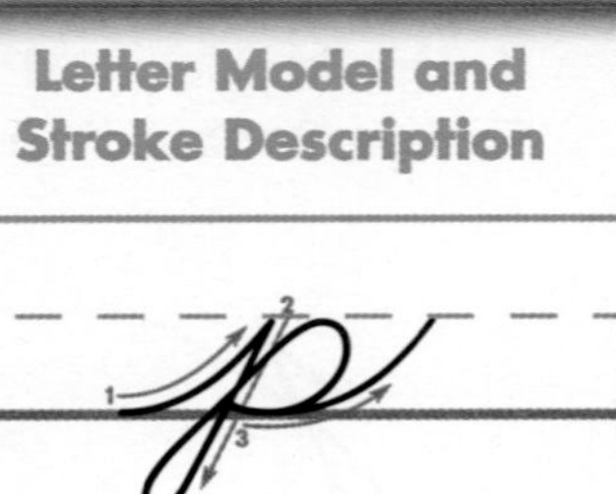

1. Undercurve.
2. Slant; loop back; overcurve; curve back.
3. Undercurve.

Objective: To practice writing lowercase cursive **p**.

p *p*

The letter *p* begins and ends with an undercurve stroke.

purple plums

purple plums

Trace and write.

p p p p p p p

Join *p* and other letters.

pi pe pl pr ph sp

Write the words.

put push beep spell

Handwriting Tutor

Stroke description to guide letter formation at home:
1. Undercurve.
2. Slant; loop back; overcurve; curve back.
3. Undercurve.

Stop and Check
Circle your best *p*.

52

1 Model

Talk about cursive **p**. Ask:

- Where does the beginning undercurve end? *(at the midline)*
- Where does the loop close? *(near the baseline)*

Write cursive **p** on guidelines on the board as you say the stroke description. Use skywriting to model writing **p** in the air. Have students stand and say the stroke description with you as they write **p** in the air.

2 Practice

Remind students to position their book and grip their pencil correctly for writing.

Ask students to begin at the green dot and carefully trace the shaded letters with pencil. Then have them write the letters, joinings, and words on the page.

Remind students that when they come to this symbol ✓, they should stop writing and circle their best letter, joining, or word.

3 Evaluate

Tell students it is important to make their writing easy for others to read. Remind them to complete all **Stop and Check** activities.

✓ **Use** these questions to help students evaluate their cursive **p**:

- Does your loop fill the descender space?
- Does your loop slant to the left?

School Home Extra Practice

Practice Masters 34, 81

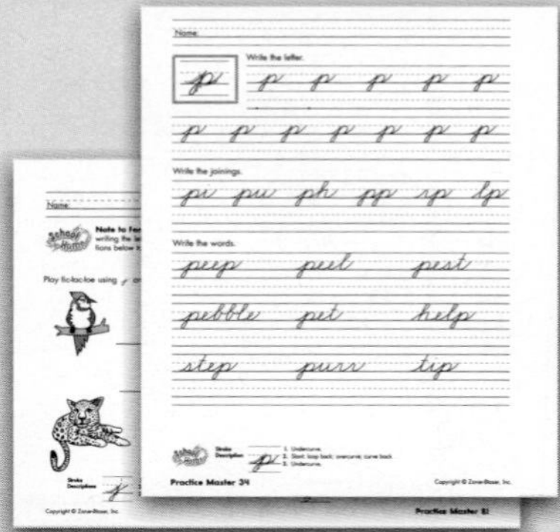

Support for English Language Learners

Additional Practice With *p* Write several words that begin with **p** on the board. Examples: **pan, penny, pint, piñata, parade,** and **parents**. Say each word as you skywrite **p** in the air. Have students say the words along with you. Invite students to share **p** words from their native launguage.

Joinings

Write the joinings and words.

Undercurve-to-Undercurve Joining
The undercurve ending swings wide to begin the following letter.

hi kit list tree

Checkstroke-to-Undercurve Joining
The checkstroke ending dips deep to begin the following letter.

we wi bus blue

Overcurve-to-Undercurve Joining
The overcurve ending crosses at the baseline and turns into a wide undercurve.

ji ju jet just

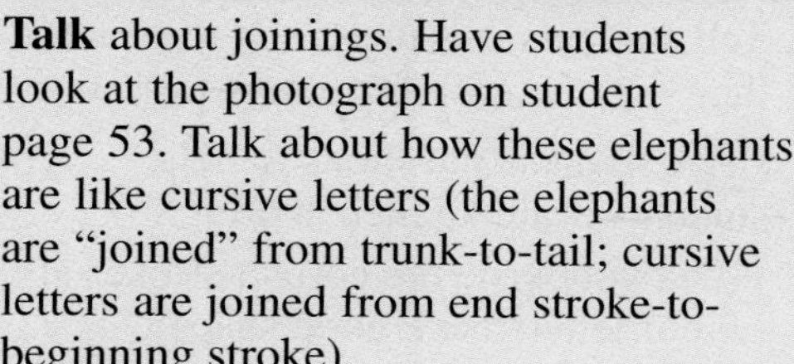

Stop and Check
Circle three words you wrote that have good joinings.

53

Objective: To write joinings and words legibly.

1 Model

Talk about joinings. Have students look at the photograph on student page 53. Talk about how these elephants are like cursive letters (the elephants are "joined" from trunk-to-tail; cursive letters are joined from end stroke-to-beginning stroke).

Write the different letter combinations and words on guidelines on the board as you emphasize the joinings. Use skywriting as you model each. Have students skywrite with you.

Ask students to use their index finger to trace the letters and joinings several times on student page 53.

2 Practice

Remind students to position their book and grip their pencil correctly for writing.

Ask students to write the joinings and words on the page.

3 Evaluate

Tell students it is important to make their writing easy for others to read. Remind them to complete all **Stop and Check** activities.

Use these questions to help students evaluate their joinings:

- Does your undercurve swing wide to begin the next letter?
- Does your checkstroke deepen a little before swinging into the undercurve of the next letter?
- Does your overcurve turn at the baseline to form an undercurve?

Support for English Language Learners

Vocabulary Building Some English Language Learners may not have a full understanding of the word **joining** and its root, **join**. Explain to students that *to join* means to bring together two or more parts. For instance, when you join a club, a team, or a class you are adding yourself to a group of people. Also explain that the word **join** is in the word **joint**; joints are parts of the body that connect other parts together, such as knees and elbows. Point out to students that the joinings in cursive handwriting are similar to the joints in the body.

Review

Objective: To review the lowercase cursive letters beginning with an undercurve stroke: **i, t, u, w, e, l, b, h, f, k, r, s, j, p**.

Review

i t u w e l b
h f k r s j p

Write these rhyming words.

keep peep jeep beep

jet pet set wet

hill bill fill will

true blue few flew

54

1 Review

Review the stroke descriptions, and model any letters students might be having difficulty writing. You might want to refer to **resources.zaner-bloser.com/hw** for more detailed stroke descriptions.

Ask a volunteer to give a verbal description of one of the letters. Challenge students to identify the letter being described and then write it on guidelines on the board.

See the **Corrective Strategies** in the Appendix for techniques in correcting common problems in your students' handwriting.

2 Practice

Remind students to position their book and grip their pencil correctly for writing.

Ask students to carefully write the rhyming words on student page 54.

3 Evaluate

Tell students it is important to make their writing easy for others to read.

Use these questions to help students evaluate their writing:

- Did you write the correct strokes so your letters have good shape?
- Did you use the guidelines to make your letters the correct size?
- Are the spaces between the letters of your words equal?
- Do your words have consistent forward slant?

Digital Tools

Go Online Printables and other free classroom resources are available at **resources.zaner-bloser.com/hw**.

Support for English Language Learners

Vowel and Consonant Recognition Review with students the difference between vowels and consonants. Write the letters **i, t, u, w, e, l, b, h, f, k, r, s, j,** and **p** on the board. Point to each letter, and have students say "vowel" or "consonant" for each letter. Then ask students to name a word that begins with each letter.

Homophones

Homophones are words that sound alike but are spelled differently. They have different meanings, too.

see
sea

Write these homophone pairs.

fur fir be bee

peer pier flew flu

its it's wheel we'll

their there sweet suite

blue blew few phew!

Stop and Check Circle your best letter.

55

Application

Homophones

Objective: To practice writing homophones legibly.

1 Review

Write several words from student page 55 on the board. Think aloud as you talk through the correct formation of several letters and joining strokes. Emphasize that students should swing wide to join letters that begin with undercurves. Ask volunteers to evaluate the words you wrote according to the Keys to Legibility.

2 Practice

Remind students to position their book and grip their pencil correctly for writing.

Ask students to carefully write the words on the page and pay close attention to their joinings.

3 Evaluate

Tell students it is important to make their writing easy for others to read.

Use these questions to help students evaluate their writing:

- Do your letters have good shape?
- Do your short letters touch both the midline and the baseline?
- Do your tall letters touch both the headline and the baseline?
- Do your joining strokes make good spacing between your letters?
- Does your writing have good slant?

Tips From an Occupational Therapist

Making Mosaics The ability to integrate the **visual and motor systems** is very important for both manuscript and cursive handwriting. Tell students they are going to create a picture called a mosaic. First, ask students to draw simple designs on construction paper. Then tell them to tear construction or tissue paper into small pieces and glue them onto their designs. Finally, ask students to give their mosaics titles. Tearing and gluing small pieces of tissue paper is a good activity to help with **muscle grading, or the ability to control how much force is needed for certain activities.** You might want to post student work in the classroom for all to enjoy.

In the Real World

Objective: To practice writing words legibly.

Cursive Writing

In the Real World

There are five words spelled incorrectly in the short story below. On the guidelines, write the misspelled words correctly and in cursive. Writing the words again will help you remember them.

On a small farm, there lived a mouse named Louisa. She slept under a pyle of hay in the barn. She poot her food behind a loose board in the wall. One day, she found that her food was gone. She was shure she had hidden a big piece of cheese their. She was so hungry her stomach was starting to hirt. So Louisa set out to discover who stole her cheese.

1.
2.
3.
4.
5.

The more you practice writing in cursive, the easier it will be!

56

1 Review

Present the activity. When students practice writing their spelling words correctly, it is easier to remember them. Learning to write cursive is very similar—the more you practice writing in cursive, the easier it will be. To make the most of their time, students can do both: practice writing their spelling words in cursive.

Read aloud the first sentence on student page 56. Then use skywriting to model writing one word from the sentence in the air.

2 Practice

Remind students to position their book and grip their pencil correctly for writing.

Ask students to find the five misspelled words in the paragraph and carefully write the corrected words on the page.

3 Evaluate

Use these questions to help students evaluate their writing:

- Does your checkstroke-to-undercurve joining on **b** and **w** connect to the next letter?
- Is your writing easy to read?
- Are the letters in your words equally spaced?

Support for English Language Learners

Homonyms Some students might have difficulty understanding the difference between *their* and *there*. Write **their** and **there** on the board, and say the words aloud. Explain to students that these words sound the same but have different meanings and spellings. **Their** means "belonging to them"; **there** usually means "at or in that place." Add **they're** to the board. Explain that this word also sounds like **their** and **there,** but it has another meaning: **they're** is a contraction that means "they are." Encourage students to write a sentence using each **their, there,** and **they're**.

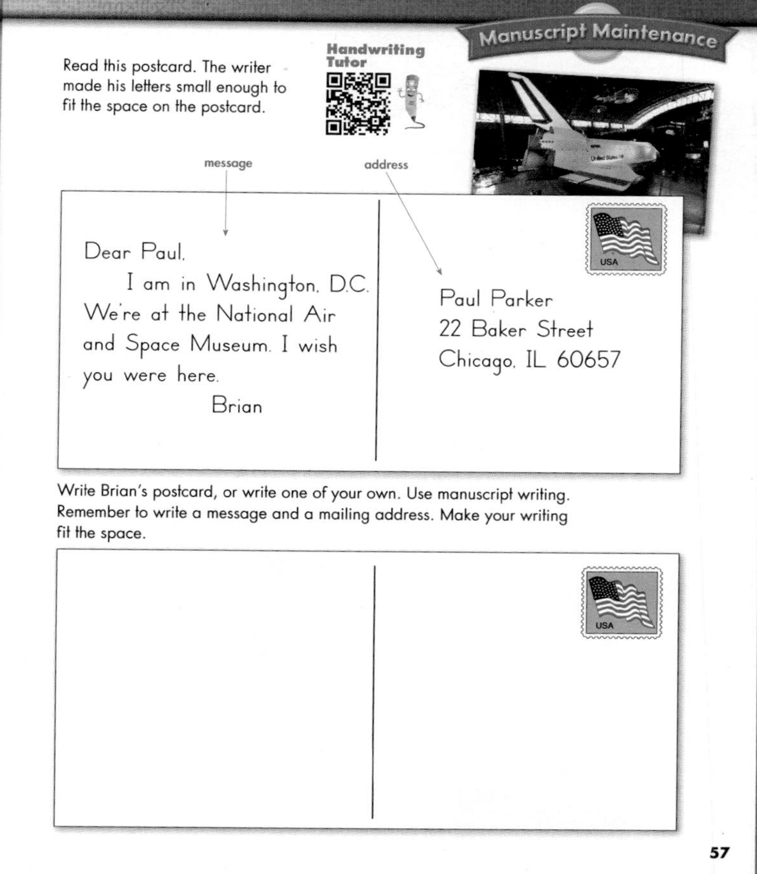

Manuscript Maintenance
Read this postcard. The writer made his letters small enough to fit the space on the postcard.
Handwriting Tutor
message
address
Dear Paul,
I am in Washington, D.C.
We're at the National Air
and Space Museum. I wish
you were here.
Brian
Paul Parker
22 Baker Street
Chicago, IL 60657
USA
Write Brian's postcard, or write one of your own. Use manuscript writing.
Remember to write a message and a mailing address. Make your writing fit the space.
USA
57

Manuscript Maintenance

Objective: To practice writing a postcard message and an address in manuscript.

1 Review

Have students look at the postcard on student page 57. Ask them to describe the Shape, Size, Spacing, and Slant of the manuscript letters and numerals.

Ask students to notice how the writer of the postcard adjusted the size of his writing to fit the smaller space. Point out that **Shape, Size, Spacing,** and **Slant** remain consistent even though the writing is smaller than usual.

2 Practice

Have students write Brian's postcard message or write one of their own. Remind them to include a mailing address on the right-hand side of the postcard, and to form their manuscript letters and numerals carefully so they will be legible.

Refer students to the Cursive and Manuscript alphabets on student pages 22 and 23 if more guidance is needed.

3 Evaluate

Tell students it is important to make their writing easy for others to read.

Use these questions to help students evaluate their writing:

- Did you write with correct strokes so your letters and numerals have good shape?
- Did you write letters and numerals with good size to fit the writing space?
- Are your short letters half the height of your tall letters?
- Did you allow good spacing?
- Did you maintain good vertical slant?

Using Technology

E-mail Have students write an e-mail about a trip they have taken. Open an e-mail program and explain the applicable fields to complete—**To:, Cc:, Subject:,** and **body**. Have students type their message in the body. Review how to start a new line after the greeting and before the closing. Have students insert the recipient's e-mail address in the **To:** field. Have students add your address in the **Cc:** field. Show students where to find the @ symbol on the keyboard, and demonstrate how to use the Shift key to access it. After the e-mail is written, suggest a good subject line (e.g., Look where I went!) and direct students to click Send to deliver their messages.

Keys to Legibility

Shape
Shape describes the strokes that form each letter and give it a unique appearance.

Size
Size describes the height of letters.

Spacing
Spacing describes the space between letters, words, and sentences.

Slant
Slant refers to the angle of writing on the paper.

Objective: To practice the four Keys to Legibility.

Write the poem.
Make your writing easy to read.

pets true
will keep
true blue
his sleep

58

Handwriting Coach

Pencil Position

Many students hold their pencils too close to the point. To help students position their fingers on the pencil, demonstrate how to wrap a rubber band tightly around the pencil at least an inch away from the point. Explain that the rubber band shows where to hold the pencil and keeps the fingers from slipping so students can more easily control the shape, size, spacing, and slant of their writing.

1 Model

Remind students that good handwriting is legible handwriting. The most important thing to remember is that readers must be able to read a message in order to understand its meaning.

Brainstorm with students qualities of legible handwriting. Write responses on the board. These might include neatness, carefully written letters, and letters that are not too crowded.

Point out to students that the basic strokes they learned earlier in the book are the basis for a letter's shape.

2 Practice

Remind students to position their book and grip their pencil correctly for writing. Ask students to carefully write the poem on student page 58 and be sure to write inside the margins.

Emphasize that all four Keys to Legibility work together. Their writing will be easy to read when they use proper Shape, Size, Spacing, and Slant.

Read and discuss with students the directions on student page 59. Then help them as needed as they complete the writing activity. Remind them to stay inside the margins.

Write your own poem.
Be sure to leave space for margins.

Pay attention to all four **Keys to Legibility** to make your writing easy to read.

Shape Circle your best letter that has an undercurve beginning.

Size Circle your best tall letter.

Spacing Circle two words that have space for \ between them.

Slant Circle a word you wrote that has good slant.

59

3 Evaluate

Tell students it is important to make their writing easy for others to read, and to be sure to pay close attention to margins.

Use these questions to help students evaluate their writing:

- Does each letter have its own clear shape?
- Are your tall letters the same height?
- Are your short letters the same height?
- Are your letters neither too close together nor too far apart?
- Does your writing have good slant?

Support for English Language Learners

Rhyming Words When writing poetry, students may need help with rhyming words. In the poem on page 58, the last words rhyme in alternating lines. In other poems, the rhyming patterns are different. Find examples of brief, easy poems to illustrate to students that there is more than one way to use rhyming words in poetry.

Some students might also look for spelling clues to tell if words rhyme, such as **true/blue** and **keep/sleep**. Provide students with examples of words that rhyme but have different spellings, such as **blue/stew** and **keep/cheap**. Encourage students to keep a list of rhyming words that they can add to throughout the year.

Downcurve Letters

Objective: To practice writing lowercase downcurve strokes.

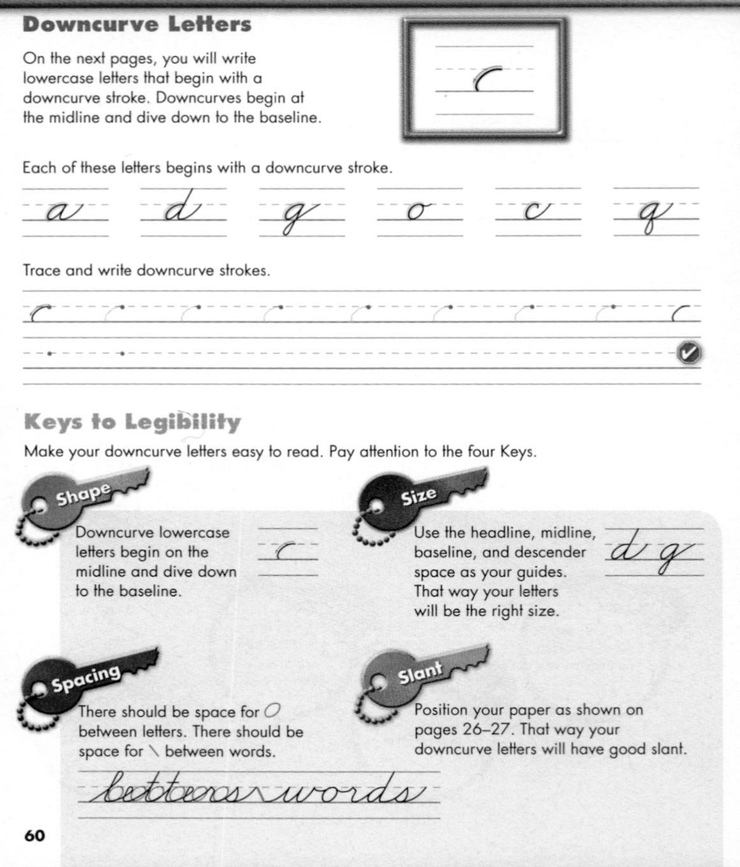

Downcurve Letters

On the next pages, you will write lowercase letters that begin with a downcurve stroke. Downcurves begin at the midline and dive down to the baseline.

Each of these letters begins with a downcurve stroke.

Trace and write downcurve strokes.

Keys to Legibility

Make your downcurve letters easy to read. Pay attention to the four Keys.

Shape Downcurve lowercase letters begin on the midline and dive down to the baseline.

Size Use the headline, midline, baseline, and descender space as your guides. That way your letters will be the right size.

Spacing There should be space for O between letters. There should be space for \ between words.

Slant Position your paper as shown on pages 26–27. That way your downcurve letters will have good slant.

60

1 Model

Point out the lowercase letters on student page 60, and explain that each one begins with a downcurve stroke. Encourage students to use their index finger to trace several of the downcurve strokes in these letters.

2 Practice

Remind students to position their book and grip their pencil correctly for writing.

Ask students to trace and write the downcurve strokes on the guidelines.

Remind students that when they come to this symbol ✓, they should stop writing and circle their best stroke.

3 Evaluate

Tell students it is important to make their writing easy for others to read. Remind them to complete the **Stop and Check** activity.

✓ **Use** these questions to help students evaluate their downcurve strokes:

- Do your downcurve strokes begin at the midline?
- Do your downcurve strokes end at the baseline?

Support for English Language Learners

Stroke Description Vocabulary Model writing the downcurve letters on the board. Recite the stroke description for each letter as you write it. Students will benefit from the visual and auditory demonstration. Invite kinesthetic learners to the board to highlight in a different color marker or piece of chalk the beginning downcurve stroke in each letter.

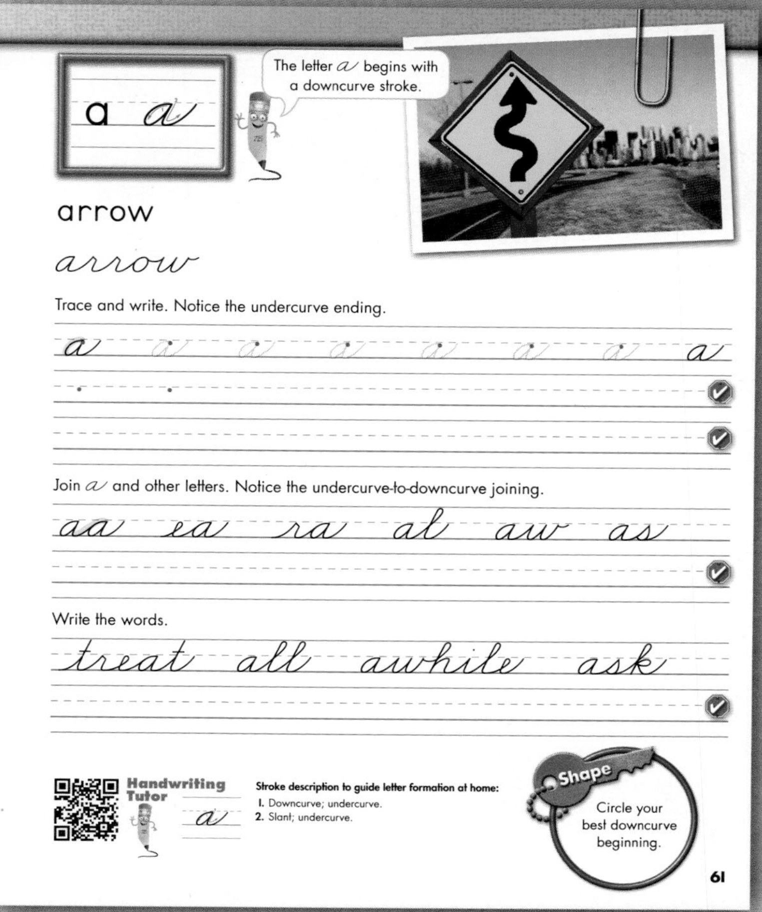
The letter *a* begins with a downcurve stroke.

a *a*

arrow

arrow

Trace and write. Notice the undercurve ending.

Join *a* and other letters. Notice the undercurve-to-downcurve joining.

aa ea ra al aw as

Write the words.

treat all awhile ask

Handwriting Tutor

Stroke description to guide letter formation at home:
1. Downcurve; undercurve.
2. Slant; undercurve.

Shape

Circle your best downcurve beginning.

61

Letter Model and Stroke Description

1. Downcurve; undercurve.
2. Slant; undercurve.

Objective: To practice writing lowercase cursive **a**.

1 Model

Talk about cursive **a**. Ask:

- How much of **i** do you see in **a**? *(all except the dot)*

Write cursive **a** on guidelines on the board as you say the stroke description. Model skywriting (see page Z21) **a** as you repeat the stroke description. Have students say the stroke description as they use their index finger to trace **a** on their desktop.

It might be helpful for students, especially auditory learners, to hear a more detailed stroke description (Go to **resources.zaner-bloser.com/hw**.)

2 Practice

Remind students to position their book and grip their pencil correctly for writing.

Ask students to begin at the green dot and carefully trace the shaded letters on student page 61 with pencil. Then have them write the letters, joinings, and words on the page.

Remind students that when they come to this symbol ✓, they should stop writing and circle their best letter, joining, or word.

3 Evaluate

Tell students it is important to make their writing easy for others to read. Remind them to complete all **Stop and Check** activities.

Proper shape makes each letter easy to read. Ask:

- Does the first downcurve of each **a** end at the baseline?
- Does each **a** end at the midline?

Writing in the Content Areas

Social Studies

Opinion Paragraph Point out the photo on page 61. Ask students what they think the sign means to drivers. Have students think of other signs they commonly see and write them. Then have students decide which street sign is the most vital to the safety of motorists, cyclists, and/or pedestrians. Ask students to write an **opinion** paragraph about their selected sign, making sure to include several solid supporting statements. Remind students to use their best cursive handwriting.

Extra Practice

Practice Masters 35, 82

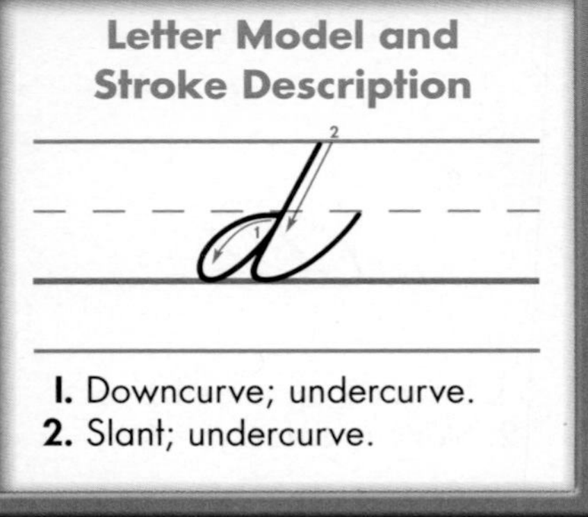

Objective: To practice writing lowercase cursive **d**.

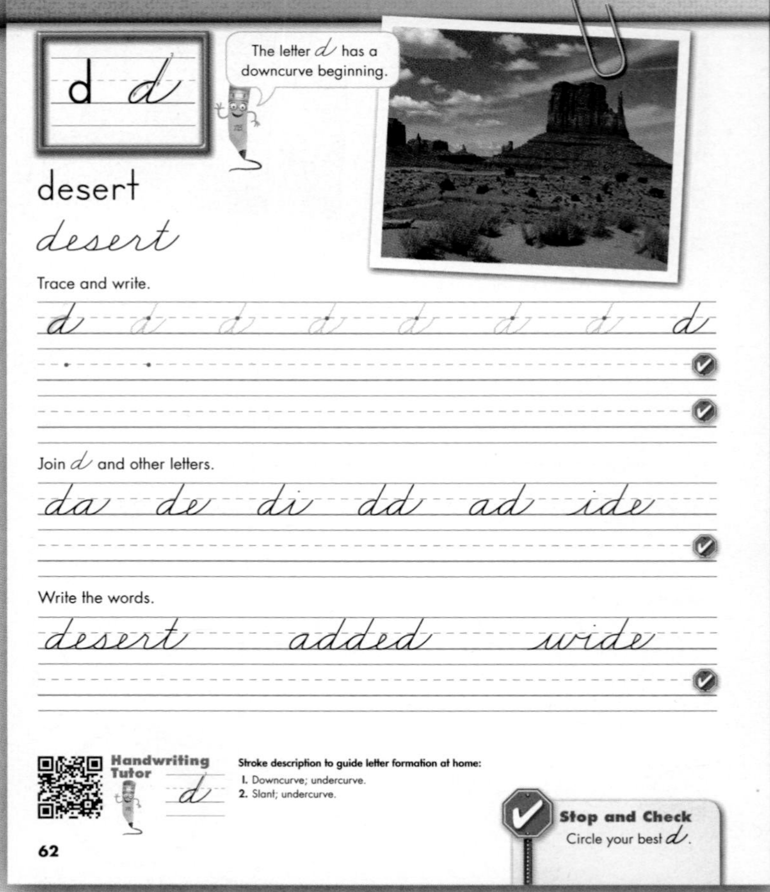

d d
The letter d has a downcurve beginning.
desert
desert
Trace and write.
Join d and other letters.
da de di dd ad ide
Write the words.
desert added wide
Handwriting Tutor
Stroke description to guide letter formation at home:
1. Downcurve; undercurve.
2. Slant; undercurve.
62
Stop and Check
Circle your best d.

1 Model

Talk about cursive **d**. Ask:

- Can you see **a** in **d**? *(yes)*

Write cursive **d** on guidelines on the board as you say the stroke description. Use skywriting to model writing the letter **d** as you repeat the stroke description. Have students say the stroke description as they skywrite **d** with you.

Ask students to use their index finger to trace **d** several times on student page 62.

2 Practice

Remind students to position their book and grip their pencil correctly for writing.

Ask students to begin at the green dot and carefully trace the shaded letters on student page 62 with pencil. Then have them write the letters, joinings, and words on the page.

Remind students that when they come to this symbol ✓, they should stop writing and circle their best letter, joining, or word.

3 Evaluate

Tell students it is important to make their writing easy for others to read. Remind them to complete all **Stop and Check** activities.

✓ **Use** these questions to help students evaluate their cursive **d**:

- Does your downcurve meet the undercurve at the midline?
- Does your **d** end at the midline?

Extra Practice

Practice Masters 36, 82

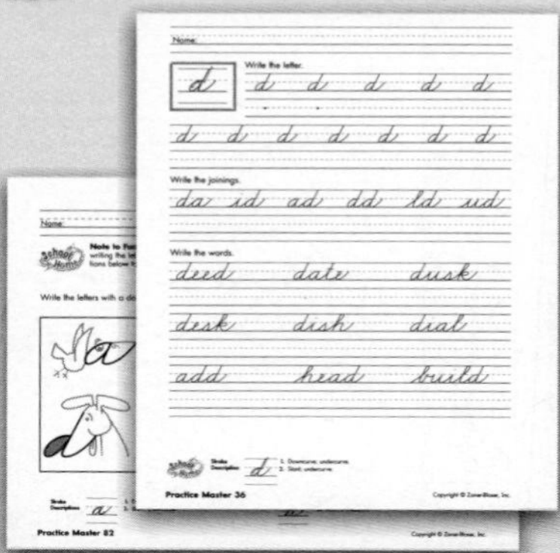

Support for English Language Learners

Additional Practice With *d* Students will benefit from hearing the letter **d** pronounced so they will recognize the same sound when it is used in words. Provide students with pictures of objects, or point to things in the classroom that begin with the letter **d**, such as **dog, daisy, desk,** and **door**. Say the words, and emphasize the **d** sound.

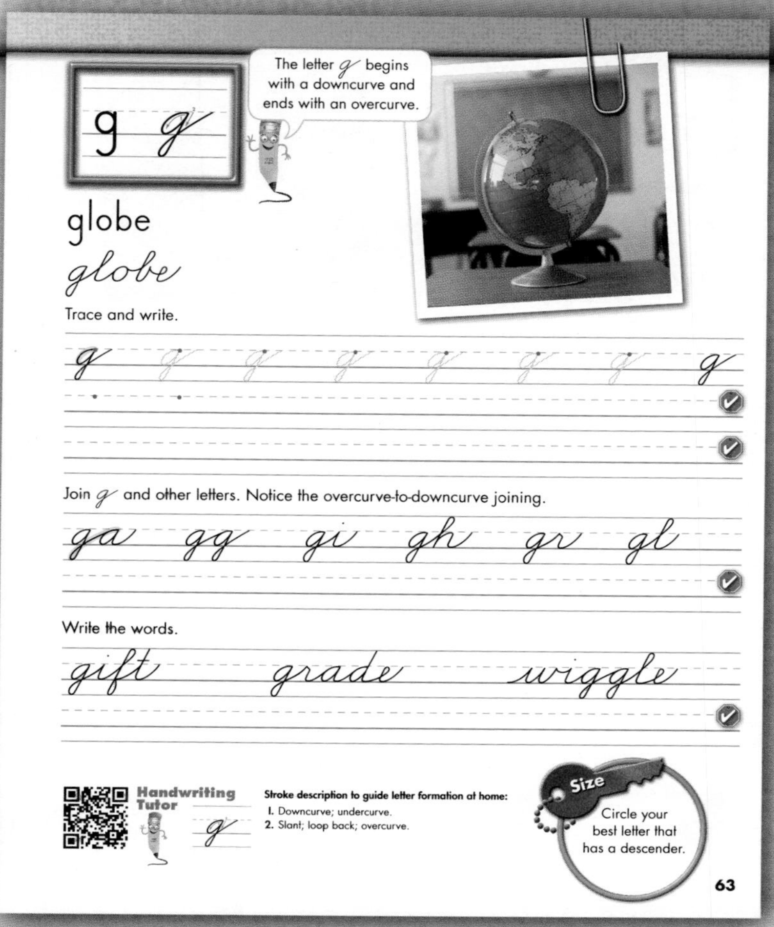

g *g*

The letter *g* begins with a downcurve and ends with an overcurve.

globe

globe

Trace and write.

g g g g g g g g

Join *g* and other letters. Notice the overcurve-to-downcurve joining.

ga gg gi gh gr gl

Write the words.

gift grade wiggle

Handwriting Tutor

Stroke description to guide letter formation at home:
1. Downcurve; undercurve.
2. Slant; loop back; overcurve.

Size

Circle your best letter that has a descender.

63

Letter Model and Stroke Description

1. Downcurve; undercurve.
2. Slant; loop back; overcurve.

Objective: To practice writing lowercase cursive **g**.

1 Model

Talk about cursive **g**. Ask:

- What stroke follows the slant? *(loop back)*
- Where does the loop in **g** close? *(near the baseline)*

Write cursive **g** on guidelines on the board as you say the stroke description. Model skywriting **g** as you repeat the stroke description. Have students say the stroke description as they use their index finger to write **g** on their desktop.

2 Practice

Remind students to position their book and grip their pencil correctly for writing.

Ask students to begin at the green dot and carefully trace the shaded letters on student page 63 with pencil. Then have them write the letters, joinings, and words on the page.

Remind students that when they come to this symbol ✓, they should stop writing and circle their best letter, joining, or word.

3 Evaluate

Tell students it is important to make their writing easy for others to read. Remind them to complete all **Stop and Check** activities.

Proper size makes each letter easy to read. Ask:

- Does each **g** begin and end at the midline?
- Does each **g** look like the model?
- Does the descender of each **g** fill the descender space?

Tips From an Occupational Therapist

Clay and Pennies Activities that require the manipulation of objects help to develop the arches of the hands, which are necessary for fine motor control and handwriting. Have students use clay or putty to make small balls. Instruct them to roll the material between their thumb and each individual finger. Or, have students use only one hand to pick up three pennies and secure them in their palm with their ring and little fingers. Then direct them to use the tips of their free fingers and thumb on the same hand to move and grasp one penny at a time from their palm and deposit it into the slot of a piggy bank. This activity requires students to transfer and manipulate objects from their palm to their fingers.

Extra Practice

Practice Masters 37, 83

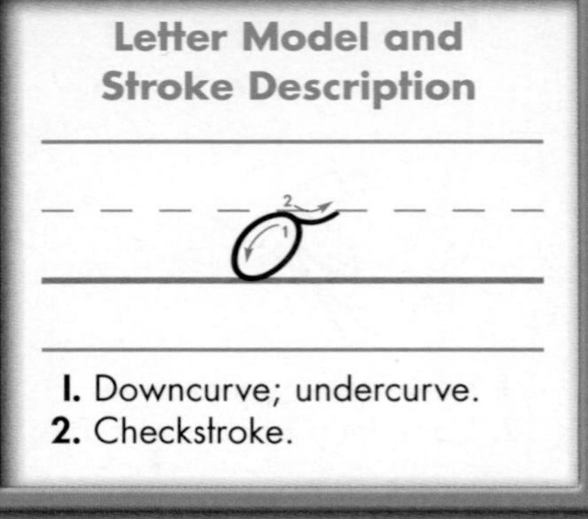

Objective: To practice writing lowercase cursive **o**.

The letter o begins with a downcurve and ends with a checkstroke.
o o
oranges
oranges
Trace and write.
Join o and other letters. Notice the checkstroke-to-downstroke joining.
od oa oo ot or oll
Write the words.
other orders boots
Handwriting Tutor
Stroke description to guide letter formation at home:
1. Downcurve; undercurve.
2. Checkstroke.
Stop and Check
Circle your best o.
64

1 Model

Talk about cursive **o**. Ask:

- Where does **o** begin? *(just below the midline)*

Write cursive **o** on guidelines on the board as you say the stroke description. Model skywriting **o** as you repeat the stroke description. Have students say the stroke description as they skywrite **o** with you.

Ask students to use their index finger to trace **o** several times on their desktop.

2 Practice

Remind students to position their book and grip their pencil correctly for writing.

Ask students to begin at the green dot and carefully trace the shaded letters on student page 64 with pencil. Then have them write the letters, joinings, and words on the page.

Remind students that when they come to this symbol , they should stop writing and circle their best letter, joining, or word.

3 Evaluate

Tell students it is important to make their writing easy for others to read. Remind them to complete all **Stop and Check** activities.

Use these questions to help students evaluate their cursive **o**:

- Is your **o** closed?
- Does your checkstroke end at the midline?

Extra Practice

Practice Masters 38, 83

Support for English Language Learners

Sound Discrimination Help students practice saying the long and short vowel sound of the letter **o**. Help students discriminate between the sound **o** makes in **hope** and the sound **o** makes in **hop**. Point out that the **e** in *hope* changes the sound of the **o**.

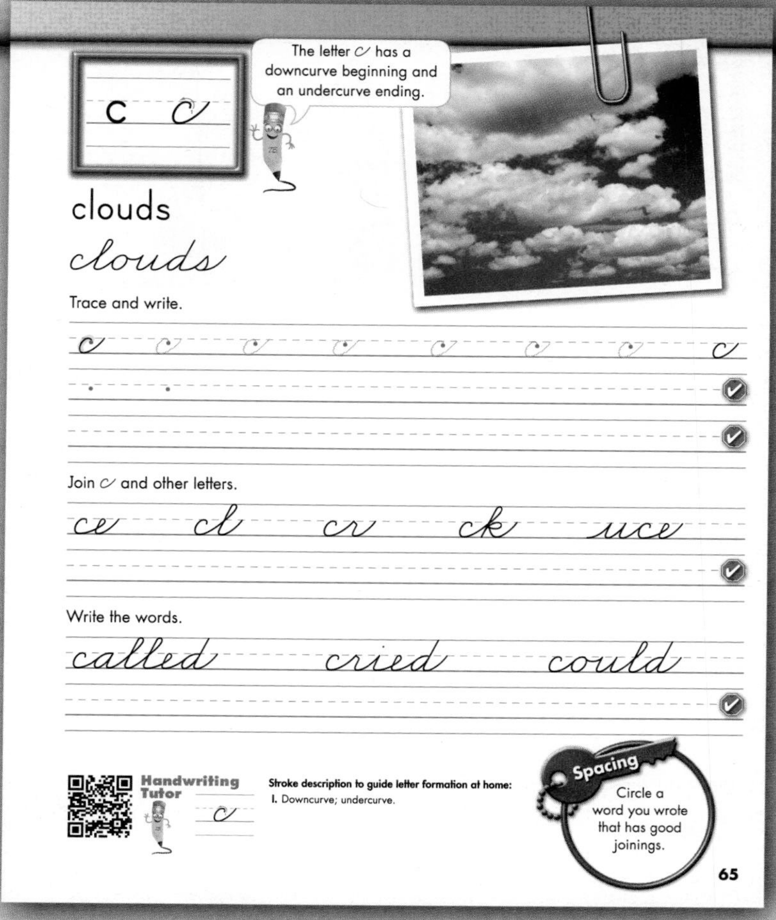

c *c*

The letter *c* has a downcurve beginning and an undercurve ending.

clouds

clouds

Trace and write.

Join *c* and other letters.

ce cl cr ck uce

Write the words.

called cried could

Handwriting Tutor

Stroke description to guide letter formation at home:
1. Downcurve; undercurve.

Spacing

Circle a word you wrote that has good joinings.

65

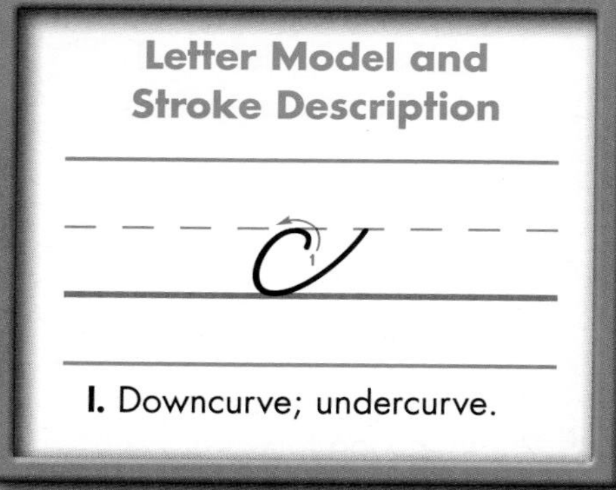

Objective: To practice writing lowercase cursive **c**.

1 Model

Talk about cursive **c**. Ask:

- Where does **c** begin? *(below the midline)*
- How does **c** end? *(with an undercurve)*

Write cursive **c** on guidelines on the board as you say the stroke description. Use skywriting to model writing **c** in the air as you repeat the stroke description. Have students say the stroke description as they use their index finger to write **c** on their desktop.

2 Practice

Remind students to position their book and grip their pencil correctly for writing.

Ask students to begin at the green dot and carefully trace the shaded letters on student page 65 with pencil. Then have them write the letters, joinings, and words on the page.

Remind students that when they come to this symbol ✓, they should stop writing and circle their best letter, joining, or word.

3 Evaluate

Tell students it is important to make their writing easy for others to read. Remind them to complete all **Stop and Check** activities.

Proper spacing makes each letter easy to read. Ask:

- Is the spacing between your joinings consistent?
- Do your letters look like the models?

Writing in the Content Areas

Science

Explanatory Paragraph Have students look at the photo on page 65. Ask, *Do all clouds look the same? How are they the same? How are they different?* Provide students with information about clouds using print or online resources. Then ask them to write a brief **informative/explanatory** paragraph that tells what they know about clouds, including the composition of a cloud and the types of clouds. Remind students to use their best cursive handwriting.

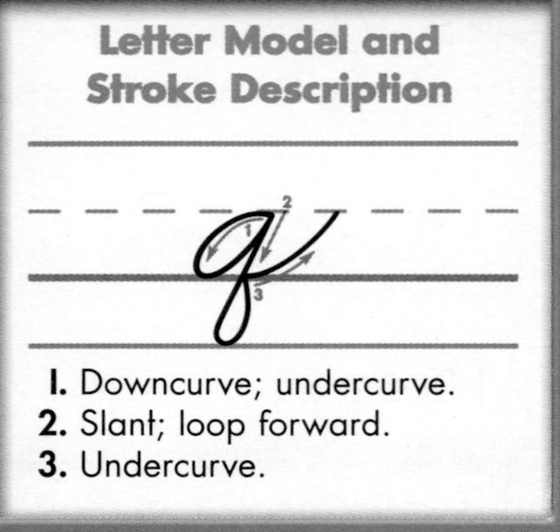

Letter Model and Stroke Description
I. Downcurve; undercurve.
2. Slant; loop forward.
3. Undercurve.

Objective: To practice writing lowercase cursive **q**.

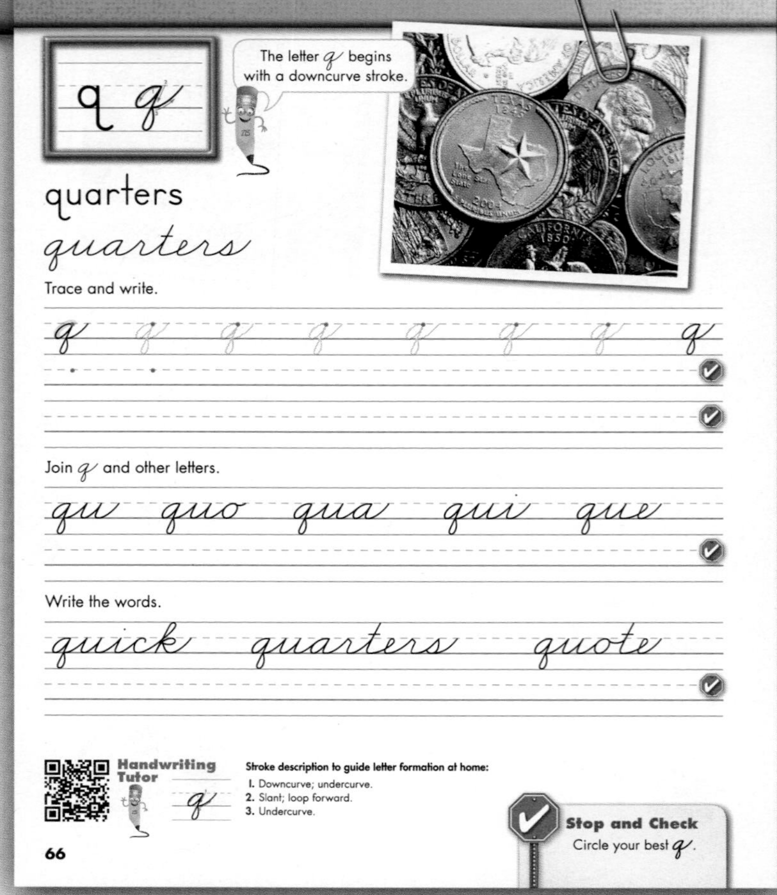

The letter q begins with a downcurve stroke.
quarters
Trace and write.
Join q and other letters.
Write the words.
Handwriting Tutor
Stroke description to guide letter formation at home:
I. Downcurve; undercurve.
2. Slant; loop forward.
3. Undercurve.
66
Stop and Check
Circle your best q.

1 Model

Talk about cursive **q**. Ask:

- Where does the loop in **q** close? *(at the baseline)*

Write cursive **q** on guidelines on the board as you say the stroke description. Model skywriting **q** as you repeat the stroke description. Have students say the stroke description as they use their index finger to write **q** on their desktop.

Ask students to use their index finger to trace **q** several times on their desktop.

2 Practice

Remind students to position their book and grip their pencil correctly for writing.

Ask students to begin at the green starting dot and carefully trace the shaded letters on student page 66 with pencil. Then have them write the letters, joinings, and words on the page.

Remind students that when they come to this symbol ✓, they should stop writing and circle their best letter, joining, or word.

3 Evaluate

Tell students it is important to make their writing easy for others to read. Remind them to complete all **Stop and Check** activities.

✓ **Use** these questions to help students evaluate their cursive **q**:

- Does your loop close at the baseline?
- Does your loop fill the descender space?

School Home Extra Practice

Practice Masters 40, 84

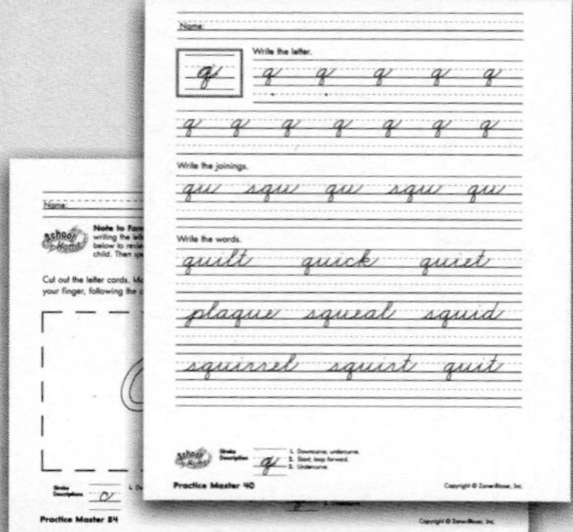

Support for English Language Learners

Additional Practice With q Write several words that begin with **q** on the board. Examples may be: **quiet, quick, quarter,** and **quack**. Discuss the meaning of each word, and point out that the second letter in all the words is **u**. Tell students that the letter **q** at the beginning of an English word is almost always followed by a **u**.

Joinings

Write the joinings and words.

Undercurve-to-Downcurve Joining
The undercurve swings wide to form the top of the downcurve of the next letter.

ea ra sa ed do call

Overcurve-to-Downcurve Joining
The overcurve crosses at the baseline and then continues up and wide to form the top of the downcurve letter.

ga ja gg go joke

Checkstroke-to-Downcurve Joining
The checkstroke ending swings wide to form the top of the downcurve letter.

oa wa oo boo bog

Stop and Check
Circle your three best joinings.

67

Objective: To write joinings and words legibly.

1 Model

Talk about joinings. Have students look at the photograph on student page 67. Talk about how these children resemble the joinings that link cursive letters.

Write the different letter combinations and words on guidelines on the board as you emphasize the joinings. Use skywriting as you model each. Have students model skywriting with you.

Ask students to use their index finger to trace the letters and joinings several times on student page 67.

2 Practice

Remind students to position their book and grip their pencil correctly for writing.

Ask students to carefully trace the letters with pencil. Then have them write the joinings and words on the page.

Remind students that when they come to this symbol ✓, they should stop writing and circle their best letter, joining, or word.

3 Evaluate

Tell students it is important to make their writing easy for others to read. Remind them to complete all **Stop and Check** activities.

✓ **Use** these questions to help students evaluate their joinings:

- Do your joinings swing wide to form the next letter?
- Are your joinings formed to allow space for a small oval?

Tips From an Occupational Therapist

Ball Buddies To develop arches of the hand and increase finger strength, have students create a "ball buddy." Cut a two-inch slit in a tennis ball to serve as a mouth. Have students decorate their ball buddies with eyes, nose, and hair. Then tell students to hold their ball buddies in one hand and squeeze to open the mouth. To incorporate both hands and a pinch grip, have students "feed" their ball buddies by picking up small beans with their free fingers, tweezers, or clothespins.

Review

Objective: To review the lowercase cursive letters beginning with a downcurve stroke: **a, d, g, o, c, q**.

Review

a d g o c q

Write the names of breakfast foods.

quiche cereal eggs

toast bagel bread

Write the phrases.

a quart of grape juice

a good breakfast

68

1 Review

Review the stroke descriptions and model any letters students might be having difficulty writing. You might want to refer to **resources.zaner-bloser.com/hw** for more detailed stroke descriptions.

Ask a volunteer to give a verbal description of one of the letters. Challenge the other students to identify the letter being described and then write it on guidelines on the board.

See the **Corrective Strategies** in the Appendix for techniques in correcting common problems in your students' handwriting.

2 Practice

Remind students to position their book and grip their pencil correctly for writing.

Ask students to carefully write the words and phrases on student page 68.

3 Evaluate

Tell students it is important to make their writing easy for others to read.

Use these questions to help students evaluate their writing:

- Do your letters look like the models?
- Is your writing easy to read?

Digital Tools

Digital Resources for Handwriting Provides interactive tools, including videos, animated letter models, practice and evaluation tools, and games.

Support for English Language Learners

Vowel and Consonant Recognition Review with students the difference between vowels and consonants. Write the letters **a, d, g, o, c,** and **q** on the board. Point to each letter, and have students say "vowel" or "consonant" for each one. Ask students to name other vowels and consonants.

Application

Nouns

Nouns are naming words. The nouns on this page name vegetables.
Write the words.

squash carrots peppers

lettuce cabbages leeks

potatoes peas broccoli

Complete the sentences. Leave space for margins.

I like to eat

I don't like to eat

Stop and Check
Circle your best word.

69

Application

Nouns

Objective: To practice writing nouns legibly.

1 Review

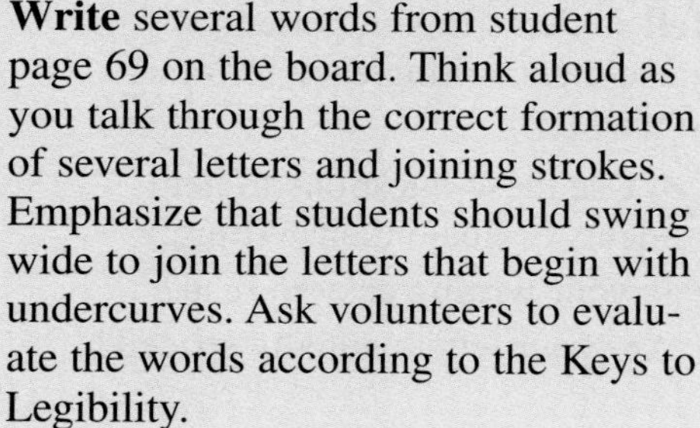

Write several words from student page 69 on the board. Think aloud as you talk through the correct formation of several letters and joining strokes. Emphasize that students should swing wide to join the letters that begin with undercurves. Ask volunteers to evaluate the words according to the Keys to Legibility.

2 Practice

Remind students to position their book and grip their pencil correctly for writing.

Ask students to carefully write the words on student page 69 and pay close attention to the margins.

3 Evaluate

Tell students it is important to make their writing easy for others to read.

Use these questions to help students evaluate their writing:

- Do your letters have good shape?
- Do your short letters touch both the midline and the baseline?
- Do your tall letters touch both the headline and the baseline?
- Did you use good spacing between letters and words?
- Does your writing have good slant?

Writing in the Content Areas

Science

Food Journals Ask students to keep track of the foods they eat during one day. Discuss with the class which types of foods in general are healthy or unhealthy. Have students write an **informative/explanatory** journal entry about which foods are healthiest and which foods they might replace in their diet with healthier choices. Remind students to use their best cursive handwriting.

Cursive Writing

In the Real World

Objective: To practice writing a list using legible cursive handwriting.

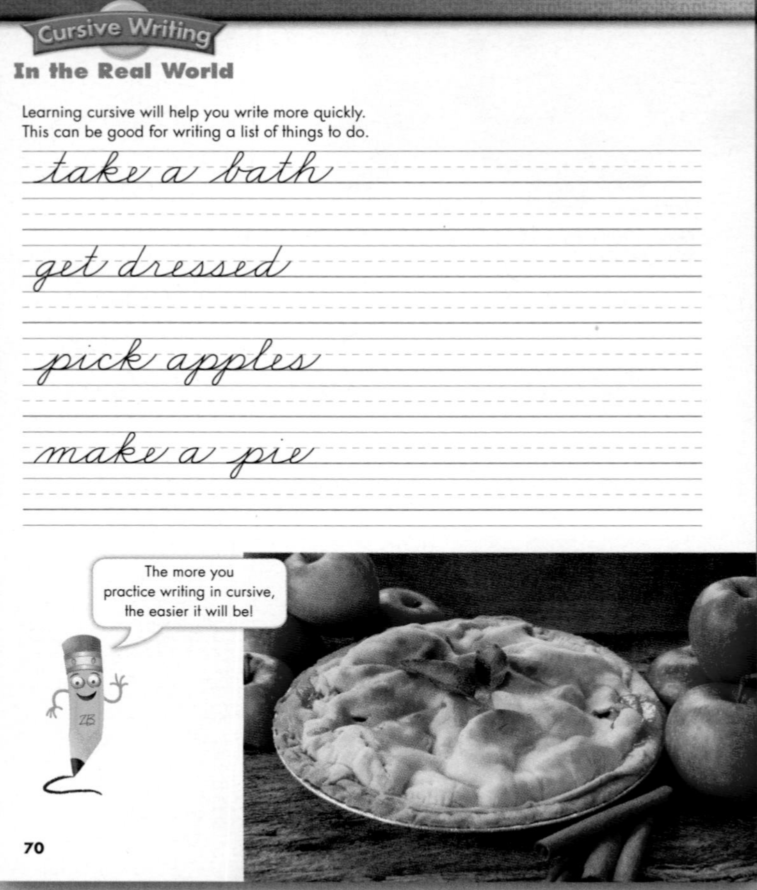

Cursive Writing
In the Real World
Learning cursive will help you write more quickly.
This can be good for writing a list of things to do.
take a bath
get dressed
pick apples
make a pie
The more you practice writing in cursive, the easier it will be!
ZB
70

1 Review

Present the activity. Tell students that writing a list is a good way to stay organized. Often they might hurry to make a list, to copy a homework assignment, or to jot something down before it's forgotten. Cursive writing will allow students to write more quickly what they need to get down on paper.

Write several words from student page 70 on the board. Think aloud as you talk through the correct formation of several letters and joining strokes.

Discuss the meaning of each word as you write it.

2 Practice

Remind students to position their book and grip their pencil correctly for writing.

Ask students to carefully write the words on the page.

3 Evaluate

Tell students it is important to make their writing easy for others to read.

Use these questions to help students evaluate their writing:

- Is your writing easy to read?
- Are your letters equally spaced?

Support for English Language Learners

Vocabulary Building To help students understand the meaning of each word on the page, call on volunteers to act out situations that illustrate each word. To make the exercise more challenging, have other students guess the word each skit demonstrates.

Overcurve Letters

On the next pages, you will write lowercase letters that begin with an overcurve stroke. Overcurves begin at the baseline and bounce up to the midline.

Each of these letters begins with an overcurve stroke.

n m y x v z

Trace and write overcurve strokes.

Keys to Legibility

Make your overcurve letters easy to read. Pay attention to the four Keys.

Shape Overcurve lowercase letters begin at the baseline and bounce up to the midline.

Size Use the midline, baseline, and descender space as your guides. That way, your letters will be the right size.

Spacing Swing wide on the last stroke of each letter to allow for good spacing as you join letters.

Slant Remember that cursive letters have a consistent forward slant.

even slant

71

Overcurve Letters

Objective: To practice writing lowercase overcurve strokes.

1 Model

Point out the lowercase letters on student page 71, and explain that each one begins with an overcurve stroke. Talk about the shape of the overcurve stroke and how its motion relates to an upward clockwise motion. Encourage students to use their index finger to trace several of the overcurve strokes in these letters.

2 Practice

Remind students to position their book and grip their pencil correctly for writing.

Ask students to trace and write the overcurve strokes on the guidelines.

Remind students that when they come to this symbol ✓, they should stop writing and circle their best strokes.

3 Evaluate

Draw attention to the letters and Keys to Legibility. Discuss how the Key information relates to the overcurve letters shown.

Tell students it is important to make their writing easy for others to read. Remind them to complete the **Stop and Check** activity.

✓ **Use** these questions to help students evaluate their overcurves:

- Do your overcurve strokes have a smooth shape?
- Do your strokes touch the midline?

Writing in the Content Areas

Language Arts

Writing About Routines Have students look at the list on page 70. Have them think about what they typically do on a Saturday or Sunday morning. Then have them write a **narrative** piece about their routines. Tell them that they can use words such as **always, usually, occasionally, sometimes, frequently,** and **often** to describe the frequency of their activities. Remind students to use their best cursive handwriting.

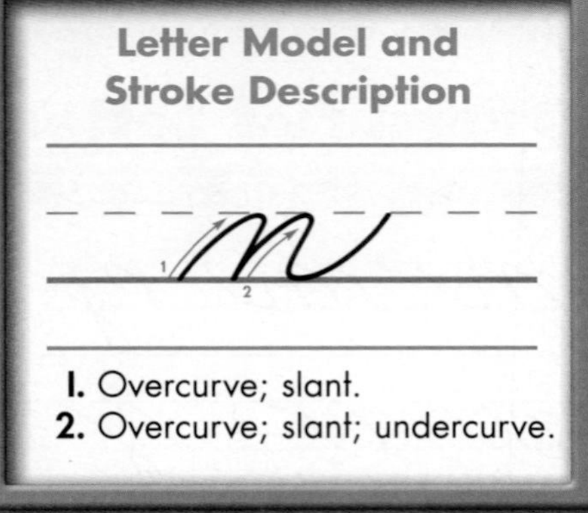

Objective: To practice writing lowercase cursive **n**.

The letter *n* begins with an overcurve stroke.

neighborhood

neighborhood

Trace and write.

Join *n* and other letters.

nn sn an na nd ne

Write the words.

newspaper band often

Handwriting Tutor

Stroke description to guide letter formation at home:
1. Overcurve; slant.
2. Overcurve; slant; undercurve.

Stop and Check
Circle your best *n*.

72

1 Model

Talk about cursive **n**. Ask:

- What stroke follows the first slant in **n**? *(overcurve)*
- How many overcurves are in **n**? *(two)*

Write cursive **n** on guidelines on the board as you say the stroke description. Use skywriting (see page Z21) to model writing **n** in the air. Have students stand and say it with you as they write **n** in the air.

2 Practice

Remind students to position their book and grip their pencil correctly for writing.

Ask students to begin at the green dot and use their index finger to trace cursive **n** several times on student page 72. Then have them carefully trace and write with pencil the letters, joinings, and words on the page.

Remind students that when they come to this symbol ✓, they should stop writing and circle their best letter, joining, or word.

3 Evaluate

Tell students it is important to make their writing easy for others to read. Remind them to complete all **Stop and Check** activities.

✓ **Use** these questions to help students evaluate their cursive **n**:

- Do your overcurves touch the midline?
- Are the tops of your **n** round?

Extra Practice

Practice Masters 41, 85

Support for
English Language Learners

Comparing Cursive *n* and *m* Students may need additional help in distinguishing **n** from **m** in cursive writing. Write about ten words on the board, some beginning with **n**, some with **m**. Make sure the list has a few words that include both **n** and **m**. The list might include: **mount, number, milk, nine, nurse, mind, music, nut, ninety, mine, mouse**. First have students identify the words that begin with **n** and those that begin with **m**. Then ask volunteers to tell which words have both letters in them (*mount, number, mind, mine*). Finally have volunteers come to the board and circle the **n**'s and **m**'s in these words.

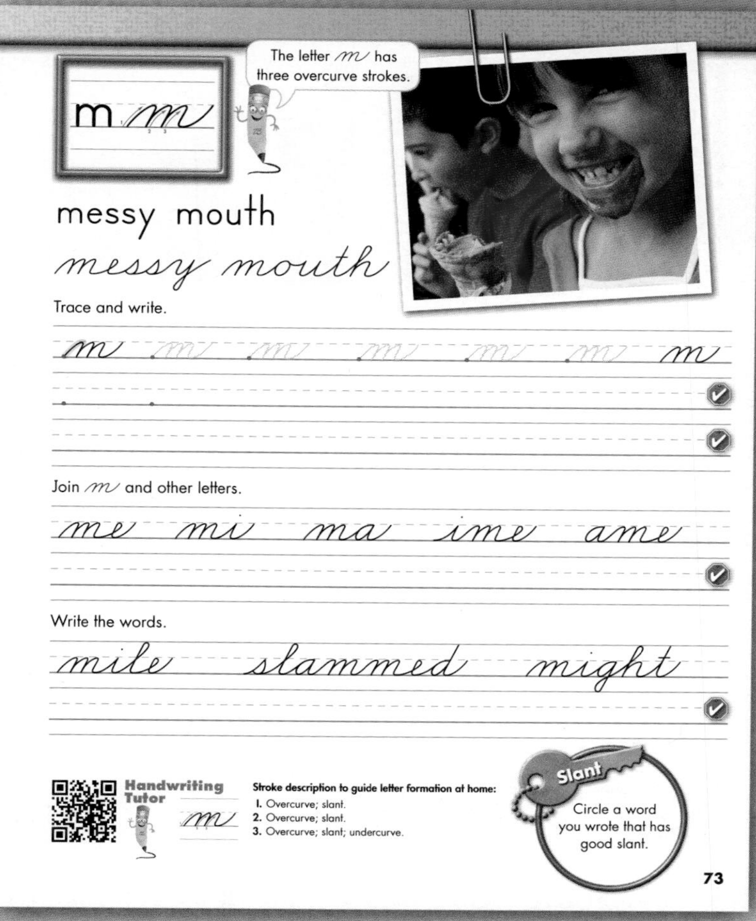

The letter *m* has three overcurve strokes.

m *m*

messy mouth

messy mouth

Trace and write.

m m m m m m m

Join *m* and other letters.

me mi ma ime ame

Write the words.

mile slammed might

Handwriting Tutor

Stroke description to guide letter formation at home:
1. Overcurve; slant.
2. Overcurve; slant.
3. Overcurve; slant; undercurve.

Slant

Circle a word you wrote that has good slant.

73

Letter Model and Stroke Description

1. Overcurve; slant.
2. Overcurve; slant.
3. Overcurve; slant; undercurve.

Objective: To practice writing lowercase cursive **m**.

1 Model

Talk about cursive **m**. Ask:

- How many slant strokes are in **m**? *(three)*
- How many times does **m** touch the midline? *(four)*

Write cursive **m** on guidelines on the board as you say the stroke description. Use skywriting to model writing **m** in the air. Have students stand and say it with you as they write **m** in the air.

It might be helpful for students, especially auditory learners, to hear a more detailed stroke description (Go to **resources.zaner-bloser.com/hw**.).

2 Practice

Remind students to position their book and grip their pencil correctly for writing.

Ask students to begin at the green dot and use their index finger to trace **m** several times on student page 73. Then have them carefully trace and write with pencil the letters, joinings, and words on the page.

Remind students that when they come to this symbol ✓, they should stop writing and circle their best letter, joining, or word.

3 Evaluate

Tell students it is important to make their writing easy for others to read. Remind them to complete all **Stop and Check** activities.

Proper slant makes each letter easy to read. Ask:

- Did you write with consistent forward slant?
- Are your slant strokes parallel?

Practice Masters 42, 85

Tips From an Occupational Therapist

Letters and Invitations For holidays or other events during the year, have students use their best cursive writing to create letters or invitations. For example, students might write letters to friends about something that's going on in school. Or, you might want to have students invite their families to an event at school. After the letters or invitations have been written and proofread, help students mail them.

Objective: To practice writing lowercase cursive **y**.

The letter *y* begins and ends with an overcurve stroke.

young puppy

young puppy

Trace and write.

Join *y* and other letters.

ym yo ye ty oy

Write the words.

yellow your city buy

Handwriting Tutor

Stroke description to guide letter formation at home:
1. Overcurve; slant; undercurve.
2. Slant; loop back; overcurve.

74

Stop and Check
Circle your best *y*.

1 Model

Talk about cursive **y**. Ask:

- How does **y** end? *(with an overcurve)*
- How many overcurves are in **y**? *(two)*

Write cursive **y** on guidelines on the board as you say the stroke description. Use skywriting to model writing **y** in the air. Have students stand and say the stroke description with you as they write **y** in the air.

2 Practice

Remind students to position their book and grip their pencil correctly for writing.

Ask students to begin at the green dot and use their index finger to trace **y** several times on student page 74. Then have them carefully trace and write with pencil the letters, joinings, and words on the page.

Remind students that when they come to this symbol ✓, they should stop writing and circle their best letter, joining, or word.

3 Evaluate

Tell students it is important to make their writing easy for others to read. Remind them to complete all **Stop and Check** activities.

✓ **Use** these questions to help students evaluate their cursive **y**:

- Does the loop of your **y** close at the baseline?
- If you turn your paper upside down, does your **y** look like an **h**?

Support for English Language Learners

Pronunciation Practice Some students may need help understanding the different pronunciations of **y**. Write the letter **y** and the words **yellow, your, city,** and **buy** on the board in cursive. Say the sound of **y** when it is the initial consonant. Point to the words **yellow** and **your** as you pronounce them, stressing the initial /y/ sound. Then tell students that when **y** appears at the end of a word, it has a vowel sound of long **i** or long **e**. Say the words **city** and **buy**. Ask which word has the /ī/ sound and which word has the /ē/ sound. Say all four words, and have students repeat each word after you.

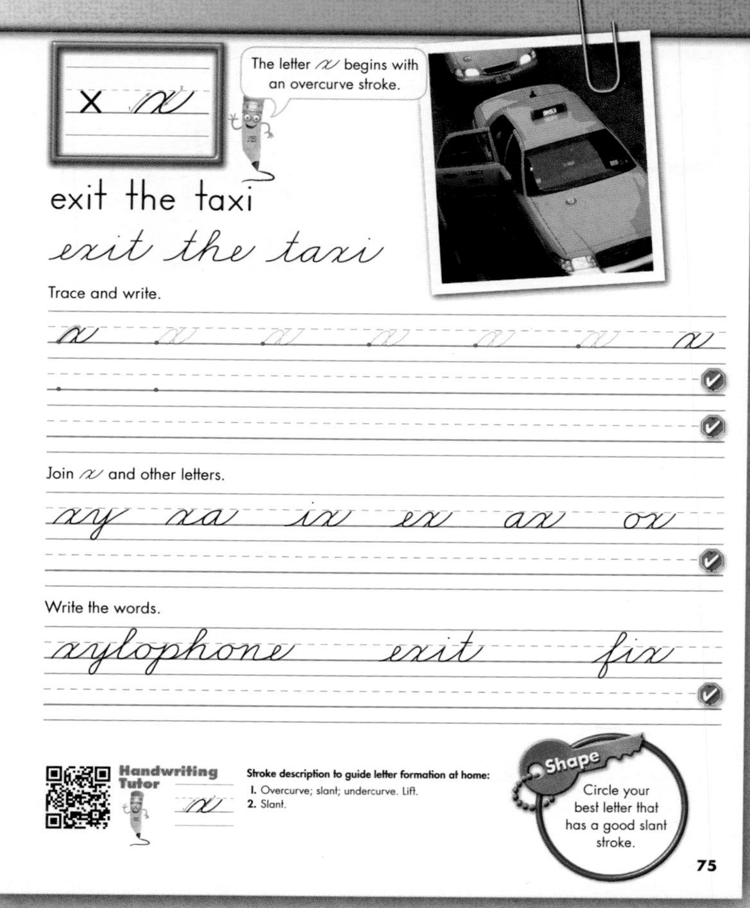

x
The letter x begins with an overcurve stroke.
exit the taxi
exit the taxi
Trace and write.
Join x and other letters.
xy xa ix ex ax ox
Write the words.
xylophone exit fix
Handwriting Tutor
Stroke description to guide letter formation at home:
1. Overcurve; slant; undercurve. Lift.
2. Slant.
Shape
Circle your best letter that has a good slant stroke.
75

Letter Model and Stroke Description

1. Overcurve; slant; undercurve. Lift.
2. Slant.

Objective: To practice writing lowercase cursive **x**.

1 Model

Talk about cursive **x**. Ask:

- Where does the overcurve of the **x** end? *(at the midline)*
- Where does the last slant stroke of the **x** end? *(at the baseline)*

Write cursive **x** on guidelines on the board as you say the stroke description. Use skywriting to model writing **x** in the air. Have students stand and say the stroke description with you as they write cursive **x** in the air.

2 Practice

Remind students to position their book and grip their pencil correctly for writing.

Ask students to begin at the green dot and use their index finger to trace **x** several times on student page 75. Then have them carefully trace and write with pencil the letters, joinings, and words on the page.

Remind students that when they come to this symbol ✓, they should stop writing and circle their best letter, joining, or word.

3 Evaluate

Tell students it is important to make their writing easy for others to read. Remind them to complete all **Stop and Check** activities.

Proper shape makes each letter easy to read. Ask:

- Does your **x** have a good overcurve?
- Is the first slant stroke on your **x** pulled toward the baseline?
- Is your **x** crossed near the middle of the first slant stroke?

Writing in the Content Areas

Social Studies

Explanatory Paragraph Point out the word **city** on page 74 and the photo of the taxi on page 75. Ask students where they might see a taxi (*in the city*). Brainstorm with students other things they might see in a big city (e.g., skyscrapers, parks, subways), and write their responses on the board. Have students write an **informative/explanatory** paragraph about what someone would see in a city. Encourage them to use sensory language in their descriptions. Remind students to use their best cursive handwriting.

School Home **Extra Practice**

Practice Masters 44, 86

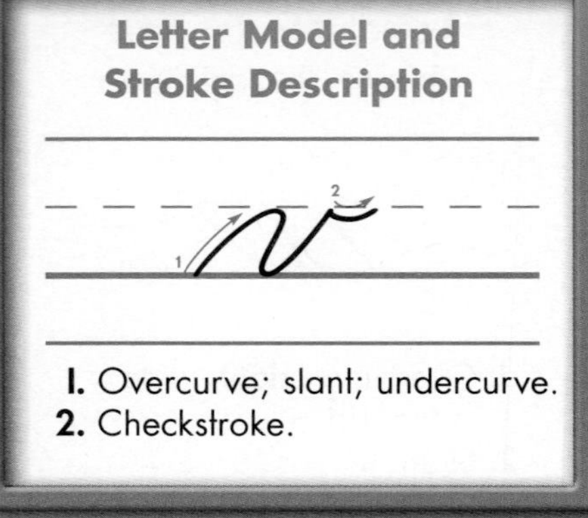

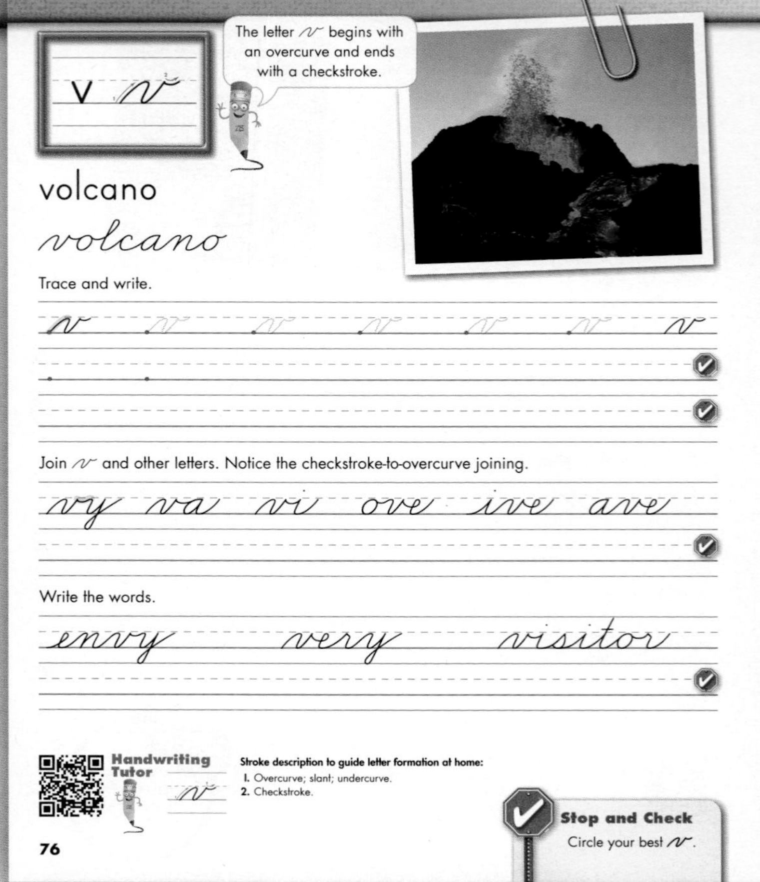

The letter v begins with an overcurve and ends with a checkstroke.

v v

volcano

volcano

Trace and write.

v v v v v v v

Join v and other letters. Notice the checkstroke-to-overcurve joining.

vy va vi ove ive ave

Write the words.

envy very visitor

Handwriting Tutor

Stroke description to guide letter formation at home:
1. Overcurve; slant; undercurve.
2. Checkstroke.

Stop and Check
Circle your best v.

76

Objective: To practice writing lowercase cursive **v**.

1 Model

Talk about cursive **v**. Ask:

- What strokes are in **v**? *(overcurve, slant, undercurve, checkstroke)*
- How does **v** end? *(with a checkstroke)*

Write cursive **v** on guidelines on the board as you say the stroke description. Use skywriting to model writing **v** in the air. Have students stand and say the stroke description with you as they write **v** in the air.

2 Practice

Remind students to position their book and grip their pencil correctly for writing.

Ask students to begin at the green dot and use their index finger to trace **v** several times on student page 76. Then have them carefully trace and write with pencil the letters, joinings, and words on the page.

Remind students that when they come to this symbol , they should stop writing and circle their best letter, joining, or word.

3 Evaluate

Tell students it is important to make their writing easy for others to read. Remind them to complete all **Stop and Check** activities.

Use these questions to help students evaluate their cursive **v**:

- Does your **v** have a good overcurve beginning?
- Does your **v** end with a checkstroke?

Extra Practice

Practice Masters 45, 87

Support for English Language Learners

Additional Practice With v Write several words that begin with or have the letter **v** in them on the board. Examples might include **vase, vine, cave, river**. Say each word as you skywrite **v** in the air. Have students say the words along with you. Encourage students to share **v** words from their native language. Add them to the list on the board.

The letter *z* begins and ends with an overcurve stroke.

z *z*

zoo zebras

zoo zebras

Trace and write.

z z z z z z z

Join *z* and other letters.

zy zi ze za ize oze

Write the words.

zebra zipper zigzag

Handwriting Tutor

Stroke description to guide letter formation at home:

1. Overcurve; slant.
2. Overcurve; curve down; loop; overcurve.

Size

Circle your best letter that has a descender.

77

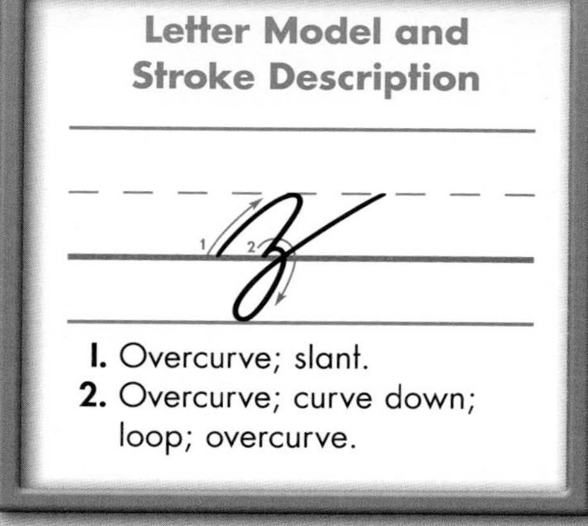

Letter Model and Stroke Description

1. Overcurve; slant.
2. Overcurve; curve down; loop; overcurve.

Objective: To practice writing lowercase cursive **z**.

1 Model

Talk about cursive **z**. Ask:

- What stroke follows the first slant in **z**? *(overcurve)*
- How does **z** end? *(with an overcurve)*

Write cursive **z** on guidelines on the board as you say the stroke description. Use skywriting to model writing **z** in the air. Have students stand and say the stroke description with you as they write **z** in the air.

2 Practice

Remind students to position their book and grip their pencil correctly for writing.

Ask students to begin at the green dot and use their index finger to trace **z** several times on student page 77. Then have them carefully trace and write with pencil the letters, joinings, and words on the page.

Remind students that when they come to this symbol ✓, they should stop writing and circle their best letter, joining, or word.

3 Evaluate

Tell students it is important to make their writing easy for others to read. Remind them to complete all **Stop and Check** activities.

Proper size makes each letter easy to read. Ask:

- Does your loop in **z** fill the descender space?
- Is your **z** the same size as the model?

Writing in the Content Areas

Science

Opinion Paragraph Have students look at the photo and words at the top of page 77. Ask students where zebras live (*zoos, Africa*). Ask students, *What are the pros and cons of keeping animals in a zoo?* Draw a T-chart on the board and record students' responses. Then have students write a paragraph stating their **opinion** about why zoos are good (or not). Make sure they include strong reasons to support their opinions. Then have students pair up with a student who had an opposing view to compare their paragraphs. Volunteers may like to debate their opinions in front of the class. Remind students to use their best cursive handwriting.

School Home

Extra Practice

Practice Masters 46, 87

Review

Objective: To review the lowercase cursive letters beginning with an overcurve stroke: **n, m, y, x, v,** and **z**.

Review

n m y x v z

Write these color words.

maroon lime orange

neon green tangerine

violet lavender silver

yellow ivory azure

pink a color mix

Complete this sentence in cursive.

My favorite color is ______.

78

1 Review

Review the stroke descriptions, and model any letters students might be having difficulty writing. You might want to refer to **resources.zaner-bloser.com/hw** for more detailed stroke descriptions.

Ask a volunteer to give a verbal description of one of the letters. Challenge students to identify the letter being described and then write it on guidelines on the board.

See the **Corrective Strategies** in the Appendix for techniques in correcting common problems in your students' handwriting.

2 Practice

Remind students to position their book and grip their pencil correctly for writing.

Ask students to carefully write the color words on student page 78 and to complete the sentence at the bottom of the page.

3 Evaluate

Tell students it is important to make their writing easy for others to read.

Use these questions to help students evaluate their writing:

- Are your beginning overcurves rounded?
- Do your letters look like the models?
- Is your writing easy to read?

Support for English Language Learners

Letter Review Write the letters **n, m, y, x, v,** and **z** on the board. Point to each letter. Have students say the name of the letter. Then ask volunteers to give an example of a word that begins with each letter. Write their words on the board. Say each word, and have students repeat it chorally after you.

Digital Tools

ZB FontsOnline Plus Go to **www.zaner-bloser.com/zb-fontsonline-plus** to access editable page templates that enable teachers to create worksheets, practice pages, and more.

Adjectives

What a great day for a picnic!
Write these phrases that describe foods you might find at a picnic.

marvelous gigantic salad

amazing icy lemonade

tasty tuna sandwiches

yummy yellow mustard

juicy pink melon

excellent cherry pie

Stop and Check
Circle your best word.

79

Application

Adjectives

Objective: To practice writing describing phrases legibly.

1 Review

Write several words from student page 79 on the board. Think aloud as you talk through the correct formation of the letters and joining strokes in each word. Emphasize that students should swing wide to join the letters that begin with undercurves. Ask volunteers to evaluate the words according to the Keys to Legibility.

2 Practice

Remind students to position their book and grip their pencil correctly for writing.

Read the directions with students, and name the items shown in the photo. Then have students carefully write the describing phrases. Remind them to write carefully with consistent slant and leave good spacing between letters and words.

3 Evaluate

Tell students it is important to make their writing easy for others to read.

Use these questions to help students evaluate their writing:

- Do your letters have good shape?
- Do your short letters touch both the midline and the baseline?
- Do your tall letters touch both the headline and the baseline?
- Do your joining strokes make good spacing between your letters?
- Does your writing have good slant?

Tips From an Occupational Therapist

What's in the Bag? In-hand manipulation is an important skill for handwriting. **This skill enables students to grasp and manipulate objects using their palm and fingertips.** It is needed every time a student picks up a pencil, eraser, ruler, or sharpener. To help students develop this skill, hide small, familiar objects in a bag. Have individual students put their hands into the bag and, using only their sense of touch, guess the objects in the bag. You might want to keep track of the number of objects each student guesses.

Keys to Legibility

Shape
Shape describes the strokes that form each letter and give it a unique appearance.

Size
Size describes the height of letters.

Spacing
Spacing describes the space between letters, words, and sentences.

Slant
Slant refers to the angle of writing on the paper.

Objective: To practice the four Keys to Legibility.

Write this to-do list.
Make your writing easy to read.

organize toys in basement

ride skateboard

read one book or more

write school book report

have best sleepover ever

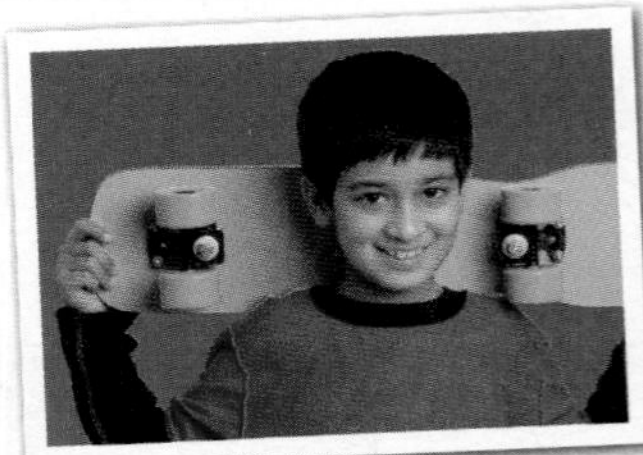

80

Handwriting Coach

Joinings Keep a record of joinings students are having problems with. Provide practice with these joinings by assigning writing exercises, such as making word lists and writing tongue twisters. Call students' attention to less common joinings when they occur in daily writing assignments.

1 Model

Remind students that good handwriting is legible handwriting. The most important thing to remember is that readers must be able to read a message in order to understand its meaning.

Brainstorm with students qualities of legible handwriting. Write responses on the board. These might include neatness, carefully written letters, and letters that are not too crowded.

Point out to students that the basic strokes they learned in the previous pages are the basis for a letter's shape.

2 Practice

Remind students to position their book and grip their pencil correctly for writing. Ask students to carefully write the phrases on the page.

Emphasize that all four Keys to Legibility work together. Their writing will be easy to read when they use proper Shape, Size, Spacing, and Slant.

Read and discuss with students the to-do list on student page 80. Then help them as needed as they complete the writing activity on student page 81.

Support for English Language Learners

Compound Words Compound words such as **skateboard** on page 80 pose difficulties for some students. Write about ten compound words on index cards, and include illustrations with each. Show students the cards. Say each word aloud as you point to its illustration. Once students understand the meanings, tell them that the words are compound words. Explain that compound words are two or more words that work together as one word. Write the compound words on the board. Draw lines to separate the words in each.

Write a to-do list of things you need to do soon.
Be sure to include a few things you want to do, too.

Is your writing easy to read?

Shape Circle your best letter that has an overcurve beginning.

Size Circle your best short letter. Underline your best tall letter.

Spacing Circle two words that have space for \ between them.

Slant Circle a word you wrote that has good slant.

81

3 Evaluate

Tell students it is important to make their writing easy for others to read.

Use these questions to help students evaluate their writing:

- Does each letter have its own clear shape?
- Are your tall letters the same height?
- Are your short letters the same height?
- Are your letters not too close together and not too far apart?
- Does your writing have good slant?

Using Technology

Calendar Applications There are many digital calendars and programs available for students to keep lists of things they need to do, either for school or personal activities. Find a suitable site for your students (enter *student online calendars* in a search engine) and show students how to create their own schedules. They can keep lists of homework tasks, family events, and activities (such as sports, dance, music lessons, and so on).

Review

Lowercase Letters

These letters begin with the undercurve stroke.

b e f
h i j
k l p
r s t
u w

These letters begin with the downcurve stroke.

a c d
g o q

These letters begin with the overcurve stroke.

m n v
x y z

Objective: To review and practice lowercase cursive letters.

Review

Lowercase Letters

a b c d e f g
n o p q r s t

Write these lowercase letters in cursive.

i t u w
e l b h f
k r s j p
a d g o c q
n m y x v z

Write these words in cursive.

cozy
happy
swift
great
young

mixed
lively
brave
juicy
quick

82

1 Review

Tell students they have now studied and written all the lowercase cursive letters. Guide them in a review of these letters by asking the following questions.

- What stroke do the letters **b, e, f, h, i, j, k, l, p, r, s, t, u,** and **w** begin with? *(undercurve)*
- What stroke do the letters **a, c, d, g, o,** and **q** begin with? *(downcurve)*
- What letters begin with the overcurve stroke? *(m, n, v, x, y, z)*
- What do the letters **f, g, j, p, q, y,** and **z** all have? *(descender)*
- What do the letters **b, o, v,** and **w** all end with? *(checkstroke)*

2 Practice

Remind students to position their book and grip their pencil correctly for writing.

Encourage students to use their best cursive handwriting as they write the lowercase letters and words on student page 82. Then have students rearrange the letters to write new words on student page 83. Remind students to consider the Keys to Legibility as they write.

h i j k l m
u v w x y z

Change the order of the letters to write a new word.

deal pat late

lead

ate trap pool

tens dear limes

nap ant gulp

own tone

My writing has good ❑
My writing has good ❑
My writing has good ❑
My writing has good ❑

83

 Evaluate

Students at this level should realize the importance of legibility beyond the daily handwriting lesson. Their skills should be transferring into all areas of the curriculum.

Remind students that the four Keys to Legibility all begin with the letter **s** (Shape, Size, Spacing, and Slant), making them easy to remember.

Use these questions to help students evaluate their writing:

- Which of your letters are satisfactory?
- Which of your letters need improvement?
- Did you use the guidelines to write letters with correct size?
- Did you dot your **i**'s and **j**'s and cross your **t**'s and **x**'s?

Note: Certificates of Progress (*Practice Master* 102) should be awarded to those students who show notable handwriting progress and **Certificates of Excellence** (*Practice Master* 103) to those who progress to the top levels of handwriting ability.

Practice Masters 102–103

Support for English Language Learners

Working in Pairs Changing the order of the letters to write new words will be difficult for some English Language Learners. Have pairs of students work together to complete student page 83. Encourage them to use a separate piece of paper to write each word in different letter combinations until they recognize one as an English word. Allow students to use a dictionary as needed to verify the new words they create.

Objective: To review and practice joinings.

Joinings

Write each joining. Then write the word.

Undercurve-to-Undercurve

ri ride ti time

Undercurve-to-Downcurve

ea eat mo moon

Undercurve-to-Overcurve

ry cry az amaze

84

1 Review

Remind students they have studied and written the lowercase cursive letters, grouped according to beginning strokes. Write the lowercase cursive alphabet on the board, as well as the category headings of the chart at right. Guide students in choosing the letters that complete each category of the chart.

Tell students joinings are formed by combining any letter from the first column with a letter from the second column. If we choose the letter **a** from the first column and write it with the letter **i** from the second column, we have joined an undercurve-ending letter and an undercurve-beginning letter to form the undercurve-to-undercurve joining **ai**.

undercurve ending letters (*a, c, d, e, f, h, i, k, l, m, n, p, q, r, s, t, u, x*)	**undercurve beginning letters** (*i, t, u, w, e, l, b, h, f, k, r, s, j, p*)
overcurve ending letters (*g, j, y, z*)	**downcurve beginning letters** (*a, d, g, o, c, q*)
checkstroke ending letters (*b, o, v, w*)	**overcurve beginning letters** (*n, m, y, x, v, z*)

Support for English Language Learners

Stroke Description Vocabulary Review with students the meanings of **over, under,** and **down**. Hold up a ball or other round object to demonstrate the motion of curving over, curving under, and curving down. Then have students say the terms **overcurve, undercurve,** and **downcurve** with you.

Overcurve-to-Undercurve

ju just ye yell

Overcurve-to-Downcurve

ga gate yo you

Overcurve-to-Overcurve

zy dizzy gy foggy

Checkstroke-to-Undercurve

wr wrote os most

Checkstroke-to-Downcurve

ba back vo voices

Checkstroke-to-Overcurve

om home ov over

85

2 Practice

Choose several of the following joinings, and list them on the board:

undercurve-to-undercurve
undercurve-to-downcurve
undercurve-to-overcurve
overcurve-to-undercurve
overcurve-to-downcurve
overcurve-to-overcurve
checkstroke-to-undercurve
checkstroke-to-downcurve
checkstroke-to-overcurve

Have students choose letter pairs to form examples of each joining. List their suggestions on the board with the proper joining label.

Remind students to position their book and grip their pencil correctly for writing.

Have students write the joinings and words on student pages 84 and 85. Remind them to consider the Keys to Legibility as they write.

3 Evaluate

Tell students it is important to make their writing easy for others to read.

Use these questions to help students evaluate their writing:

- Which of your joinings are satisfactory?
- Which of your joinings need improvement?

Tips From an Occupational Therapist

Finger Exercises One of the biggest differences between early printing and cursive is the need for fine motor endurance. Not only are students learning a new way to write, they are also writing more and for longer periods of time. Therefore, include some warm-up activities before the handwriting lesson. **Have the class do wall pushups and finger exercises to warm up their hands before they begin.**

Numeral Models and Stroke Descriptions

1. Slant.

1. Slant.
2. Curve forward; slant.
3. Curve right.

1. Slant.
2. Curve forward and back.
3. Curve forward and back.

1. Slant.
2. Slide right. Lift.
3. Slant.

1. Slant.
2. Curve forward and back. Lift.
3. Slide right.

1. Curve down and forward; loop.

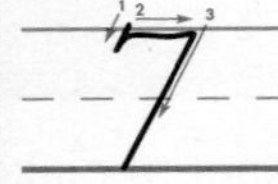
1. Slant.
2. Doublecurve.
3. Slant.

1. Curve back and down; curve back; slant up.

1. Downcurve; undercurve.
2. Slant.

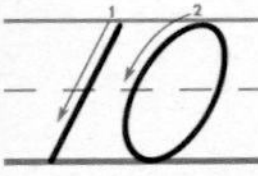
1. Slant. Lift.
2. Downcurve; undercurve.

Objective: To practice writing cursive numerals.

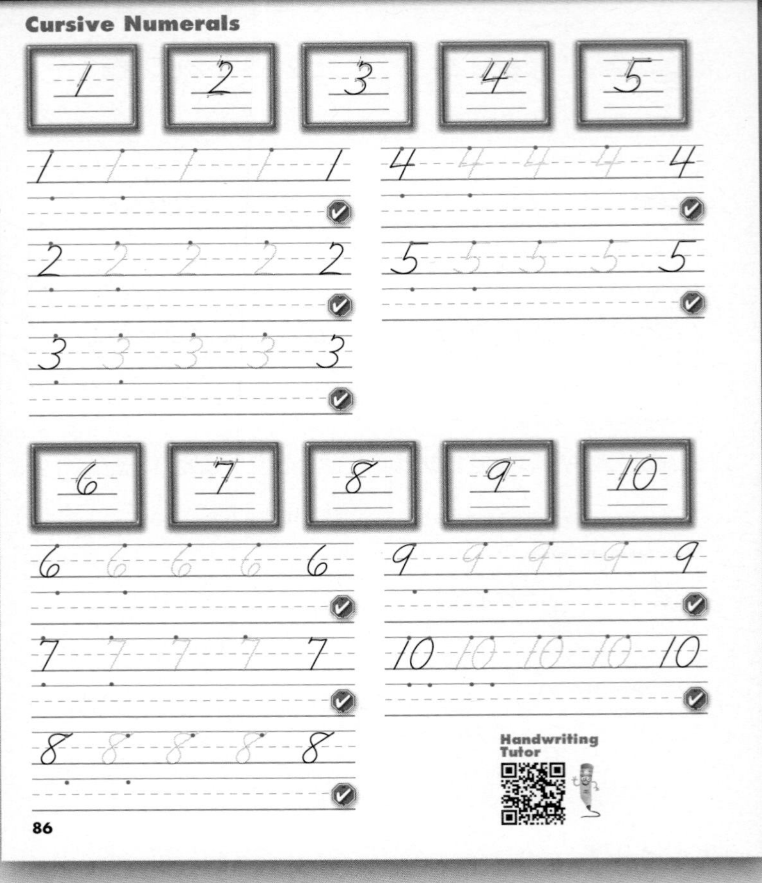
Cursive Numerals

1 2 3 4 5

1 1 1 1 1

4 4 4 4 4

2 2 2 2 2

5 5 5 5 5

3 3 3 3 3

6 7 8 9 10

6 6 6 6 6

9 9 9 9 9

7 7 7 7 7

10 10 10 10 10

8 8 8 8 8

Handwriting Tutor

86

1 Model

Write the numeral **1** on guidelines as you say the stroke description. Use skywriting (see page Z21) to model writing **1** in the air as you repeat the stroke description. Have students say it as they skywrite **1** with you.

2 Practice

Remind students to position their book and grip their pencil correctly for writing.

Ask students to begin at the green dot and carefully trace with pencil the shaded numeral **1**s on student page 86. Then have them write **1**s on the line below.

Remind students that when they come to this symbol ✓, they should stop writing and circle their best numeral.

Repeat steps 1 Model and 2 Practice for numerals 2–10. Finally have students respond to the questions on student page 87 by writing the correct times on the guidelines. Point out and explain the use of the colon in writing times.

Sam's Busy Day

9:00	Reading
10:30	Math
11:30	Social Studies
12:30	Lunch
1:15	Gym
2:00	Science
3:00	School's Out
4:00	Homework
5:00	Violin Lesson
6:00	Dinner
7:00	Free Time
9:00	Sleep

1. When does Sam start his homework? ________
2. When does Sam eat lunch? ________
3. When does Sam have math? ________
4. When does Sam go home? ________
5. When does Sam go to sleep? ________
6. When does Sam have his violin lesson? ________

3 Evaluate

Tell students it is important to make their writing easy for others to read.

Use these questions to help students evaluate their writing:

- Does your **1** begin at the headline?
- Does your **1** have correct slant?
- Does your **2** begin with a short slant stroke?
- Are the top and bottom of your **3** about the same size?
- Is the slide right of your **4** on the midline?
- Does your **5** touch both the headline and the baseline?
- Does the loop of your **6** end at the baseline?
- Does the top of your **7** have a slight doublecurve?
- Does your **8** begin just below the headline?
- Is your **9** written with correct slant?
- Is there correct space between the **1** and the **0** in your **10**?

Support for English Language Learners

Additional Practice With Numerals Review the name of each numeral with students. As you say each name, have students repeat it after you. Have students work with a partner. Ask them to write each numeral, 1–10, on an index card. Have students go through the stack of cards several times and say each number orally. Then tell students to shuffle the cards. Direct students to take turns showing their partner a card and asking, "What number am I?" One partner says the name of the number, and then the pair reverses roles.

Extra Practice

Practice Masters 73–74

Manuscript Maintenance

Objective: To write a recipe in manuscript.

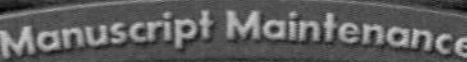

Read this recipe for a fruit salad. The writer made her letters small enough to fit the space on the recipe card.

Handwriting Tutor

Grandma's Fruit Salad
1. chop peaches and apples
2. slice strawberries and bananas
3. add both red and green grapes
4. dip all fruit in pineapple juice
5. mix together in a bowl and serve

Copy the recipe here. Use your best manuscript writing.
Make your writing fit the space.

88

1 Review

Write several words from student page 88 in manuscript on the board. Think aloud as you talk through the correct formation of several letters.

Ask volunteers to evaluate the words according to the Keys to Legibility.

2 Practice

Remind students to position their book and grip their pencil correctly for writing.

Ask students to carefully write the recipe on student page 88 for each step. Point out the period that follows the numeral.

 Evaluate

Tell students it is important to make their writing easy for others to read.

Use these questions to help students evaluate their writing:

- Do your letters have good shape?
- Does each numeral rest on the baseline and touch the headline?
- Is there good spacing between your letters and words?
- Does your writing have proper vertical slant?

Support for English Language Learners

Vocabulary Building Provide pictures of the foods listed on student page 88. Review the name of each food, and have students repeat it with you. Invite students to share the name for each food in their native language.

The steps for this recipe are out of order. Write the steps in the correct order on the recipe card below. Use your best manuscript writing, and make your writing fit the space.

Grandpa's Tortilla Casserole
5. pour salsa and sprinkle cheese over top
1. to begin, fill tortilla with shredded cheese
6. cook until cheese has melted
4. sprinkle cheese between rolled tortillas
3. stuff and roll more tortillas until dish is full
2. roll up tortilla and place in cooking dish

Did you use the space wisely? Is your manuscript writing easy to read?

89

Objective: To write a recipe in manuscript.

1 Review

Write several words from student page 89 in manuscript on the board. Think aloud as you talk through the correct formation of several letters.

Ask volunteers to evaluate the words according to the Keys to Legibility.

2 Practice

Remind students to position their book and grip their pencil correctly for writing.

Ask students to carefully write the recipe on student page 89 and put the steps in the correct order.

3 Evaluate

Tell students it is important to make their writing easy for others to read.

Use these questions to help students evaluate their writing:

- Do your letters have good shape?
- Does each numeral rest on the baseline and touch the headline?
- Is there good spacing between your letters and words?
- Does your writing have proper vertical slant?

Writing in the Content Areas

Traditional Family Foods Point out the words **Grandma's** and **Grandpa's** on the recipe cards on pages 88–89. Tell students that family recipes are passed down from one generation to the next. Ask students to think about the special foods their family makes, either for holidays or for other occasions. Then have them choose their favorite food and write a recipe for it. Make sure they include the ingredients they can remember and simple steps for making the dish. If students get stuck, allow them to consult a recipe online and then rewrite it in their own words. Remind students to use their best manuscript handwriting.

Writing Uppercase Cursive Letters

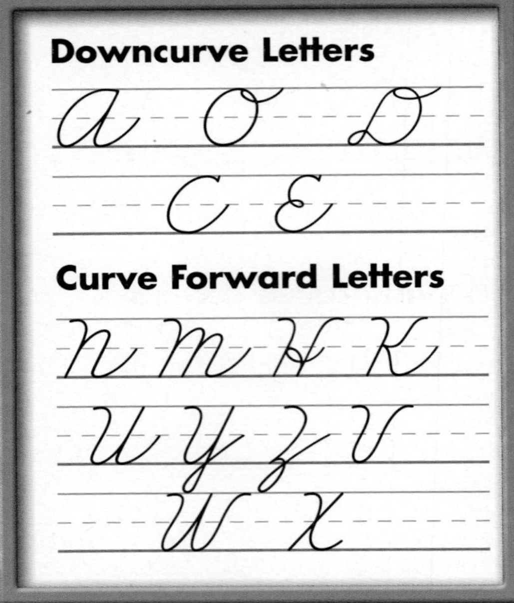

Objective: To practice downcurve and curve forward strokes.

Writing Uppercase Cursive Letters

Downcurve Letters
You will learn to write these uppercase letters.
Each letter has a downcurve stroke.

Trace and write downcurve strokes.

Curve Forward Letters
You will learn to write these uppercase letters.
Each letter begins with a curve forward stroke.

Trace and write curve forward-slant strokes.

Stop and Check
Circle your best downcurve stroke.
Circle your best curve forward-slant stroke.

90

1 Model

Point out the uppercase letters on student page 90. Explain that the following letters are associated with specific strokes:

- **A, O, D, C,** and **E** begin with a downcurve stroke.
- **N, M, H, K, U, Y, Z, V, W,** and **X** begin with a curve forward stroke.

Have students trace the downcurve and curve forward strokes in these letters.

2 Practice

Remind students to position their book and grip their pencil correctly for writing. Have students write the downcurve and curve forward strokes.

Direct students to notice this symbol at the end of the writing grid. Remind them this symbol tells them to stop and check their writing. Then guide students in circling their best downcurve and curve forward stroke.

3 Evaluate

Tell students it is important to make their writing easy for others to read.

Use these questions to help students evaluate their writing:

- Does your downcurve begin at the headline and end at the baseline?
- Does your curve forward stroke begin at the headline and slant down toward the baseline?

Support for English Language Learners

Stroke Description Vocabulary Write the word **curve** on the board. Explain to students that the word means *a line that bends in one direction*. Share with students other words that have similar meanings to *curve*, such as *bend*, *turn*, *arch*, and *curl*.

Overcurve Letters
You will learn to write these uppercase letters. Each letter begins with an overcurve stroke.

Trace and write overcurve strokes.

Undercurve-Loop Letters
You will learn to write these uppercase letters. Each letter begins with an undercurve and a loop stroke.

Trace and write undercurve-loop strokes.

Doublecurve Letters
You will learn to write these uppercase letters. Each letter has a doublecurve stroke.

Trace and write doublecurve strokes.

Undercurve-Slant Letters
You will learn to write these uppercase letters. Each letter begins with an undercurve and a slant stroke.

Trace and write undercurve-slant strokes.

91

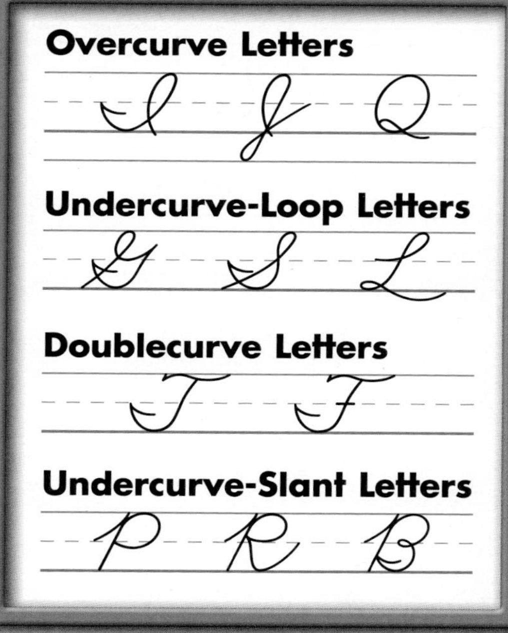

Objective: To practice overcurve, undercurve-loop, doublecurve, and undercurve-slant strokes.

1 Model

Point out the uppercase letters on student page 91. Explain that the following letters are associated with specific strokes:

- **I, J,** and **Q** begin with an overcurve stroke.
- **T** and **F** have doublecurve strokes.
- **G, S,** and **L** begin with an undercurve and loop stroke.
- **P, R,** and **B** begin with an undercurve and slant stroke.

Have students trace the overcurve, doublecurve, undercurve-loop, and undercurve-slant strokes in these letters.

2 Practice

Remind students to position their book and grip their pencil correctly for writing.

Have students write the overcurve and doublecurve strokes. Have them write the undercurve-loop and undercurve-slant strokes.

Remind students that when they come to this symbol, ✓ they should stop writing and circle their best strokes.

3 Evaluate

Tell students it is important to make their writing easy for others to read.

✓ **Use** these questions to help students evaluate their writing:

- Does your overcurve begin at the baseline and end at the headline?
- Does your doublecurve begin at the headline and end at the baseline?
- Does your undercurve and loop stroke begin at the baseline?
- Does your undercurve and slant stroke end on the baseline?

Using Technology

Digital Journals There are numerous digital journaling applications and programs for children. Find a suitable site for your students (enter *online journals for children* in a search engine) and show students how to start their own journals. You might also introduce web logs, or blogs, which are a type of online journal that can be shared with friends or kept private. Have students use the digital journaling tool you selected to write a travel journal entry about a trip they would like to take.

Downcurve Letters

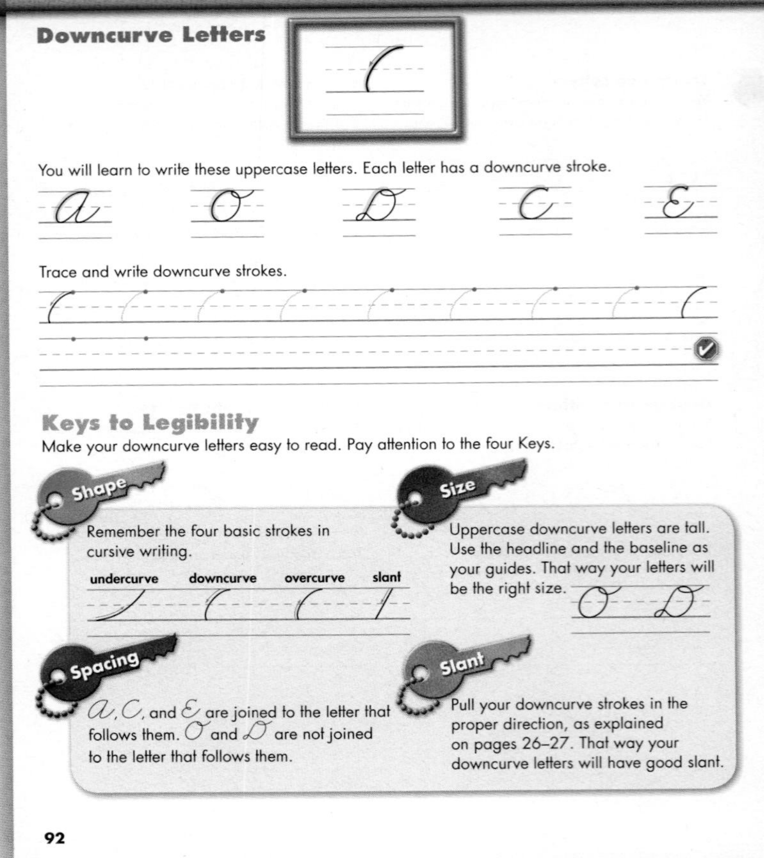

Downcurve Letters
You will learn to write these uppercase letters. Each letter has a downcurve stroke.
Trace and write downcurve strokes.
Keys to Legibility
Make your downcurve letters easy to read. Pay attention to the four Keys.
Shape
Remember the four basic strokes in cursive writing.
undercurve
downcurve
overcurve
slant
Size
Uppercase downcurve letters are tall. Use the headline and the baseline as your guides. That way your letters will be the right size.
Spacing
, and are joined to the letter that follows them. and are not joined to the letter that follows them.
Slant
Pull your downcurve strokes in the proper direction, as explained on pages 26–27. That way your downcurve letters will have good slant.
92

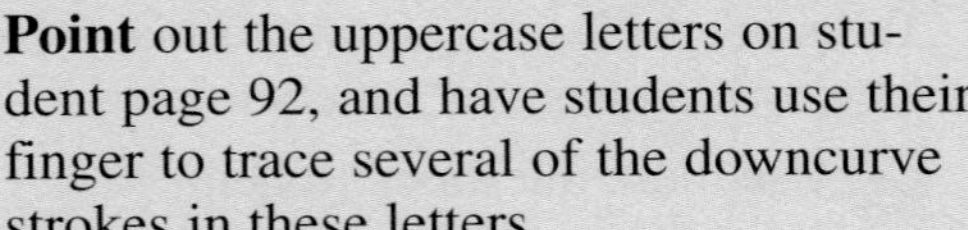

Objective: To practice writing uppercase downcurve strokes.

1 Model

Point out the uppercase letters on student page 92, and have students use their finger to trace several of the downcurve strokes in these letters.

2 Practice

Remind students to position their book and grip their pencil correctly for writing.

Ask students to start at the green dot and carefully trace the downcurve strokes with pencil.

Remind students that when they come to this symbol , they should stop writing and circle their best downcurve stroke.

3 Evaluate

Tell students it is important to make their writing easy for others to read. Remind them to complete all **Stop and Check** activities.

Point out to students the four keys on student page 92. Remind them to pay attention to all four keys as they write, in order to have legible handwriting.

Support for English Language Learners

Stroke Description Vocabulary Write the four basic strokes in cursive writing **(undercurve, downcurve, overcurve,** and **slant)** on the board. Name each stroke, and have students repeat each one several times. Have students think of an object that has the same shape as each stroke. Ask them to draw a picture of the object next to each stroke on a sheet of lined writing paper.

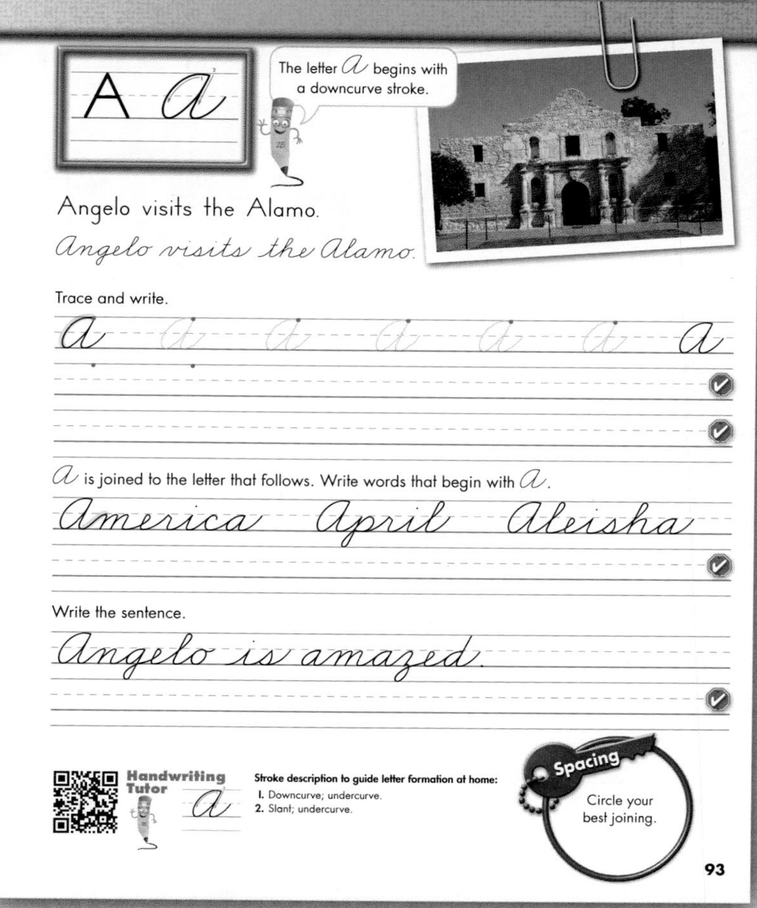

A *a*

The letter *a* begins with a downcurve stroke.

Angelo visits the Alamo.

Angelo visits the Alamo.

Trace and write.

a a a a a a a

a is joined to the letter that follows. Write words that begin with *a*.

America April Aleisha

Write the sentence.

Angelo is amazed.

Handwriting Tutor

Stroke description to guide letter formation at home:
1. Downcurve; undercurve.
2. Slant; undercurve.

Spacing

Circle your best joining.

93

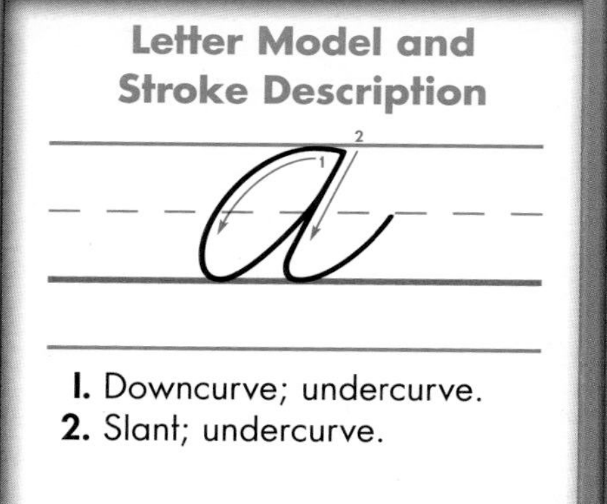

Letter Model and Stroke Description
1. Downcurve; undercurve.
2. Slant; undercurve.

Objective: To practice writing uppercase cursive **A**.

1 Model

Point out that uppercase cursive **A** begins with a downcurve. Write **A** on guidelines as you say the stroke description.

Repeat the stroke description as students use their finger to trace the letter on their desktop.

It might be helpful for students, especially auditory learners, to hear a more detailed stroke description (Go to **resources.zaner-bloser.com/hw**.).

2 Practice

Remind students to position their book and grip their pencil correctly for writing.

Ask students to begin at the green dot and carefully trace the letters on student page 93 with pencil. Then have them write the letters, words, and sentence on the page.

Remind students that when they come to this symbol ✓, they should stop writing and circle their best letter, joining, or word.

3 Evaluate

Tell students it is important to make their writing easy for others to read. Remind them to complete all **Stop and Check** activities.

Proper spacing makes each letter easy to read. Ask:

- Is your **A** joined to the letter that follows?
- Did you use proper spacing between your letters and words?

Writing in the Content Areas

Social Studies

Describing a Place Have students look at the photo of the Alamo on page 93. Tell them that this location was the site of a battle between the Mexican army and supporters of Texan independence. Show students some other photos of the Alamo. Have them write an **informative/explanatory** piece to describe the physical features of the Alamo. Encourage them to use vivid adjectives and other sensory words to help them describe it. Remind students to use their best cursive handwriting.

Extra Practice

Practice Masters 47, 88

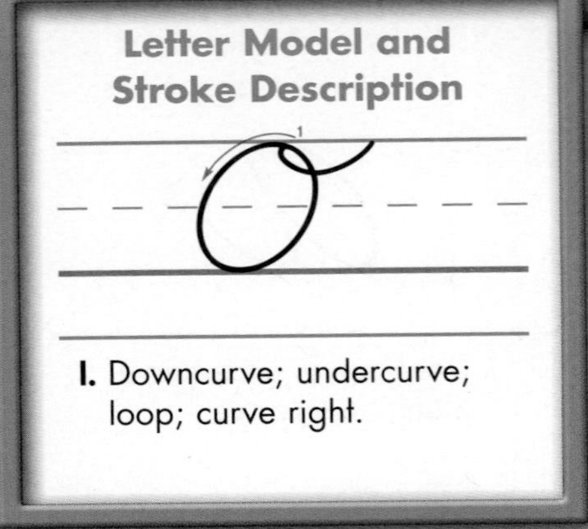

The letter O begins with a downcurve stroke.
Olivia loves October.
Olivia loves October.
Trace and write.
O is not joined to the letter that follows. Write words that begin with O.
Oregon Ohio October
Write the sentence.
Olivia likes cool weather.
Handwriting Tutor
Stroke description to guide letter formation at home:
I. Downcurve; undercurve; loop; curve right.
Stop and Check
Circle your best O.
94

Objective: To practice writing uppercase cursive **O**.

1 Model

Talk about cursive **O**. Ask:

- Where does **O** begin? *(just below the headline)*
- How many pauses are there in **O**? *(none)*

Write cursive **O** on guidelines on the board as you say the stroke description. Use skywriting (see page Z21) to model writing **O** in the air. Have students stand and say the stroke description with you as they write cursive **O** in the air.

2 Practice

Remind students to position their book and grip their pencil correctly for writing.

Ask students to start at the green dot and carefully trace the shaded letters on student page 94 with pencil. Then have them write the letters, words, and sentence on the page.

Remind students that when they come to this symbol , they should stop writing and circle their best letter, joining, or word.

3 Evaluate

Tell students it is important to make their writing easy for others to read.

 **Use** these questions to help students evaluate their writing:

- Does your **O** begin at the headline?
- Does your **O** end at the headline?

Extra Practice

Practice Masters 48, 88

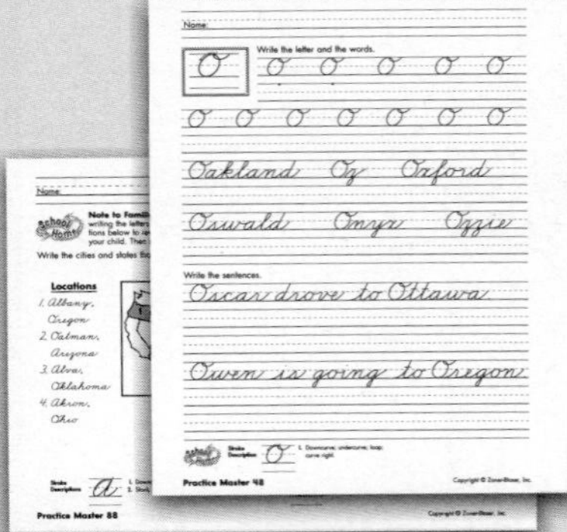

Support for English Language Learners

Cognates You can relate the first language of some students to English by comparing words with the same cognates (words that share a common origin), with similar pronunciations, and with similar meanings to corresponding English words. For example, you can use cognates from Romance languages, such as Spanish, to teach the months of the year (*enero/January, febrero/February, marzo/March, abril/April, mayo/May, junio/June, julio/July, agosto/August, septiembre/September, octubre/October, noviembre/November, diciembre/December*).

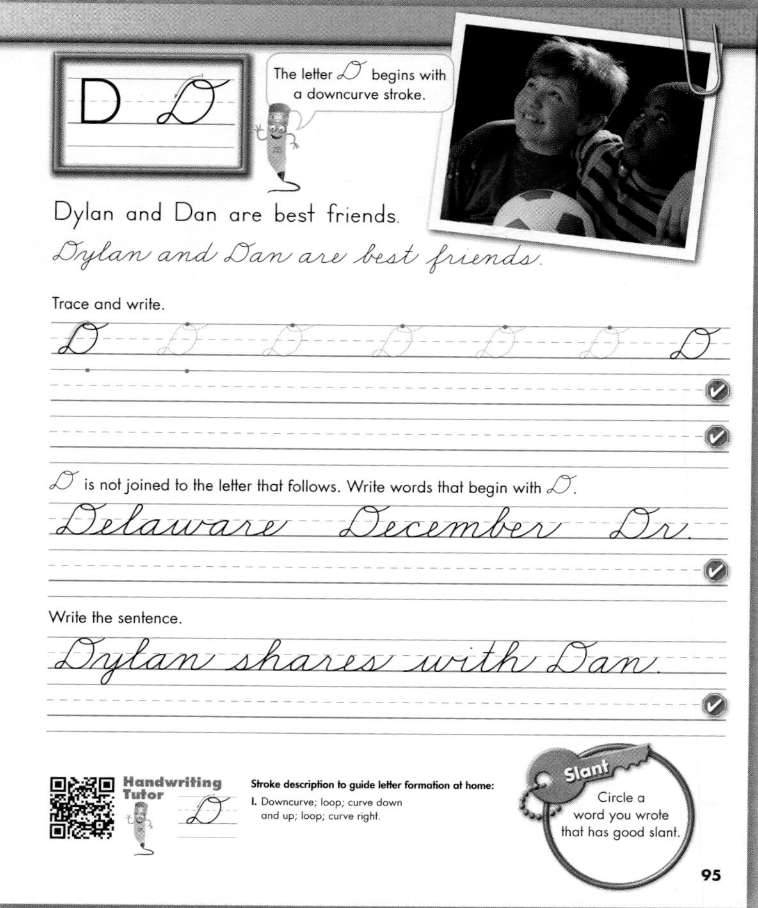
D *D*

The letter *D* begins with a downcurve stroke.

Dylan and Dan are best friends.

Dylan and Dan are best friends.

Trace and write.

D D D D D D D

D is not joined to the letter that follows. Write words that begin with *D*.

Delaware December Dr.

Write the sentence.

Dylan shares with Dan.

Handwriting Tutor

Stroke description to guide letter formation at home:

1. Downcurve; loop; curve down and up; loop; curve right.

Slant

Circle a word you wrote that has good slant.

95

Letter Model and Stroke Description

1. Downcurve; loop; curve down and up; loop; curve right.

Objective: To practice writing uppercase cursive **D**.

Handwriting Tutor

1 Model

Talk about cursive **D**. Ask:

- How many times does cursive **D** touch the baseline? *(two)*
- How many loops are in **D**? *(two)*

Write cursive **D** on guidelines on the board as you say the stroke description. Use skywriting to model writing **D** in the air. Have students stand and say the stroke description with you as they write **D** in the air.

2 Practice

Remind students to position their book and grip their pencil correctly for writing.

Ask students to begin at the green dot and use their index finger to trace **D** on student page 95. Then have them carefully trace and write with pencil the letters, words, and sentence on the page.

Remind students that when they come to this symbol ✓, they should stop writing and circle their best letter, joining, or word.

3 Evaluate

Tell students it is important to make their writing easy for others to read. Remind them to complete all **Stop and Check** activities.

Proper slant makes each letter easy to read. Ask:

- Does your **D** have correct slant?
- Do all your letters have consistent forward slant?

Writing in the Content Areas

Language Arts

Describing a Friend Point out the picture of the boys on page 95. Have students think about their friends. What is important about being a good friend? Ask students to write a **narrative** piece describing what makes a good friend. Have them include what they like to do with their friends. Encourage the use of sensory words in their descriptions. Remind students to use their best cursive handwriting.

School Home

Extra Practice

Practice Masters 49, 89

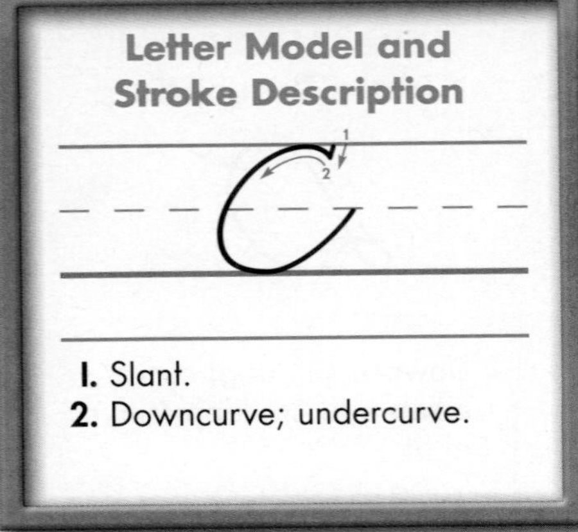

Objective: To practice writing uppercase cursive **C**.

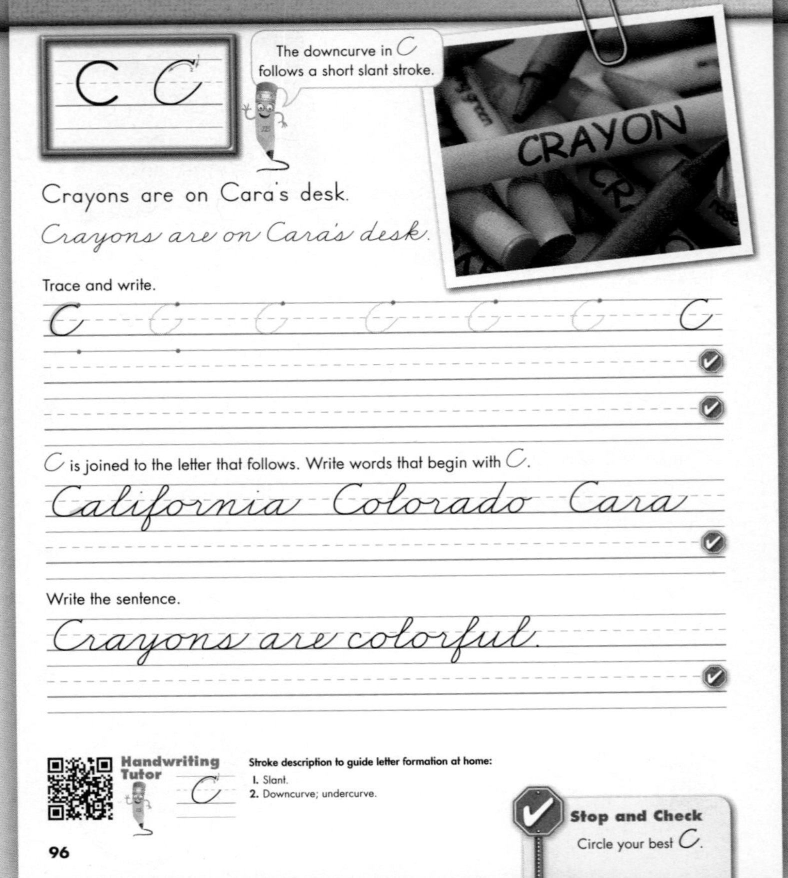

The downcurve in C follows a short slant stroke.
Crayons are on Cara's desk.
Crayons are on Cara's desk.
CRAYON
Trace and write.
C is joined to the letter that follows. Write words that begin with C.
California Colorado Cara
Write the sentence.
Crayons are colorful.
Handwriting Tutor
Stroke description to guide letter formation at home:
1. Slant.
2. Downcurve; undercurve.
Stop and Check
Circle your best C.
96

1 Model

Talk about cursive **C**. Ask:

- How does **C** begin? *(with a slant)*
- What follows the slant? *(a downcurve)*

Write cursive **C** on guidelines on the board as you say the stroke description. Use skywriting to model writing **C** in the air. Have students stand and say it with you as they write cursive **C** in the air.

2 Practice

Remind students to position their book and grip their pencil correctly for writing.

Ask students to begin at the green dot and use their index finger to trace **C** several times on student page 96. Then have them carefully trace and write with pencil the letters, words, and sentence on the page.

Remind students that when they come to this symbol , they should stop writing and circle their best letter, joining, or word.

3 Evaluate

Tell students it is important to make their writing easy for others to read. Remind them to complete all **Stop and Check** activities.

Use these questions to help students evaluate their writing:

- Does your **C** have correct slant?
- Does your **C** end at the midline?

Extra Practice

Practice Masters 50, 89

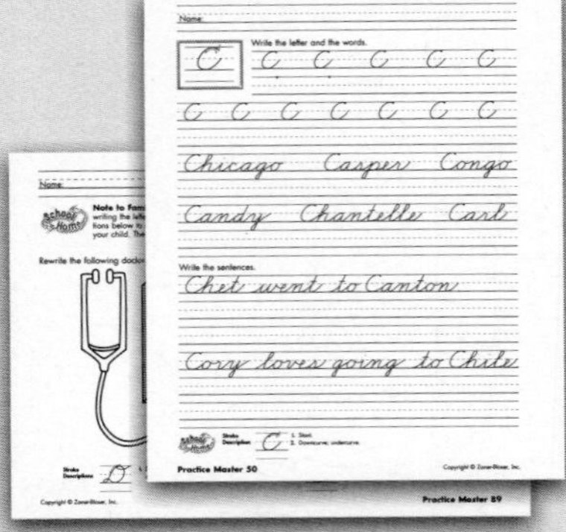

Support for English Language Learners

Vocabulary Building Use the photo on student page 96 to practice naming colors with students. Point to each crayon in the book, and hold up a crayon of the matching color. Say: "The color of this crayon is ____." Have students repeat each sentence chorally after you.

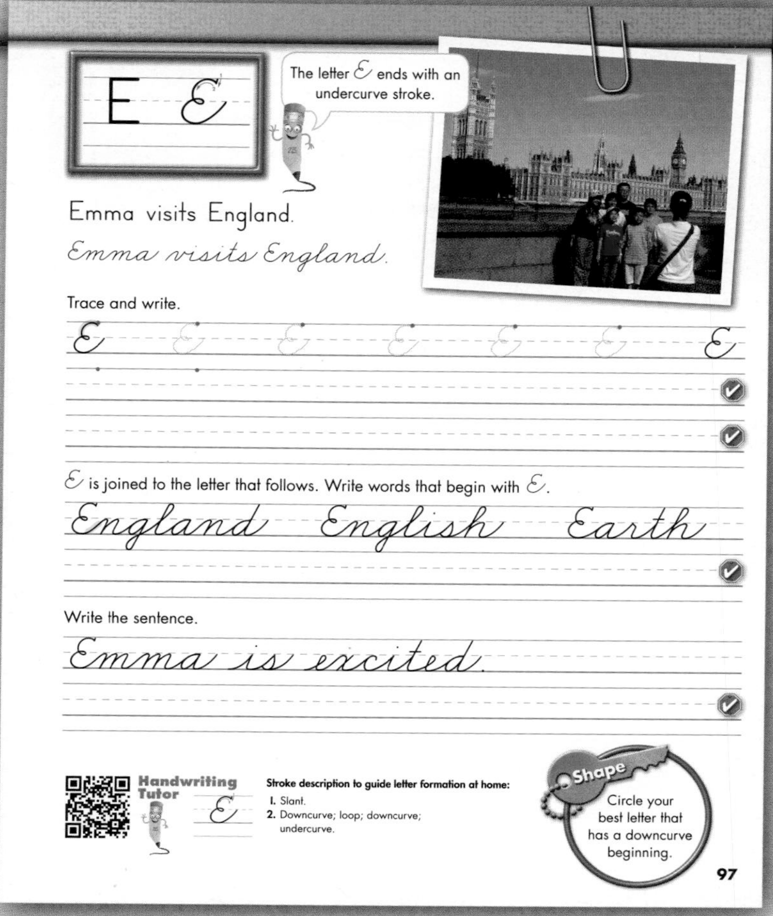

E ℰ

The letter ℰ ends with an undercurve stroke.

Emma visits England.

Emma visits England.

Trace and write.

ℰ is joined to the letter that follows. Write words that begin with ℰ.

England English Earth

Write the sentence.

Emma is excited.

Handwriting Tutor

Stroke description to guide letter formation at home:
1. Slant.
2. Downcurve; loop; downcurve; undercurve.

Shape — Circle your best letter that has a downcurve beginning.

97

Letter Model and Stroke Description

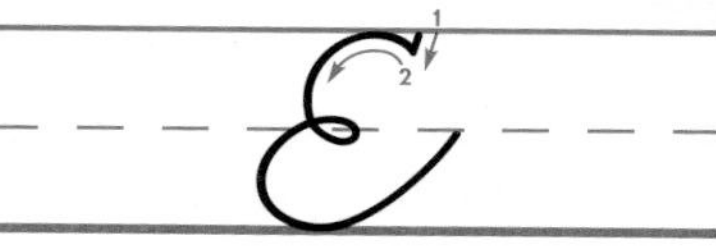

1. Slant.
2. Downcurve; loop; downcurve; undercurve.

Objective: To practice writing uppercase cursive **E**.

1 Model

Talk about cursive **E**. Ask:

- How many loops are in **E**? *(one)*
- Where does **E** end? *(at the midline)*

Write cursive **E** on guidelines on the board as you say the stroke description. Use skywriting to model writing **E** in the air. Have students stand and say it with you as they write **E** in the air.

2 Practice

Remind students to position their book and grip their pencil correctly for writing.

Ask students to begin at the green dot and use their index finger to trace **E** several times on student page 97. Then have them carefully trace and write with pencil the letters, words, and sentence on the page.

Remind students that when they come to this symbol ✓, they should stop writing and circle their best letter, joining, or word.

3 Evaluate

Tell students it is important to make their writing easy for others to read. Remind them to complete all **Stop and Check** activities.

Proper shape makes each letter easy to read. Ask:

- Is the loop of your **E** at the midline?
- Are the downcurves of your **E** the correct shape?

Tips From an Occupational Therapist

Rest Breaks When students first begin to connect letters and complete longer written assignments, provide them with rest breaks. Slowly increase the length of the assignments so they can build up their **fine motor endurance**.

Extra Practice

Practice Masters 51, 90

Review

Objective: To review uppercase cursive **A, O, D, C,** and **E.**

Review

A O D C E

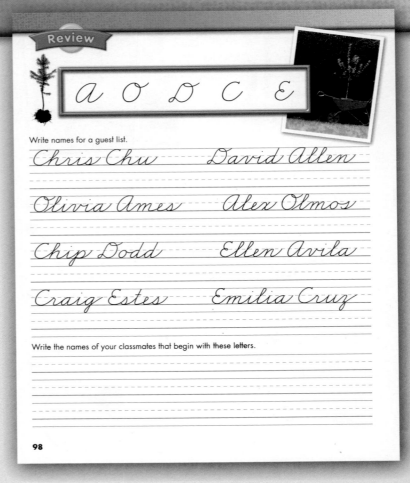

Write names for a guest list.

Chris Chu David Allen

Olivia Ames Alex Olmos

Chip Dodd Ellen Avila

Craig Estes Emilia Cruz

Write the names of your classmates that begin with these letters.

98

1 Review

Point out that letters **A, O, D, C,** and **E** begin with a downcurve or a short slant followed by a downcurve. Review the stroke descriptions and model any letters students might be having difficulty writing.

Ask a volunteer to give a verbal description of one of the letters. Challenge students to identify the letter being described and then write it on guidelines on the board.

See the **Corrective Strategies** in the Appendix for techniques in correcting common problems in your students' handwriting.

2 Practice

Remind students to position their book and grip their pencil correctly for writing.

Ask students to carefully write the names on student page 98. Remind them to form their letters with correct strokes so they will have proper shape.

3 Evaluate

Tell students it is important to make their writing easy for others to read.

Use these questions to help students evaluate their writing:

- Did you write with correct strokes so your letters have good shape?
- Are your letters about the same width as the models?
- Is your **A** closed?
- Does your **O** end at the headline?
- Is the loop in your **E** at the midline?

Digital Tools

ZB Handwriting App
Available through the iTunes Store for English Manuscript, English Cursive, Spanish Manuscript, and Spanish Cursive.

Support for English Language Learners

Capitalizing Proper Nouns Write the full name of a student on the board. Point to the uppercase letters that begin the student's first and last name. Review with students that in the English language, proper nouns, such as names, begin with an uppercase letter. Have students provide other proper nouns that begin with **A, O, D, C,** or **E.** Ask students to practice writing some of them.

Application

Come One, Come All!
Celebrate Arbor Day

At: Chris Edson's house
Address: 5 Ocean Avenue

Date: April 29
Don't bring any treats.

Writing an Invitation

Write the invitation. Leave space for margins.

Stop and Check
Circle your best uppercase letter.

99

Application

Writing an Invitation

Objective: To write an invitation.

1 Review

Read aloud the text of the invitation on student page 99, and review the *What?*, *Who?*, *Where?*, and *When?* information.

2 Practice

Remind students to position their book and grip their pencil correctly for writing.

Ask students to carefully write the invitation within the margins. Remind them to form their letters with correctly written stokes so they will have good shape.

3 Evaluate

Tell students it is important to make their writing easy for others to read. Remind them to complete all **Stop and Check** activities.

Proper Shape, Size, Spacing, and Slant make words easy to read. Ask:

- Do your letters look like the models?
- Are your short letters half the height of your tall letters?
- Is there proper spacing between each letter and word?
- Did you use proper slant?

Using Technology

Create an Invitation Have students open a painting program. Model how to insert a text box and how to resize the box to accommodate the text. Have students type the invitation on page 99 into the text box. Show students where to find the Apostrophe key and how to insert an exclamation point by holding down the Shift key and then selecting the I or ! key. Repeat for the colon. Remind students that after each line, they should select the Enter or Return key to start a new line. After the text has been added, show students how they can decorate their Arbor Day invitation by adding shapes (such as trees), filling the shapes with color, using different brushes to draw designs, and so on.

Curve Forward Letters

Curve Forward Letters

You will learn to write these uppercase letters. Each letter begins with a curve forward stroke.

Trace and write curve forward-slant strokes.

Keys to Legibility

Make your curve forward letters easy to read. Pay attention to the four Keys.

Shape Curve forward-slant strokes begin at the headline and sweep down.

Size Remember that all uppercase letters are tall letters. Some uppercase letters have descenders that go below the baseline and touch the next headline.

Spacing V, W, and X are not joined to the letter that follows.

Slant Shift your paper as you write, as explained on pages 26–27. That way your curve forward letters will have good slant.

100

1 Model

Point out the uppercase letters on student page 100, and explain that each one begins with a curve forward stroke. In most of the letters, the curve forward is followed by a slant stroke. Encourage students to use their index finger to trace several of the curve forward strokes in these letters.

Practice

Remind students to position their book and grip their pencil correctly for writing.

Have them trace with pencil and write the curve forward-slant strokes on the guidelines.

Remind students that when they come to this symbol ✓, they should stop writing and circle their best stroke.

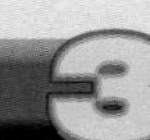

Evaluate

Tell students it is important to make their writing easy for others to read. Remind them to complete all **Stop and Check** activities.

Point out to students the four keys on student page 100. Remind them to pay attention to all four keys as they write, in order to have legible handwriting.

Support for
English Language Learners

Vocabulary Building Review the words **headline, midline,** and **baseline** with students. Label the headline, midline, and baseline on guidelines on the board. Help students remember each by associating the headline with a "head" or the top-most part of a person's body. Help students associate the midline with the "middle," and the baseline with the "base," or "bottom."

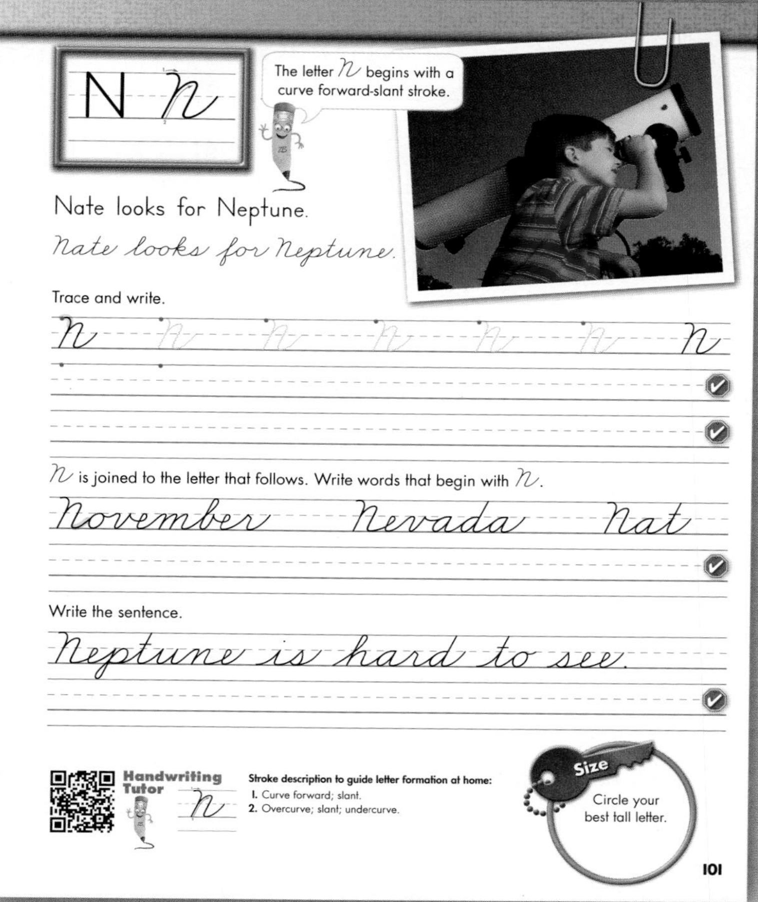
N 𝓃

The letter 𝓃 begins with a curve forward-slant stroke.

Nate looks for Neptune.

Nate looks for Neptune.

Trace and write.

𝓃 is joined to the letter that follows. Write words that begin with 𝓃.

November Nevada Nat

Write the sentence.

Neptune is hard to see.

Handwriting Tutor

Stroke description to guide letter formation at home:
1. Curve forward; slant.
2. Overcurve; slant; undercurve.

Size

Circle your best tall letter.

101

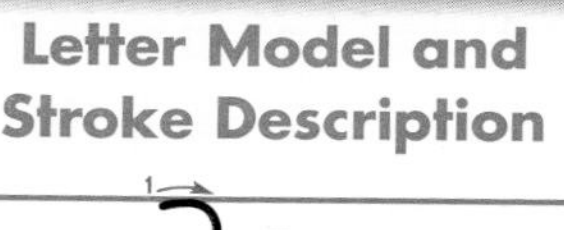

Letter Model and Stroke Description

1. Curve forward; slant.
2. Overcurve; slant; undercurve.

Objective: To practice writing uppercase cursive **N**.

1 Model

Talk about cursive **N**. Ask:

- What stroke follows the first slant? *(overcurve)*
- How many slant strokes are in **N**? *(two)*

Write cursive **N** on guidelines as you say the stroke description. Use skywriting (see page Z21) to model writing **N** in the air as you say the stroke description. Have students say the words as they use their index finger to write large **N**'s on the board.

2 Practice

Remind students to position their book and grip their pencil correctly for writing.

Ask students to begin at the green dot and carefully trace the shaded letters on student page 101 with pencil. Then have them write the letters, words, and sentence on the page.

Remind students that when they come to this symbol ✓, they should stop writing and circle their best letter, joining, or word.

3 Evaluate

Tell students it is important to make their writing easy for others to read. Remind them to complete all **Stop and Check** activities.

Proper size makes each letter easy to read. Ask:

- Does your curve forward stroke begin at the headline?
- Does the top of your overcurve hit between the midline and the headline?

Science

Writing in the Content Areas

Observation Point out the photo on page 101. Ask students if they have ever looked through a telescope or visited an observatory. Ask them what sorts of things they might see through a telescope. Since most students have looked at the moon, have them write a paragraph about what they observed. They might discuss the moon's shape and phases, its colors, formations on the moon's surface, and so on. Remind students to use their best cursive handwriting.

Extra Practice

Practice Masters 52, 90

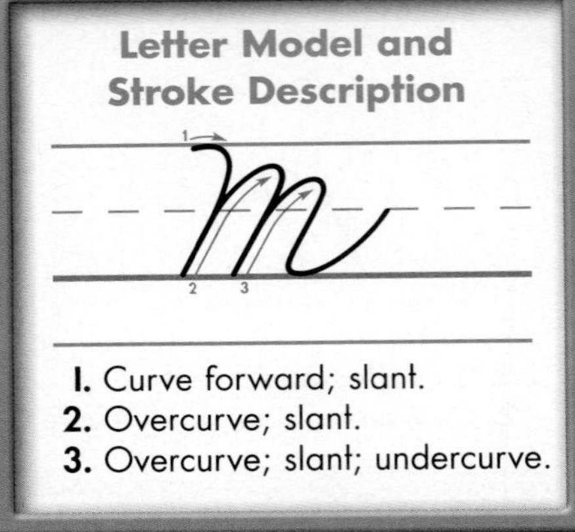

Objective: To practice writing uppercase cursive **M**.

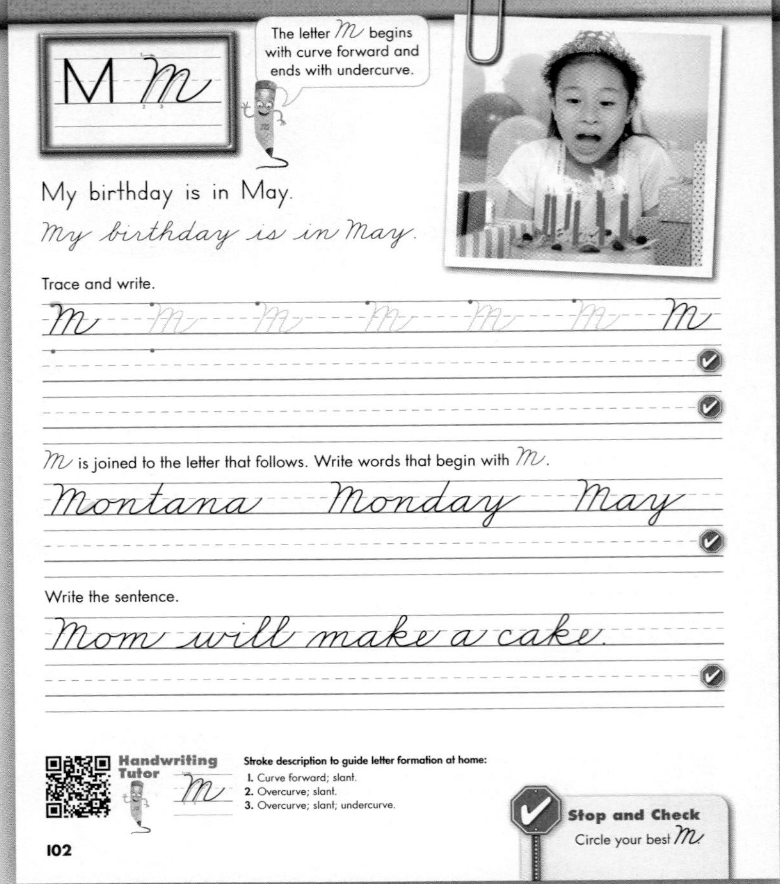

The letter M begins with curve forward and ends with undercurve.
My birthday is in May.
Trace and write.
M is joined to the letter that follows. Write words that begin with M.
Montana Monday May
Write the sentence.
Mom will make a cake.
Handwriting Tutor
Stroke description to guide letter formation at home:
1. Curve forward; slant.
2. Overcurve; slant.
3. Overcurve; slant; undercurve.
Stop and Check
Circle your best M
102

1 Model

Talk about cursive **M**. Ask:

- How many slant strokes are in **M**? *(three)*
- Where does **M** end? *(at the midline)*

Write cursive **M** on guidelines on the board as you say the stroke description. Use skywriting to model writing **M** in the air as you repeat the stroke description. Have students say the stroke description as they use their index finger to write **M** on their desktop.

2 Practice

Remind students to position their book and grip their pencil correctly for writing.

Ask students to begin at the green dot and carefully trace the shaded letters on student page 102 with pencil. Then have them write the letters, words, and sentence on the page.

Remind students that when they come to this symbol , they should stop writing and circle their best letter, joining, or word.

3 Evaluate

Tell students it is important to make their writing easy for others to read. Remind them to complete all **Stop and Check** activities.

Use these questions to help students evaluate their cursive **M**:

- Does the undercurve stroke of your **M** end at the midline?
- Is your second overcurve shorter than your first?

Extra Practice

Practice Masters 53, 91

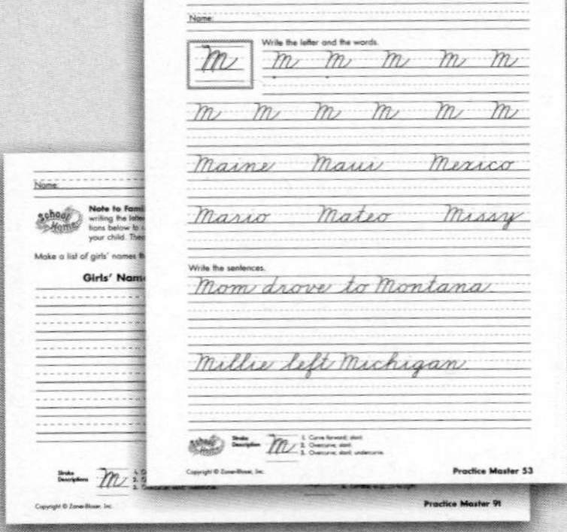

Support for English Language Learners

Cultural Awareness Teachers should be attuned to English Language Learners' sensitivities regarding birthdays. Some students who have immigrated from other countries may not have official documentation of birth and may not know their true dates of birth. Some students might come from cultures in which birthdays are not emphasized as they are in the United States. Upon enrollment in their U.S. school, some students might have been placed in a different grade from their chronological age group and therefore could be sensitive to discussions of birthdays.

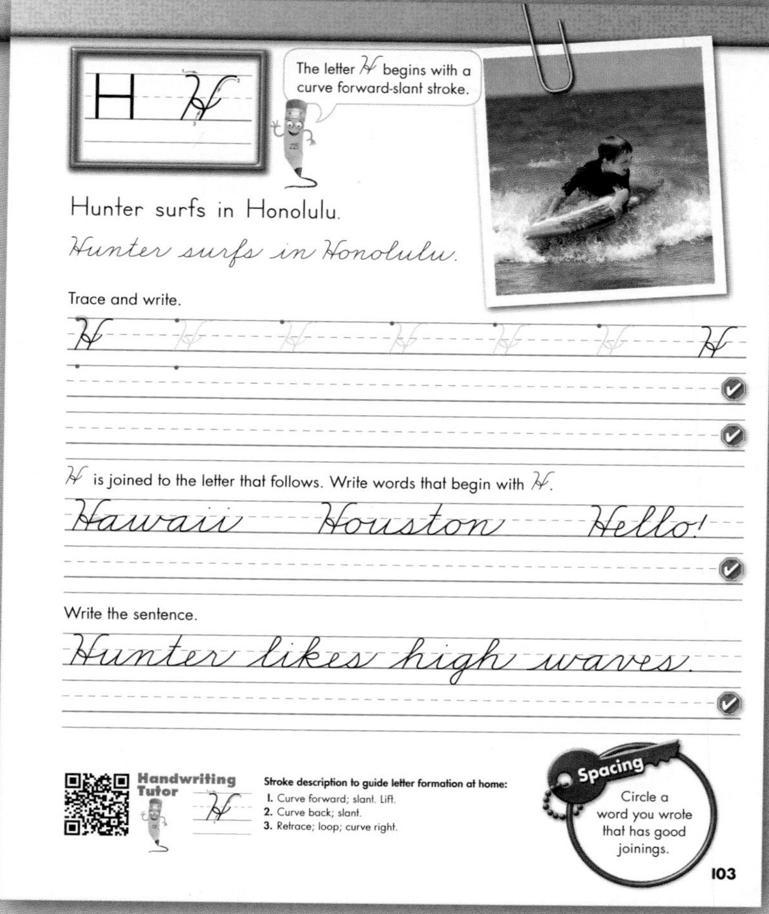

The letter 𝓗 begins with a curve forward-slant stroke.

Hunter surfs in Honolulu.

Hunter surfs in Honolulu.

Trace and write.

H H H H H H H

𝓗 is joined to the letter that follows. Write words that begin with 𝓗.

Hawaii Houston Hello!

Write the sentence.

Hunter likes high waves.

Handwriting Tutor

Stroke description to guide letter formation at home:
1. Curve forward; slant. Lift.
2. Curve back; slant.
3. Retrace; loop; curve right.

Spacing

Circle a word you wrote that has good joinings.

103

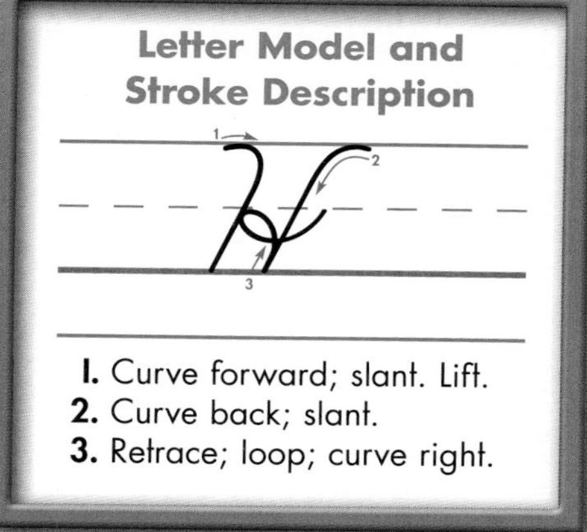

Letter Model and Stroke Description

1. Curve forward; slant. Lift.
2. Curve back; slant.
3. Retrace; loop; curve right.

Objective: To practice writing uppercase cursive **H**.

1 Model

Talk about cursive **H**. Ask:

- How many loops are in **H**? *(one)*
- How many lifts are in **H**? *(one)*

Write cursive **H** on guidelines on the board as you say the stroke description. Use skywriting to model writing **H** in the air as you repeat the stroke description. Have students say the stroke description as they use their index finger to write large **H**'s on their desktop.

It might be helpful for students, especially auditory learners, to hear a more detailed stroke description (Go to **resources.zaner-bloser.com/hw**.).

2 Practice

Remind students to position their book and grip their pencil correctly for writing.

Ask students to begin at the green dot and carefully trace the shaded letters on student page 103 with pencil. Then have them write the letters, words, and sentence on the page.

Remind students that when they come to this symbol , they should stop writing and circle their best letter, joining, or word.

3 Evaluate

Tell students it is important to make their writing easy for others to read. Remind them to complete all **Stop and Check** activities.

Proper spacing makes each letter easy to read. Ask:

- Is your **H** joined to the letter that follows?

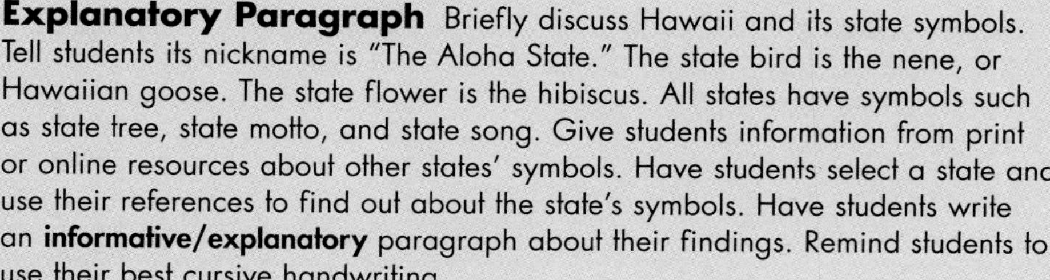

Writing in the Content Areas

Explanatory Paragraph Briefly discuss Hawaii and its state symbols. Tell students its nickname is "The Aloha State." The state bird is the nene, or Hawaiian goose. The state flower is the hibiscus. All states have symbols such as state tree, state motto, and state song. Give students information from print or online resources about other states' symbols. Have students select a state and use their references to find out about the state's symbols. Have students write an **informative/explanatory** paragraph about their findings. Remind students to use their best cursive handwriting.

School Home

Extra Practice

Practice Masters 54, 91

Hartford Hudson Holland

Hines Hoya Heather

Are they in Havana?

He is in Hamden.

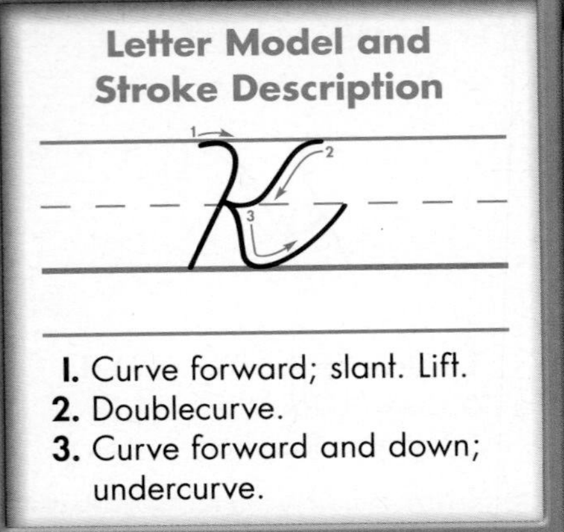

Objective: To practice writing uppercase cursive **K**.

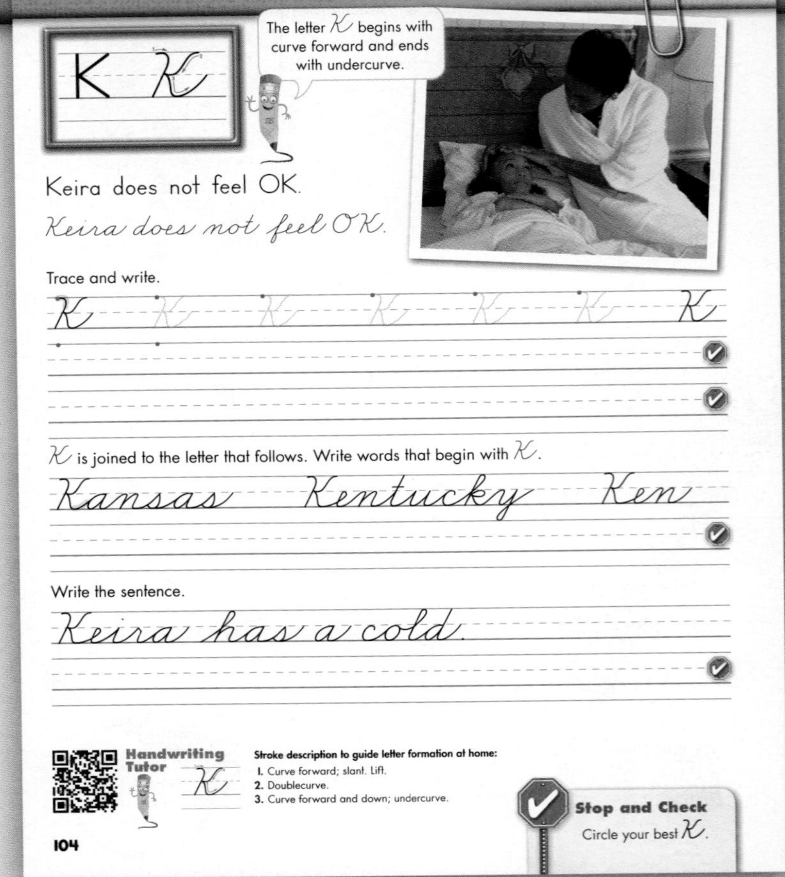

The letter K begins with curve forward and ends with undercurve.
Keira does not feel OK.
Keira does not feel OK.
Trace and write.
K is joined to the letter that follows. Write words that begin with K.
Kansas Kentucky Ken
Write the sentence.
Keira has a cold.
Handwriting Tutor
Stroke description to guide letter formation at home:
1. Curve forward; slant. Lift.
2. Doublecurve.
3. Curve forward and down; undercurve.
Stop and Check
Circle your best K.
104

1 Model

Talk about cursive **K**. Ask:

- Where is the lift in **K**? *(after the slant)*
- What stroke follows the lift in **K**? *(doublecurve)*

Write cursive **K** on guidelines on the board as you say the stroke description. Use skywriting to model writing **K** in the air as you repeat the stroke description. Have students say the stroke description as they use their index finger to write large **K**'s on their desktop.

2 Practice

Remind students to position their book and grip their pencil correctly for writing.

Ask students to begin at the green dot and carefully trace the shaded letters on student page 104 with pencil. Then have them write the letters, words, and sentence on the page.

Remind students that when they come to this symbol ✓, they should stop writing and circle their best letter, joining, or word.

3 Evaluate

Tell students it is important to make their writing easy for others to read.

✓ **Use** these questions to help students evaluate their writing:

- Does your **K** rest on the baseline?
- Does the undercurve stroke of your **K** end at the midline?

Extra Practice

Practice Masters 55, 92

Support for English Language Learners

Abbreviations Some students may not be familiar with the abbreviation *OK*. Explain that it is a shortened form of the word **okay**, and that it is pronounced the same way it is spelled: O-K. Mention **TV** as a second example of an abbreviation pronounced the same way it is spelled: T-V.

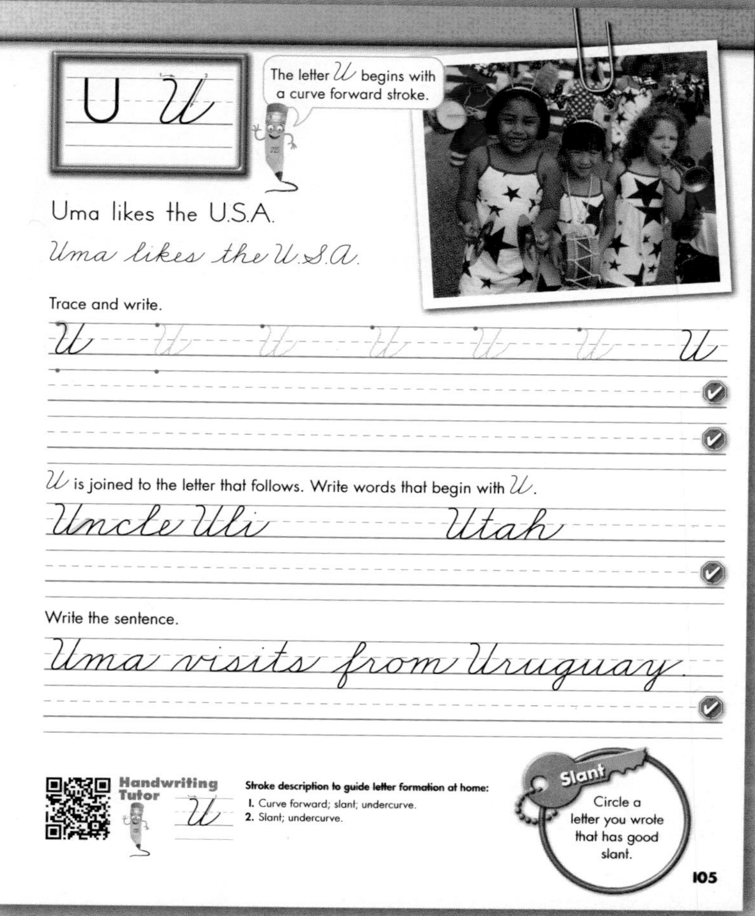

The letter U begins with a curve forward stroke.
Uma likes the U.S.A.
Trace and write.
U is joined to the letter that follows. Write words that begin with U.
Uncle Uli Utah
Write the sentence.
Uma visits from Uruguay.
Handwriting Tutor
Stroke description to guide letter formation at home:
1. Curve forward; slant; undercurve.
2. Slant; undercurve.
Slant
Circle a letter you wrote that has good slant.
105

Letter Model and Stroke Description

1. Curve forward; slant; undercurve.
2. Slant; undercurve.

Objective: To practice writing uppercase cursive **U**.

1 Model

Talk about cursive **U**. Ask:

- How many undercurve strokes are in **U**? *(two)*
- Where does the first undercurve end in **U**? *(at the headline)*

Write cursive **U** on guidelines on the board as you say the stroke description. Use skywriting to model writing **U** in the air as you repeat the stroke description. Have students say the stroke description as they use their index finger to write large **U**'s on their desktop.

2 Practice

Remind students to position their book and grip their pencil correctly for writing.

Ask students to begin at the green dot and carefully trace the shaded letters on student page 105 with pencil. Then have them write the letters, words, and sentence on the page.

Remind students that when they come to this symbol ✓, they should stop writing and circle their best letter, joining, or word.

3 Evaluate

Tell students it is important to make their writing easy for others to read. Remind them to complete all **Stop and Check** activities.

Proper slant makes each letter easy to read. Ask:

- Do your slant strokes have proper slant?
- Can you determine by looking at your writing that your paper was positioned properly?

Tips From an Occupational Therapist

Pick It Up This activity helps students practice in-hand manipulation and promotes mature pencil grasp. Give each student about a dozen small items, such as coins, pencil erasers, or paper clips. Have students pick up items one at a time with the thumb, forefinger, and middle finger. Then direct students to transfer and hold each item in the space between the last two fingers and the palm of the same hand. Make a game of this activity by seeing who can hold the most items.

School Home Extra Practice

Practice Masters 56, 92

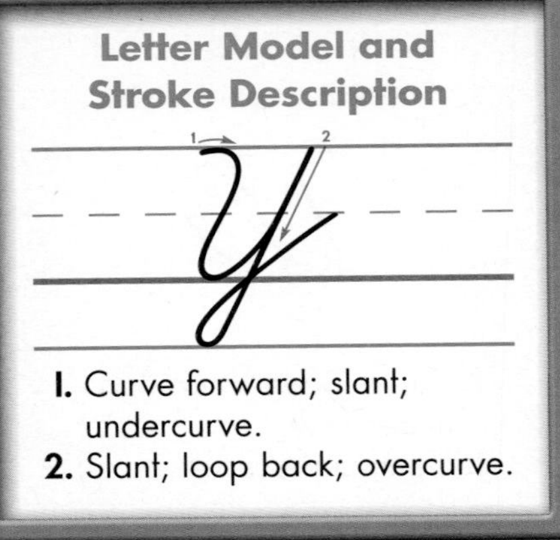

Objective: To practice writing uppercase cursive **Y**.

The letter Y ends with an overcurve stroke.
Yasmin is in Yellowstone.
Yasmin is in Yellowstone.
Trace and write.
Y is joined to the letter that follows. Write words that begin with Y.
Yosemite Yorktown
Write the sentence.
Yellowstone is a big park.
Handwriting Tutor
Stroke description to guide letter formation at home:
1. Curve forward; slant; undercurve.
2. Slant; loop back; overcurve.
106
Stop and Check
Circle your best Y.

1 Model

Talk about cursive **Y**. Ask:

- How does **Y** end? *(with an overcurve)*
- Where does the loop in **Y** close? *(near the baseline)*

Write cursive **Y** on guidelines on the board as you say the stroke description. Use skywriting to model writing **Y** in the air as you repeat the stroke description. Have students say the stroke description as they use their index finger to write large **Y**'s on their desktop.

2 Practice

Remind students to position their book and grip their pencil correctly for writing.

Ask students to begin at the green dot and carefully trace the shaded letters on student page 106 with pencil. Then have them write the letters, words, and sentence on the page.

Remind students that when they come to this symbol , they should stop writing and circle their best letter, joining, or word.

3 Evaluate

Tell students it is important to make their writing easy for others to read.

 **Use** these questions to help students evaluate their writing:

- Is your **Y** about the same size as the model?
- Does your loop fill the descender space and close near the baseline?

Extra Practice

Practice Masters 57, 93

Support for English Language Learners

Multiple-Meaning Words Point out that the word **park** in the sentence on student page 106 is used as a naming word (a noun), but the same word is also an action word (a verb). Provide an example sentence. Write some other examples on the board of words that are both verbs and nouns (such as **plant**, **turn**, **brush**). Then write two sentences for each word, one with the word as a verb and another with the word as a noun. Ask students to identify which sentences use the words as a verb or a noun.

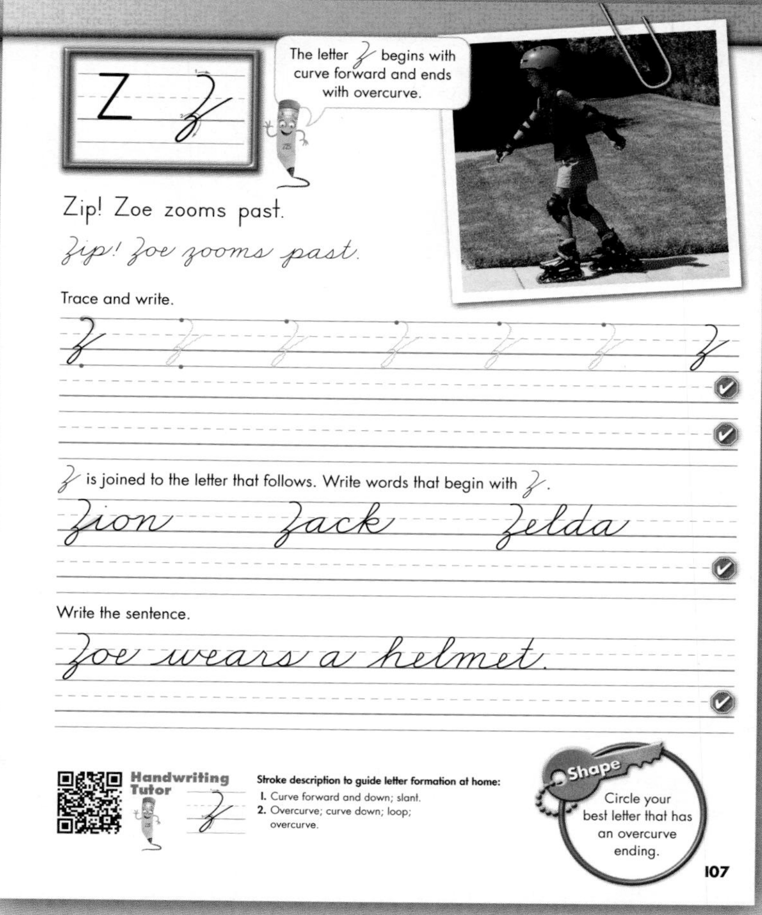

The letter Z begins with curve forward and ends with overcurve.

Z Z

Zip! Zoe zooms past.

Zip! Zoe zooms past.

Trace and write.

Z is joined to the letter that follows. Write words that begin with Z.

Zion Zack Zelda

Write the sentence.

Zoe wears a helmet.

Handwriting Tutor

Stroke description to guide letter formation at home:

1. Curve forward and down; slant.
2. Overcurve; curve down; loop; overcurve.

Shape

Circle your best letter that has an overcurve ending.

107

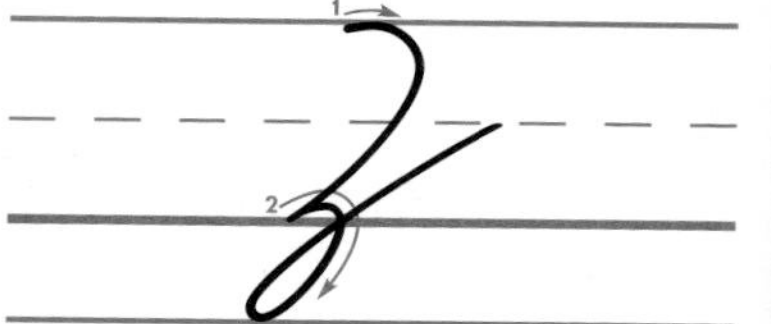

Letter Model and Stroke Description

1. Curve forward and down; slant.
2. Overcurve; curve down; loop; overcurve.

Objective: To practice writing uppercase cursive **Z**.

1 Model

Talk about cursive **Z**. Ask:

- How many loops are in **Z**? *(one)*
- How does **Z** end? *(with an overcurve)*

Write cursive **Z** on guidelines on the board as you say the stroke description. Use skywriting to model writing **Z** in the air as you repeat the stroke description. Have students say the stroke description as they use their index finger to write large **Z**'s on their desktop.

2 Practice

Remind students to position their book and grip their pencil correctly for writing.

Ask students to begin at the green dot and carefully trace the shaded letters on student page 107 with pencil. Then have them write the letters, words, and sentence on the page.

Remind students that when they come to this symbol ✓, they should stop writing and circle their best letter, joining, or word.

3 Evaluate

Tell students it is important to make their writing easy for others to read.

Proper shape makes each letter easy to read. Ask:

- Does your loop in **Z** close near the baseline?
- Do your strokes look like the model?

Writing in the Content Areas

Language Arts

Onomatopoeia Point out that the word **zip** is a word whose name suggests its meaning, just as the words **pop, snap,** and **click** sound like the noises they describe. Brainstorm other examples of onomatopoeia (e.g., **boom, beep, croak, quack, cluck, zoom, splat**) and write them on the board. Then have students select a few of the words and use them in a poem. Challenge students to use a theme in their poems (e.g., **cars:** *We see cars zoom down the road; We hear the cars beep at each other*). Ask volunteers to share their poems with the group. Remind students to use their best cursive handwriting.

Extra Practice

Practice Masters 58, 93

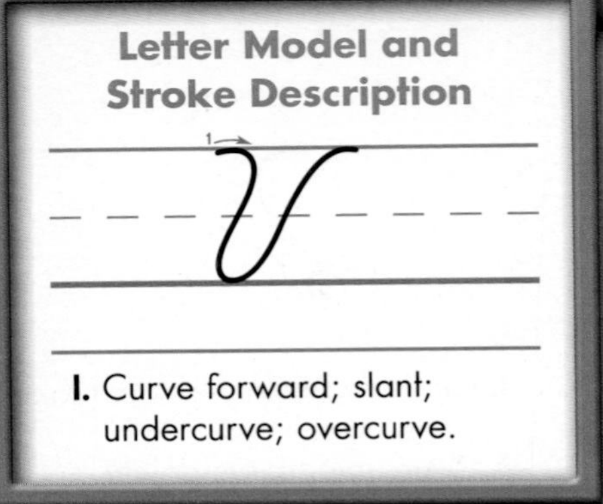

Objective: To practice writing cursive uppercase **V**.

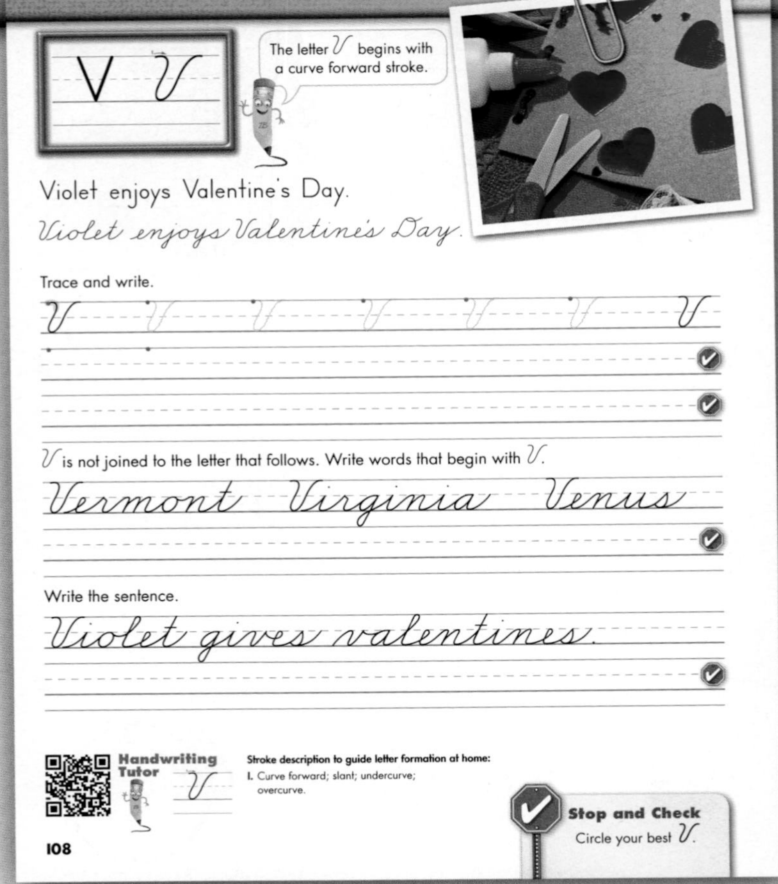

The letter V begins with a curve forward stroke.
Violet enjoys Valentine's Day.
Violet enjoys Valentine's Day.
Trace and write.
V is not joined to the letter that follows. Write words that begin with V.
Vermont Virginia Venus
Write the sentence.
Violet gives valentines.
Handwriting Tutor
Stroke description to guide letter formation at home:
I. Curve forward; slant; undercurve; overcurve.
Stop and Check
Circle your best V.
108

1 Model

Talk about cursive **V**. Ask:

- How does **V** begin? *(with a curve forward, slant)*
- Where does **V** end? *(just below the headline)*

Write cursive **V** on guidelines on the board as you say the stroke description. Model skywriting **V** in the air as you repeat the stroke description. Have students say the stroke description as they use their index finger to write large **V**'s on their desktop.

2 Practice

Remind students to position their book and grip their pencil correctly for writing.

Ask students to begin at the green dot and carefully trace the shaded letters on student page 108 with pencil. Then have them write the letters, words, and sentence on the page.

Remind students that when they come to this symbol , they should stop writing and circle their best letter, joining, or word.

3 Evaluate

Tell students it is important to make their writing easy for others to read.

Use these questions to help students evaluate their writing:

- Is your **V** about the same size as the model?
- Is the bottom of your **V** round?

Extra Practice

Practice Masters 59, 94

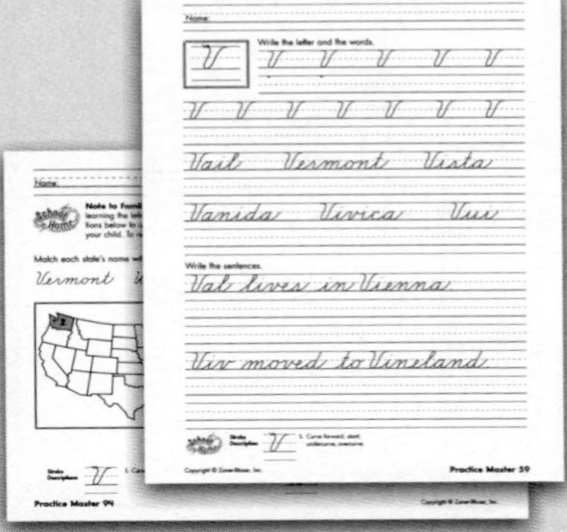

Support for
English Language Learners

Using the Apostrophe Some students may need help understanding the use of the apostrophe in **Valentine's Day**. First, point out that on this holiday, people exchange cards called valentines. In this use, **valentines** is a plural noun and has no apostrophe before the **s**. Provide other examples of plural nouns, such as *cards*.

In **Valentine's Day,** however, the word **Valentine's** tells the name of the person the holiday was named after—Saint Valentine. We think of it as a day "for" him or "belonging to" him, so we use the apostrophe and **s** to show possession. Provide other examples of possessive nouns, such as **Mark's** *cards*.

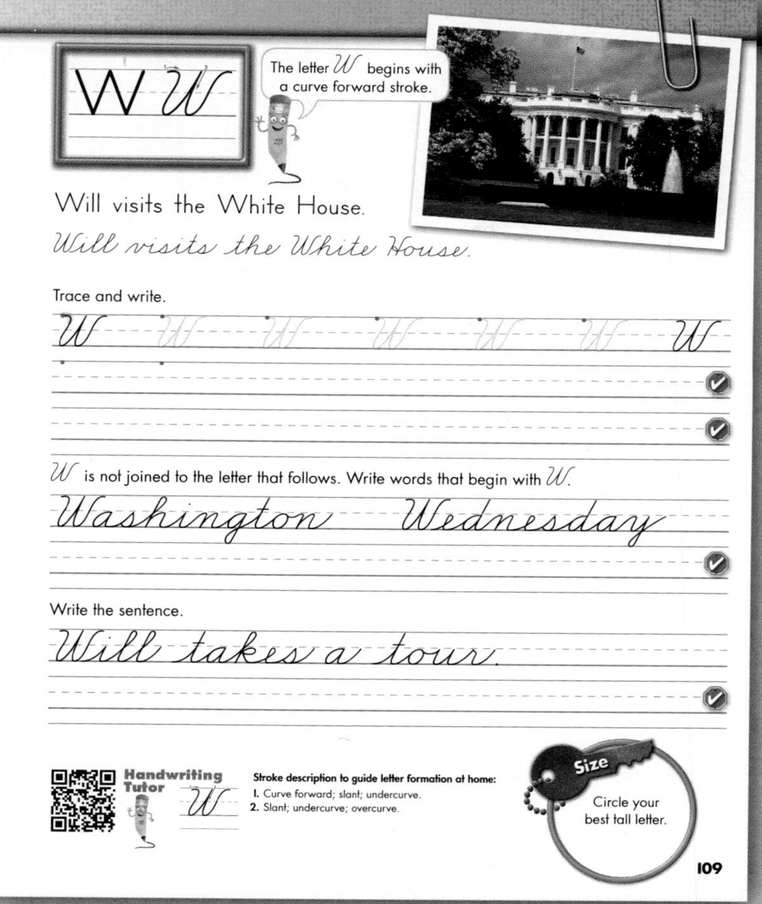
The letter *W* begins with a curve forward stroke.

Will visits the White House.

Will visits the White House.

Trace and write.

W W W W W W W

W is not joined to the letter that follows. Write words that begin with *W*.

Washington Wednesday

Write the sentence.

Will takes a tour.

Handwriting Tutor

Stroke description to guide letter formation at home:
1. Curve forward; slant; undercurve.
2. Slant; undercurve; overcurve.

Size

Circle your best tall letter.

109

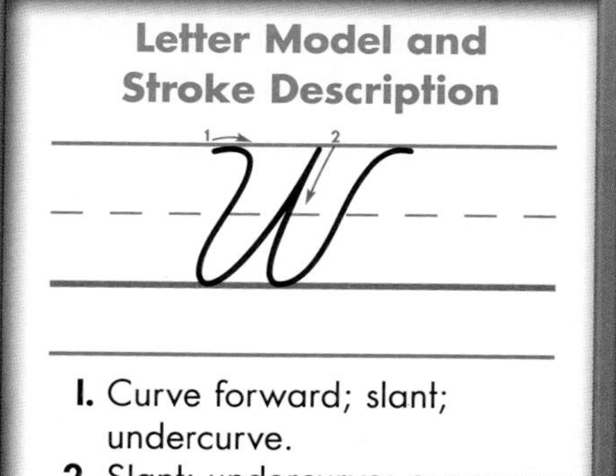
Letter Model and Stroke Description

1. Curve forward; slant; undercurve.
2. Slant; undercurve; overcurve.

Objective: To practice writing uppercase cursive **W**.

1 Model

Talk about cursive **W**. Ask:

- Where does **W** begin? *(just below the headline)*
- How many undercurves are in **W**? *(two)*

Write cursive **W** on guidelines on the board as you say the stroke description. Use skywriting to model writing **W** in the air as you repeat the stroke description. Have students say the stroke description as they use their index finger to write large **W**'s on their desktop.

2 Practice

Remind students to position their book and grip their pencil correctly for writing.

Ask students to begin at the green dot and carefully trace the shaded letters on student page 109 with pencil. Then have them write the letters, words, and sentence on the page.

Remind students that when they come to this symbol ✓, they should stop writing and circle their best letter, joining, or word.

3 Evaluate

Tell students it is important to make their writing easy for others to read. Remind them to complete all **Stop and Check** activities.

Proper size makes each letter easy to read. Ask:

- Is your **W** about the same width as the model?
- Does your **W** touch the headline three times?

Tips From an Occupational Therapist

Focusing With Music Some students have a hard time maintaining concentration while writing. **Rhythmic activities can help stimulate the nervous system and keep students focused.** After modeling instructions for a lesson, try playing music while students are practicing and writing. Choose jazz or classical music with an obvious, simple rhythm that is not too fast. Avoid music with lyrics so students are not distracted from the words they are writing.

Extra Practice

Practice Masters 60, 94

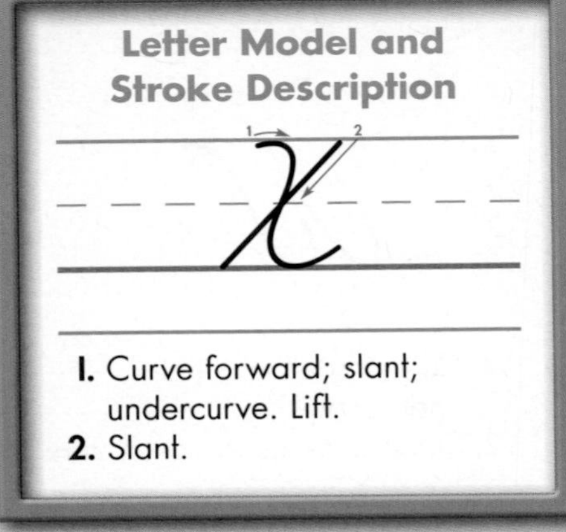
Letter Model and Stroke Description
1. Curve forward; slant; undercurve. Lift.
2. Slant.

Objective: To practice writing cursive uppercase **X**.

Handwriting Tutor

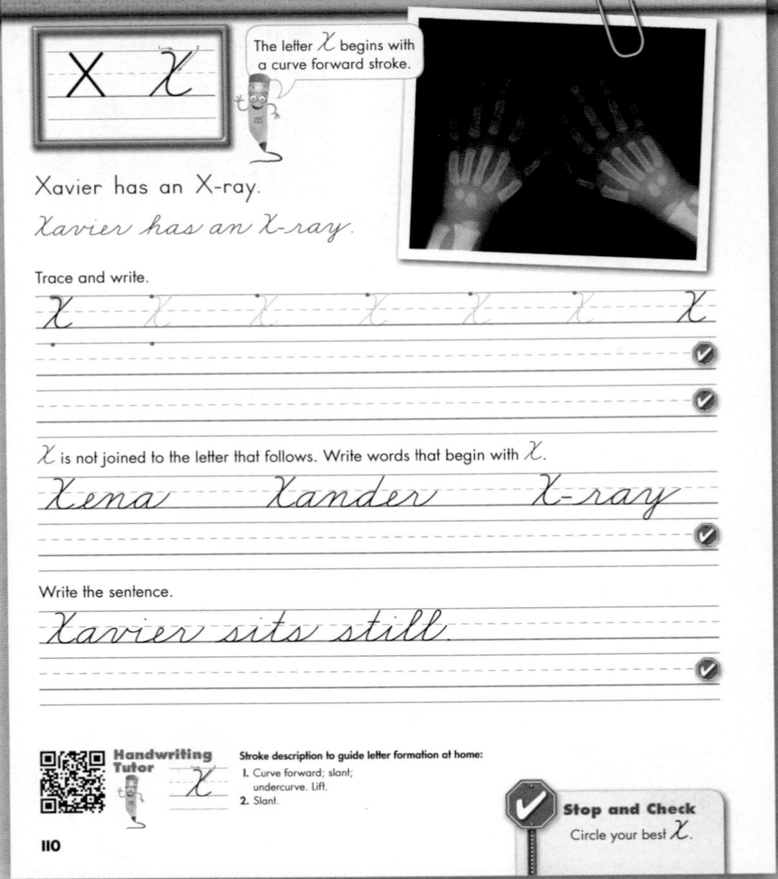
The letter X begins with a curve forward stroke.

Xavier has an X-ray.

Xavier has an X-ray.

Trace and write.

X is not joined to the letter that follows. Write words that begin with X.

Xena Xander X-ray

Write the sentence.

Xavier sits still.

Handwriting Tutor

Stroke description to guide letter formation at home:
1. Curve forward; slant; undercurve. Lift.
2. Slant.

Stop and Check
Circle your best X.

110

1 Model

Talk about cursive **X**. Ask:

- How does **X** begin? *(with a curve forward)*
- Where is the lift? *(after the undercurve)*

Write cursive **X** on guidelines as you say the stroke description. Use skywriting to model writing **X** in the air as you say the stroke description. Have students say the words as they use their index finger to write large **X**'s on the board.

2 Practice

Remind students to position their book and grip their pencil correctly for writing.

Ask students to begin at the green dot and carefully trace the shaded letters on student page 110 with pencil. Then have them write the letters, words, and sentence on the page.

Remind students that when they come to this symbol ✓, they should stop writing and circle their best letter, joining, or word.

3 Evaluate

Tell students it is important to make their writing easy for others to read. Remind them to complete all **Stop and Check** activities.

✓ **Use** these questions to help students evaluate their writing:

- Does your **X** rest on the baseline?
- Are your curve strokes smooth?

Extra Practice

Practice Masters 61, 95

Support for English Language Learners

The Sounds of x Help students understand that sometimes the letter **x** makes the /z/ sound, as in **Xavier, Xena,** and **Xander** on this page. (The word **X-ray**, however, does not follow this rule.) Write two lists of words on the board, one with words beginning with **x** that use the /z/ sound **(xylophone, Xena)** and the other with words that end in **x** in which the letter is pronounced as /x/ **(box, tax)**.

Joinings

Write the joinings.

Joining n and m

n and m are joined to the letter that follows. The undercurve ending must be wide enough to allow room for joining to the next letter.

Ne Mi No Ma My

Joining H and K

H and K are joined to the letter that follows. The loop in H swings across the letter and slightly down to allow room for joining to the next letter.

He Ki Ha Ko Hu

Joining U, Y, and Z

U, Y, and Z are joined to the letter that follows. The overcurve ending in Y and Z crosses at the baseline, then continues up and wide to form the next letter.

Ue Ya Zo Ye Zu

The cursive letters V, W, and X are not joined to the letter that follows.

Stop and Check Circle your three best joinings.

111

Objective: To write joinings.

1 Model

Talk about the joinings. Ask:

- What do **N, M, H, K, U, Y,** and **Z** have in common? *(They all join the letter that follows.)*
- Which letters are not joined to the letter that follows? *(**V, W,** and **X**)*

Write the different joinings on guidelines on the board as you say the stroke descriptions. Use skywriting as you model each. Have students skywrite with you.

Ask students to use their index finger to trace the joinings several times on student page 111.

2 Practice

Remind students to position their book and grip their pencil correctly for writing.

Ask students to write the letters and joinings on the page.

Remind students that when they come to this symbol ✓, they should stop writing and circle their best joining.

3 Evaluate

Tell students it is important to make their writing easy for others to read. Remind them to complete all **Stop and Check** activities.

✓ **Use** these questions to help students evaluate their joinings:

- Is the spacing between your letters consistent?
- Do your letters and joinings look like the models?

Using Technology

Optical Character Recognition (OCR) Explain that when handwritten ideas and writings are scanned to a computer, optical character recognition (or OCR) "recognizes" what the person has written and can convert it to text for use in a digital format. To go a step further, handwriting recognition software allows writers to use a stylus to handwrite directly onto a tablet or touchpad. Discuss how these technologies might not work if the writer's handwriting is not legible. If time permits, have students experiment with OCR and handwriting recognition software to test the readability of their cursive handwriting.

Review

Objective: To review uppercase cursive letters beginning with a curve forward stroke: **N, M, H, K, U, Y, Z, V, W,** and **X**.

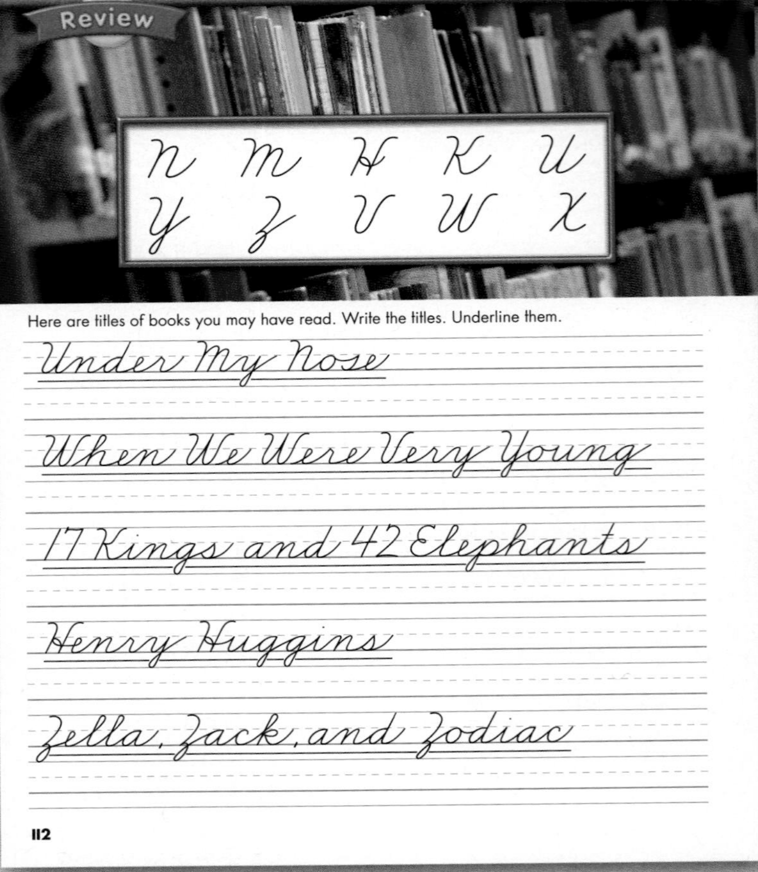

Review
N M H K U
Y Z V W X
Here are titles of books you may have read. Write the titles. Underline them.
Under My Nose
When We Were Very Young
17 Kings and 42 Elephants
Henry Huggins
Zella, Zack, and Zodiac
112

1 Review

Review the stroke descriptions and model any letters students might be having difficulty writing.

Ask a volunteer to give a verbal description of one of the letters. Challenge the other students to identify the letter being described and then write it on guidelines on the board.

See the **Corrective Strategies** in the Appendix for techniques in correcting common problems in your students' handwriting.

2 Practice

Remind students to position their book and grip their pencil correctly for writing.

Ask students to carefully write the titles on student page 112. Remind students to underline each title and leave space for margins.

3 Evaluate

Tell students it is important to make their writing easy for others to read.

 **Use** these questions to help students evaluate their writing:

- Did you underline the book titles?
- Do your short letters touch both the midline and the baseline?
- Do your tall letters touch both the headline and the baseline?
- Do your short letters with descenders touch the headline of the next writing space?

Support for English Language Learners

Using Authentic Texts Authentic literature exposes students to American culture and teaches elements of language. Use authentic literature to teach those elements that best address students' needs. For example, if your focus is on pronunciation and intonation, read the story aloud. When choosing a story, determine how much background you need to provide to make it intelligible. Allow students to read the story in their native language first. Reading in a student's first language builds comprehension. Then when students read the story in English, they can focus on fluency rather than decoding.

Digital Tools

Go Online Printables and other free classroom resources are available at **resources.zaner-bloser.com/hw**.

Application

Writing a Book Review

Henry Huggins meets a funny dog. He likes the dog right away. While on their way to Henry's house, they have lots of adventures. What a great book! You should read it.

Complete this book review in *cursive* handwriting. Leave room for margins.

Title: Henry Huggins
Author: Beverly Cleary
What Happened:

Stop and Check
Circle your best uppercase letter.

Application

Writing a Book Review

Objective: To write a book review using complete sentences and appropriate margins.

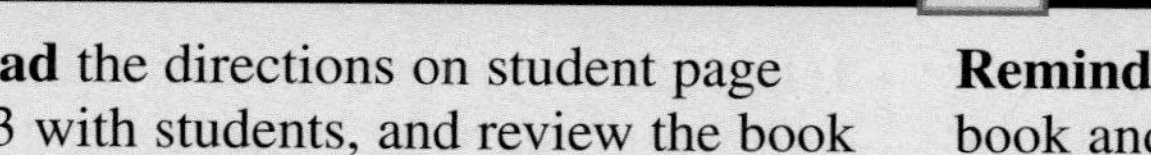

1 Review

Read the directions on student page 113 with students, and review the book review.

Write several words from the student page on the board. Think aloud as you talk through the correct formation of several letters and joining strokes that connect uppercase to lowercase letters. Ask volunteers to evaluate the words according to the Keys to Legibility.

2 Practice

Remind students to position their book and grip their pencil correctly for writing.

Ask students to carefully copy the book review on student page 113 and pay close attention to margins.

3 Evaluate

Tell students it is important to make their writing easy for others to read.

Use these questions to help students evaluate their writing:

- Do your letters look like the models?
- Is each letter the correct size?
- Are your letters, words, and sentences properly spaced?
- Is your slant correct?

Writing in the Content Areas

Response to Literature Ask students to think about a book they have recently finished reading. Have them write a response to literature. Make sure they include the title of the book (underlined) and author's name in the first paragraph of their reviews. They should also describe the characters and the setting and give a summary of the plot. Have them include another paragraph telling whether they like the book and several reasons to support their opinion. Remind students to use their best cursive handwriting.

Cursive Writing

In the Real World

Objective: To practice writing a phone message legibly.

Cursive Writing

In the Real World

Learning cursive will help you write more quickly. This can be good for writing a phone message. Write this note in your best cursive writing.

The more you practice writing in cursive, the easier it will be!

A lady named Val called. Do you want to join the exercise group? Bring a friend along. Call 555-9843. She is in a hurry to sign people up. Look at the website for an example of the exercises you'll do.

114

1 Model

Present the activity. Explain to students that we sometimes need to write quickly, before we forget something or lose a thought. Writing quickly is important when taking a phone message, but so is writing legibly—others need to be able to read what you have written.

Read aloud the first sentence on student page 114. Then use skywriting to model writing one word from the sentence.

2 Practice

Remind students to position their book and grip their pencil correctly for writing.

Ask students to carefully write the note on the page.

3 Evaluate

Tell students it is important to make their writing easy for others to read.

Use these questions to help students evaluate their writing:

- Did you write with correct strokes so your letters have good shape?
- Did you use the guidelines to make letters with correct size?
- Do your uppercase letters join with the following letters properly?
- Did you write with consistent slant?

Support for English Language Learners

Note Taking Help students develop the skill of taking notes or writing down important information while someone is speaking. Organize students into pairs. Have one student play the role of speaker and the other of note-taker. Give speakers a few note cards with sentences, such as the following:

- **Please call Terry at 309-555-2985.**
- **Can Uncle John borrow your drill?**
- **Pick up Tom at 4:30.**

Have speakers say the messages at a normal pace while the note-takers write them down. After a few tries, have students reverse roles.

Manuscript Maintenance

On most forms, you see the words **Please print**.
Use manuscript to complete the information form below.

Handwriting Tutor

School Library
Information Form

Please print.

Name ______________________

Grade ______________________

Favorite book ______________________

Write which kinds of books you like to read.

history | science fiction | biography
mystery | folktales | plays

Check how many books you would like to take out each week.

☐1 ☐2 ☐3 ☐4

How many times a week do you like to visit the library?

On which day would you like to come for reading club?

115

Manuscript Maintenance

Objective: To practice filling out a form using manuscript writing.

1 Model

Have students look at the writing they did on student page 114. Review the stroke descriptions, and model any letters or joinings students might be having difficulty with. Refer students to the Cursive and Manuscript alphabets on student pages 22 and 23 for more guidance.

2 Practice

Have students fill in the form on student page 115 with their own information. Remind students to form their letters and numerals carefully so they will be legible. Point out that the guidelines on this form have only a baseline, not a headline or a midline.

3 Evaluate

Tell students it is important to make their writing easy for others to read.

✓ **Use** these questions to help students evaluate their writing:

- Did you write with correct strokes so your letters and numerals have good shape?
- Did you write letters and numerals with good size to fit the writing space?
- Did you allow good spacing?
- Did you maintain good vertical slant?

Tips From an Occupational Therapist

Tennis Practice This activity will help students develop strong wrists, which are important for stabilization while writing. Bring a tennis racket and a tennis ball into class. Have students take turns trying to balance the ball on the racket. They should hold the racket flat and in front of them, about chest-high. Have them hold the racket steady for about a minute so the ball doesn't fall off.

Keys to Legibility

Shape
Shape describes the strokes that form each letter and give it a unique appearance.

Size
Size describes the height of letters.

Spacing
Spacing describes the space between letters, words, and sentences.

Slant
Slant refers to the angle of writing on the paper.

Objective: To practice the four Keys to Legibility.

Keys to Legibility
Slant
Spacing
Size
Shape
Write the paragraph about the sun.
Make your writing easy to read. Pay attention to the margins.
Earth circles the sun.
Our sun is a large star.
A star is a really hot
ball of gas that gives off
light and heat.
116

Handwriting Coach

Keys to Legibility

Pressure Point Encourage discussion about how hard to push on the point of a pencil when writing. List disadvantages of using too much or too little pressure. *(Writing that is too light or too dark may be illegible. Too much pressure may tear the paper.)*

Ask students to experiment with different amounts of writing pressure and describe the ideal amount of pressure to exert. Explain that the pencil should not be gripped or squeezed. The pressure should be light and easy, but the pencil must press the paper firmly enough to produce legible writing.

Invite volunteers to show samples of smooth, even writing that has been written with the correct amount of pressure.

1 Review

Remind students that good handwriting is legible handwriting. The most important thing to remember is that readers must be able to read a message in order to understand its meaning.

Brainstorm with students a list of errors they commonly make in their handwriting. Write responses on the board. These might include not making descenders go below the baseline, or writing letters that are too large or too small.

Point out to students which of the Keys to Legibility they can apply to each of these common errors.

2 Practice

Remind students to position their book and to grip their pencil correctly for writing.

Ask students to carefully write the paragraph within the margins on student page 116. Then have students write their own paragraph on student page 117. Remind them to leave space for margins.

Support for English Language Learners

Additional Writing Practice As their knowledge of English increases, students can begin extended writing tasks. Appropriate activities include writing about a field trip, retelling a story, and creating original stories, poems, and descriptions.

Write your own paragraph about the sun.
Be sure to leave space for margins.

Our sun is very important because

Is your writing easy to read?

Shape Circle your best letter that has a downcurve beginning.

Size Circle your best tall letter.

Spacing Circle two words that have space for \ between them.

Slant Circle a word you wrote that has good slant.

117

3 Evaluate

Tell students it is important to make their writing easy for others to read.

Use these questions to help students evaluate their writing:

- Does each letter have its own clear shape?
- Are tall letters the same height?
- Are short letters the same height?
- Are letters neither too close together nor too far apart?
- Does your writing have good slant?

Tips From an Occupational Therapist

Stacking Cubes To help students refine wrist, thumb, and finger interaction as well as increase hand-eye coordination, try this activity: Have students hold a pencil cap eraser with the thumb and index finger of each hand (make sure thumbs are on top). Ask students to use the open ends of the cap eraser to grip a small cube, such as a counting block. The goal is to stack and then unstack ten cubes.

Overcurve and Doublecurve Letters

Objective: To practice writing overcurve and doublecurve strokes.

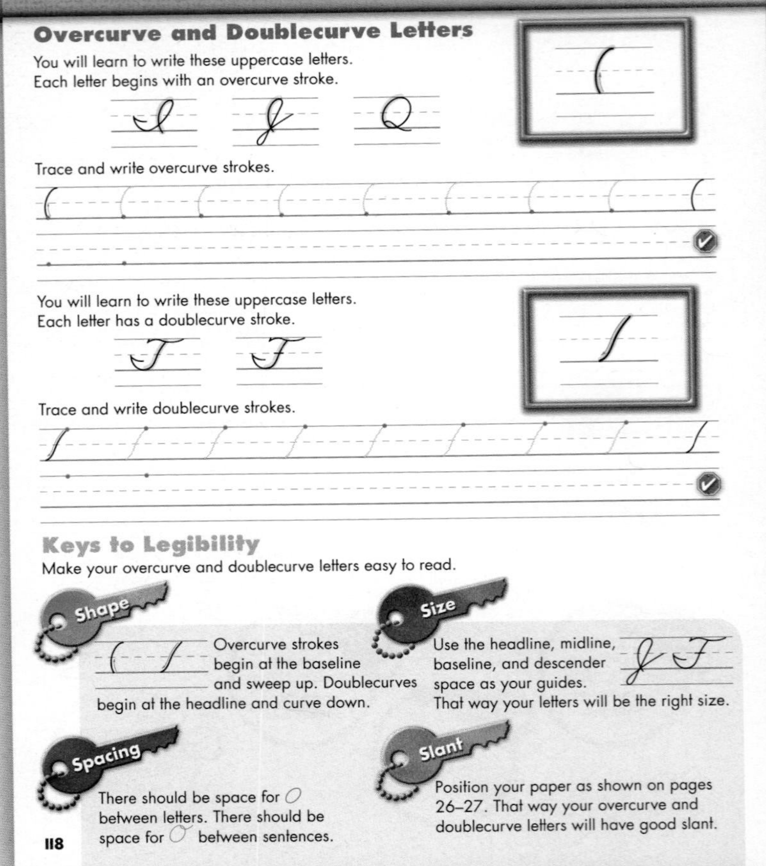

Overcurve and Doublecurve Letters

You will learn to write these uppercase letters.
Each letter begins with an overcurve stroke.

Trace and write overcurve strokes.

You will learn to write these uppercase letters.
Each letter has a doublecurve stroke.

Trace and write doublecurve strokes.

Keys to Legibility

Make your overcurve and doublecurve letters easy to read.

Shape Overcurve strokes begin at the baseline and sweep up. Doublecurves begin at the headline and curve down.

Size Use the headline, midline, baseline, and descender space as your guides. That way your letters will be the right size.

Spacing There should be space for O between letters. There should be space for O between sentences.

Slant Position your paper as shown on pages 26–27. That way your overcurve and doublecurve letters will have good slant.

118

1 Model

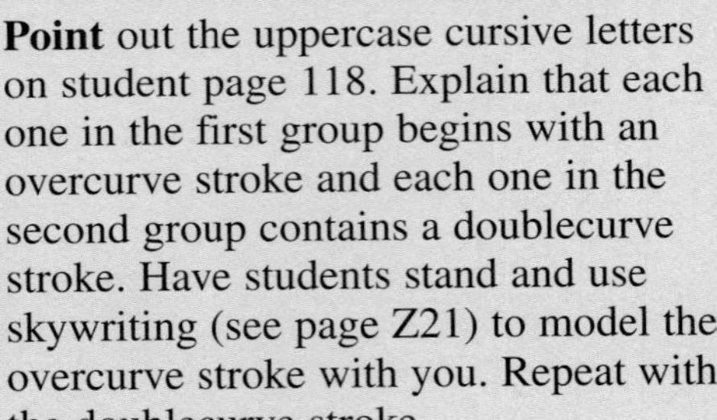

Point out the uppercase cursive letters on student page 118. Explain that each one in the first group begins with an overcurve stroke and each one in the second group contains a doublecurve stroke. Have students stand and use skywriting (see page Z21) to model the overcurve stroke with you. Repeat with the doublecurve stroke.

2 Practice

Remind students to position their book and grip their pencil correctly for writing.

Have students begin at the green dot and carefully trace the shaded strokes with pencil. Then have them write the overcurve strokes on the guidelines. Repeat with the doublecurve strokes.

Remind students that when they come to this symbol ✔, they should stop writing and circle their best overcurve stroke and doublecurve stroke.

3 Evaluate

Draw attention to the letters and the Keys to Legibility. The Spacing Key gives them a model for evaluating the spacing between letters and sentences.

Point out to students the four keys on student page 118. Remind them to pay attention to all four keys as they write, in order to have legible handwriting.

Support for
English Language Learners

Stroke Descriptions Students will benefit from hearing the stroke descriptions as you use them to write uppercase overcurve and doublecurve letters. Model strokes for students on the board while describing them aloud. Have students say the stroke descriptions with you as you write each letter.

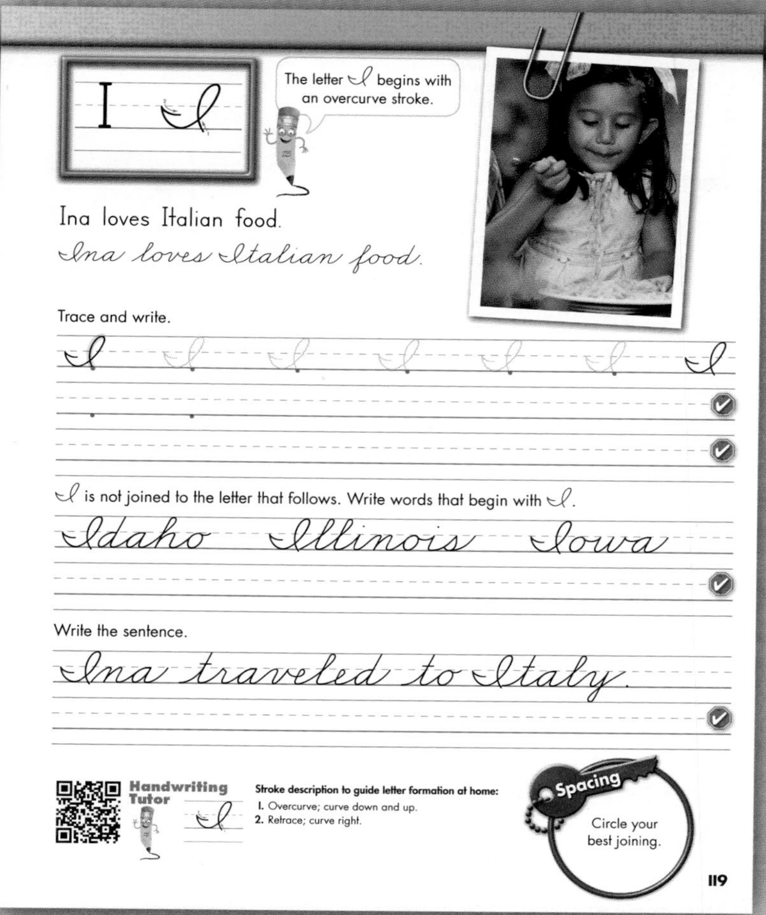

I *I*

The letter *I* begins with an overcurve stroke.

Ina loves Italian food.

Ina loves Italian food.

Trace and write.

I I I I I I I

I is not joined to the letter that follows. Write words that begin with *I*.

Idaho Illinois Iowa

Write the sentence.

Ina traveled to Italy.

Handwriting Tutor

Stroke description to guide letter formation at home:
1. Overcurve; curve down and up.
2. Retrace; curve right.

Spacing

Circle your best joining.

119

Letter Model and Stroke Description

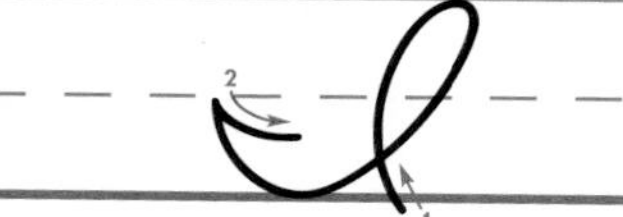

1. Overcurve; curve down and up.
2. Retrace; curve right.

Objective: To practice writing uppercase cursive **I**.

1 Model

Talk about uppercase cursive **I**. Ask:

- Where does **I** begin? *(just below the baseline)*
- Where is the pause in **I**? *(at the midline, before the retrace)*

Write cursive **I** on guidelines as you say the stroke description. Use skywriting (see page Z21) to model writing **I** in the air. Have students stand and say the stroke description with you as they write **I** in the air. Ask students to use their finger to trace cursive **I** several times on student page 119.

2 Practice

Remind students to position their book and grip their pencil correctly for writing.

Ask students to begin at the green dot and carefully trace the shaded letters with pencil. Then have them write the letters, words, and sentence on the page.

Remind students that when they come to this symbol ✓, they should stop writing and circle their best letter, joining, or word.

3 Evaluate

Tell students it is important to make their writing easy for others to read. Remind them to complete all **Stop and Check** activities.

Proper spacing makes each letter easy to read. Ask:

- Did you use proper spacing between letters and words?
- Where is your best joining?

Writing in the Content Areas

Math

Writing About Distance Tell students they are going to plan a trip itinerary that includes several of the locations listed on page 119. Locate a distance calculator program or application online. Have partners enter two locations to find the distance between them. Then have them find the distance to a third location. Have partners write a short **informative/explanatory** paragraph about their itinerary, including the location names and the distances between each. As a concluding sentence, have students tell how many total miles (or nautical miles or kilometers) they would travel. Remind students to use their best cursive handwriting.

Extra Practice

Practice Masters 62, 95

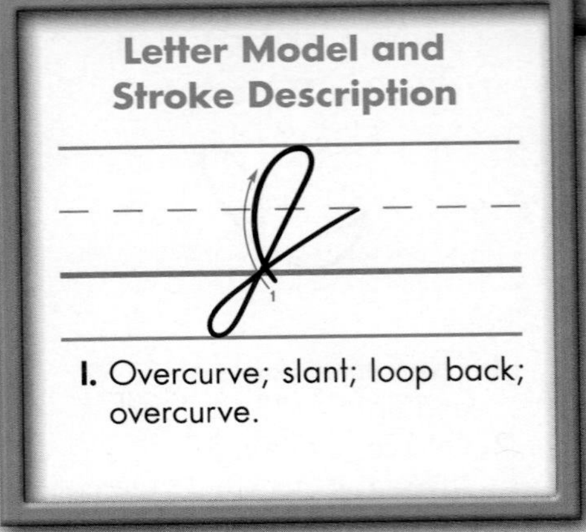

Objective: To practice writing uppercase cursive **J**.

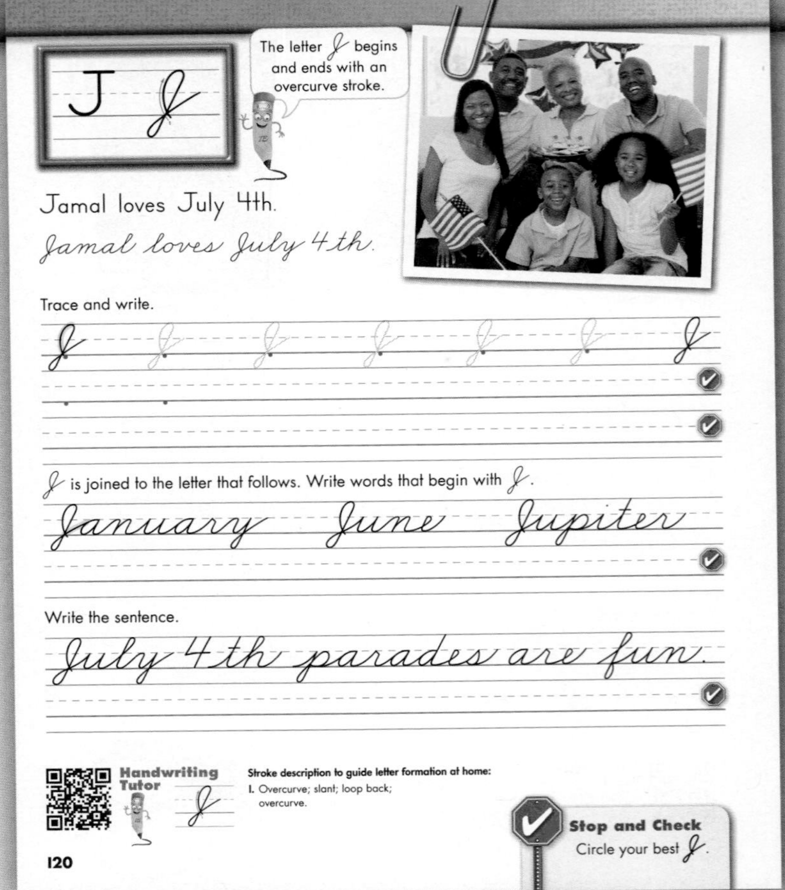

The letter J begins and ends with an overcurve stroke.
Jamal loves July 4th.
Jamal loves July 4th.
Trace and write.
J is joined to the letter that follows. Write words that begin with J.
January June Jupiter
Write the sentence.
July 4th parades are fun.
Handwriting Tutor
Stroke description to guide letter formation at home:
1. Overcurve; slant; loop back; overcurve.
Stop and Check
Circle your best J.
120

1 Model

Talk about uppercase cursive **J**. Ask:

- Where does **J** begin? *(just below the baseline)*
- Where do the two loops close? *(near the baseline)*

Write cursive **J** on guidelines on the board as you say the stroke description. Model skywriting **J** in the air. Have students say the stroke description as they use their index finger to trace **J** several times on student page 120.

2 Practice

Remind students to position their book and grip their pencil correctly for writing.

Ask students to begin at the green dot and carefully trace the shaded letters with pencil. Then have them write the letters, words, and sentence on the page.

Remind students that when they come to this symbol ✓, they should stop writing and circle their best letter, joining, or word.

3 Evaluate

Tell students it is important to make their writing easy for others to read. Remind them to complete all **Stop and Check** activities.

✓ **Use** these questions to help students evaluate their cursive **J**:

- Do the loops of your **J** close near the baseline?
- Does your first overcurve touch the headline?
- Does your descender fill the descender space and touch the next headline?

Extra Practice

Practice Masters 63, 96

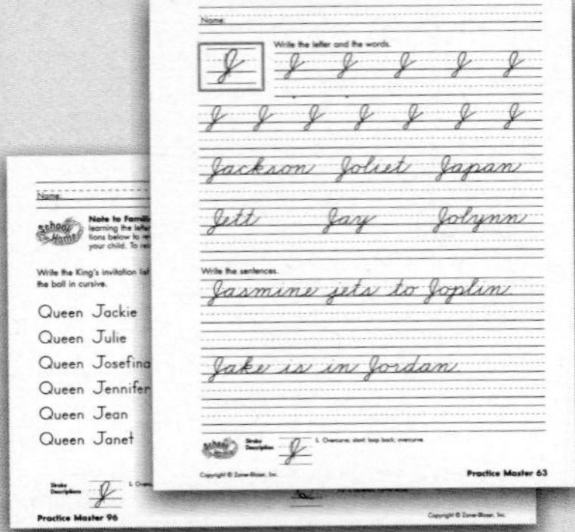

Support for English Language Learners

Additional Practice Write **January, June,** and **July** on the board. Say each month, and have students repeat after you. Invite one or more volunteers to say the remaining months of the year. Encourage students to say the months of the year in their first language as they point to the corresponding months listed on the board.

The letter Q begins with an overcurve stroke.

Quinn saw Queensland.

Quinn saw Queensland.

Trace and write.

Q is not joined to the letter that follows. Write words that begin with Q.

Quentin Quimby Quito

Write the sentence.

Where is Queensland?

Handwriting Tutor

Stroke description to guide letter formation at home:
I. Curve back; overcurve; curve down; retrace; curve forward; curve under.

Slant

Circle a word you wrote that has good slant.

121

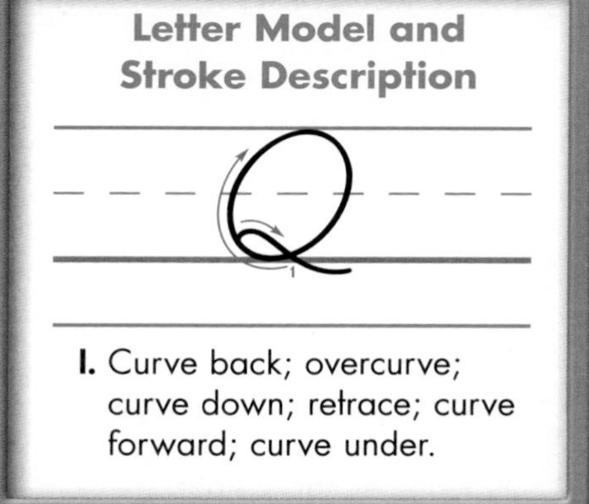

Letter Model and Stroke Description
I. Curve back; overcurve; curve down; retrace; curve forward; curve under.

Objective: To practice writing uppercase cursive **Q**.

Handwriting Tutor

1 Model

Talk about uppercase cursive **Q**. Ask:

- Where does **Q** begin? *(at the baseline)*
- How does **Q** end? *(with a curve under)*

Write cursive **Q** on guidelines on the board as you say the stroke description. Use skywriting to model writing **Q** in the air. Have students stand and say the stroke description with you as they write **Q** in the air. Ask students to use their finger to trace cursive **Q** several times on student page 121.

2 Practice

Remind students to position their book and grip their pencil correctly for writing.

Ask students to begin at the green dot and carefully trace the shaded letters with pencil. Then have them write the letters, words, and sentence on the page.

Remind students that when they come to this symbol ✓, they should stop writing and circle their best letter, joining, or word.

3 Evaluate

Tell students it is important to make their writing easy for others to read. Remind them to complete all **Stop and Check** activities.

Proper slant makes each letter easy to read. Ask:

- Does your **Q** have correct forward slant?
- Do all your letters have consistent slant?

Tips From an Occupational Therapist

Going Fishing Playing with toys that stick together can help strengthen finger muscles, improve dexterity, and develop fine motor control. Magnetic fishing toys can be made by tying one end of a string to a dowel rod and the other end to a magnet. For the pond, place packing peanuts in a dishpan. Mix a few iron or steel objects with the packing peanuts (bolts, nuts, paper clips, and so on). For fun, you might tape a picture of a fish to each of the magnetic objects. Then have students fish for objects by holding the fishing rod and lowering the magnet into the pond.

Extra Practice

Practice Masters 64, 96

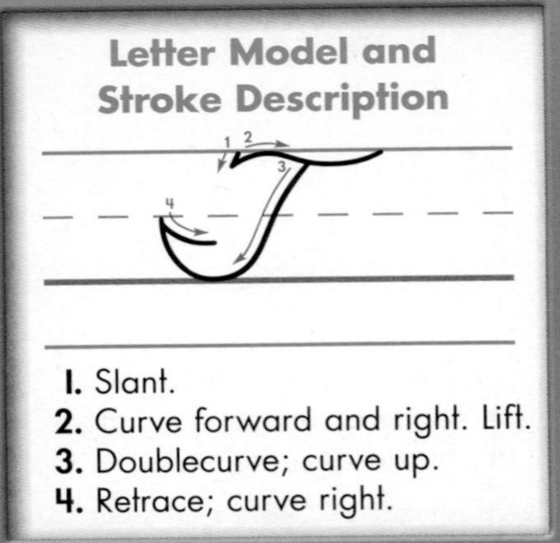

Objective: To practice writing uppercase cursive **T**.

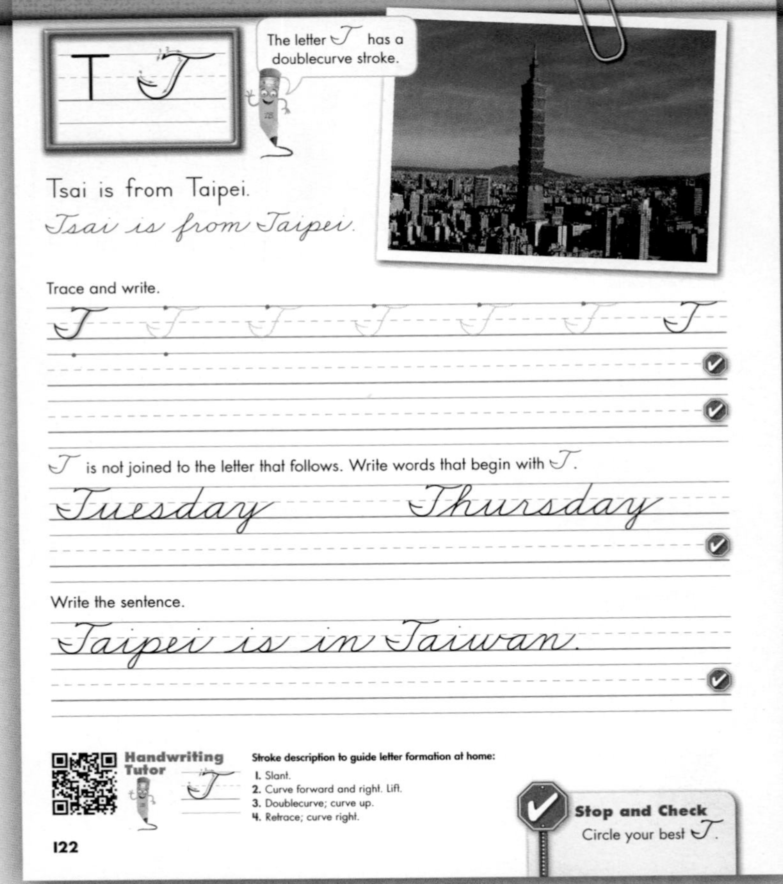

The letter T has a doublecurve stroke.

Tsai is from Taipei.

Tsai is from Taipei.

Trace and write.

T T T T T T T

T is not joined to the letter that follows. Write words that begin with T.

Tuesday Thursday

Write the sentence.

Taipei is in Taiwan.

Handwriting Tutor

Stroke description to guide letter formation at home:

1. Slant.
2. Curve forward and right. Lift.
3. Doublecurve; curve up.
4. Retrace; curve right.

Stop and Check
Circle your best T.

122

1 Model

Talk about cursive **T**. Ask:

- Where does **T** begin? *(at the headline)*
- What is the first stroke in **T**? *(slant)*

Write cursive **T** on guidelines on the board as you say the stroke description. Use skywriting to model writing **T** in the air. Have students stand and say the stroke description with you as they write cursive **T** in the air. Ask students to use their finger to trace **T** several times on student page 122.

2 Practice

Remind students to position their book and grip their pencil correctly for writing.

Ask students to begin at the green dot and carefully trace the shaded letters with pencil. Then have them write the letters, words, and sentence on the page.

Remind students that when they come to this symbol ✓, they should stop writing and circle their best letter, joining, or word.

3 Evaluate

Tell students it is important to make their writing easy for others to read. Remind them to complete all **Stop and Check** activities.

✓ **Use** these questions to help students evaluate their cursive **T**:

- Does your **T** begin at the headline?
- Does your last stroke curve right?

Extra Practice

Practice Masters 65, 97

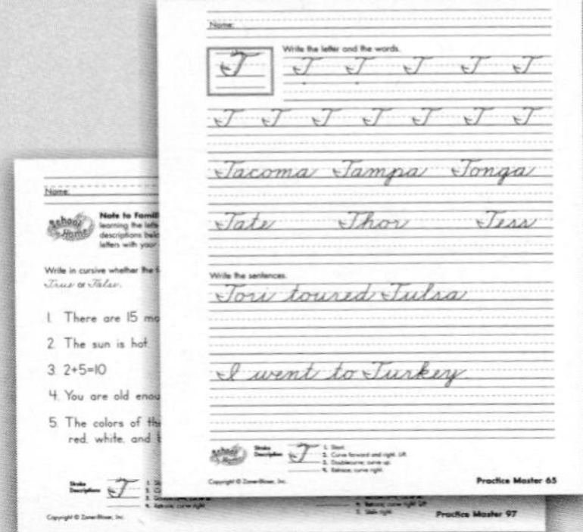

Support for English Language Learners

Additional Practice Write **Tuesday** and **Thursday** on the board. Say each word, and have students repeat them. Invite one or more volunteers to say the days of the week, beginning with **Sunday,** and add them to the board. Encourage students to say the days of the week in their native language as they point to the corresponding days listed on the board. Ask students to write the names of the days that begin with **T**.

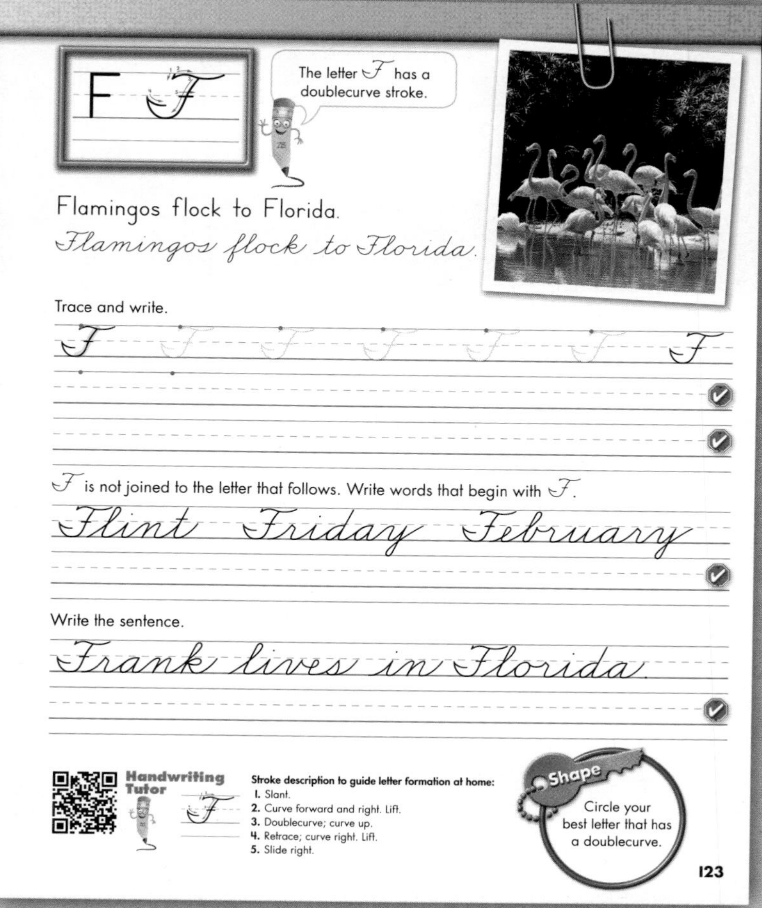

F F

Flamingos flock to Florida.

Flamingos flock to Florida.

Trace and write.

F F F F F F F

F is not joined to the letter that follows. Write words that begin with F.

Flint Friday February

Write the sentence.

Frank lives in Florida.

Handwriting Tutor

Stroke description to guide letter formation at home:
1. Slant.
2. Curve forward and right. Lift.
3. Doublecurve; curve up.
4. Retrace; curve right. Lift.
5. Slide right.

Shape

Circle your best letter that has a doublecurve.

123

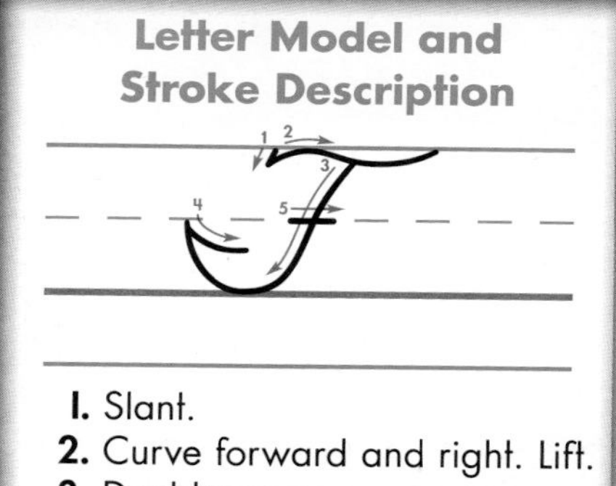

1. Slant.
2. Curve forward and right. Lift.
3. Doublecurve; curve up.
4. Retrace; curve right. Lift.
5. Slide right.

Objective: To practice writing uppercase cursive **F**.

1 Model

Talk about cursive **F**. Ask:

- How are **T** and **F** alike? *(There is a* ***T*** *in* ***F****.)*
- How are they different? *(In* ***F****, the last stroke is a slide right.)*

Write cursive **F** on guidelines on the board as you say the stroke description. Use skywriting to model writing **F** in the air. Have students stand and say the stroke description with you as they write **F** in the air. Ask students to use their finger to trace cursive **F** several times on student page 123.

2 Practice

Remind students to position their book and grip their pencil correctly for writing.

Ask students to begin at the green dot and carefully trace the shaded letters with pencil. Then have them write the letters, words, and sentence on the page.

Remind students that when they come to this symbol , they should stop writing and circle their best letter, joining, or word.

3 Evaluate

Tell students it is important to make their writing easy for others to read. Remind them to complete all **Stop and Check** activities.

Proper shape makes each letter easy to read. Ask:

- Does your **F** rest on the baseline?
- Is your slide right stroke at the midline?

Writing in the Content Areas

Compare and Contrast Sentences Have students look at the photo on page 122. Tell them the tall building they see in the photo is called Taipei 101 and that it is one of the tallest buildings in the world. Show photos of the world's five tallest buildings. List the names and heights of the buildings on the board. Have students write compare/contrast sentences using the information. For example, **The Burj Khalifa is over 2,700 feet tall. Taipei 101 is 1,100 feet shorter than the Burj Khalifa.** Remind students to use their best cursive handwriting.

School Home **Extra Practice**
Practice Masters 66, 97

Review

Objective: To review the uppercase cursive letters beginning with an overcurve: **I, J, Q**; and with a doublecurve: **T, F**.

Review

I J Q T F

Write the sentence.

I read about presidents.

Write these names of American presidents.

Third President: Thomas Jefferson

Sixth President: John Quincy Adams

Tenth President: John Tyler

Thirteenth President: Millard Fillmore

124

1 Review

Ask students what they remember about the shape of the letters **I, J, Q, T,** and **F**. *(**I, J,** and **Q** contain an overcurve; **T** and **F** contain a doublecurve.)*

Review any letters students might be having difficulty writing.

Ask a volunteer to give a verbal description of one of the letters. Challenge students to identify the letter being described and write it on guidelines on the board.

See the **Corrective Strategies** in the Appendix for techniques in correcting common problems in your students' handwriting.

2 Practice

Remind students to position their book and grip their pencil correctly for writing.

Ask students to carefully write the sentence and the names of the presidents on student page 124. Remind them to form letters with correct shape and size and use good spacing.

3 Evaluate

Tell students it is important to make their writing easy for others to read.

Use these questions to help students evaluate their writing:

- Did you write with correct strokes so your letters have good shape?
- Did you use the guidelines to make your letters with correct size?
- Are your letters and words written with good spacing?
- Do all your letters have consistent forward slant?

Digital Tools

Digital Resources for Handwriting Provides interactive tools, including videos, animated letter models, practice and evaluation tools, and games.

Support for English Language Learners

Letter Review Write the letters **I, J, Q, T, F** on the board. Point to each letter, and have students name a person or place that begins with each letter. Write their responses on the board. Say each word, and have students chorally repeat it after you. Encourage students to share words from their native language, as well as English.

Writing Facts

Application

Jupiter is a large planet.
Io is a moon of Jupiter.
Earth has one moon.
The sun is just a star.
Fixed stars are far off.
Quasars are big and shiny.

Write the facts about space in *cursive* handwriting. Leave room for margins.

Stop and Check
Circle your best word.

Application

Writing Facts

Objective: To practice writing factual sentences legibly.

1 Model

Write several words on the board from the sentences that begin with **I, J, Q, T,** and **F** on student page 125. Think aloud as you talk through the correct formation of several letters. Emphasize that **J** is the only letter in this grouping that joins to the letter that follows. Students should swing wide to join uppercase **J** to the letter that follows.

2 Practice

Remind students to position their book and grip their pencil correctly for writing.

Ask students to carefully write the sentences on student page 125 and pay close attention to margins. Remind them to write carefully with consistent slant and leave good spacing between their letters and words.

3 Evaluate

Tell students it is important to make their writing easy for others to read.

Use these questions to help students evaluate their writing:

- Do your letters have good shape?
- Do your short letters touch both the midline and the baseline?
- Do your tall letters touch both the headline and the baseline?
- Do your joining strokes make good spacing between your letters?
- Does your writing have good slant?

Using Technology

Collaborative Writing Have students use an online collaborative writing tool to produce a piece of writing as a group. For example, place students in groups of three and provide each group with information about a particular planet. Have students find out the planet's radius and mass, distance from the sun, rotation period, surface temperature, and number of moons. There are many easy-to-use tools for collaborative writing, some of which do not require software to be downloaded. Collaborative writing increases student participation, engages critical thinking, and combines the strengths of individual writers to produce a solid piece of writing. Have groups compare their planets.

Undercurve-Loop and Undercurve-Slant Letters

Undercurve-Loop and Undercurve-Slant Letters

You will learn to write these uppercase letters.
Each letter begins with an undercurve and a loop stroke.

Trace and write undercurve-loop strokes.

You will learn to write these uppercase letters.
Each letter begins with an undercurve and a slant stroke.

Trace and write undercurve-slant strokes.

Keys to Legibility

Make your undercurve-loop and undercurve-slant letters easy to read.

Shape An undercurve stroke can begin at the baseline or the midline.

Size Use the headline, midline, baseline, and descender space as your guides. That way your letters will be the right size.

Spacing R is joined to the letter that follows. Swing wide to join to the next letter. That way your letters will have good spacing.

Slant Cursive letters have a consistent forward slant.

126

1 Model

Point out the uppercase letters on page 126 of the student book. Explain that each letter in the first group begins with an undercurve-loop stroke and each letter in the second group begins with a undercurve-slant stroke. Talk about the shape of the undercurve stroke and how its motion relates to an upward counter-clockwise motion. Encourage students to use their index finger to trace several undercurve-loop and undercurve-slant strokes.

2 Practice

Remind students to position their book and grip their pencil correctly for writing.

Ask students to begin at the green dot and carefully trace the shaded undercurve-loop strokes with pencil. Then have them write undercurve-loop strokes on the guidelines. Repeat the exercise with the undercurve-slant stroke.

Remind students that when they come to this symbol ✓, they should stop writing and circle their best undercurve-loop and undercurve-slant strokes.

3 Evaluate

Tell students it is important to make their writing easy for others to read. Remind them to complete all **Stop and Check** activities.

Point out to students the four keys on student page 126. Remind them to pay attention to all four keys as they write, in order to have legible handwriting.

Support for

English Language Learners

Stroke Descriptions Students will benefit from hearing the stroke description as you use them to write the uppercase undercurve-loop and under-curve-slant letters. Model strokes for students on the board while describing them aloud. Have students say the stroke descriptions with you as you write each letter.

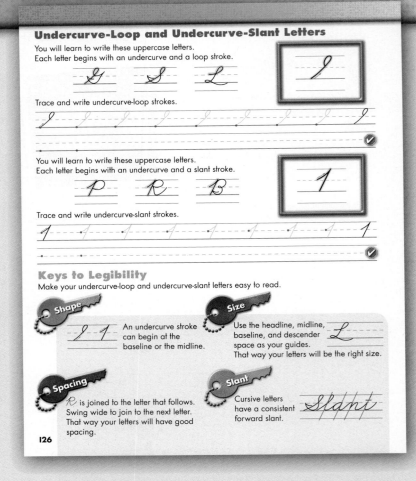

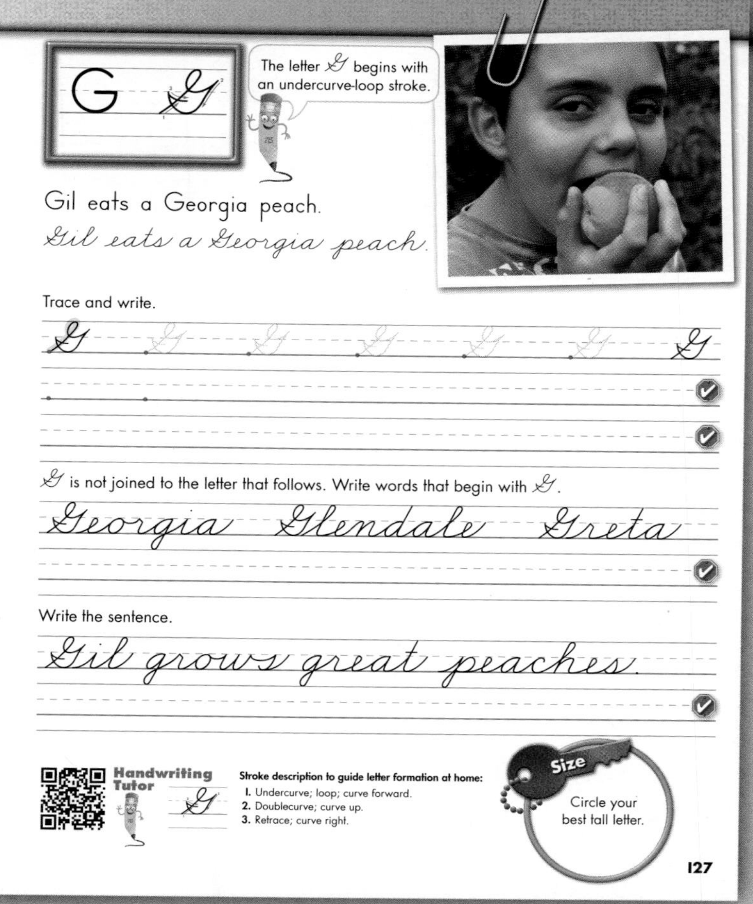

The letter *G* begins with an undercurve-loop stroke.

Gil eats a Georgia peach.

Gil eats a Georgia peach.

Trace and write.

G is not joined to the letter that follows. Write words that begin with *G*.

Georgia Glendale Greta

Write the sentence.

Gil grows great peaches.

Handwriting Tutor

Stroke description to guide letter formation at home:
1. Undercurve; loop; curve forward.
2. Doublecurve; curve up.
3. Retrace; curve right.

Size

Circle your best tall letter.

127

Letter Model and Stroke Description

1. Undercurve; loop; curve forward.
2. Doublecurve; curve up.
3. Retrace; curve right.

Objective: To practice writing uppercase cursive **G**.

Handwriting Tutor

1 Model

Talk about uppercase **G**. Ask:

- Where does **G** begin? *(at the baseline)*
- Where does the retrace begin? *(at the midline)*

Write cursive **G** on guidelines on the board as you say the stroke description. Use skywriting (see page Z21) to model writing **G** in the air. Have students stand and say the stroke description with you as they write **G** in the air. Ask students to use their finger to trace **G** several times on student page 127.

2 Practice

Remind students to position their book and grip their pencil correctly for writing.

Ask students to begin at the green dot and carefully trace the shaded letters with pencil. Then have them write the letters, words, and sentence on the page.

Remind students that when they come to this symbol ✓, they should stop writing and circle their best letter.

3 Evaluate

Tell students it is important to make their writing easy for others to read. Remind them to complete all **Stop and Check** activities.

Proper size makes each letter easy to read. Ask:

- Is your loop written from the headline to the midline?
- Is your **G** about the same size as the model?

Tips From an Occupational Therapist

Partner Stories This activity can be used to increase endurance and develop fine motor skills. Pair students, and have each pair create a story. The first student writes the beginning sentence on a sheet of paper and then gives the paper to his or her partner. The partner continues the story by adding a new sentence. The partners take turns until each student has written at least three sentences. Each pair may create an entire story if this activity is done several days in a row. Remind students to use legible handwriting so their finished story can be read by others. Allow students to draw pictures to accompany their story.

Extra Practice

Practice Masters 67, 98

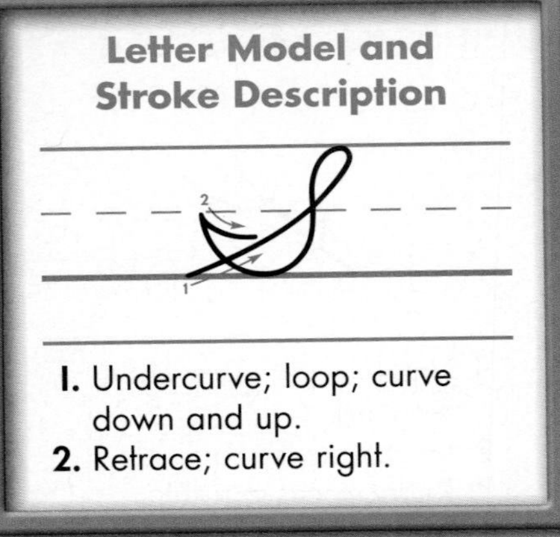
Letter Model and Stroke Description
1. Undercurve; loop; curve down and up.
2. Retrace; curve right.

Objective: To practice writing uppercase cursive **S**.

Handwriting Tutor

The letter S begins with an undercurve-loop stroke.
Summers are hot in San Antonio.
Summers are hot in San Antonio.
Trace and write.
S is not joined to the letter that follows. Write words that begin with S.
Saturday Sunday Sam
Write the sentence.
Sophie goes to the pool.
Handwriting Tutor
Stroke description to guide letter formation at home:
1. Undercurve; loop; curve down and up.
2. Retrace; curve right.
Stop and Check
Circle your best S.
128

1 Model

Talk about uppercase cursive **S**. Ask:

- Where does **S** begin? *(at the baseline)*
- How many loops are in **S**? *(one)*

Write cursive **S** on guidelines on the board as you say the stroke description. Use skywriting to model writing **S** in the air. Have students stand and say the stroke description with you as they write **S** in the air. Ask students to use their index finger to trace cursive **S** several times on student page 128.

2 Practice

Remind students to position their books and grip their pencil correctly for writing.

Ask students to begin at the green dot and carefully trace the shaded letters with pencil. Then have them write the letters, words, and sentence on the page.

Remind students that when they come to this symbol ✓, they should stop writing and circle their best letter, joining, or word.

3 Evaluate

Tell students it is important to make their writing easy for others to read. Remind them to complete all **Stop and Check** activities.

✓ **Use** these questions to help students evaluate their cursive **S**:

- Does your **S** have correct slant?
- Does your curve right stop before the undercurve?
- Does your loop close at the midline?

School Home

Extra Practice

Practice Masters 68, 98

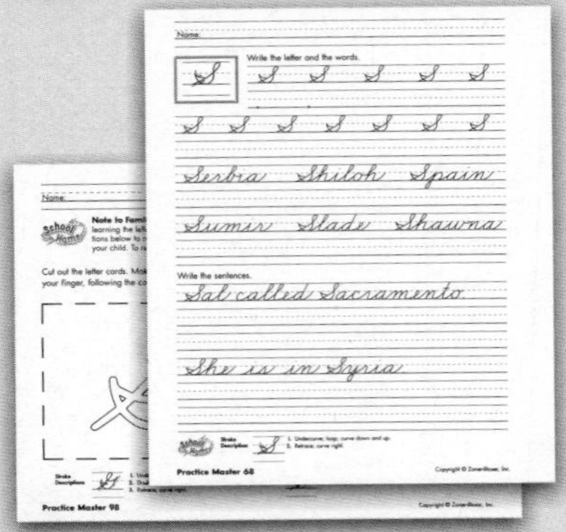
Serbia Shiloh Spain
Sumer Slade Shawna
Sal called Sacramento
She is in Syria
Practice Master 68
Practice Master 98

Support for English Language Learners

Additional Practice Write **Saturday** and **Sunday** on the board. Say each word, and have students repeat after you. Invite one or more volunteers to say the days of the week, beginning with **Sunday**. Encourage students to say the days of the week in their first language as they point to the days listed in English on the board. Invite students to think of things they do on Saturdays and Sundays that begin with the letter **s**.

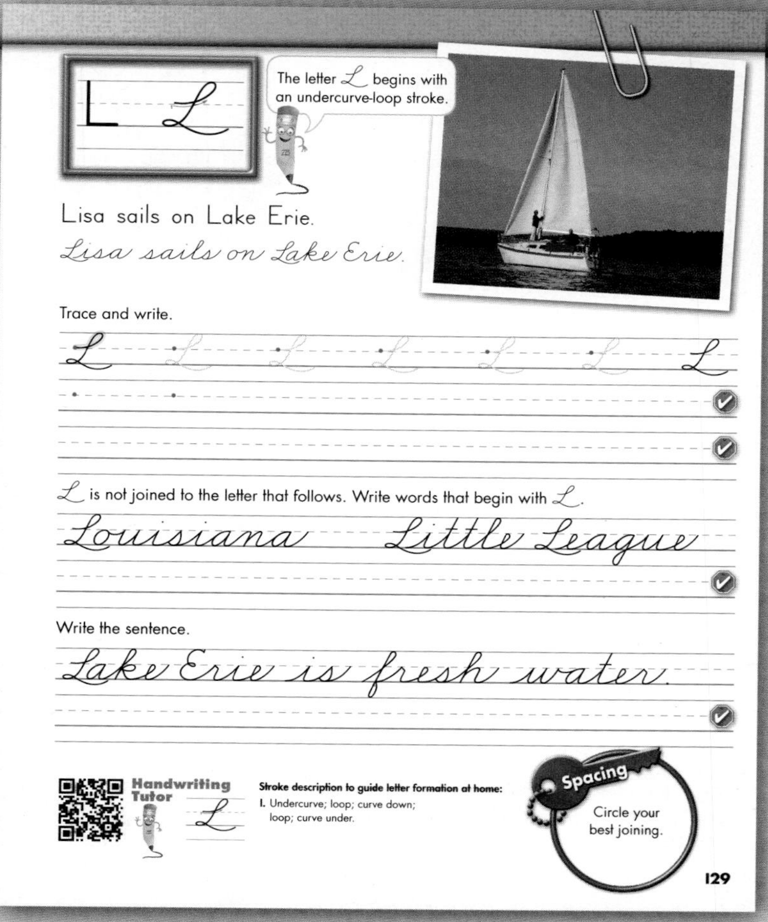

The letter L begins with an undercurve-loop stroke.
Lisa sails on Lake Erie.
Lisa sails on Lake Erie.
Trace and write.
L is not joined to the letter that follows. Write words that begin with L.
Louisiana Little League
Write the sentence.
Lake Erie is fresh water.
Handwriting Tutor
Stroke description to guide letter formation at home:
I. Undercurve; loop; curve down; loop; curve under.
Spacing
Circle your best joining.
129

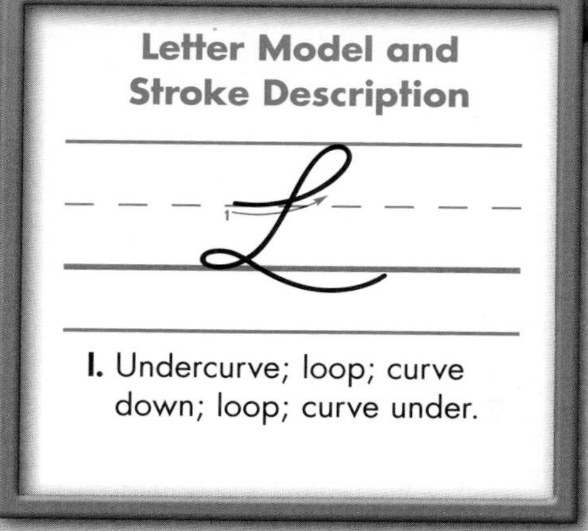

Objective: To practice writing uppercase cursive **L**.

1 Model

Talk about uppercase cursive **L**. Ask:

- How many loops are in **L**? *(two)*
- Where does **L** end? *(just below the baseline)*

Write cursive **L** on guidelines on the board as you say the stroke description. Use skywriting to model writing **L** in the air. Have students stand and say the stroke description with you as they write **L** in the air. Ask students to use their index finger to trace cursive **L** several times on student page 129.

2 Practice

Remind students to position their book and grip their pencil correctly for writing.

Ask students to begin at the green dot and carefully trace the shaded letters with pencil. Then have them write the letters, words, and sentence on the page.

Remind students that when they come to this symbol ✓, they should stop writing and circle their best letter, joining, or word.

3 Evaluate

Tell students it is important to make their writing easy for others to read. Remind them to complete all **Stop and Check** activities.

Proper spacing makes each letter easy to read. Ask:

- Did you use proper spacing between your letters and words?
- Is the spacing between your joinings consistent?

Writing in the Content Areas

Science

Explanatory Paragraph Tell students that Lake Erie is one of the five Great Lakes. Point out the Great Lakes on a map. Tell students that lakes are almost always bodies of fresh water and that all states have lakes. Some states have very few natural lakes while other states have thousands. Have students write an explanatory paragraph about lakes. They might write about how a natural lake was formed (*How was Lake Okeechobee formed?*), manmade vs. natural lakes (*Why are there so many manmade lakes in Ohio?*), or about the plants and animals that live in lakes (*What freshwater fish live in the lakes of Minnesota?*). Remind students to use their best cursive handwriting.

Extra Practice

Practice Masters 69, 99

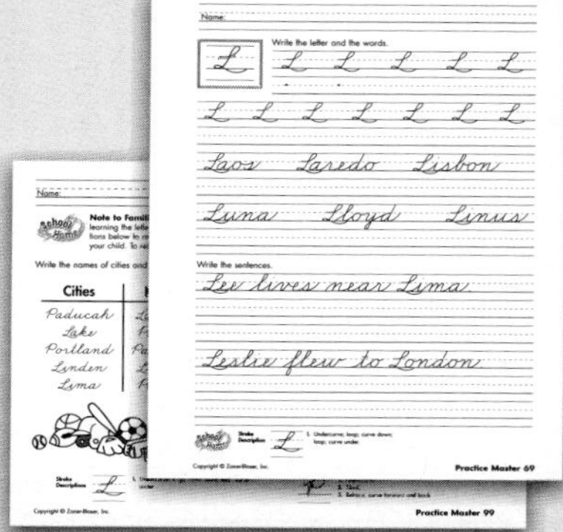

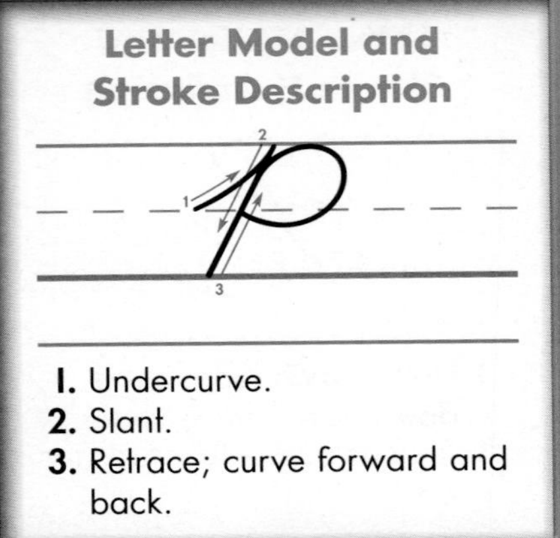

Objective: To practice writing uppercase cursive **P**.

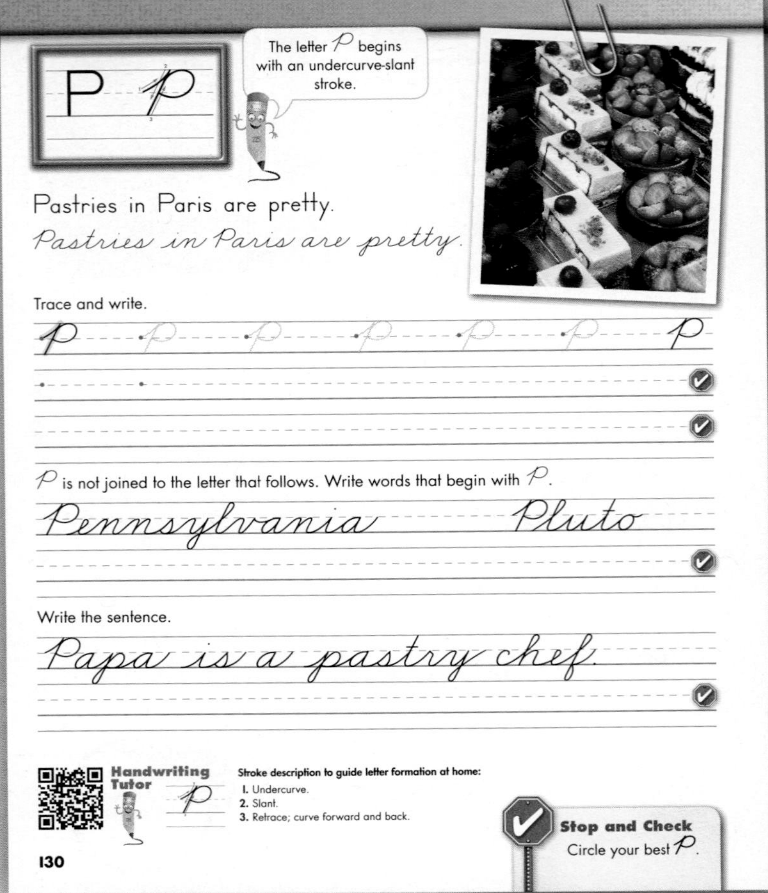

P P
The letter P begins with an undercurve-slant stroke.
Pastries in Paris are pretty.
Pastries in Paris are pretty.
Trace and write.
P is not joined to the letter that follows. Write words that begin with P.
Pennsylvania Pluto
Write the sentence.
Papa is a pastry chef.
Handwriting Tutor
Stroke description to guide letter formation at home:
1. Undercurve.
2. Slant.
3. Retrace; curve forward and back.
Stop and Check
Circle your best P.
130

1 Model

Talk about uppercase cursive **P**. Ask:

- Where does **P** begin? *(at the midline)*
- What stroke begins **P**? *(an undercurve)*

Write cursive **P** on guidelines on the board as you say the stroke description. Use skywriting to model writing **P** in the air. Have students stand and say the stroke description with you as they write cursive **P** in the air. Ask students to use their finger to trace **P** several times on student page 130.

2 Practice

Remind students to position their book and grip their pencil correctly for writing.

Ask students to begin at the green dot and carefully trace the shaded letters with pencil. Then have them write the letters, words, and sentence on the page.

Remind students that when they come to this symbol , they should stop writing and circle their best letter, joining, or word.

3 Evaluate

Tell students it is important to make their writing easy for others to read. Remind them to complete all **Stop and Check** activities.

Use these questions to help students evaluate their cursive **P**:

- Is your **P** about the same width as the model?
- Is your **P** closed?
- Does your forward oval curve below the midline?

Practice Masters 70, 99

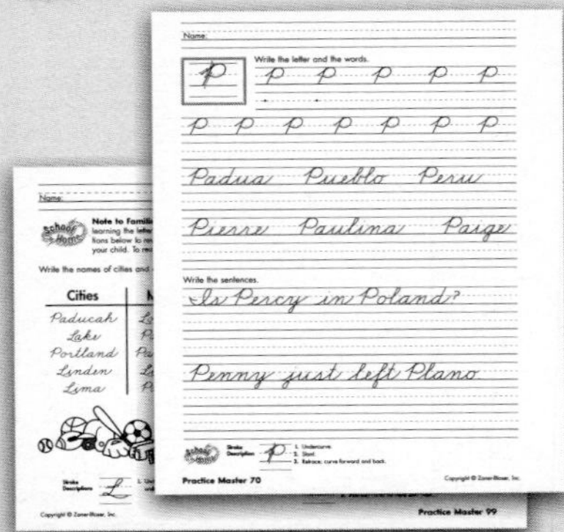

Support for
English Language Learners

Capitalization Rules Write the words **Papa** and **Mama** on the board. Ask students if they know other English words that have the same meaning as these words *(Father, Dad, Pop, Mother, Mom, Mommy, Ma)*, and write them on the board. Tell students all of these words are capitalized when they replace a person's name in a sentence. Write this sentence on the board: **I asked Papa for my allowance.** Demonstrate the rule by crossing out *Papa* and writing **Hector** in its place to show that a person's name can replace *Papa*. Then write on the board: **I asked my papa for my allowance.** Explain that *papa* is lowercase because it cannot be replaced by a person's name. It would not make sense to write **my Hector**.

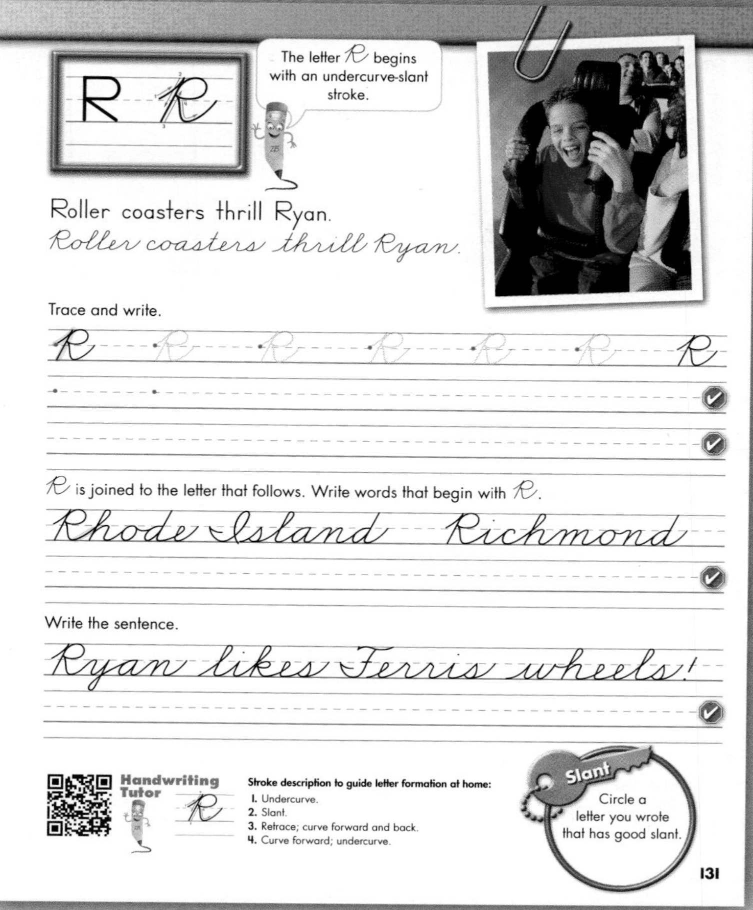

R *R*

The letter *R* begins with an undercurve-slant stroke.

Roller coasters thrill Ryan.
Roller coasters thrill Ryan.

Trace and write.

R R R R R R R

R is joined to the letter that follows. Write words that begin with *R*.

Rhode Island Richmond

Write the sentence.

Ryan likes Ferris wheels!

Handwriting Tutor

Stroke description to guide letter formation at home:
1. Undercurve.
2. Slant.
3. Retrace; curve forward and back.
4. Curve forward; undercurve.

Slant

Circle a letter you wrote that has good slant.

131

Letter Model and Stroke Description

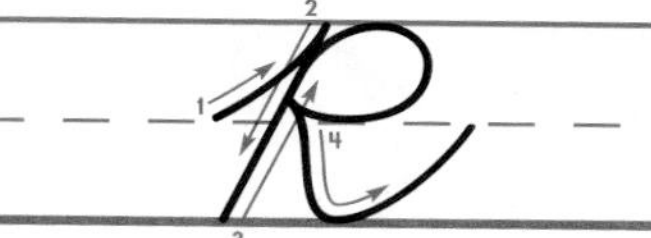

1. Undercurve.
2. Slant.
3. Retrace; curve forward and back.
4. Curve forward; undercurve.

Objective: To practice writing uppercase cursive **R**.

1 Model

Talk about uppercase cursive **R**. Ask:

- Where does **R** end? *(at the midline)*
- What is the ending stroke? *(undercurve)*

Write cursive **R** on guidelines on the board as you say the stroke description. Use skywriting to model writing **R** in the air. Have students stand and say the stroke description with you as they write cursive **R** in the air. Ask students to use their index finger to trace **R** several times on student page 131.

2 Practice

Remind students to position their book and grip their pencil correctly for writing.

Ask students to begin at the green dot and carefully trace the shaded letters with pencil. Then have them write the letters, words, and sentence on the page.

Remind students that when they come to this symbol ✓, they should stop writing and circle their best letter, joining, or word.

3 Evaluate

Tell students it is important to make their writing easy for others to read. Remind them to complete all **Stop and Check** activities.

Proper slant makes each letter easy to read. Ask:

- Does your **R** have correct slant?
- Do your letters have consistent slant?

Writing in the Content Areas

Language Arts

Personal Narrative Point out the photo on page 131 and explain the word **thrill**. Ask students what they have done that gave them a thrill. Have them write a short personal **narrative** about the experience. Make sure they include when and where the event happened, who they were with, and how they felt before, during, and after. Remind students to use their best cursive handwriting.

Extra Practice

School Home

Practice Masters 71, 100

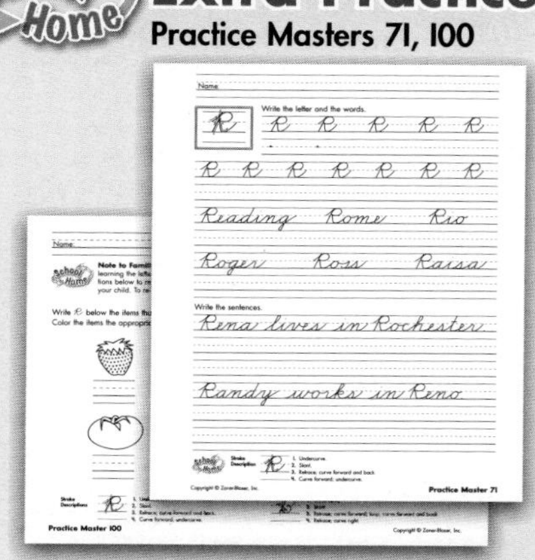

Write the letter and the words.

Reading Rome Rio

Roger Ross Raisa

Write the sentences.

Rina lives in Rochester.

Randy works in Reno.

Practice Master 71

Practice Master 100

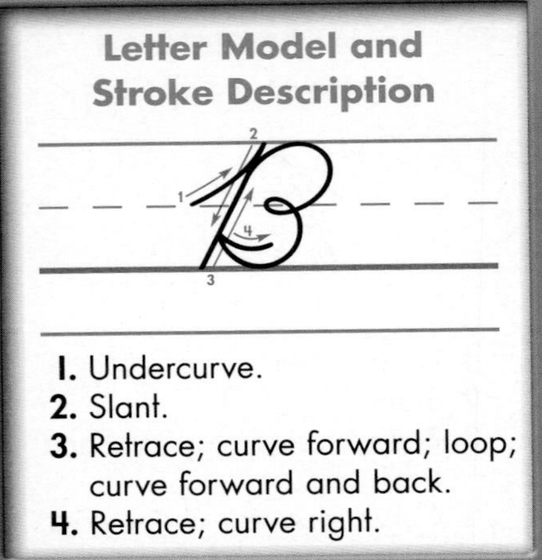
Letter Model and Stroke Description
1. Undercurve.
2. Slant.
3. Retrace; curve forward; loop; curve forward and back.
4. Retrace; curve right.

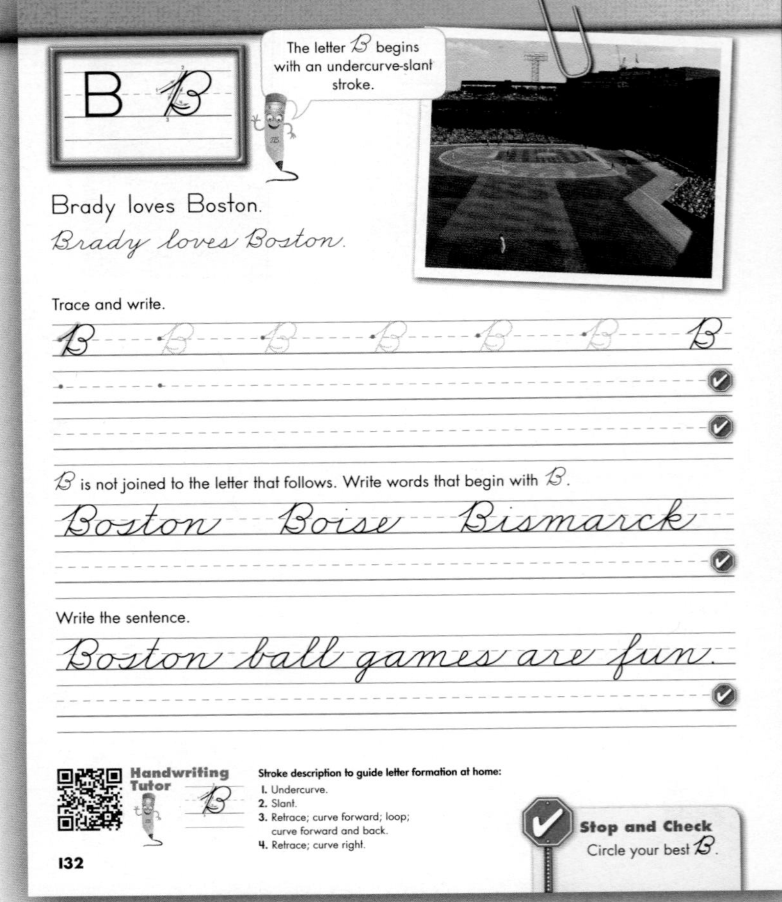
B
The letter B begins with an undercurve-slant stroke.

Brady loves Boston.
Brady loves Boston.

Trace and write.

B is not joined to the letter that follows. Write words that begin with B.

Boston Boise Bismarck

Write the sentence.

Boston ball games are fun.

Handwriting Tutor

Stroke description to guide letter formation at home:
1. Undercurve.
2. Slant.
3. Retrace; curve forward; loop; curve forward and back.
4. Retrace; curve right.

132

Stop and Check
Circle your best B.

Objective: To practice writing uppercase cursive **B**.

Handwriting Tutor

1 Model

Talk about uppercase cursive **B**. Ask:

- How are **B** and **R** alike? *(They have the same beginning.)*
- Where does the loop on **B** close? *(near the midline)*

Write cursive **B** on guidelines on the board as you say the stroke description. Model skywriting **B**. Have students say the stroke description with you as they use their index finger to trace cursive **B** several times on student page 132.

2 Practice

Remind students to position their book and grip their pencil correctly for writing.

Ask students to begin at the green dot and carefully trace the shaded letters with pencil. Then have them write the letters, words, and sentence on the page.

Remind students that when they come to this symbol ✓, they should stop writing and circle their best letter, joining, or word.

3 Evaluate

Tell students it is important to make their writing easy for others to read. Remind them to complete all **Stop and Check** activities.

✓ **Use** these questions to help students evaluate their cursive **B**:

- Does your **B** have correct slant?
- Does your **B** rest on the baseline?
- Does the ending stroke in **B** touch the slant stroke?

School Home Extra Practice

Practice Masters 72, 100

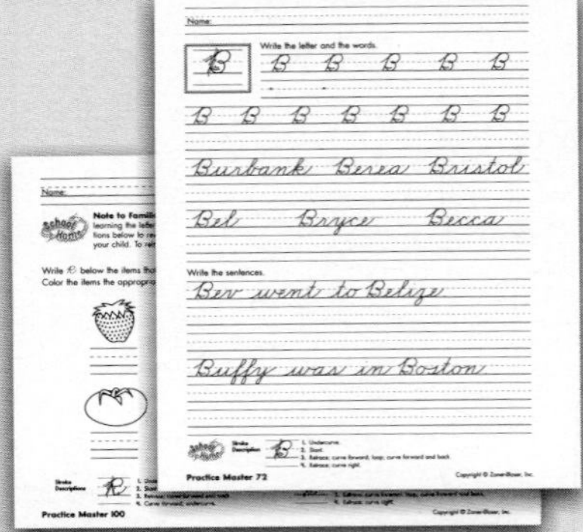
Burbank Berea Bristol
Bel Bryce Becca
Bev went to Belize.
Buffy was in Boston.
Practice Master 72
Practice Master 100

Support for English Language Learners

Pronunciation Practice Write **Boise** on the board and explain that this is the name of a city. Underline the letters **oi,** and circle the letters **se**. Say the word **Boise**. Explain that the /oi/ sound is the same as in the word **boy** and that the letter **s** is pronounced with the /z/ sound as in the word **dessert**. Say the word **Boise** again, and have students repeat it after you. Ask students if they can think of another word that rhymes with **Boise** *(noisy)*. Encourage students to think of a rhyming word from their native language.

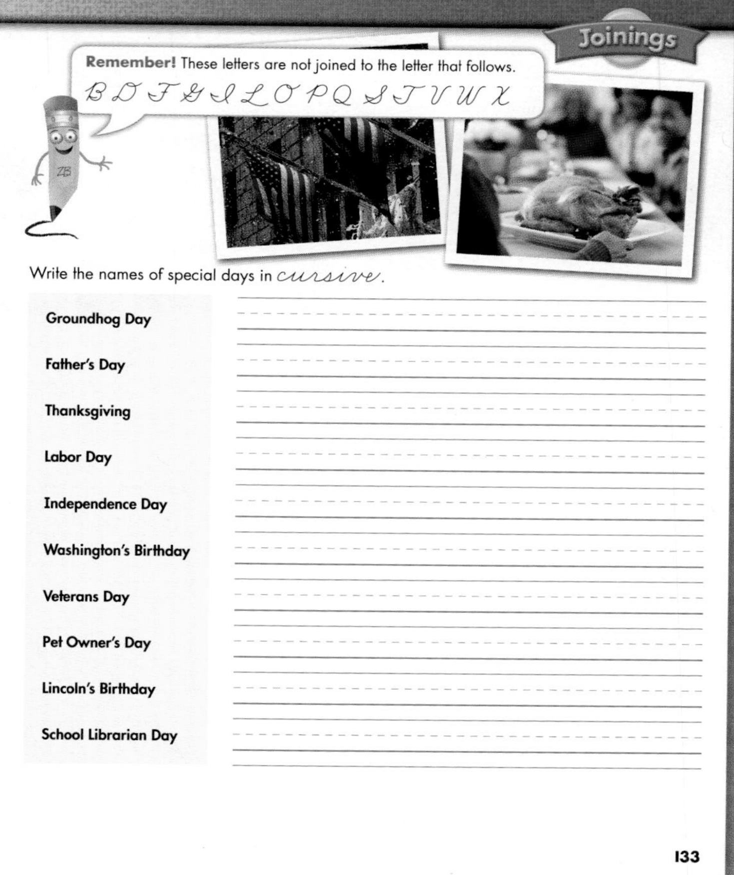

Joinings

Remember! These letters are not joined to the letter that follows.

B D F G I L O P Q S T V W X

Write the names of special days in *cursive*.

Groundhog Day

Father's Day

Thanksgiving

Labor Day

Independence Day

Washington's Birthday

Veterans Day

Pet Owner's Day

Lincoln's Birthday

School Librarian Day

133

Joinings

Objective: To write joinings and words.

1 Model

Talk about **joinings**. Ask:

- Which uppercase letters are not joined to the letter that follows? ***(B, D, F, G, I, L, O, P, Q, S, T, V, W, X)***
- Which uppercase letters are joined to the letter that follows? ***(A, C, E, H, J, K, M, N, R, U, Y, Z)***

Write the words **Memorial Day** as an example. Ask students if uppercase **M** or **D** is joined to the letter that follows it. *(**D** is not joined to the letter following, but **M** is joined.)*

2 Practice

Remind students to position their book and grip their pencil correctly for writing.

Point out **Remember!** and remind students that the uppercase letters listed in the box are not joined to the letter that follows.

Encourage students to use their best cursive handwriting and apply the four Keys to Legibility (Shape, Size, Spacing, and Slant) as they write the special days on student page 133.

3 Evaluate

Tell students it is important to make their writing easy for others to read.

Use these questions to help students evaluate their writing:

- Which of your uppercase letters with joinings are satisfactory?
- Which of your uppercase letters without joinings are satisfactory?
- Which of your letters need improvement?

Tips From an Occupational Therapist

Papier-mâché Globes A fun fine motor activity for students is to create a papier-mâché globe. Have students tear strips of newspaper and dip them in a glue and water mixture to make papier-mâché. Next have them wrap the wet strips around a simple mold, such as an inflated balloon. Once the strips of newspaper are dry and rigid, the balloon inside can be popped by inserting a pin through the papier-mâché. Finally have students paint oceans and continents on their globe. **This activity allows students to strengthen finger muscles by tearing and practice hand manipulation by wrapping the strips and painting the globe.**

Review

Objective: To review the uppercase cursive letters beginning with an undercurve-loop stroke—**G, S, L**—and with an undercurve-slant stroke—**P, R, B**.

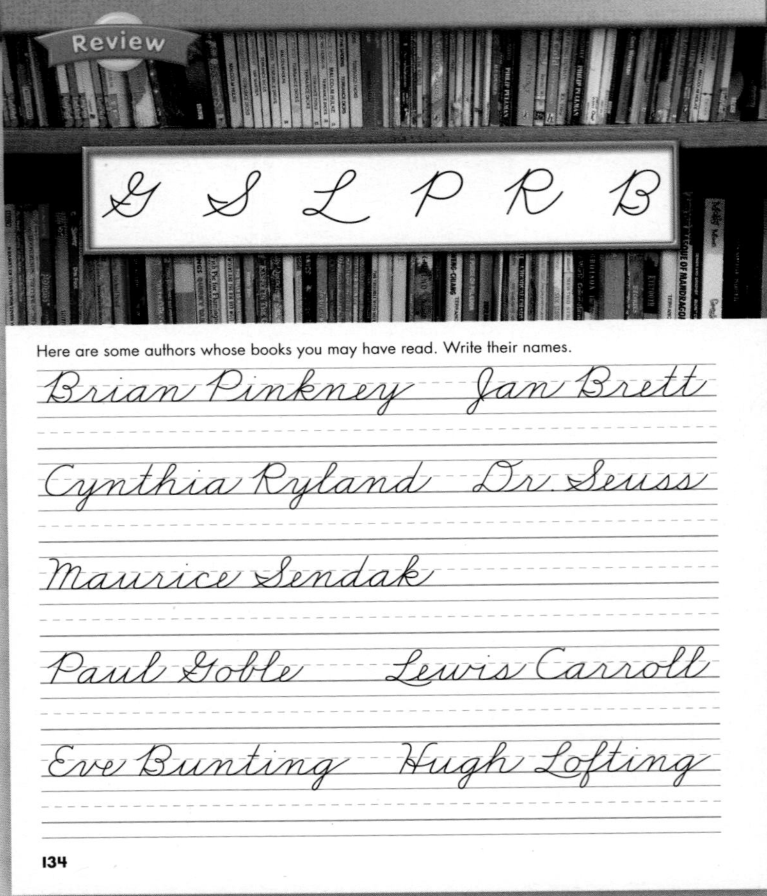

Review
G S L P R B
Here are some authors whose books you may have read. Write their names.
Brian Pinkney Jan Brett
Cynthia Ryland Dr. Seuss
Maurice Sendak
Paul Goble Lewis Carroll
Eve Bunting Hugh Lofting
134

1 Review

Ask students what they remember about the shape of these letters. *(All begin with an undercurve-loop or an undercurve-slant stroke.)*

Review any letters students might be having difficulty writing.

Ask a volunteer to give a verbal description of one of the review letters. Challenge other students to identify the letter being described and write it on guidelines on the board.

See the **Corrective Strategies** in the Appendix for techniques in correcting common problems in your students' handwriting.

2 Practice

Remind students to position their book and grip their pencil correctly for writing.

Ask students to carefully write the names of the authors on student page 134 and remember to form their letters with correct Shape, Size, Spacing, and Slant.

3 Evaluate

Tell students it is important to make their writing easy for others to read.

Use these questions to help students evaluate their writing:

- Did you write with correct strokes so your letters have good shape?
- Did you use the guidelines to make your letters with correct size?
- Did you use good spacing between your letters and words?
- Does your writing have consistent forward slant?

Digital Tools

ZB FontsOnline Plus Go to **www.zaner-bloser.com/zb-fontsonline-plus** to access editable page templates that enable teachers to create worksheets, practice pages, and more.

Support for English Language Learners

Letter Review Write the letters **G, S, L, P, R, B** in cursive on the board. Point to each letter, and have students name a person or a place that begins with each letter. Write their responses on the board. Say the words, and have students chorally repeat them after you.

Application

Writing About a Book Character

I love to read exciting Dr. Doolittle stories. He is a doctor who can talk to the animals. He understands what they say. He helps them feel better.

Write the paragraph about Dr. Doolittle. Leave space for margins.

Stop and Check
Circle your best word.

135

Application

Writing About a Book Character

Objective: To practice writing in cursive a paragraph about a book character.

1 Model

Read aloud the paragraph about Dr. Doolittle on student page 135. Write on the board the words that begin with uppercase letters from the sentences on the page *(I, Dr. Doolittle, He)*. Think aloud as you talk through the correct formation of *He*. Emphasize swinging wide to join uppercase **H** to lowercase **e**. Ask volunteers to evaluate the words according to the Keys to Legibility.

2 Practice

Remind students to position their book and grip their pencil correctly for writing.

Read the directions aloud. Then have students read and follow the directions. Remind them to write carefully and remember to follow the Keys to Legibility so their writing will be easy to read.

Ask students to pay close attention to margins. Remind them to write with consistent slant and leave good spacing between their letters and words.

3 Evaluate

Tell students it is important to make their writing easy for others to read.

Use these questions to help students evaluate their writing:

- Do your letters have good shape?
- Do your short letters touch both the midline and the baseline?
- Do your tall letters touch both the headline and the baseline?
- Do joining strokes make good spacing between your letters?
- Does your writing have good slant?

Writing in the Content Areas

Character Description Have students name a character from a storybook they have recently read. Have them write a **narrative** to describe that character. Make sure they include details about his or her physical appearance, personality, friends or family, and motivations in the story. Remind students to use their best cursive handwriting.

In the Real World

Objective: To practice writing a book summary legibly in cursive.

Cursive Writing

In the Real World

The Mitten by Jan Brett

It is a snowy winter day. A boy drops his mitten. One by one, eight animals climb inside. There is always enough room. But when the bear sneezes, all the animals bounce back out.

Use cursive to write the book summary. Leave space for margins.

136

1 Model

Present the activity. Explain to students that much of the work they will do for school will be done on a computer, but not everything. When they write by hand, students can write anywhere; they don't have to be tied down to a computer. But their handwriting needs to be neat and legible.

Write the first line of the book summary on student page 136 on the board. Ask volunteers to evaluate the words in the sentences according to the Keys to Legibility.

2 Practice

Remind students to position their book and grip their pencil correctly for writing.

Ask students to carefully write the book summary on student page 136 and pay close attention to margins.

3 Evaluate

Tell students it is important to make their writing easy for others to read.

Use these questions to help students evaluate their writing:

- Do my words look like the model?
- Do my joining strokes make good spacing between letters?
- Does my writing have good slant?
- Is my writing easy to read?

Support for English Language Learners

Word Knowledge Say and then write the words **mitten, sneezes,** and **bounce** on the board. Pronounce sounds students might have difficulty with. Have students say the words and clap for each syllable heard in each word *(***mit•ten** *is two claps;* **sneez•es** *is two claps; and* **bounce** *is one clap).* Ask volunteers to describe the meaning of each word and use each in an original sentence.

Uppercase Cursive Review

Write these uppercase letters in *cursive*.

A B C D E F G H I

J K L M N O P Q R

S T U V W X Y Z

Remember! These letters are joined to the letter that follows.

A C E H J K M N R U Y Z

Write these song titles in *cursive*.

"Kumbaya"

"Yankee Doodle"

"Clementine"

"My Bonnie"

"Are You Sleeping?"

"Home on the Range"

"John Henry"

137

Uppercase Cursive Review

Objective: To review all uppercase cursive letters.

1 Review

Tell students they now have studied and written all of the uppercase cursive letterforms. Guide them in a review of these letters with the following activity.

- Letters **A, C, E, N, M, K, H, U, Y, Z, J,** and **R** are _______ to the letter that follows. *(joined)*
- Letters **O, V, X, W, T, F, I, Q, G, S, L, D, P,** and **B** are _________ to the letter that follows. *(not joined)*
- All uppercase letters are _____ letters. *(tall)*
- Uppercase letters with descenders are _____. *(J, Y, Z)*

Have students review and practice the basic cursive strokes.

2 Practice

Remind students to position their book and grip their pencil correctly for writing.

Point out on student page 137 **Remember!** and the list of letters that are joined. Remind students that all other uppercase letters are not joined to the letter that follows.

Read the directions aloud with students. Encourage them to use their best cursive handwriting as they write the song titles.

Remind them to write carefully with consistent slant and leave good spacing between their letters and words.

3 Evaluate

Tell students it is important to make their writing easy for others to read.

Use these questions to help students evaluate their writing:

- Which of your letters are satisfactory?
- Which of your letters need improvement?
- Which of your joinings are satisfactory?
- Which of your joinings need improvement?

Using Technology

Keyboarding Game Play a version of "Simon Says." Have students open a word-processing program and then follow along as you give instructions. Here are some examples to get you started:

*Simon says, "Press and hold the **Shift** key with your left pinky finger."*
*Simon says, "Press **H** with your right index finger."*
"Lift up your left pinky finger." Simon says, "Lift up your left pinky finger."
*Simon says, "Press **i** with your right middle finger."*
Simon says, "Press the period with your right ring finger."
"Say the word." Simon says, "Say the word."

Keys to Legibility

Shape
Shape describes the strokes that form each letter and give it a unique appearance.

Size
Size describes the height of letters.

Spacing
Spacing describes the space between letters, words, and sentences.

Slant
Slant refers to the angle of writing on the paper.

Objective: To practice the four Keys to Legibility.

Keys to Legibility

Slant Spacing Size Shape

Write these tips for healthy eating.
Make your writing easy to read.

Drink enough water.

Always wash vegetables.

Cook meat well.

Support local farmers!

138

Handwriting Coach

Practice If students have not mastered a particular handwriting skill, provide additional instruction and practice. Reinforce instruction with activities geared to each student's modality strengths—visual, auditory, or kinesthetic. Then help them evaluate their writing.

1 Review

Remind students that good handwriting is legible handwriting. Brainstorm with students the qualities of legible handwriting. Write responses on the board. These might include neatness, carefully written letters, and letters that are not too crowded.

Point out and discuss the tips for healthy eating on student page 138. Encourage students to provide and discuss additional tips.

2 Practice

Remind students to position their book and grip their pencil correctly for writing. Ask students to carefully write the sentences on student page 138.

Emphasize that all four Keys to Legibility work together. Students' writing will be easy to read when they use proper Shape, Size, Spacing, and Slant.

Read and discuss the persuasive letter on student page 139. Have students complete the writing activity on that page, and provide help as needed.

Support for English Language Learners

Opinion Writing Some students might need additional help on student page 139 with writing an opinion letter about eating well. Say and then write the word **opinion** on the board. Tell students the purpose of their letter is to convince someone, or get someone to believe, that eating healthy foods is the right thing to do. Explain that using strong words or stating facts is a way of stating your opinion. Have students think about why eating healthy foods is important. Encourage them to give their reasons and list them on the board in legible cursive handwriting before writing their letter.

Finish this letter stating your opinion about eating well.
Be sure to leave space for margins.

Dear ,
It is important to eat well because

Shape Circle your best letter that has an undercurve beginning.

Size Circle your best tall letter.

Spacing Circle two words that have space for \ between them.

Is your writing easy to read?

Slant Circle a word you wrote that has good slant.

139

3 Evaluate

Tell students it is important to make their writing easy for others to read.

Use these questions to help students evaluate their writing:

- Does each letter have its own clear shape?
- Are your tall letters the same height?
- Are your short letters the same height?
- Are your letters neither too close together nor too far apart?
- Does your writing have good slant?

Tips From an Occupational Therapist

Towel-Scrunching Towel-scrunching is an activity that helps increase individual finger strength. This activity works best sitting at a table, where forearms can be supported. Lay a dish towel flat on the table, with the short side toward the student. Have students keep their arms flat on the table and place one hand on the end of the towel. Instruct students to "walk" their fingers up the towel, "scrunching" (or gathering) it into their hand as they go. When they are gripping as much of the towel as they can hold, have them reverse the process by flicking away parts of the towel with their fingers. Then switch and "scrunch" with the other hand. The activity may also be perfomed using tissue paper.

Manuscript Maintenance

Objective: To practice writing a personal narrative in manuscript.

Manuscript Maintenance

Read the personal narrative.
Write the narrative in your best manuscript.
Remember to leave space for margins.

Last summer was great. My father and mother took me to visit our family in Mexico. I had never been to another country. I got to see how my little cousins live. Those children have so much fun!

140

1 Model

Point out and discuss the sentences on student page 140. Emphasize that each sentence begins with an uppercase letter and ends with a period. Ask:

- Which uppercase letter begins with a curve forward-slant? *(**M** as in **My**)* What is the manuscript stroke description for **M**? *(1. Pull down straight. Lift. 2. Slant right. Slant up. Pull down straight.)*
- Which word beginning with an uppercase letter starts with an undercurve-loop stroke? *(Last)* What is the manuscript stroke description for the letter **L**? *(1. Pull down straight. Slide right.)*

Review manuscript stroke descriptions, and model any letters students might be having difficulty writing.

2 Practice

Remind students to position their book and grip their pencil correctly for writing. Ask students to carefully write the sentences on the page.

Emphasize that their writing will be easy to read when they follow the four Keys to Legibility and use proper Shape, Size, Spacing, and Slant.

3 Evaluate

Tell students it is important to make their writing easy for others to read.

✓ **Use** these questions to help students evaluate their writing:

- Does each letter have the correct size and shape?
- Is your spacing between letters and between words correct?
- Does your writing have good slant?

Support for English Language Learners

Word Order Some students might need additional help with the order of words in a sentence. Ask students to find the subject in each sentence on student page 140. Then ask them to identify the verb in each sentence. Write additional sentences on the board, and have volunteers come to the board and circle the subject and underline the verb.

Read the diary entry in cursive.
Use manuscript to write the passage below.
Remember to leave space for margins.

Sometimes I like to paint.
I am done with this picture.
I painted a big ship sailing
below a black, starry sky.
My mom thought it was beautiful.

Is your manuscript writing easy to read?

141

Objective: To practice writing a diary entry in manuscript.

1 Model

Talk about a diary entry. Ask:

- What is a diary? *(It is a book in which a writer records his or her thoughts, actions, and feelings.)*
- Why do people write in diaries? *(Diaries can help a person express feelings and thoughts privately.)*

Review manuscript stroke descriptions, and model any letters students might be having difficulty writing.

2 Practice

Remind students to position their book and grip their pencil correctly for writing. Ask students to carefully write the diary entry on student page 141 in manuscript.

Emphasize that their writing will be easy to read when they follow the four Keys and use proper Shape, Size, Spacing, and Slant.

3 Evaluate

Tell students it is important to make their writing easy for others to read.

Use these questions to help students evaluate their writing:

- Are your tall letters the same height?
- Are your short letters the same height?
- Does each letter have its own clear shape and size?
- Does your writing have good slant?

Writing in the Content Areas

Historical Narrative Point out the diary activity on page 141 and answer any questions students might have about diaries. Explain that one way we learn about history is to read the diaries of people who lived during important events. Choose a topic from American history, and have students read a section from their social studies book about it. Have students select a figure who participated in the event and write a diary entry about the event from that person's point of view. Remind students to use their best cursive handwriting.

Narrative

Friendly Letter

Objective: To practice writing a friendly letter.

Narrative

Friendly Letter

Use cursive to write the letter.
Write as quickly and neatly as you can.
Be sure to leave room for margins.

Dear Papa and Mama,
Soccer camp is fun! Coach says I did something great in today's game—I scored the winning goal. Alex almost stole the ball from me, but I ran faster. Coach began to shout from the side of the field. It felt like a scene from a movie. Now I need to wash the dirt off my uniform so I can wear it again tomorrow. I'll write more later!
Love,
Jada

142

1 Present the Activity

Point out and discuss the friendly letter. Explain that in a friendly letter the writer shares an interesting experience with the reader. Add that a friendly letter includes important events and descriptive words that tell about the experience.

Read and discuss the letter on student page 142. Ask:

- What is the letter about? *(a girl's experience at soccer camp)*
- What does the girl do? *(She scored the winning goal.)*

2 Practice

Remind students to position their book and grip their pencil correctly for writing. Ask students to quickly and neatly write the friendly letter on student pages 142–143 in cursive.

Emphasize that their writing will be easy to read when they use proper Shape, Size, Spacing, and Slant.

Support for

English Language Learners

Friendly Letter Writing Some students may need additional help with friendly letters. Explain that a friendly letter is a casual letter written to a friend or family member. A friendly letter might be written to send a message, invite someone to a party, or to thank someone for a gift. The friendly letter on student page 142 has four parts: a **greeting,** which includes the name of the person or people to whom the letter is written; a **body,** which includes the message; a **closing,** which includes a friendly way to say goodbye; and a **signature,** which is the name of the writer. Invite students to identify these four parts in the letter on the page.

Stop and Check
Circle your best word.

143

3 Evaluate

Tell students it is important to make their writing easy for others to read.

Use these questions to help students evaluate their writing:

- Do your letters have good shape?
- Do your short letters touch both the midline and the baseline?
- Do your tall letters touch both the headline and the baseline?
- Do your joining strokes make good spacing between letters?

Writing in the Content Areas

Business Letters Now that students have written a friendly letter, have them write a more formal business letter. Tell students they might write a business letter to a company, a newspaper, or an acquaintance. A business letter looks a lot like a friendly letter, but it includes the name and address of the business as well as the address of the writer. Have students think of a topic and recipient for a business letter. Find samples of business letters for students to reference as they write their own. Remind students to use their best cursive handwriting.

Compare and Contrast

Objective: To write an informative/explanatory piece that compares and contrasts two animals.

Informative/Explanatory

Compare and Contrast

Draw and identify two types of animals.

Animal 1

Animal 2

144

Handwriting Coach

Guidelines Review with students the use of guidelines for correct letter formation. Draw guidelines on the board using colored chalk or markers. Identify the headline, the midline, the baseline, and the descender space. Invite volunteers to write words on the guidelines, paying close attention to the size of their letters.

1 Present the Activity

Tell students that comparing and contrasting two things means describing how those things are alike and different. Compare and contrast two foods.

Invite volunteers to provide additional facts that show how the foods are alike and how they are different. Encourage students to state each fact as a complete sentence.

Direct students' attention to student pages 144 and 145. Point out the directions and spaces for response. Then read the directions with students, making sure they understand the task.

2 Write

Direct students to draw and identify two animals on student page 144. Then prompt them to use facts to compare and contrast the animals on student page 145. Remind students to write each letter clearly. Instruct them to indent the first line of each paragraph they write and leave space for margins.

Tips From an Occupational Therapist

Practicing Strokes Provide large sheets of construction paper and a marker to each student. Have students tape their paper to the board or wall and practice each of the beginning strokes—**undercurve, downcurve,** and **overcurve**—in large, sweeping motions. Encourage them to practice each stroke several times and feel the motion that each one involves.

Write about how these animals are alike and how they are different. Be sure to include facts and details about each animal. Remember to indent the first line of each paragraph you write and leave space for margins.

145

3 Evaluate

Use these questions to help students evaluate the shape of their letters:

- Does each letter have its own clear shape?
- Did you form your letters using correct strokes?

Handwriting Coach

Guidelines for Writing Partners

Provide students with a copy of these guidelines when they work with a writing partner.

1. Listen carefully to your partner.
2. Give positive feedback first.
3. Ask questions that will help your partner.
4. Be honest and kind when making suggestions about your partner's work.

Support for

English Language Learners

Using a Dictionary Remind students that a dictionary will help them spell and pronounce words correctly and understand what words mean. Give each student or pair of students a dictionary. Practice finding a few words together as a class. Direct students to use the guide words at the top of each page to locate the word they are looking for. Review the information included in an entry. Then give students a short list of words to find with a partner, taking turns spelling and pronouncing the words. Have students write a sentence using each word. It might be helpful to have students create their own word banks.

Fiction or Nonfiction?

Objective: To write an opinion about fiction and nonfiction texts, support the opinion with reasons, and include a concluding statement.

Fiction or Nonfiction?

Which type of text do you like to read better: fiction (imagined) or nonfiction (real)? Write your opinion, reasons to support your opinion, and a concluding statement. Remember to indent the first line of each paragraph you write and leave space for margins.

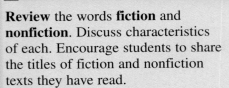

Handwriting Coach

Practice Students who have mastered the skill of writing the lowercase and uppercase cursive letters without models should be given writing activities that will challenge them and require thinking. Reteaching, for any student who still needs it, will be most effective if practice is given in the student's dominant learning modality.

1 Present the Activity

Review the words **fiction** and **nonfiction**. Discuss characteristics of each. Encourage students to share the titles of fiction and nonfiction texts they have read.

Direct students' attention to student pages 146 and 147. Point out the directions and spaces for response. Then read the directions with students, making sure they understand the task.

2 Write

Direct students to determine which type of text they enjoy reading better: fiction or nonfiction. Prompt them to write their opinion, supporting reasons, and a concluding statement on student pages 146 and 147. Remind them to write their letters carefully on the guidelines so their writing will be easy to read. Instruct them to indent the first line of each paragraph they write and leave space for margins.

Tips From an Occupational Therapist

Large Puzzles Provide a large puzzle on a table as a fine motor activity for students to choose during free time. Manipulating the pieces requires **individual finger movement,** while finding the appropriate spot for each piece requires a high degree of **visual perceptual skills**.

3 Evaluate

Use these questions to help students evaluate the size of their letters:

- Do your short letters touch both the midline and the baseline?
- Do your tall letters touch both the headline and the baseline?
- Do your letters with descenders go below the baseline?

Handwriting Coach

Using the Board Continue to use the board for teaching and practicing basic strokes, letters, and numerals. Students who have difficulty with their motor skills might benefit from the increased space the board provides. Since erasing is easy, identification and correction of errors becomes a simpler task.

Support for English Language Learners

Word Order Because sentence word order is different in different languages, some students might need additional help with the order of words in English sentences. Write on the board the words **subject-verb-object** and the sentence **Jacob likes books**. Briefly review the meaning of **subject, verb,** and **object**. Ask volunteers to name the subject, verb, and object in the sentence. Provide additional examples to reinforce the concept and help students feel confident enough to write their opinion.

Last Weekend

Objective: To write a narrative about the weekend, making sure to include temporal words to show the order of events.

Narrative

Last Weekend

Write about what you did last weekend. Be sure to include temporal words (such as *first, next, then, later, finally*) to show the order of events. Remember to indent the first line of each paragraph you write and leave space for margins.

148

Handwriting Coach

Automaticity The ability to write letters and words automatically allows student to spend more time thinking about the content of their writing. To make sure students are gaining automaticity, ask them to demonstrate correct letter formation with their eyes closed.

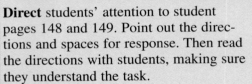

1 Present the Activity

Direct students' attention to student pages 148 and 149. Point out the directions and spaces for response. Then read the directions with students, making sure they understand the task.

Work with students to brainstorm a list of temporal words commonly used in narrative writing (*first, next, then, later, finally*). Explain that students should use these words in their writing to signal event order.

2 Write

Direct students to write about what they did last weekend on student pages 148 and 149. Prompt them to use temporal words to show the order of events. Remind students to use proper spacing between letters, words, and sentences. Instruct them to indent the first line of each paragraph they write and leave space for margins.

Support for English Language Learners

Capitalization Be aware that capitalization rules vary by language. Teach English capitalization rules to help students determine when and how to use uppercase letters.

Model capitalization rules with examples on the board. Using the names of students in your class, write sentences to model correct and incorrect capitalization. For example, write **My name is Giselle Lozano. I live in Texas.** and **My name is giselle lozano. I live in texas.** Have students write their own sentences.

149

Evaluate

Use these questions to help students evaluate their spacing:

- Are your letters neither too close together nor too far apart?
- Did you use proper spacing between your letters, words, and sentences?

Handwriting Coach

Sitting Position Correct body position allows students to write smoothly. Encourage students to sit comfortably erect with their feet flat on the floor and their hips touching the back of the chair. Both arms should rest on the desk.

Tips From an Occupational Therapist

Eraser Practice Students who have difficulty using the eraser on their pencil efficiently will benefit from this activity. Make ten small circles on a piece of writing paper. Have the student color in the first circle, rotate the pencil by turning it with the thumb and fingertips of the writing hand so the eraser is pointing down, erase the second circle, and so on.

How To

Objective: To write an informative/explanatory piece that explains how to complete an activity or make a food.

Informative/Explanatory

How To

Explain how to complete a favorite activity or make a special food. List each step in order. Use linking words (such as *and*, *but*, *or*) to connect ideas. Remember to indent the first line of each paragraph you write and leave space for margins.

150

1 Present the Activity

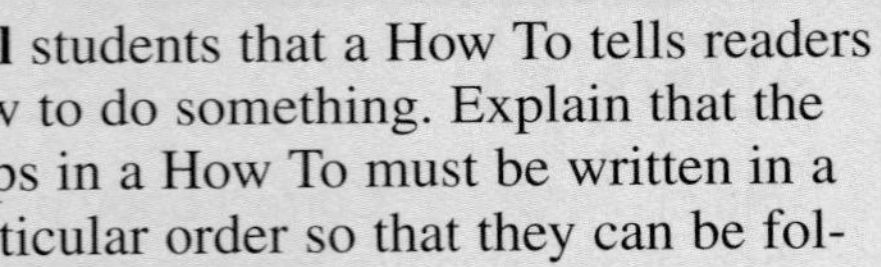

Tell students that a How To tells readers how to do something. Explain that the steps in a How To must be written in a particular order so that they can be followed correctly.

Direct students' attention to student page 150. Point out the directions and spaces for response. Then read the directions with students, making sure they understand the task.

2 Write

Direct students to write a How To on student page 150. Remind students to use proper spacing. Instruct them to leave space for margins.

3 Evaluate

Use these questions to help students evaluate the slant of their letters:

- Does your writing have uniform forward slant?
- Did you pull your downstrokes in the proper direction?

Support for English Language Learners

Lesson Management Create a balance between rote activities and those that develop higher-order thinking skills. Use rote learning to develop letter and word recognition, teach spelling rules, improve aural discrimination, and help students achieve handwriting fluency. To help students develop higher-order thinking skills, create a classroom environment in which students are encouraged to share their thoughts, ask questions, and have many opportunities to write essays, stories, and poems.

Informative/Explanatory

Handwriting and the Writing Process

Write a Paragraph

A paragraph is a group of sentences about one subject.
Write a paragraph about your school.

1. Prewriting
Prewriting means gathering ideas and planning before you write. List your ideas on a piece of paper. Then plan your paragraph, telling the subject and in what order you will write your ideas.

2. Drafting
Drafting means putting your thoughts into written sentences for the first time. Use the ideas you listed in Prewriting to draft your paragraph. Write your first draft.

3. Revising
Revising means changing your writing to make it say exactly what you mean. Read your draft. Mark any changes you want to make.

Does your writing include all the information readers want to know?	Yes	No

4. Editing
Editing means checking your revised writing for errors in spelling, punctuation, capitalization, and handwriting.

Are all words spelled correctly?	Yes	No
Have you used uppercase letters and punctuation correctly?	Yes	No
Do your letters have good shape and size?	Yes	No
Does your writing have good spacing?	Yes	No
Does your writing have good slant?	Yes	No
Is your writing easy to read?	Yes	No

5. Publishing
Publishing means using your best handwriting to make a good copy of your writing. Share your writing with others.

151

Handwriting and the Writing Process

As students participate in the writing process, let them know that good handwriting is always important. Notes, Webs, story drafts, and published pieces that are easy to read reduce confusion in the classroom. Legible handwriting also helps students express their ideas clearly and confidently.

Review with students the five steps in the writing process identified on student page 151. Encourage discussion on the importance of following each step as students develop their writing.

Objective: To write a paragraph using the writing process while practicing cursive writing.

Prewriting

What should I write?

During prewriting, students plan for their writing by making notes, lists, and webs. Carelessly written prewriting work may cause confusion throughout the writing process, but easy-to-read notes and webs smooth the way for students, teachers, and writing partners.

Drafting

I write my ideas in sentences.

Students' best handwriting isn't necessary for a first draft. In fact, concentrating on handwriting may take students' attention away from the content of their writing. However, a "sloppy" draft makes revising and editing more difficult. As students develop a consciousness about legibility, their writing will be fluent and easy to read.

Revising

What should I change?

As students revise their drafts, remind them to begin each sentence with an uppercase letter and use end marks. The revising stage is also a good time to check slant and spacing in the writing. As they revise, students should continue to be aware of the need for legibility.

Editing

How can I improve my spelling and handwriting?

To complete the writing process, have students edit their drafts, checking spelling, punctuation, and handwriting. Thinking about legibility should always be part of the editing stage of the writing process. The Keys to Legibility—Shape, Size, Spacing, Slant—help students know what to look for.

Publishing

How will I share my work?

When publishing writing, it's especially important for students to use their best handwriting. Neat, legible writing shows courtesy to readers. It makes a good first impression, and it ensures that readers will understand the writer's message.

Support for
English Language Learners

Writing Process The writing process can be intimidating for English Language Learners. Have students complete prewriting activities, such as brainstorming, in their first language. Then help students create comparable lists of English words and phrases, and encourage them to use the words and phrases in their writing. This strategy prevents limitations in fluency from stifling creativity.

Writing Quickly

Discuss with students various times when being able to write quickly might be helpful or necessary. These might include taking notes in class; copying a friend's address or telephone number; jotting down ideas as they come to mind; writing words for a spelling test; and writing a story. Emphasize the importance of maintaining legibility even when writing quickly. Describe a time when you wrote important information quickly and were unable to read it later.

Objective: To practice writing quickly and legibly.

Writing Quickly

Writing quickly is a skill that will help when you need to write a story, take a timed test, or take notes.

Writing that is done quickly should still be easy to read. With practice, you will learn how to write quickly and still have legible handwriting.

Handwriting Tutor

Read the saying. Write it quickly and legibly.

In fourteen hundred ninety-two Columbus sailed the ocean blue.

Now write the lines again.
Try to write them faster this time.

Handwriting Tutor

152

Handwriting Coach

Writing Quickly

Tell students that the goal of handwriting instruction is to help them write legibly with ease and fluency. It is important, however, not to stress fluency (speed) too early. Students should master writing the lowercase and uppercase alphabets before being concerned with speed. By the end of third grade, students should be able to write legibly, without stress, approximately 40 letters per minute. Based on this estimate, students should be able to write the saying on the student page, legibly and without stress, in about one minute and fifteen seconds.

1 Practice

Direct students to look at the saying on the student page and read it aloud with you. Review any letters that still present difficulties for any students. When all students seem comfortable with the task, have them write the saying the first time. Ask them to write more quickly than usual but make sure their letters are easy to read.

Note: To make this an actual timed writing, have students begin at your signal. After exactly one minute, have students stop and put a mark, such as a star or a check mark, after the letter they just completed. Then have them finish the saying.

Count the letters in each student's marked passage. Most third-graders can be expected to write about 40 letters legibly in one minute. Then have them write the saying a second time. You might want to repeat the timed writing procedure.

2 Evaluate

Encourage them to evaluate their letters and words by comparing them to the models. Ask questions such as these:

- Do your letters have good shape?
- Do your tall letters touch the headline?
- Do your short letters touch the midline?
- Do your **f** and **y** go below the baseline and touch the next headline?
- Do your words have good letter spacing?
- Is there good spacing between your words?
- Does your writing have consistent forward slant?

Write the saying two more times.
Try to write it even faster, but keep it easy to read.

Now read your final writing. Circle Yes or No to respond to each statement. Then show your writing to another reader, either a classmate or your teacher. Ask that person to circle Yes or No beside each statement.

	My Evaluation	My Classmate's or Teacher's Evaluation
The writing is easy to read.	Yes No	Yes No
The writing has good Shape	Yes No	Yes No
The writing has good Size	Yes No	Yes No
The writing has good Spacing	Yes No	Yes No
The writing has good Slant	Yes No	Yes No

153

Write More Quickly

Direct students to look at the writing space on student page 153. Point out that this space is where they are to write the saying two more times. Encourage students to try to write faster than they did during the other two times, but caution them not to sacrifice legibility for the sake of speed.

For timed writing, follow the procedure recommended earlier in this lesson. Help students evaluate their writing by comparing it to the models and their previous attempts in this lesson. Then have them respond to each statement on the evaluation checklist at the bottom of the page.

Evaluation

Explain that self-evaluation is an important step in the handwriting process. By identifying their own handwriting strengths and weaknesses, students become independent learners. The steps in the self-evaluation process are as follows:

Question Students should ask themselves questions such as these: "Does my writing have the correct slant?" "Do my letters rest on the baseline?"

Compare Students should compare their handwriting to the models.

Evaluate Students should determine strengths and weaknesses in their handwriting based on the Keys to Legibility.

Diagnose Students should diagnose the cause of any difficulties. Possible causes include incorrect paper or pencil position, inconsistent pressure on the pencil, and incorrect strokes.

Improve Self-evaluation should include a means of improvement through additional instruction and continued practice.

Writing Easily

Now that students have been introduced to the formation of all the cursive letters, they can begin to increase the ease with which they write. The ability to write letters and words automatically allows students to spend more time thinking about the content of their writing.

Objective: To practice narrative writing in cursive in order to increase the ease of writing legibly.

Narrative

Writing Easily

As you write stories and essays for school papers and tests, it is important that your handwriting flows easily. When you automatically know how to write legibly, you don't have to worry about your handwriting. You are free to think about what you want your writing to say. With practice, you will learn how to make your writing easy, quick, and legible.

Read the writing prompt below. Respond to it by writing on the lines. Let your handwriting flow easily as you think and write.

Think about a time when you were surprised by someone or something.

Write a story about what happened when you were surprised. Include details to make your writing interesting.

154

1 Present the Activity

Direct students to the writing prompt and the related photo on student page 154. Encourage discussion about the specific text type being used (narrative writing), and have volunteers name and describe the writing process steps to help them begin planning their writing. (You might want to refer to page T151.)

2 Practice

Ask students to respond to the prompt on the page by writing a story about a time when they were surprised. Remind students that their handwriting should be legible, flowing easily, and their focus should be on the content of the narrative they're writing.

Support for English Language Learners

Working in Pairs English Language Learners who have some fluency in English are often reluctant to share their creative writing. These students might use only a limited number of sentence patterns, and they often have problems with sentence structure, organization, word choice, and word order.

Encourage students to work with a writing buddy to complete the activity on the student page. As a student tells his or her story, the writing buddy records it verbatim. When the story is complete, the writing buddy reads it back as the storyteller follows along. The storyteller can then go back and read the story independently and copy it in his or her own handwriting.

Now read your writing. Circle Yes or No to respond to each statement. Then show your writing to another reader, either a classmate or your teacher. Ask that person to circle Yes or No beside each statement.

	My Evaluation		My Classmate's or Teacher's Evaluation	
The writing is easy to read.	Yes	No	Yes	No
The writing has good Shape	Yes	No	Yes	No
The writing has good Size	Yes	No	Yes	No
The writing has good Spacing	Yes	No	Yes	No
The writing has good Slant	Yes	No	Yes	No

155

Evaluate

Point out the evaluation checklist on student page 155. Read the statements with students, and encourage them to evaluate their writing and respond to the evaluation comments. Then have them show their writing to a classmate or you for additional evaluation.

Writing Practice

Reinforce both cursive and manuscript writing by having students do many different kinds of writing. Activities might include the following:

- Label pictures and objects.
- Make lists of things in categories.
- Write about field trips.
- Write facts.
- Retell a story in writing.
- Write about books.
- Write stories, poems, and descriptions.
- Write the names of friends and pets.
- Prepare invitations to parties.
- List games for parties.
- Send holiday greetings to parents and friends.

Objective: To write a poem in cursive and compare it to the pretest written at the beginning of the school year.

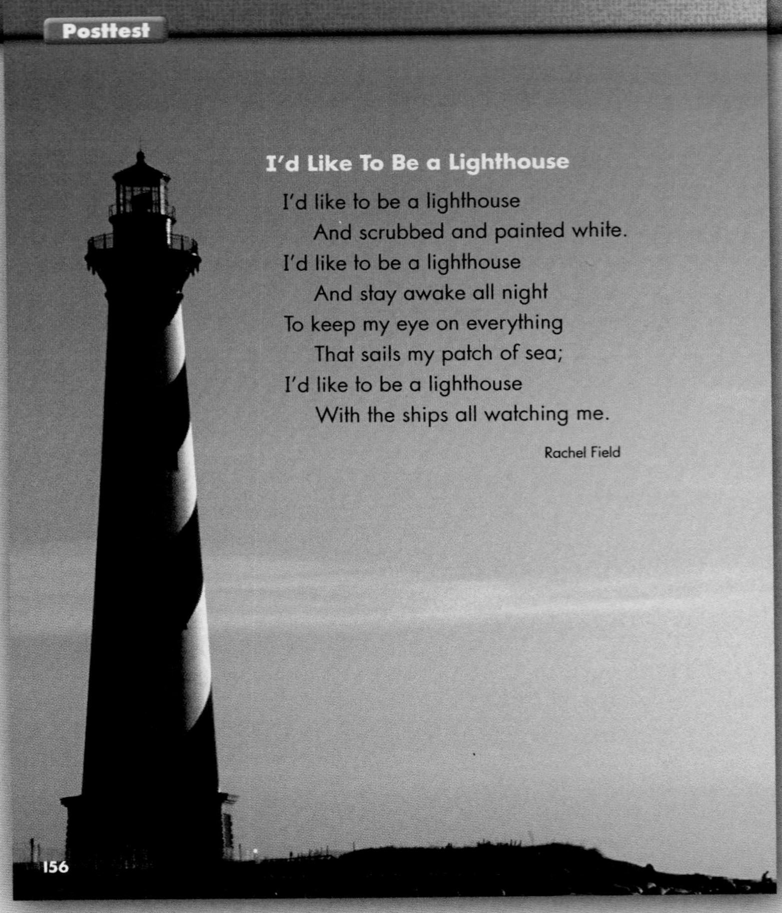

Posttest
I'd Like To Be a Lighthouse
I'd like to be a lighthouse
And scrubbed and painted white.
I'd like to be a lighthouse
And stay awake all night
To keep my eye on everything
That sails my patch of sea;
I'd like to be a lighthouse
With the ships all watching me.
Rachel Field
156

1 Review

Remind students to use the four Keys to Legibility—Shape, Size, Spacing, and Slant—as a rubric for evaluating their handwriting.

2 Posttest

Remind students that at the beginning of the school year they wrote this poem as a pretest and evaluated their handwriting. Read the poem aloud with students. Then point out the writing area on student page 157 where they are to write the poem again. As they write the poem in cursive as a posttest, remind them to use correct letter shape and size, correct spacing, and uniform slant.

Support for English Language Learners

Build Background Before you read aloud the poem on student page 156, show pictures of lighthouses. Ask students what they know about lighthouses. Explain that lighthouses are tall buildings or towers with special lights at the top. They are located near the shore of lakes, rivers, or oceans. Sailors and ship captains use the bright lights from lighthouses to aid them in navigation. The lights also warn of nearby dangers, such as rocks or sandbars.

Write the poem in your best cursive handwriting. Be sure to leave space for margins.

157

Evaluate

Have students use the Keys to Legibility to evaluate their handwriting. Suggest that they compare this writing to their writing on the pretest on student page 19 and discuss how their writing has changed. Meet individually with students to help them assess their progress.

Note: Zaner-Bloser's *Evaluation Guide* for Grade 3 handwriting is a useful tool for evaluating students' writing. The evaluation criteria are the Keys to Legibility. Samples of students' handwriting, ranging in quality from excellent to poor, provide a helpful comparison for evaluation.

Write the Sentence

Use the following lesson to provide students with extra practice or as an additional posttest.

Objective: To write a sentence that incorporates each letter of the alphabet.

Write the Sentence

The quick brown fox jumps over the lazy dog.

The quick brown fox jumps over the lazy dog.

158

1 Present the Activity

Read aloud the sentence on student page 158. Tell students that writing the sentence will allow them to practice writing each letter of the alphabet. Explain that it will also help them evaluate the shape and size of their letters, slant of their writing, and spacing between their letters and words.

Write

Ask students to write the sentence in their best manuscript and cursive handwriting. Remind them to write their letters carefully on the guidelines so their writing will be easy to read.

3 Evaluate

Have students use the Keys to Legibility to evaluate their handwriting. Ask the following questions:

- Did you write with correct strokes so your letters have good shape?
- Are your letters the correct size?
- Did you use proper spacing?
- Did you write with correct slant?

Support for English Language Learners

Handwriting Fluency For students whose first language does not use the Roman alphabet, the time needed to achieve handwriting fluency may be longer than that needed by students who have more familiarity with Roman letters and numerals. To build vocabulary and promote ease in writing, label pictures and objects and have students create picture dictionaries.

Record of Student's Handwriting Skills

Cursive

	Needs Improvement	Shows Mastery
Sits correctly	❑	❑
Positions paper correctly	❑	❑
Holds pencil correctly	❑	❑
Writes undercurve strokes	❑	❑
Writes downcurve strokes	❑	❑
Writes overcurve strokes	❑	❑
Writes slant strokes	❑	❑
Writes *i, t, u, w*	❑	❑
Writes *e, l, b, h, f, k*	❑	❑
Writes *r, s, j, p*	❑	❑
Writes *a, d, g, o, c, q*	❑	❑
Writes *n, m, y, x, v, z*	❑	❑
Writes numerals *1–10*	❑	❑
Writes *A, O, D, C, E*	❑	❑
Writes *N, M, H, K*	❑	❑
Writes *U, Y, Z*	❑	❑
Writes *V, W, X*	❑	❑
Writes *I, J, Q*	❑	❑
Writes *T, F*	❑	❑
Writes *G, S, L*	❑	❑
Writes *P, R, B*	❑	❑

	Needs Improvement	Shows Mastery
Writes the undercurve-to-undercurve joining	❑	❑
Writes the undercurve-to-downcurve joining	❑	❑
Writes the undercurve-to-overcurve joining	❑	❑
Writes the checkstroke-to-undercurve joining	❑	❑
Writes the checkstroke-to-downcurve joining	❑	❑
Writes the checkstroke-to-overcurve joining	❑	❑
Writes the overcurve-to-undercurve joining	❑	❑
Writes the overcurve-to-downcurve joining	❑	❑
Writes the overcurve-to-overcurve joining	❑	❑
Writes with correct shape	❑	❑
Writes with correct size	❑	❑
Writes with correct spacing	❑	❑
Writes with correct slant	❑	❑
Regularly checks written work for legibility	❑	❑

159

Record of Student's Handwriting Skills

The **Record of Student's Handwriting Skills** serves to indicate each student's progress in mastering the skills presented. The chart lists the essential skills in the program. After the skills that are listed have been practiced and evaluated, you will be able to mark the **Record of Student's Handwriting Skills** for either *Shows Mastery* or *Needs Improvement.*

Objective: To indicate progress in mastering handwriting skills.

Needs Improvement

If a student has not mastered a skill, provide additional basic instruction and practice. First, determine the student's specific needs. Then return to the initial teaching steps of the lesson for ways to help the student. To improve letterforms, have the student practice writing the letter in isolation and within words and sentences. Reinforce instruction through activities geared to the student's modality strengths. Ask the student to evaluate his or her writing with you. Reevaluate the student's writing following practice over time. When mastery of the skill is achieved, check *Shows Mastery.*

Note: *The* **Record of Student's Handwriting Skills** *is reproduced on Practice Master 101.*

Shows Mastery

Mastery of written letterforms is achieved when the student writes the letters using correct basic strokes. Compare the student's written letterforms with the letter models shown in the book. Keep in mind the Keys to Legibility (**Shape, Size, Spacing, Slant**) when evaluating letters, numerals, punctuation marks, words, and sentences for mastery of skill. Observation will indicate whether a student has mastered such skills as pencil and paper position.

Check the appropriate box for each skill.

Checklist for Handwriting Instruction

Developed by Steve Graham, Arizona State

Directions: This checklist is a tool for assessing handwriting instruction. Place a check next to each item that describes a feature of instruction in your classroom. When completed, a review of this checklist can assist you in maintaining and improving the effectiveness of your current handwriting program. It can also help you identify instructional procedures that are effective in improving the legibility and fluency of students who experience difficulty mastering the handwriting process.

I promote handwriting development by

- ☐ making sure that each student—left-handed and right-handed—employs proper sitting, paper, and pencil positions for writing.
- ☐ teaching students to identify and name the letters of the alphabet.
- ☐ allotting approximately 15 minutes per day to handwriting instruction.
- ☐ providing students with plenty of opportunities to use different types of writing instruments and paper.
- ☐ asking students to set goals for improving specific aspects of their handwriting.
- ☐ monitoring students' handwriting, paying special attention to their instructional needs in letter formation, spacing, slant, alignment, size, and line quality.
- ☐ helping students develop a positive attitude about handwriting.

I teach students how to write each letter by

- ☐ showing them how it is formed.
- ☐ describing how it is similar to and different from other letters.
- ☐ using visual cues, such as numbered arrows, as a guide for letter formation.
- ☐ providing practice tracing, copying, and writing the letter from memory.
- ☐ asking them to identify or circle their best formed letter or letters.
- ☐ encouraging them to correct or rewrite poorly formed letters.
- ☐ reinforcing their successful efforts and providing corrective feedback as needed.

I help students become more fluent in handwriting by

- ☐ providing them with plenty of opportunities to write.
- ☐ having them copy a short passage several times, trying to write it a little faster each time.
- ☐ encouraging them to make all final drafts of papers neat and legible.

I assist students who are experiencing difficulty by

- ☐ organizing my class so that I can provide additional handwriting instruction to students who need it.
- ☐ identifying and addressing roadblocks that may impede a student's success in handwriting.
- ☐ talking with parents and soliciting their advice about how to improve their child's handwriting.
- ☐ coordinating my handwriting instruction with the efforts of other professionals, such as an occupational therapist.
- ☐ placing special emphasis on the teaching of difficult letters, such as **a, j, k, n, q, u,** and **z,** as well as reversals.
- ☐ ensuring that the student masters one style of handwriting before introducing a second style.

I make sure that I

- ☐ maintain my belief that I can teach each student in my class how to write fluently and legibly.
- ☐ set high but realistic expectations for the handwriting performance of each student in my class.
- ☐ maintain a balanced perspective on the role of handwriting in learning to write.

Cursive Evaluation Rubric

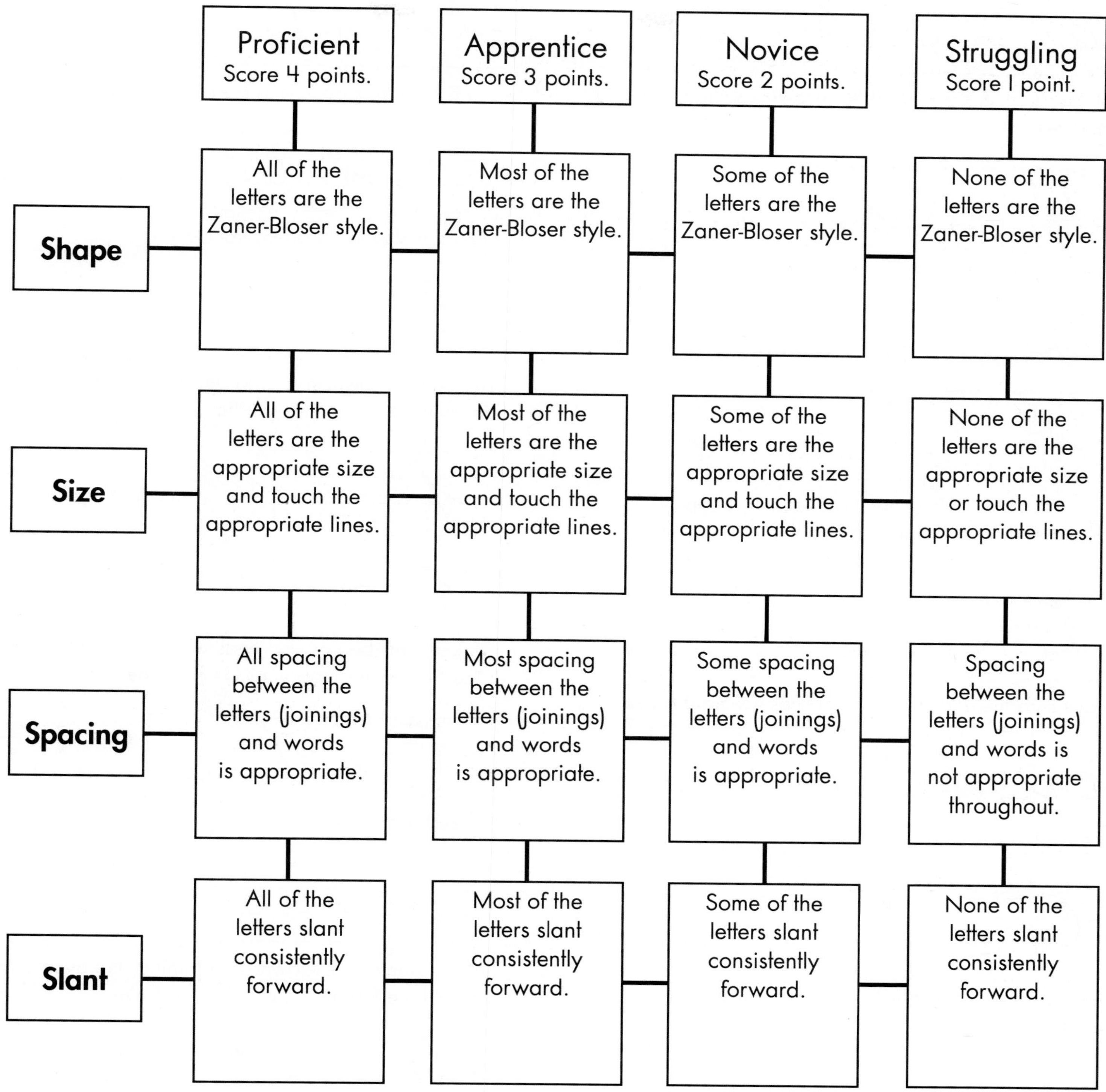

	Proficient Score 4 points.	Apprentice Score 3 points.	Novice Score 2 points.	Struggling Score 1 point.
Shape	All of the letters are the Zaner-Bloser style.	Most of the letters are the Zaner-Bloser style.	Some of the letters are the Zaner-Bloser style.	None of the letters are the Zaner-Bloser style.
Size	All of the letters are the appropriate size and touch the appropriate lines.	Most of the letters are the appropriate size and touch the appropriate lines.	Some of the letters are the appropriate size and touch the appropriate lines.	None of the letters are the appropriate size or touch the appropriate lines.
Spacing	All spacing between the letters (joinings) and words is appropriate.	Most spacing between the letters (joinings) and words is appropriate.	Some spacing between the letters (joinings) and words is appropriate.	Spacing between the letters (joinings) and words is not appropriate throughout.
Slant	All of the letters slant consistently forward.	Most of the letters slant consistently forward.	Some of the letters slant consistently forward.	None of the letters slant consistently forward.

Manuscript Evaluation Rubric available at **resources.zaner-bloser.com/hw**

Corrective Strategies for Cursive Letters

a not a

Pull the slant stroke toward the baseline with a good retrace.

A not A

Pause before writing the slant stroke.

be not be

b not b

In the checkstroke-to-undercurve joining, deepen the checkstroke before swinging into the undercurve. The second undercurve in **b** ends at the midline.

B not B

Make sure the ending stroke touches the slant stroke.

ci not ci

Swing wide on the undercurve-to-undercurve joining.

C not C

The first stroke is a short slant that begins at the headline.

d not d

Pull the slant stroke toward the baseline with a good retrace.

D not D

The first loop is open and rests on the baseline.

e not e

The loop should be open, not closed.

E not E

The bottom downcurve is larger than the top downcurve, and a little farther to the left.

f not f

f not f

Make sure **f** begins and ends with an undercurve. Close the lower loop near the baseline.

F not F

Pause before the retrace.

ga not ga

In the overcurve-to-downcurve joining, the overcurve ends at the beginning of the downcurve.

G not G

Pause before the retrace.

h not h

Close the loop near the midline and keep slant strokes parallel.

H not H

Retrace before the loop.

i not i

Pull the slant stroke toward the baseline and pause before making the undercurve ending.

I not I

Pause after the curve at the midline and retrace slightly.

ji not ji

Make sure the overcurve ending stops at the baseline to blend with the undercurve beginning.

J not J

Make sure the descender fills the space.

k not k

The curve under stroke is followed by a pause, slant right, and undercurve.

K not K

Curve forward and down before the undercurve ending.

l not l

Close the loop just below the midline.

L not L

The lower loop is horizontal and rests on the baseline.

m not m

Make sure there is enough space between the overcurves.

M not M

Pause after the first and second slant strokes.

n not n

Make sure there is enough space between the overcurves.

N not N

Make sure the overcurve is round.

oa not oa

The checkstroke swings wide to join a downcurve.

O not O

Dip the loop down slightly; then curve right to end at the headline.

Corrective Strategies for Cursive Letters (continued)

p not *p*

Close the loop near the baseline.

P not *P*

The forward oval curves around and goes below the midline.

q not *q*

Close the loop near the baseline.

Q not *Q*

The curve under stroke ends below the baseline.

r not *r*

Pause after the first undercurve and then slant right.

R not *R*

Pause at the slant stroke before beginning the second curve forward.

s not *s*

The final undercurve rests on the baseline.

S not *S*

Close the loop at the midline.

it not *it*

Swing wide on the undercurve-to-undercurve joining.

T not *T*

The first stroke begins at the headline.

u not *u*

Pause at the midline before writing the slant strokes.

U not *U*

Pause before retracing to write the second slant stroke.

v not *v*

The overcurve stroke curves up and over.

V not *V*

The undercurve is round, not pointed.

wi not *wi*

Deepen the retrace in the checkstroke before swinging into the undercurve of the next letter.

W not *W*

Parallel slant strokes will keep the undercurves open.

x not *x*

After writing the overcurve, be sure to slant left toward the baseline.

X not *X*

The second slant stroke crosses the first near the midline.

y not *y*

The overcurve ending crosses the slant stroke at the baseline.

Y not *Y*

Pause after the undercurve, to avoid looping.

z not *z*

Close the loop near the baseline.

Z not *Z*

The loop in **Z** should fill the descender space.

Corrective Strategies for Cursive Writing

break weather

Demonstrate the checkstroke joinings and explain the strokes as you write them.

Use the stroke description "retrace and curve right" as students practice these letters.

Point out the letters that change slightly when they are preceded by a checkstroke.

boat amount

Remind students to begin the downcurve stroke just below the midline. Encourage students to practice deep undercurve strokes to connect with the downcurve strokes.

too small

Instruct students to use ruled paper with a midline or to rule a midline on notebook paper. Explain that short letters should touch the midline.

Write freely

Show students how to evaluate their writing for size by drawing a horizontal line across the tops of letters that should be the same height.

laboratory

Remind students to shift both the paper and the hand as the writing progresses. The paper moves toward the student, and the hand moves away.

Show students how improving joinings will automatically improve letter spacing.

flight

Remind students to check their paper position and to pull strokes in the proper direction. Show students how to evaluate slant by drawing lines through the slant strokes of their letters. The lines should be parallel.

Glossary of Handwriting Terms

backward oval
an oval motion made in a counterclockwise direction, as in *a*

baseline
the guideline on which letters rest

basic manuscript strokes
lines that make up all manuscript letters: vertical, horizontal, circle, slant

basic cursive strokes
lines that make up all cursive letters: undercurve, downcurve, overcurve, slant

checkstroke
the modified undercurve that ends *b*, *o*, *v*, and *w*

circle back line
counterclockwise circle that begins at 1:00 position

circle forward line
clockwise circle that begins at 9:00 position

continuous-stroke manuscript alphabet
Zaner-Bloser alphabet that requires few or no lifts of the writing tool

cursive
slanted writing in which the letters are connected

descender
the part of a letter that extends below the baseline, as in **g** and *g*

directionality
top-to-bottom and left-to-right movement of eyes, hands, and writing tool when reading and writing

downcurve
a downward counterclockwise motion, such as the beginning stroke in *a*

downstroke
any stroke that is pulled downward

fine motor skills
movements such as grasping, releasing, tearing, cutting, drawing, and writing that depend on development of the small muscles such as those found in the hands and wrists; strength and control of the hand support a student's ability to write

forward oval
an oval motion made in a clockwise direction, as in *p*

grip
method of holding a writing tool; three-finger (tripod) grip is preferred

guideline
a line used for the placement of handwritten letters: headline, midline, baseline

hand preference
tendency to choose one dominant and more skilled hand (right or left) for tasks such as writing or throwing a ball

headline
guideline at the top of the writing space

helper hand
non-dominant or non-writing hand that steadies paper and other materials while dominant hand performs the task

Keys to Legibility
elements used to evaluate handwriting: shape, size, spacing, slant

lowercase letter
letter that is not uppercase or capital, sometimes referred to as a "small" letter

manuscript
writing in which the letters are vertical, are made up of lines and circles, and are not joined

midline
guideline which is halfway between the headline and the baseline

multisensory practice
writing practice that engages auditory, visual, and kinesthetic activities

overcurve
stroke made with an upward clockwise motion, as in *n*

pull down stroke
a vertical line written from top to bottom

retrace
backtracking or tracing over the same line

reversal
a writer's tendency to confuse letters of mirror-opposite shapes, such as **b** and **d**

shape
the form of a letter, determined by the basic strokes; one of the Keys to Legibility

short letter
letter that doesn't extend above the midline

size
the height of a letter, either short or tall, measured by the space it occupies above the baseline; one of the Keys to Legibility

skywriting
method of using large arm muscles to trace a letter's shape in the air before writing it on paper

slant
degree of tilt, or verticality, in written letters; one of the Keys to Legibility

slide line
horizontal line written from left to right or right to left

spacing
the distance between letters, words, and sentences; the distance between lines of writing; one of the Keys to Legibility

tall letter
letter that is of the greatest height from the baseline up; letter that touches the headline (in Grades K–4)

undercurve
a stroke made with an upward counterclockwise motion, as in *i*

uppercase letter
letter that is not lowercase, sometimes referred to as a capital letter or "big" letter

verticality
degree to which letters are written vertically

Glossary of Handwriting-Related Occupational Therapy Terms

bilateral skill
any activity or skill that requires both sides of the body or both hands to complete successfully

bimanual skill
any activity or skill that requires the use of both hands working cooperatively (e.g., opening a bottle top)

compensation technique
a different (and usually less complex) way to complete an activity

directionality
refers to the way that letters are formed when written on the page (e.g., English writing is read from left to right)

dominant hand
the preferred hand used during writing activities

dynamic movement
this movement refers to the ability of the fingers and wrist to move in a coordinated, yet independent manner; for example, a dynamic pencil grip refers to the ability to use the wrist and fingers to move the pencil, in contrast to moving the pencil using the whole arm while holding the wrist and fingers statically

fine motor endurance
the ability to maintain coordination of small muscle groups (such as in the hands, fingers, and wrists) to complete an activity that may take a long time; in handwriting, it is the ability to maintain a proper grasp pattern and proper writing mechanics over a long period of time or during lengthy writing assignments

fine motor skill
the coordination of small muscle groups (e.g., in the fingers) required to manipulate small objects

gross motor skill
the coordination of large muscle groups required to perform movement (e.g., raising your arms or walking)

hand-eye coordination
the ability to use visual input or information to help guide movements of the hand or arm (e.g., catching a ball)

in-hand manipulation
the ability to hold or move an object within one hand

intrinsic muscles
the deep, small muscles within the hand

letter formation
the ability to correctly connect lines or curves using upward, downward, horizontal, or diagonal movements of the pencil to cohesively create a letter

midline
refers to an imaginary line that runs vertically down the middle of the body; "crossing midline" refers to the action of reaching one's arm across the body to help complete a task presented on the other side of the body (e.g., reaching one's right arm across the body to the left side)

opposition
the movement of the thumb to reach across to connect with the pad of each finger (e.g., when the thumb is opposed to the pointer finger, one can make the "okay" sign)

perceptual skill
the ability to interpret and organize information that is received

prehension
the act of gripping or holding something in one's hand

pressure
the amount of force exerted with the pencil when writing on paper

recessive hand
the non-dominant hand, or the hand not usually used during writing activities

seating adaptation
any substitute made to a current seating position that helps to improve posture, attention, and ultimately handwriting (e.g., sitting on a therapy ball chair or placing an air-inflated disc on a regular school chair)

sensory feedback
any additional information received from the sensory system to further support acquiring a new skill (e.g., tracing letters on a student's back provides the child with tactile sensory feedback to help learn formation of new letters)

spatial skill
the ability to visualize what something looks like (e.g., knowing that a triangle is still a triangle even when it is turned upside down; knowing where to write a letter within the lines on a piece of paper)

stability
(in handwriting) having the firm support and proper alignment of the arm and shoulder needed to produce efficient written output

stereognosis
the ability to recognize items using only the sense of touch

tactile cue
any aid that can be felt that triggers or reminds the student of specific rules or positions to use while writing or performing fine motor tasks

tripod grasp
a holding pattern in which the writing utensil is held between the tips of the thumb and pointer finger with the utensil resting on the middle finger; the thumb and pointer finger should form a circle

visual cue
any aid that can be seen that triggers or reminds the student of specific rules or positions to use while writing or performing fine motor tasks

visual memory
the ability to remember a form/letter/shape after it has been removed from sight; in handwriting, the ability to remember how to correctly form letters without a visual guide

visual-motor integration
the ability to interpret visual information into written output (i.e., the ability to copy from the board in a classroom)

visual perceptual skill
the cognitive ability to correctly interpret visual information

visual tracking
the ability to follow an object through space with the eyes (e.g., tracking a thrown football)

web space
refers to the circular opening that is formed when the tip of the thumb and index finger are touching

weight bearing
any activity that requires one's body to work against gravity while putting pressure on the palms of the hands, arms, and shoulders

Scope and Sequence

	Grade K	Grade 1	Grade 2M	Grade 2C (manuscript/cursive)
Basic Strokes	15–36	14–21	10–13	10–11, 52–55, 60–61, 104–105
A, a	47–48, 51, 52, 60, 68, 78, 88, 96, 104, 105	56–57, 60–61	30–31, 32–33, 34, 78	18–19/82, 88, 100–101, 106, 112, 148
B, b	73–74, 77, 78, 88, 96, 104, 105	86–87, 90–91	54–55, 56–57, 62, 78	28–29/68, 70, 100–101, 143, 144, 148
C, c	53–54, 59, 60, 68, 78, 88, 96, 104, 105	64–65, 70–71	38–39, 40–41, 46, 78	20–21/86, 88, 100–101, 109, 112, 148
D, d	49–50, 51, 52, 60, 68, 78, 88, 96, 104, 105	58–59, 60–61	30–31, 32–33, 34, 78	18–19/83, 88, 100–101, 108, 112, 148
E, e	55–56, 59, 60, 68, 78, 88, 96, 104, 105	66–67, 70–71	38–39, 40–41, 46, 78	20–21/66, 70, 100–101, 110, 112, 148
F, f	57–58, 59, 60, 68, 78, 88, 96, 104, 105	68–69, 70–71	38–39, 40–41, 46, 78	22–23/74, 80, 100–101, 135, 136, 148
G, g	61–62, 67, 68, 78, 88, 96, 104, 105	72–73, 78–79	42–43, 44–45, 46, 78	22–23/84, 88, 100–101, 138, 144, 148
H, h	85–86, 87, 88, 96, 104, 105	98–99, 100–101	58–59, 60–61, 62, 78	32–33/73, 80, 100–101, 117, 120, 148
I, I	39–40, 43, 44, 52, 60, 68, 78, 88, 96, 104, 105	46–47, 52–53	26–27, 28–29, 34, 78	14–15/62, 70, 100–101, 131, 136, 148
J, j	63–64, 67, 68, 78, 88, 96, 104, 105	74–75, 78–79	42–43, 44–45, 46, 78	24–25/78, 80, 100–101, 132, 136, 148
K, k	99–100, 103, 104, 105	114–115, 118–119	70–71, 72–73, 74, 78	38–39/75, 80, 100–101, 118, 120, 148
L, l	37–38, 43, 44, 52, 60, 68, 78, 88, 96, 104, 105	44–45, 52–53	26–27, 28–29, 34, 78	14–15/67, 70, 100–101, 140, 144, 148
M, m	83–84, 87, 88, 96, 104, 105	96–97, 100–101	58–59, 60–61, 62, 78	32–33/91, 96, 100–101, 116, 120, 148
N, n	81–82, 87, 88, 96, 104, 105	94–95, 100–101	58–59, 60–61, 62, 79	30–31/90, 96, 100–101, 115, 120, 149
O, o	45–46, 51, 52, 60, 68, 78, 88, 96, 104, 105	54–55, 60–61	30–31, 32–33, 34, 79	16–17/85, 88, 100–101, 107, 112, 149
P, p	75–76, 77, 78, 88, 96, 104, 105	88–89, 90–91	54–55, 56–57, 62, 79	28–29/79, 80, 100–101, 141, 144, 149
Q, q	65–66, 67, 68, 78, 88, 96, 104, 105	76–77, 78–79	42–43, 44–45, 46, 79	24–25/87, 88, 100–101, 133, 136, 149
R, r	79–80, 87, 88, 96, 104, 105	92–93, 100–101	54–55, 56–57, 62, 79	30–31/76, 80, 100–101, 142, 144, 149
S, s	71–72, 77, 78, 88, 96, 104, 105	84–85, 90–91	50–51, 52–53, 62, 79	26–27/77, 80, 100–101, 139, 144, 149
T, t	41–42, 43, 44, 52, 60, 68, 78, 88, 96, 104, 105	48–49, 52–53	26–27, 28–29, 34, 79	16–17/63, 70, 100–101, 134, 136, 149
U, u	69–70, 77, 78, 88, 96, 104, 105	82–83, 90–91	50–51, 52–53, 62, 79	26–27/64, 70, 100–101, 119, 120, 149
V, v	89–90, 95, 96, 104, 105	104–105, 110–111	66–67, 68–69, 74, 79	34–35/94, 96, 100–101, 124, 128, 149
W, w	93–94, 95, 96, 104, 105	108–109, 110–111	66–67, 68–69, 74, 79	36–37/65, 70, 100–101, 125, 128, 149
X, x	97–98, 103, 104, 105	112–113, 118–119	70–71, 72–73, 74, 79	36–37/93, 96, 100–101, 126, 128, 149
Y, y	91–92, 95, 96, 104, 105	106–107, 110–111	66–67, 68–69, 74, 79	34–35/92, 96, 100–101, 122, 128, 149
Z, z	101–102, 103, 104, 105	116–117, 118–119	70–71, 72–73, 74, 79	38–39/95, 96, 100–101, 123, 128, 149
Numerals	109–120, 121, 122–123	9, 30–43, 122–123	22–25, 80–83	40–41/46–47, 102–103
Assessment and Evaluation	9, 37–42, 45–50, 53–58, 61–66, 69–76, 79–86, 89–94, 97–102, 106, 107, 109–118, 141–142, 143, T145	6, 7, 15, 17, 18, 19, 21, 30, 31, 32, 33, 34, 35, 36, 37, 44, 46, 48, 50, 53, 54, 56, 58, 61, 64, 66, 68, 71, 72, 74, 76, 79, 82, 84, 86, 88, 91, 92, 94, 96, 98, 101, 104, 106, 108, 111, 112, 114, 116, 119, 140, 141, 142, 143, T6, T106, T122, T145	6, 7, 10, 11, 12, 13, 22, 23, 26, 28, 30, 32, 38, 40, 42, 44, 47, 50, 52, 54, 56, 58, 60, 63, 66, 68, 70, 72, 75, 116, 117, 118, 119, T6, T14, T33, T84, T114, T118, T121	6, 7, 14, 16, 18, 20, 22, 24, 26, 28, 30, 31, 32, 34, 36, 38, 40–41, 42–43, 52, 53, 54–55, 60, 61, 62, 63, 64, 65, 66, 67, 68, 69, 71, 73, 74, 75, 76, 77, 78, 79, 81, 82, 83, 84, 85, 86, 87, 90, 91, 92, 93, 94, 95, 102, 104, 105, 106, 107, 108, 109, 110, 111, 115, 116, 117, 118, 119, 122, 123, 124, 125, 126, 127, 131, 132, 133, 134, 135, 138, 139, 140, 141, 142, 143, 164, 165, 166, 167, T7, T152, T161, T164, T169
Automaticity		138–139, T96, T138	112–113, 114–115, T112	160–161, 162–163, T160
Corrective Strategies	T146–T149	T146–T149	T122–T125	T170–T173
ELL Support	T11, T13, T15, T17, T19, T21, T23, T25, T27, T29, T31, T33, T35, T37, T39, T41, T43, T45, T47, T49, T51, T53, T55, T57, T59, T61, T63, T65, T67, T69, T71, T73, T75, T77, T79, T81, T83, T85, T87, T89, T91, T93, T95, T97, T99, T101, T103, T106, T109, T111, T113, T115, T117, T119, T121, T123, T125, T127, T129, T131, T133, T135, T137, T139, T141	T7, T9, T11, T13, T15, T17, T19, T21, T23, T25, T27, T29, T31, T33, T35, T37, T39, T41, T43, T45, T47, T49, T51, T53, T55, T57, T59, T61, T63, T65, T67, T69, T71, T73, T75, T77, T79, T81, T83, T85, T87, T89, T91, T93, T95, T97, T99, T101, T103, T105, T107, T109, T111, T113, T115, T117, T119, T121, T123, T125, T127, T129, T131, T135, T139, T141	T7, T9, T11, T13, T15, T17, T19, T21, T25, T27, T29, T31, T33, T35, T37, T39, T41, T43, T45, T47, T49, T51, T53, T55, T57, T59, T61, T63, T65, T67, T69, T71, T73, T75, T77, T79, T81, T83, T85, T87, T89, T91, T93, T95, T97, T99, T101, T103, T105, T107, T109, T113, T115, T117	T6, T10, T11, T12, T14, T16, T18, T20, T22, T24, T26, T28, T30, T32, T34, T36, T38, T40, T42, T44, T46, T48, T51, T52, T53, T54, T55, T56, T57, T58, T59, T60, T62, T64, T66, T68, T70, T72, T74, T76, T78, T80, T82, T84, T86, T88, T90, T92, T94, T96, T98, T100, T102, T104, T106, T108, T110, T112, T114, T116, T118, T120, T122, T124, T126, T128, T130, T132, T134, T136, T138, T140, T142, T144, T146, T148, T150, T152, T154, T156, T158, T162, T164

	Grade 3	Grade 4	Grade 5	Grade 6
Basic Strokes	7, 28–32, 36–52, 60–66, 71–77, 90–98, 100–110, 118–121	12–14, 18, 19, 21–24, 26–29, 39–41, 32–34, 46, 50–54, 68, 69	6, 8, 10–13, 16–18, 22–24, 28–30	6–8, 10–15, 18–20, 24–26
A, a	9, 22, 61, 82, 90, 92, 93, 137	8, 9, 18, 32, 48, 50, 51	7, 22, 38	7, 18, 34
B, b	12, 22, 45, 82, 91, 126, 132, 137	8, 9, 18, 26, 46, 50, 73, 78	7, 13, 55	7, 13, 49
C, c	10, 22, 65, 82, 90, 92, 96, 137	8, 9, 18, 34, 46, 50, 53, 78	7, 24, 39	7, 20, 35
D, d	9, 22, 62, 82, 90, 92, 95, 137	8, 9, 18, 32, 46, 50, 53, 78	7, 22, 39	7, 18, 35
E, e	10, 22, 43, 82, 90, 92, 97, 137	8, 9, 18, 23, 46, 50, 54, 78	7, 12, 39	7, 12, 35
F, f	10, 22, 47, 82, 91, 118, 123, 137	8, 9, 18, 27, 46, 50, 69, 78	7, 16, 51	7, 13, 45
G, g	11, 22, 63, 82, 91, 126, 127, 137	8, 9, 18, 33, 46, 50, 72, 78	7, 23, 54	7, 19, 48
H, h	13, 23, 46, 83, 90, 100, 103, 137	8, 9, 18, 26, 46, 50, 60, 78	7, 13, 43	7, 13, 39
I, I	8, 23, 39, 83, 91, 118, 119, 137	8, 9, 18, 21, 46, 50, 68, 78	7, 10, 50	7, 10, 44
J, j	11, 23, 51, 83, 91, 118, 120, 137	8, 9, 18, 29, 46, 50, 68, 78	7, 18, 50	7, 15, 44
K, k	15, 23, 48, 83, 90, 100, 104, 137	8, 9, 18, 27, 46, 50, 60, 78	7, 16, 43	7, 14, 39
L, l	8, 23, 44, 83, 91, 126, 129, 137	8, 9, 18, 23, 46, 50, 72, 78	7, 12, 54	7, 12, 48
M, m	13, 23, 73, 83, 90, 100, 102, 137	8, 9, 18, 39, 46, 50, 59, 78	7, 28, 42	7, 24, 38
N, n	13, 23, 73, 82, 90, 100, 102, 137	8, 9, 18, 39, 46, 50, 59, 78	7, 28, 42	7, 24, 38
O, o	9, 23, 64, 82, 90, 92, 94, 137	8, 9, 18, 33, 46, 50, 51, 78	7, 23, 38	7, 19, 34
P, p	12, 23, 52, 82, 91, 126, 130, 137	8, 9, 18, 29, 46, 50, 73, 78	7, 18, 55	7, 15, 49
Q, q	11, 23, 66, 82, 91, 118, 121, 137	8, 9, 18, 34, 46, 50, 68, 78	7, 24, 50	7, 20, 44
R, r	13, 23, 49, 82, 91, 126, 131, 137	8, 9, 18, 28, 46, 50, 73, 78	7, 17, 55	7, 14, 49
S, s	12, 23, 50, 82, 91, 126, 128, 137	8, 9, 18, 28, 46, 50, 72, 78	7, 17, 54	7, 14, 48
T, t	8, 23, 40, 82, 91, 118, 122, 137	8, 9, 18, 21, 46, 50, 69, 78	7, 10, 51	7, 10, 45
U, u	12, 23, 41, 83, 90, 100, 105, 137	8, 9, 18, 22, 46, 50, 61, 78	7, 11, 44	7, 11, 40
V, v	14, 23, 76, 83, 90, 100, 108, 137	8, 9, 18, 41, 46, 50, 64, 78	7, 30, 45	7, 26, 41
W, w	14, 23, 42, 83, 90, 100, 109, 137	8, 9, 18, 22, 46, 50, 65, 78	7, 11, 46	7, 11, 41
X, x	15, 23, 75, 83, 90, 100, 110, 137	8, 9, 18, 40, 46, 50, 65, 78	7, 29, 46	7, 25, 41
Y, y	14, 23, 74, 83, 90, 100, 106, 137	8, 9, 18, 40, 46, 50, 61, 78	7, 29, 44	7, 25, 40
Z, z	15, 23, 77, 83, 90, 100, 107, 137	8, 9, 18, 41, 46, 50, 64, 78	7, 30, 45	7, 26, 40
Numerals	23, 86, 87	8, 9, 48, 49	7, 80	7
Assessment and Evaluation	5, 8–15, 18–19, 28–31, 36–53, 55, 60–67, 69, 71–77, 79, 83, 86, 90–97, 99–111, 113, 118–123, 125–132, 135, 143, 153, 155–159, T19, T153, T161	5–7, 12, 13, 18, 21–23, 25, 31–37, 39–43, 52–57, 59–65, 68, 69, 72, 73, 82–85, 87–89, 91, 94, 105, 107–109, 111, T7, T109, T113	4, 5, 10–13, 15–18, 20, 22–24, 27–30, 34, 35, 38, 39, 41–46, 48–55, 57, 61, 67–75, 91, 93–95, T5, T97	5, 10–15, 18–20, 22–26, 29, 31, 34, 35, 37, 38–41, 43–45, 47–49, 51, 53, 57, 60, 61, 75, 77–79, T5
Automaticity	152–155, T142, T148, T152–T155	104–107, T91, T104–T107	90–93, T90	74–77, T74
Corrective Strategies	T162–T165	T114–T117	T98–T101	T82–T85
ELL Support	T7, T8, T10, T12, T14, T16, T20, T22, T24, T27–T36, T38, T40, T42, T44, T46, T48, T50, T52–T54, T56, T59, T60, T62, T64, T66, T68, T70, T72, T74, T76, T78, T80, T83, T84, T87, T88, T90, T92, T94, T96, T98, T100, T102, T104, T106, T108, T110, T112, T114, T116, T118, T120, T122, T124, T126, T128, T130, T132, T134, T136, T138, T140, T142, T145, T147, T148, T150, T151, T154–T156, T158	T8, T12, T14–T18, T20, T22, T24, T26, T28, T30, T32, T34, T36, T38, T40, T42, T44, T46, T48, T50, T52, T54, T56, T58, T60, T62, T64, T66, T68, T70, T72, T74, T76, T78, T80, T82, T84, T86, T88, T90, T92, T94, T97, T99, T100, T101, T103, T104, T106, T108, T109	T6, T8, T10, T12, T14, T16, T18, T20, T22, T24, T26, T28, T30, T32, T34, T36, T38, T40, T42, T44, T46, T48, T50, T52, T54, T56, T58, T60, T62, T64, T66, T68, T70, T72, T74, T76, T78, T80, T82, T84, T87, T90, T92	T6, T8, T10, T12, T14, T16, T18, T20, T22, T24, T26, T28, T30, T32, T34, T36, T38, T40, T42, T44, T46, T48, T50, T52, T54, T56, T58, T60, T62, T64, T66, T69, T71, T74, T76

Scope and Sequence (continued)

	Grade K	Grade 1	Grade 2M	Grade 2C (manuscript/cursive)
Handwriting Coaching Tips	T6, T8, T10, T12, T14, T16, T18, T20, T22, T24, T26, T28, T30, T32, T34, T36, T38, T40, T44, T46, T48, T52, T54, T56, T60, T62, T64, T68, T70, T72, T74, T78, T80, T82, T84, T88, T90, T92, T96, T98, T100, T104, T105, T112, T116, T120, T122, T124, T128, T130, T132, T134, T136, T138, T140	T6, T8, T10, T12, T14, T16, T18, T20, T22, T24, T26, T28, T44, T46, T48, T50, T54, T56, T58, T62, T64, T66, T68, T72, T74, T76, T80, T82, T84, T86, T88, T92, T94, T96, T98, T102, T104, T106, T08, T112, T114, T116, T120, T122, T124, T126, T128, T130, T132, T134, T136, T138, T140, T142	T6, T8, T10, T12, T14, T20, T28, T32, T36, T38, T44, T48, T52, T58, T64, T66, T70, T76, T82, T84, T88, T90, T92, T94, T98, T100, T102, T104, T106, T108, T110, T112, T114, T116, T118	T7, T8, T12, T44, T46, T48, T56, T58, T60, T72, T98, T100, T104, T111, T114, T130, T146, T150, T151, T152, T153, T154, T158, T160, T161, T162, T163, T164
Indentation and Margin Practice		131, 133, 135	6–7, 35, 36–37, 47, 48–49, 63, 64–65, 75, 76–77, 83, 91, 93, 95, 97, 99, 101, 103, 105, 107, 109, 110, 112–113, 114–115, 116–117	6–7, 42–43, 114, 130, 146, 147, 151, 153, 154–155, 156, 158–159, 160–161, 162–163
Joinings				69, 111, 127, T111, T114
Keys to Legibility		13, 22–23, 24–25, 26–27, 28–29, 45, 47, 49, 51, 55, 57, 59, 62–63, 65, 67, 69, 73, 75, 77, 80–81, 83, 85, 87, 89, 93, 95, 97, 99, 102–103, 105, 107, 109, 113, 115, 117, 120–121, 123, 125, 127, 141, T13, T22, T24, T26, T28, T62, T74, T80, T102, T123, T125, T127, T138	5, 14–15, 16–17, 18–19, 20–21, 27, 29, 31, 33, 37, 39, 41, 43, 45, 49, 51, 53, 55, 57, 59, 61, 65, 69, 71, 73, 77, 79, 81, 83, 87, 89, 91, 93, 95, 97, 99, 101, 103, 115, 117, T14, T16, T18, T20, T36, T48, T64, T76, T77, T91, T99, T102, T110, T118	5, 12, 13, 15, 17, 19, 21, 23, 25, 27, 29, 31, 33, 35, 37, 39, 43, 56, 57, 58, 59, 63, 65, 67, 73, 75, 77, 79, 83, 85, 87, 89, 91, 93, 95, 97, 99, 101, 103, 107, 109, 113, 115, 117, 119, 120, 121, 123, 125, 129, 131, 133, 135, 141, 143, 145, 147, 149, 163, 165, T12, T42, T56, T57, T58, T59, T98, T146, T147
Manuscript Maintenance			78–79	
Occupational Therapist Tips	T11, T13, T15, T17, T19, T21, T23, T25, T27, T29, T31, T33, T35, T37, T39, T41, T43, T45, T47, T49, T51, T53, T55, T57, T59, T61, T63, T65, T67, T69, T71, T73, T75, T77, T79, T81, T83, T85, T87, T89, T91, T93, T95, T97, T99, T101, T103, T106, T109, T111, T113, T115, T117, T119, T121, T123, T125, T127, T129, T131, T133, T135, T137, T139, T141	T7, T9, T11, T13, T15, T17, T19, T21, T23, T25, T27, T29, T31, T33, T35, T37, T39, T41, T43, T45, T47, T49, T51, T53, T55, T57, T59, T61, T63, T65, T67, T69, T71, T73, T75, T77, T79, T81, T83, T85, T87, T89, T91, T93, T95, T97, T99, T101, T103, T105, T107, T109, T111, T113, T115, T117, T119, T121, T123, T125, T127, T129, T131, T133, T135, T139, T141	T7, T9, T11, T13, T15, T17, T19, T21, T25, T27, T29, T31, T33, T35, T37, T39, T41, T43, T45, T47, T49, T51, T53, T55, T57, T59, T61, T63, T65, T67, T69, T71, T73, T75, T77, T79, T81, T83, T85, T87, T89, T91, T93, T95, T97, T99, T101, T103, T105, T107, T109, T113, T115, T117	T13, T15, T21, T27, T33, T39, T49, T61, T67, T73, T79, T85, T89, T97, T99, T109, T111, T117, T127, T133, T139, T145, T151, T153, T159, T166
Positions: Paper, Pencil, Sitting	12–13, T10, T11, T25, T27, T35, T49, T65, T70, T89, T90, T101, T134	10–11, T10, T15, T19, T21, T31, T44, T46, T49, T68, T89, T107, T124, T133, T134	8–9, 21, T8, T9, T20, T43, T88, T104, T108	8–9, 50–51, 59, T8, T48, T51, T72, T130
Technology	T10, T12, T34, T36, T38, T40, T44, T46, T48, T52, T54, T56, T59, T60, T62, T64, T68, T70, T72, T74, T77, T78, T80, T82, T84, T87, T88, T90, T92, T96, T98, T100, T104, T108, T110, T112, T114, T116	T7, T10, T11, T12, T22, T23, T24, T26, T28, T30, T32, T34, T36, T44, T46, T48, T53, T54, T56, T58, T64, T66, T68, T71, T72, T74, T76, T81, T82, T84, T86, T88, T92, T94, T96, T98, T101, T103, T104, T106, T108, T111, T112, T114, T116	T5, T7, T8, T14, T16, T18, T19, T20, T22, T23, T26, T28, T30, T32, T35, T38, T40, T42, T44, T50, T52, T54, T56, T58, T60, T63, T65, T66, T68, T70, T72, T75, T95, T115	T5, T8, T14, T15, T16, T17, T18, T19, T20, T21, T22, T23, T24, T25, T26, T27, T28, T29, T30, T31, T32, T33, T34, T35, T36, T37, T38, T39, T40, T41, T47, T50, T56, T57, T58, T59, T62, T63, T64, T65, T66, T67, T68, T73, T74, T75, T76, T77, T78, T79, T82, T83, T84, T85, T86, T87, T90, T91, T92, T93, T94, T102, T103, T106, T107, T108, T109, T110, T115, T116, T117, T118, T119, T122, T123, T124, T125, T126, T131, T132, T133, T134, T135, T138, T139, T140, T141, T142, T143, T147
Writing in the Content Areas	T43, T51, T67, T95, T119	T25, T27, T29, T43, T61, T63, T79, T91, T119, T121	T15, T17, T21, T37, T47, T49, T77, T79	T7, T17, T23, T29, T31, T37, T41, T45, T63, T69, T71, T77, T81, T83, T91, T93, T95, T101, T107, T113, T115, T119, T121, T123, T125, T129, T131, T137, T141, T143, T149, T161, T163, T165
Writing in the Text Types (Narrative, Informative/ Explanatory, Opinion, Argument)	129, 130, 131, 132, 133–134, 135–136, 137–138, T128, T129, T130, T131, T132–T133, T134–T135, T136–T137, T138	128, 129, 130, 131, 132, 133, 134, 135, 136, 137, T25, T29, T61, T63, T79	104, 105, 106, 107, 108, 109, 110, 111, T15, T17, T47, T77	150, 151, 152, 153, 154, 155, 156, 157, T17, T23, T31, T37, T69, T71, T77, T83, T93, T95, T101, T113, T121, T129, T131, T137, T163, T165

	Grade 3	Grade 4	Grade 5	Grade 6
Handwriting Coaching Tips	T7, T19, T32, T34, T58, T80, T116, T138, T144, T145, T146, T147, T148, T149, T152, T153, T155	T6–T9, T14, T16, T20, T44, T76, T80–T83, T85, T86, T88–T101, T104, T106, T109	T5, T7–T9, T25, T32, T36, T47, T56, T64	T5, T7, T9, T27, T32, T54, T74, T76, T80, T90, T92
Indentation and Margin Practice	19, 56, 58, 59, 69, 99, 113, 114, 116, 117, 125, 135, 136, 139–143, 145–150	25, 31, 37, 43, 56–58, 62, 63, 66, 70, 74, 77, 87–89, 91, 94, 96–103, 106, 107	15, 21, 26, 27, 32, 33, 35, 37, 41, 49, 53, 61–63, 65, 67, 72, 78, 82–85, 87–88, 90, 91, 92, 93	17, 23, 31, 33, 37, 43, 47, 53, 55, 56, 58–60, 63, 66–69, 71–72, 74–77
Joinings	53, 67, 84, 85, 92, 100, 111, 126, 133, T80	20–24, 26–30, 32–36, 39–42, 46, 52–55, 59–61, 64, 65, 68, 69, 72, 73, 79, T20, T97, T100	10–13, 16–18, 22–24, 28–30, 32, 33, 38, 39, 42–46, 50, 51, 54–57, 63, 64, T9, T32, T54–T56	17, 28, 29, 31, 50, 51, T43
Keys to Legibility	5, 7–15, 32–35, 38, 39, 41, 43, 45, 47, 49, 51, 58–61, 63, 65, 71, 73, 75, 77, 80, 81, 83, 92, 93, 97, 100, 101, 103, 107, 109, 116–119, 123, 126, 127, 129, 138, 139, 153, 155, T32, T34, T116	5, 14–17, 21, 23, 25, 27, 30, 33, 36, 39, 41, 42, 44, 45, 56, 59, 61, 62, 65, 69, 73, 76, 77, 82–85, 87–89, 91, 94, 105, 107, T14, T16, T44, T76, T82, T83, T85, T101, T108	4, 8–10, 12, 16, 18, 20, 22, 24, 26, 30, 34, 36, 37, 46, 48, 52, 54, 58, 64, 65, 67, 70, 72–75, 78, 91, 93, T8, T36, T64	4, 8, 9, 16, 22, 30, 32, 33, 36, 42, 46, 52, 54, 55, 58, 59, 63, 75, 77, T20, T24, T26, T32, T54
Manuscript Maintenance	6–17, 57, 88, 89, 115, 140, 141, T7	47, 80, T80	19, 25, 31, 47, 76, 80, T19, T25, T31, T76, T80, T86, T88	21, 27, T27
Occupational Therapist Tips	T13, T19, T25, T37, T41, T47, T55, T63, T67, T73, T79, T85, T97, T105, T109, T115, T117, T121, T127, T133, T139, T144, T146, T149	T13, T19, T27, T31, T37, T43, T49, T55, T61, T67, T73, T79, T85, T91, T96, T98, T102, T107, T110	T7, T13, T19, T25, T31, T35, T39, T45, T47, T51, T57, T63, T67, T73, T79, T81, T83, T85, T86, T88, T93	T7, T13, T19, T25, T31, T35, T41, T47, T53, T57, T63, T65, T67, T68, T70, T72, T77
Positions: Paper, Pencil, Sitting	6, 26, 27, 35, T35, T58, T149	10, 11, 17, T81, T96	6, T7, T47, T88	6, T27
Technology	T5, T6, T8–T15, T23, T24, T26, T32–T35, T39–T52, T57, T61–T66, T72–T77, T81, T86, T88, T91, T93–T97, T99, T101–T111, T115, T119–T123, T125, T127–T132, T137, T140, T152	T5, T9–T10, T14–T17, T21–T24, T26–T30, T32–T34, T36, T39–T42, T47–T49, T51–T54, T56, T59–T62, T64–T66, T68–T70, T72–T74, T77, T80, T81, T83, T84, T93, T95, T104	T4, T6, T8–T20, T22–T26, T28–T31, T33, T37–T39, T42–T47, T50, T51, T55, T59, T61, T69, T71, T75, T76, T80, T90	T4, T8, T11, T15, T16, T18–T27, T29, T30, T33–T36, T38–T42, T44–T46, T48, T49, T51, T52, T55, T59, T61, T74
Writing in the Content Areas	T9, T11, T15, T17, T21, T39, T49, T51, T61, T65, T69, T71, T75, T77, T89, T93, T95, T101, T103, T107, T113, T119, T123, T129, T131, T135, T141, T143	T21, T25, T33, T35, T41, T45, T47, T53, T57, T59, T63, T65, T69, T71, T75, T87, T89, T105, T109	T11, T17, T21, T27, T29, T41, T43, T49, T53, T55, T65, T77, T91, T94	T17, T21, T27, T37, T39, T43, T45, T49, T75, T78
Writing in the Text Types (Narrative, Informative/ Explanatory, Opinion, Argument)	142–151, 154–155, T15, T61, T65, T69, T71, T75, T77, T93, T95, T103, T129, T131, T135, T141–T147, T148, T150, T151, T154, T155	92–103, T33, T35, T41, T47, T53, T65, T69, T71, T89	77–79, 81–89, 92, 93, T27, T29, T41, T43, T49, T53, T55, T65, T77–T79, T81–T89, T91–T93	58, 59, 62, 63, 65–73, 76, 77, T17, T21, T33, T39, T45, T49, T58, T59, T62–T73, T75–T77

Index

Alphabet, T22–T23, T82–T83, T137

Automaticity, T5, T148; *See* Writing Easily; Writing Quickly

Basic strokes
- cursive
  - curve forward, T90, T100–T110
  - doublecurve, T91, T118, T122, T123
  - downcurve, T29, T32, T37, T60–T66, T90, T92–T97
  - overcurve, T30, T32, T37, T71–T77, T91, T118–T121
  - slant, T31, T32
  - undercurve, T28, T32, T36, T38–T52
  - undercurve-loop, T91, T126–T129
  - undercurve-slant, T91, T126, T130–T132
- manuscript, T7

Corrective Strategies, T162–T165

Cursive writing, *See* Letter groupings; Letters
- introducing, T20–T23
- reading, T24–T25

Cursive Writing in the Real World, T56, T70, T114, T136

English Language Learners, Support for, T7, T8, T10, T12, T14, T16, T20, T22, T24, T27–T36, T38, T40, T42, T44, T46, T48, T50, T52–T54, T56, T59, T60, T62, T64, T66, T68, T70, T72, T74, T76, T78, T80, T83, T84, T87, T88, T90, T92, T94, T96, T98, T100, T102, T104, T106, T108, T110, T112, T114, T116, T118, T120, T122, T124, T126, T128, T130, T132, T134, T136, T138, T140, T142, T145, T147, T148, T150, T151, T154, T156, T158

Evaluation
- Cursive Evaluation Rubric, T161
- posttest, T156–T157
- pretest, T18–T19
- Record of Student's Handwriting Skills, T159
- self-evaluation, T8–T17, T28–T31, T36–T57, T59, T60–T79, T81, T85, T86, T87, T88, T89, T90–T115, T117–T137, T139, T140, T141, T153

Glossary
- Handwriting terms, T166, T167
- Occupational therapy terms, T168, T169

Grammar, usage, and mechanics
- adjectives, T79
- homophones, T55, T56
- nouns, T69

Handwriting Coach, T7, T19, T32, T34, T58, T80, T116, T138, T144–T149, T152, T153, T155

Handwriting Instruction, Checklist for, T160

Indentation and margin practice, T18, T58, T59, T69, T99, T112, T113, T116, T125, T135, T136, T139, T142, T143, T145–T148, T150, T152–T155, T157

Joinings
- lowercase, T53, T67, T84, T85
- uppercase, T111, T133

Keys to Legibility
- shape, T5, T7, T8, T12, T32, T39, T47, T58–T61, T71, T75, T80, T81, T83, T92, T97, T100, T107, T116–T118, T123, T126, T138, T139, T153, T155
- size, T5, T7, T9, T13, T33, T41, T49, T58–T60, T63, T71, T77, T80, T81, T83, T92, T100, T101, T109, T116–T118, T126, T127, T138, T139, T153, T155
- slant, T5, T7, T11, T15, T35, T45, T58–T60, T71, T73, T80, T81, T83, T92, T95, T100, T105, T116–T118, T121, T126, T131, T138, T139, T153, T155
- spacing, T5, T7, T10, T14, T34, T43, T51, T58–T60, T65, T71, T80, T81, T83, T92, T93, T100, T103, T116–T119, T126, T129, T138, T139, T153, T155

Left-handed writers, T6, T26, T35

Legibility, *See* Keys to Legibility

Letter groupings
- cursive
  - lowercase beginning strokes
    - downcurve letters, T29, T37, T60–T66
    - overcurve letters, T30, T37, T71–T77
    - undercurve letters, T28, T36, T38–T52
  - uppercase beginning strokes
    - curve forward letters, T90, T100–T110
    - doublecurve letters, T91, T118, T122, T123
    - downcurve letters, T29, T90, T92–T98
    - overcurve letters, T30, T91, T118–T121
    - undercurve-loop letters, T91, T126–T129
    - undercurve-slant letters, T91, T126, T130–T132
- manuscript
  - lowercase, T8–T15
  - uppercase, T8–T15

Letters
- lowercase, **a:** T9, T22, T61, T82; **b:** T12, T22, T45, T82; **c:** T10, T22, T65, T82; **d:** T9, T22, T62, T82; **e:** T10, T22, T43, T82; **f:** T10, T22, T47, T82; **g:** T11, T22, T63, T82; **h:** T13, T23, T46, T82; **i:** T8, T23, T39, T82; **j:** T11, T23, T51, T82; **k:** T15, T23, T48, T82; **l:** T8, T23, T44, T82; **m:** T13, T23, T73, T82; **n:** T13, T23, T72, T82; **o:** T9, T23, T64, T82; **p:** T12, T23, T52, T82; **q:** T11, T23, T66, T82; **r:** T13, T23, T49, T82; **s:** T12, T23, T50, T82; **t:** T8, T23, T40, T82; **u:** T12, T23, T41, T82; **v:** T14, T23, T76, T82; **w:** T14, T23, T42, T82; **x:** T15, T23, T75, T82; **y:** T14, T23, T74, T82; **z:** T15, T23, T77, T82
- uppercase, **A:** T9, T22, T90, T92, T93, T137; **B:** T12, T22, T91, T126, T132, T137; **C:** T10, T22, T90, T92, T96, T137; **D:** T9, T22, T90, T92, T95, T137; **E:** T10, T22, T90, T92, T97, T137; **F:** T10, T22, T91, T118, T123, T137; **G:** T11, T22, T91, T126, T127, T137; **H:** T13, T23, T90, T100, T103, T137; **I:** T8, T23, T91, T118, T119, T137; **J:** T11, T23, T91, T118, T120, T137; **K:** T15, T23, T90, T100, T104, T137; **L:** T8, T23, T91, T126, T129, T137; **M:** T13, T23, T90, T100, T102, T137; **N:** T13, T23, T90, T100, T101, T137; **O:** T9, T23, T90, T92, T94, T137; **P:** T12, T23, T91, T126, T130, T137; **Q:** T11, T23, T91, T118, T121, T137;

R: T13, T23, T91, T126, T131, T137; **S:** T12, T23, T91, T126, T128, T137; **T:** T8, T23, T91, T118, T122, T137; **U:** T12, T23, T90, T100, T105, T137; **V:** T14, T23, T90, T100, T108, T137; **W:** T14, T23, T90, T100, T109, T137; **X:** T15, T23, T90, T100, T110, T137; **Y:** T14, T23, T90, T100, T106, T137; **Z:** T15, T23, T90, T100, T107, T137

Manuscript Maintenance, T57, T88, T89, T115, T140, T141

Manuscript Review, T6–T17

Numerals, T23, T86, T87

Occupational Therapist, Tips From an, T13, T19, T25, T37, T41, T47, T55, T63, T67, T73, T79, T85, T97, T105, T109, T115, T117, T121, T127, T133, T139, T144, T146, T149

Poetry, T18, T58, T59, T156

Posttest, T156–T157

Pretest, T18–T19

Record of Student's Handwriting Skills, T159

References, T176

Review, T16, T54, T68, T78, T82–T83, T98, T112, T124, T134, T137

Right-handed writers, T6, T27, T35

Rubric, Cursive Evaluation, T161

Scope and Sequence, T170–T173

Technology
- Digital Tools, T54, T68, T78, T98, T112, T124, T134
- Handwriting Tutor, T5, T6, T8–T15, T24, T26, T32–T35, T39–T52, T57, T61–T66, T72–T77, T86, T88, T93–T97, T101–T110, T115, T119–T123, T127–T132, T140, T152
- Using Technology, T23, T43, T45, T57, T81, T91, T99, T111, T125, T137

Writing applications, T17, T99, T113, T125, T135

Writing Easily, T154, T155

Writing in the Content Areas
- Language Arts, T11, T17, T21, T49, T71, T95, T107, T113, T131, T135, T143
- Math, T51, T119, T123
- Science, T15, T39, T65, T69, T77, T101, T129
- Social Studies, T9, T61, T75, T89, T93, T103, T141

Writing in the text types
- Informative/Explanatory, T15, T65, T69, T75, T93, T103, T119, T129, T144, T145, T150, T151
- Narrative, T71, T95, T131, T135, T141–T143, T148, T149, T154, T155
- Opinion, T61, T77, T146, T147

Writing positions
- cursive
  - paper, T26, T27, T35
  - pencil, T26, T27, T58
  - sitting, T26, T27
- manuscript
  - paper, T6
  - pencil, T6

Writing process, T151

Writing Quickly, T142, T152, T153